J.H. Stairie

The chess player's chronicle

J.H. Stairie

The chess player's chronicle

ISBN/EAN: 9783742874313

Manufactured in Europe, USA, Canada, Australia, Japa

Cover: Foto ©Andreas Hilbeck / pixelio.de

Manufactured and distributed by brebook publishing software
(www.brebook.com)

J.H. Stairie

The chess player's chronicle

THE

CHESS PLAYER'S CHRONICLE.

(THIRD SERIES.)

1859.

LONDON:

PUBLISHED BY J. H. STARIE,

PHILIDORIAN CHESS ROOMS,

46, RATHBONE PLACE, OXFORD STREET.

M.DCCC.LX.

LONDON:
PRINTED BY F. PICKTON,
PERRY'S PLACE, 29, OXFORD STREET.

PREFACE.

WHEN the third series of THE CHESS PLAYER'S CHRONICLE made its appearance on the First of January, 1859, English Chess had been without a representative during three years. It is true that several of our weekly newspapers published, during that time, some excellent games and problems, but the want of a publication entirely devoted to Chess, was nevertheless strongly felt by the entire Chess community. In order to supply this want, rather than with any expectation of pecuniary gain, we undertook the task. A year has since elapsed, and the first volume is completed. We have remained true to our programme, given in the introduction to our first number, and this Magazine has throughout continued to be solely devoted to Chess, and chiefly to English Chess. There is scarcely an English player of note, some of whose games have not found their way into this periodical. Nor can we be accused of remissness in procuring for our readers games played by Foreign Chess celebrities.

A selection of one hundred and eighty games by English and Foreign Chess notabilities is here offered to the public. The Problems are all original, not one of them has been taken from another publication. The same may be said of the Games, with the exception of those played by Mr. Morphy. In respect to original matter, games, problems, or articles, no other Chess publication can enter the lists with us. If, however withal, we have fallen short of what we intended to do, the fault does not lay entirely with us. The obstacles we had to overcome were many, and one of the chief difficulties is, perhaps, the split which unfortunately exists among the English Chess matadores.

We must finally apologize to our readers for the typographical errors which, especially in the earlier numbers, are rather numerous; but which in most cases can be easily corrected by the reader; our utmost vigilance shall be exercised to prevent a recurrence in future numbers.

CONTENTS.

GENERAL MATTER.

GAMES.

MATCHES.

BLINDFOLD PLAY.

CONSULTATION GAMES.

OPENINGS CLASSIFIED.

PROBLEMS.

The Chess Player's Chronicle.

THIRD SERIES.

INTRODUCTION.

The Chess Player's Chronicle need not say much respecting British Chess. It would not avail us to point to our Clubs, our places of public resort, our list of strong players, to prove that we must furnish matter for no common class of readers. Such topics might be suitable to a new journal struggling into existence, and predisposed to court, in an indirect manner, general favor. They are not adapted to the old representative of Chess in this country. It was after the death of M'Donnell, and the retirement of Lewis and Fraser, that the publication of this magazine was first contemplated. What was the state of British Chess at that time? "Poor England almost afraid to know herself," (her best and bravest champion defeated in an encounter with a foreign combatant; another of her finest amateurs, beaten by a leader of the same foreign school) looked with longing eyes for some rallying-point, some centre of gravitation, towards which the falling bodies of her players might be attracted. Such a centre was offered by this magazine. The prospects of English Chess, notwithstanding the adversity it had suffered, were disposed to brighten, if the opportunity were seized with promptness and decision. The skilful amateur, of foreign extraction (to whom had been assigned by general consent the superiority over his fellows in this country), had, after a very arduous contest, been defeated by an English player by the odd game. That English player—ambitious of success, over-jealous of reputation, by the style of his game, free from what was flashy, preferring solidity to brilliancy, depth to ingenuity—seemed likely to enhance the fame of a rising school, and to maintain its pretensions against able rivals. Starting with somewhat of a miscellaneous character, the Chess Player's Chronicle soon found it necessary to devote the whole of its attention to pure Chess. Club after Club rose in the provinces, not a little aided, we may say boldly, by the existence of a central organ in the metropolis. The London Chess Societies regained their pristine vigour; practical play assumed a more and more definite form; analytical play obtained a new-born appreciation; the composition of problems, not content any longer with mere invention, demanded the higher qualifications of depth and soundness of principle. Match-play, in other words, *play in which each man does his best*, became the rule, rather than the exception. Thereupon ensued, on a foreign soil, a contest between an eminent English player and an able leader of a con-tinental school, with success attending our comparatively recent institu-tions. Such, we feel, was the legitimate result, when the energy of our country was fairly awakened. In the mean time, side by side with our own, another school, destined to fill no mean place in the annals of Chess, had arisen to dispute the superiority claimed by one of the con-tinental nations. Profound in its leaders, brilliant in its followers, with greater erudition but less exactness and self-reliance than the British, this school, by its analysis, its constant practice, with seven amateurs of distinction continually playing against one another, challenged public notice. We, satisfied with previous successes, and contented with ob-serving the skilful manner in which an English master defeated two able disciples of this school, rested upon our laurels. Our national habit has been the same in every pursuit. A British navy never shows itself to advantage until the decks of its ships are cleared for action. In spite, however, of all our national carelessness in practice—in spite of the obvious fact that our best players had ceased to play against one another—we pursued our analytical course, with a fitful rivalry, sometimes at home, sometimes abroad; but perceiving, with the greatest satisfaction, that the illustrious school to which we have alluded, at length founded an organ of their own. With this journal at once the most friendly communications were established—our continental friends bor-rowing English matter of importance from us, and we, of course, with due acknowledgment, inserting occasionally the best specimens of play of foreign masters. English players, however, did not avoid coming into collision with this important school; and it is satisfactory to state, that they have not been worsted when they engaged in *set matches*. What, then, occasioned for a time the suspension of the CHESS PLAYER'S CHRONICLE? The illness of those engaged on the first two series, and the impossibility of finding, at the last moment, successors with proper qualifications, were necessary causes of our temporary retirement from the scene of action. Even as it was, an accomplished Cambridge scholar, if coadjutors could have been found in the hurry and confusion which attend ill health, would have undertaken for a time the management of this magazine. We need not, therefore, be asked, what will be the policy of our new series? It will be the development of the ideas of its predecessors—the organization of British Chess; not unaccompanied by attention to the skill displayed in our game by Continental and American players. In a marked manner we shall give notice of the gradual progress of Chess in our Colonial dependencies, considering them to form part of our own school. Besides the games and problems, we shall publish leading articles, reviews of books, and other literary matter. These articles being independent of one another, will be written by different hands, and be intended to defend the general interests of Chess. In this department we shall strictly consult the wish of the writer, whether he prefer to give his name to the public or remain anonymous. It is certainly time that a central organ should be restored to Great Britain and Ireland. Prussia retains her Magazine; America has established upon a firm basis her own Chess monthly; whilst the voice of the British Chess circle, taken as a whole, is silent. True it is that we have many excellent games and problems published in our weekly newspapers, which are not affected by an incompetent acquaintance, to be found in some instances, with the British language, but paper competing with paper. We want that union between condensed and diffused matter that can be cemented by a monthly magazine alone. To the British school we offer our main services: the games of its clubs and subscription rooms, whether in London or in the country, the problems of its composers, and original matter of a literary nature, will be welcomed cordially by us, and, when carefully sifted, be published, if salutary to the interests of Chess. The only standard by which we shall judge, is that of excellence, our motto shall ever be

Palmam qui meruit ferat.

THE AMERICAN STAR AND THE ENGLISH LIONS.

It has been the popular belief for centuries, that the appearance of a comet is portentous of some extraordinary events. The year which has just closed its account with Time, has had to boast, if astronomers are to be credited, of three of those enigmatical stars, one of which

only was visible to the naked or vulgar eye. By scrutinizing the
political horizon of the elapsed 365 days ever so closely, there is nothing to be found in it to justify the ominous aspect of a comet; it is,
therefore, supposed that, like the star of old that conducted the wise
men of the East to Bethlehem, our comet had simply the mission to
announce a coming man, who in due time will make his appearance
before the world at large. But Chess players have a world of their
own; and, though astrology is at present a sadly neglected science with
the general public, not so with our Chess player, who makes it an
invariable rule to set, at least in his own mind, the horoscope of every
neophyte that enters the arena. This secret predilection for the forbidden fruit, and the contemporaneous appearance of the comet in
the heavens, and of the American star, Paul Morphy, on the Chess
horizon, are the only reasons we can assign for the extraordinary,
unprecedented, and unqualified enthusiasm with which Mr. Morphy
has been received by the great majority of Chess players, and especially
of Chess writers. Morphy is the greatest Chess player that has been,
is, or will be; such was the war-cry of the slavish admirers of the
new star. We do not mean to depreciate at all Mr. Morphy's high
qualities, whatever they may be; but it is in the interest of Chess, in the
interest of Mr. Morphy himself, that we should not blindly admire,
but soundly criticise Mr. Morphy's play, in order to assign to him his
place in the annals of Chess according to his merits. This is a duty we
owe to our readers in general, and to those of the English Chess players
in particular, who for years have fought in the foremost ranks, and
who, at the present moment, form a phalanx numerous and strong as
no other country can boast of.

In estimating Mr. Morphy's play, we must consider him under two
different aspects—as a blindfold player, and over the chessboard.

The great admiration Mr. Morphy's blindfold play has excited in
England we can easily understand and readily sympathize with; for he
has done what no other Chess player, *at his age*, has done before him:
he has played at Birmingham with eight players of a respectable force
at once without seeing the board, and won six games, drew one, and
lost one. Now, we give him full credit for this, the more frankly too,
as we are fully aware that no English player can compete with him—
nay, not even approach him in that line. The practical English mind
cannot bend its stubborn sense so far as to undertake to do blindfold
what it can do but imperfectly with both eyes open, that is, to play a
very good game at Chess. But, though admiring Mr. Morphy's blindfold play, we cannot on that account alone call him, as many of the
chess writers do, an extraordinary phenomenon; for has not Mr.
Paulsen, in America, played twelve games at once blindfold; and has not
Mr. Harrwitz, lately in Paris, astonished a large and chosen company by

playing eight games blindfold, beginning at seven o'clock in the evening, and finishing at two in the morning, winning six, drawing one, and losing one?

Leaving blindfold play to future consideration, let us look at Mr. Morphy over the Chessboard. There are two ways of appreciating the strength of a first-rate Chess player: first, by comparing him with former great masters; and, secondly, by registering his successes with present adepts of the science. If we compare Mr. Morphy's games with those of former masters, it will be found that most of them are his superiors in style and depth; an assertion which we are ready to prove in future numbers; but candour obliges us to admit that Mr. Morphy is young enough to improve his style, and that strong Chess players rise with their opponents; we therefore dismiss, for the present, the first way of appreciating Mr. Morphy's strength altogether, and adopt the second, by registering his successes with present adepts of the game.

It seems to be the general opinion that there is no antagonist worthy of measuring swords with Mr. Morphy to be found in England. Let us see how far this is founded upon fact. We will take twelve of the leading English players in the metropolis—Messrs. Staunton, Buckle, Brien, Campbell, Wyvill, Slous, Boden, Bird, Greenaway, Barnes, Mongredien, and Medley (a); but of this number four only had the pleasure of encountering Mr. Morphy, namely, Messrs. Boden, Bird, Barnes, and Medley; true, they were beaten by a large majority of games, but not in a set match, and only in skittling parties; they were neither prepared to encounter so formidable a foe, nor could they boast of any previous practice, so necessary to success in Chess, and of which the American champion had all the advantage. Now, although the acknowledged champion of English Chess, Mr. Staunton, will not at present encounter Mr. Morphy (and we think him fully justified in not doing it, for it would have been the fight of a knight leaving the ball-room with nothing but his drawing-room sword, to encounter another armed de pied en cap), we have good reason to believe that Mr. Morphy, if he wishes to do so, will find among the rest a willing and worthy opponent.

Having registered Mr. Morphy's successes with the metropolitan players, let us pass to the country players, and take twelve of the leading ones among them—Messrs. Ranken, Kennedy, Gordon, Owen, Kipping, Pindar, Newham, Wormald, Wilkinson, Withers, Hodges, Wayte (b): two only of these Mr. Morphy has encountered and beaten, Mr. Kipping and Mr. Owen; and to the latter he has successfully given Pawn and move—a feat which, we consider, as yet, his greatest performance in England. Speaking of Pawn and move, we cannot omit to allude here to the fact, that some papers have mentioned that Mr.

Morphy offered Mr. Staunton Pawn and move; if this be the case, we are authorised to state, that *several* of the pupils of Mr. Staunton are ready to take up the challenge, if Mr. Morphy will communicate time and conditions. The victories of Mr. Morphy, therefore, extend over six out of twenty-four strong players. A very fair result indeed; but were those six the strongest of the twenty-four, or only the most willing to be beaten?

So far Mr. Morphy has certainly the best of it, for he is fairly entitled to say, " I have beaten every one in England with whom I have played;" but it must not be forgotten that England is an exceptional country, and our metropolis an exceptional town. Although there are more Chess clubs, Chess rooms, and Chess players in this city than in any other in the world, the members of the different clubs never meet, and the strong players of the same circle scarcely ever play together. It is not long ago that one of the above-mentioned first-rate players, who knows the *Handbook* by heart, asked us, " What sort of man is Mr. Staunton?" *Non credat Americanus*. It requires an extraordinary stimulus to bring an Englishman before the public, but, once fairly launched, he is sure to steer, in spite of wind and weather. Mr. Staunton had a hard fight for the championship, but, once established in it, nobody thought of disputing his laurels. It was the very hardihood of the beardless young athlete from over the seas, to throw the gauntlet to England, that astonished the dormant energy of our gladiators for a moment; but, once fully awake to the threatening disgrace, and, in spite of the defeats of the Löwenthals, Harrwitzes, and Anderssens, the English Chess player will do his duty.

(*a*) We do not include here our glorious veterans who have some time since given up Chess—Messrs. Lewis, G. Walker, Fraser, &c.

(*b*) We are fully aware that there is a great number of strong players, besides the above-named twelve gentlemen, in the country; but they will, we hope, pardon us for not mentioning their names, on account of space.

MATCH BETWEEN MR. MORPHY AND HERR ANDERSSEN.

PARIS has, at the close of the year, witnessed a great match. The combatants were Mr. Morphy and Herr Anderssen. The former is acknowledged to be the best player in America, and has increased his fame in Europe by the defeat of Herren Harrwitz and Löwenthal, two very strong players, and by his successful encounters in light games with all other amateurs whom he has met; the latter won the first prize in the tournament of 1851, beating Messrs. Wyvill and Staunton, and Herren Szen and Kieseritzki. Both are players of unquestionable genius, and of great erudition. Indeed, so far as learning is concerned, they are unrivalled, unless Der Lasa and Löwenthal may bear comparison with them. The score of the match, just terminated in favour of Mr. Morphy, is given or page 30.

GAME I.

White. (Mr. MORPHY.)	*Black.* (HERR ANDERSSEN.)
1. P. to K. fourth	1. P. to K. fourth
2. Kt. to K. B. third	2. Kt. to Q. B. third
8. B. to Q. B. fourth	3. B. to Q. B. fourth
4. P. to Q. Kt. fourth	4. B. takes Kt. P.
5. P. to Q. B. third	5. B. to Q. R. fourth
6. P. to Q. fourth	6. P. takes P.
7. Castles	7. Kt. to K. B. third (a)
8. P. to K. fifth	8. P. to Q. fourth
9. K. B. to Q. Kt. fifth	9. Kt. to K. fifth
1J. P. takes P.	10. Castles
11. B. takes Kt.	11. P. takes B.
12. Q. to Q. R. fourth	12. B. to Q. Kt. third
13. Q. takes Q. B. P.	13. B. to K. Kt. fifth
14. B. to Q. Kt. second	14. B. takes Kt.
15. P. takes B.	15. Kt. to K. Kt. fourth
16. Kt. to Q. second	16. R. to K. square (b)
17. K. to R. square	17. Kt. to K. R. sixth
18. P. to K. B. fourth (c)	18. Q. to K. R. fifth
19. Q. takes Q. P.	19. Kt. takes K. B. P. (check)
20. K. to Kt. square	20. Kt. to Q. sixth
21. B. to Q. B. third	21. Kt. takes P. at K. B. fourth
22. Q. to K. B. third	22. Kt. to R. sixth (check)
23. K. to R. square	23. Kt. to. K. Kt. fourth
24. Q. to K. Kt. second	24. Q. R. to Q. square
25. R. to K. Kt. square	25. P. to K. R. third
26. Q. R. to K. B. square	26. Q. to K. R. sixth (d)
27. Q. to Q. B. sixth	27. Q. to Q. second
28. Q. to K. Kt. second	28. B. takes Q. P.
29. B. takes B.	29. Q. takes B.
30. Kt. to K. B. third	30. Q. to Q. fourth
31. P. to K. R. fourth	31. Kt. to K. third
32. Q. to K. Kt. fourth	32. Q. to Q. B. third
33. R. to K. Kt. second	33. R. to Q. sixth
34. Q. to K. B. fifth	34. K. R. to Q. square
35. Q. to K. R. sixth	35. Q. to Q. fourth
36. Q. to K. B. fifth	36. R. to Q. eighth

37. R. takes R.	37. Q. takes R. (check)
38. K. to R. second	38. R. to Q. sixth
39. R. to K. B. second	39. R. to K. sixth
40. Kt. to Q. second	40. R. to K. seventh
41. Q. takes K. B. P. (check)	41. K. to R. square
42. Kt. to K. fourth	42. R. takes R. (check)
43. Kt. takes R.	43. Q. to Q. fourth
44. Kt. to K. Kt. fourth	44. Q. takes Q. R. P. (check)
45. K. to Kt. third	45. Q. to Q. Kt. sixth (check)
46. K. to R. second	46. Q. to B. seventh (check)
47. K. to Kt. third	47. Q. to Q. B. sixth (check)
48. K. to R. second	48. Q. to Q. B. third (e)
49. P. to K. R. fifth	49. P. to Q. R. fourth
50. Kt. to K. B. sixth	50. P. takes Kt.
51. Q. takes P. (check)	51. K. to Kt. square
52. Q. to K. Kt. sixth (check)	52. K. to B. square
53. Q. takes R. P. (check)	53. K. to his square
54. Q. to K. Kt. sixth (check)	54. K. to Q. second
55. P. to K. R. sixth	55. Q. to Q. fourth
56. P. to K. R. seventh	56. Q. takes P. (check)
57. K. to Kt. square	57. Kt. to K. Kt. fourth
58. P. to R. eighth (queens)	58. Q. takes Q.
59. Q. takes Kt.	59. Q. to Q. fifth (check)

And Black eventually won.

This game lasted to the 72nd move.

Notes. (*By* HERR FALKBEER *of the* Sunday Times.)

(*a*) Professor Anderssen, in an elaborate analysis of this opening, published in the *Berlin Schachzeitung*, has proved that either the move in the text, or "P. to Q. third," at this juncture, admits of a sound defence.

(*b*) "B. to Q. R. fourth" looks promising, but the move adopted by Anderssen is undoubtedly stronger. The reply to the former would have been "B. to Q. B. third."

(*c*) Quite characteristic of Morphy's style. Rather than be embarrassed by a tedious defence, he chances a Pawn, even against so strong an antagonist, to maintain the attack.

(*d*) It is obvious that Black could not have taken the P. without the loss of the exchange.

(*e*) All these manœuvres, although they appear to lose time, are very deep, it being Black's intention to establish his Queen at her B. third, to protect the Kt., used at the same time to prevent the check of the Q. followed by the sacrifice of the Kt., which might have resulted in a drawn game.

GAME II.

White. (Herr ANDERSSEN.)	*Black.* (Mr. MORPHY.)
1. P. to K. fourth	1. P. to K. fourth
2. K. Kt. to B. third	2. Q. Kt. to B. third
3. K. B. to Q. Kt. fifth	3. P. to Q. R. third
4. B. to Q. R. fourth	4. Kt. to K. B. third
5. P. to Q. third	5. B. to Q. B. fourth
6. P. to Q. B. third	6. P. to Q. Kt. fourth
7. B. to Q. B. second	7. P. to Q. fourth
8. P. takes P.	8. Kt. takes P.
9. P. to K. R. third	9. Castles
10. Castles	10. P. to K. R. third
11. P. to Q. fourth	11. P. takes P.
12. P. takes P.	12. B. to Q. Kt. third
13. Kt. to Q. B. third	13. K. Kt. to Q. Kt. fifth
14. B. to Q. Kt. square (*a*)	14. Q. B. to K. third
15. P. to Q. R. third	15. Kt. to Q. fourth
16. Q. Kt. to K. second	16. Kt. to K. B. third
17. Q. B. to K. third	17. R. to K. square
18. Kt. to K. Kt. third	18. B. to Q. B. fifth
19. Kt. to K. B. fifth	19. B. takes R.
20. Q. takes B.	20. Q. Kt. to K. second
21. K. Kt. to R. fourth	21. Kt. takes Kt.
22. Kt. takes Kt.	22. Q. to Q. second
23. B. takes K. R. P.	23. P. takes B.
24. Q. to Q. B.	24. K. B. takes P.
25. Q. takes K. R. P.	25. R. to K. eighth (check)
26. K. to R. second	26. Kt. to K. fifth
27. B. takes Kt.	27. R. takes B.
28. Q. to K. Kt. fifth (check)	28. K. to B. square
29. Q. to K. R. sixth (check)	29. K. to his square
30. Kt. takes B.	30. Q. to Q. third (check)
31. Q. takes Q.	31. P. takes Q.
32. R. to Q. square	32. K. to B. square
33. R. to Q. second	33. Q. R. to Q. square
34. P. to K. Kt. fourth	34. Q. R. to K. fourth
35. P. to K. B. third	35. R. to K. eighth
36. P. to K. R. fourth	36. R. to Q. fourth

37. K. to Kt. third	37. P. to Q. R. fourth
38. P. to K. R. fifth	38. K. to Kt. square
39. K. to B. second	39. R. to K. square
40. K. to Kt. third	40. R. to K. second
41. K. to B. fourth	41. K. to R. second
42. K. to Kt. third	42. R. to K. sixth
43. K. to B. fourth	43. R. to K. square
44. K. to Kt. third	44. R. to K. second

Both parties persisting in these moves, the game was given up as drawn.

"The brilliancy of this game," says Mr. Falkbeer, "one of the best which has been played since the arrival of Mr. MORPHY in Europe, reflects great credit both on the American champion and on his renowned antagonist. The spirited and energetic manner in which White followed up his attack, and also the tenacity of Black's defence, are equally deserving of admiration."

————

Notes.

(a) Had he advanced the Q.'s Pawn instead of this move, to avoid the apparent loss of a Pawn, the following variation, which would have resulted in Black's favor, might have arisen.

White.	Black.
14. P. to Q. fifth	14. Kt. to K. second
15. B. to K. fourth	15. P. to K. B. fourth
16. P. to Q. sixth	16. P. takes B.
17. P. takes Kt.	17. Q. takes P.
18. Kt. to Q. fifth	18. Kt. takes Kt.
19. Q. takes Kt.	19. B. to K. third
20. Q. takes P.	20. Q. to K. B. third

With the better game.

Or,

16. Q. to Q. Kt. third	16. P. takes K. B.
17. P. to Q. sixth (disc. check)	17. K. to R. square
18. Q. takes Kt.	18. Q. takes P.
19. Q. takes Q. (best)	19. P. takes Q.
20. Kt. takes K. P.	20. P. to Q. fourth
21. Q. Kt. to Q. second	

This move being compulsory to save the Q. R. P. Black has decidedly the better game.

If, however, White at his fourteenth move had preferred to protect his Q. P. with the Bishop, the annexed interesting variation would have probably occurred.

White.	Black.
14. Q. B. to K. third	14. Kt. takes B.
15. Q. takes Kt.	15. Kt. takes P.
16. P. takes Kt.	16. B. takes B.
17. Q. R. to Q. square	17. P. to Q. B. fourth
18. Kt. takes B.	18. P. takes Kt.
19. Q. to K. fourth	

With a good game.

GAME III.

White. (Mr. MORPHY.)	Black. (Herr ANDERSSEN.)
1. P. to K. fourth	1. P. to K. fourth
2. K. Kt. to B. third	2. Q. Kt. to B. third
3. K. B. to Q. Kt. fifth	3. K. Kt. to B. third (a)
4. P. to Q. fourth	4. Kt. takes P.
5. Kt. takes Kt.	5. P. takes Kt.
6. P. to K. fifth	6. P. to Q. B. third (b)
7. Castles	7. P. takes B.
8. Q. B. to K. Kt. fifth	8. K. B. to K. second
9. P. takes Kt.	9. B. takes P.
10. R. to K. square (check)	10. K. to B. square
11. B. takes B.	11. Q. takes B.
12. P. to Q. B. third	12. P. to Q. fourth
13. P. takes P.	13. Q. B. to K. third
14. Q. Kt. to B. third	14. P. to Q. R. third
15. R. to K. fifth	15. R. to Q. square
16. Q. to Q. Kt. third	16. Q. to K. second (c)
17. Q. R. to K. square	17. P. to K. Kt. fourth
18. Q. to her square	18. Q. to K. B third
19. Q. R. to K. third	19. K. R. to K. Kt. square (d)
20. R. takes B.	20. P. takes R.
21. R. to K. B. third	

And Black surrenders.

Notes.

(*a*) This defence, although recommended by the German *Handbook*, has been of late closely analysed, and found defective.

(*b*) A novel move, but of rather doubtful soundness.

(*c*) A move of questionable merit, evidently made with the intention of preventing the hostile Queen from checking.

(*d*) Obviously an oversight; Pawn to K. Kt.'s fifth, might yet have saved the game.

GAME IV.

White. (HERR ANDERSSEN.)	*Black.* (MR. MORPHY.)
1. P. to K. fourth	1. P. to K. fourth
2. Kt. to K. B. third	2. Kt. to Q. B. third
3. B. to Q. Kt. fifth	3. P. to Q. R. third
4. B. to Q. R. fourth	4. Kt. to K. B. third
5. P. to Q. third (*a*)	5. B. to Q. B. fourth
6. P. to Q. B. third	6. P. to Q. Kt. fourth
7. B. to Q. B. second	7. P. to Q. fourth
8. P. takes P.	8. Kt. takes P.
9. P. to K. R. third	9. Castles
10. Castles	10. P. to K. R. third
11. P. to Q. fourth (*b*)	11. P. takes P.
12. P. takes P.	12. B. to Q. Kt. third
13. Kt. to Q. B. third	13. K. Kt. to Q. Kt. fifth
14. B. to Q. Kt. (*c*)	14. Q. B. to K. third
15. P. to Q. R. third	15. Kt. to Q. fourth
16. Q. B. to K. third	16. Kt. to K. B. third
17. Q. to Q. second	17. R. to K. square
18. R. to Q. square	18. B. to Q. fourth
19. Kt. to K. fifth	19. Q. to Q. third
20. Q. to Q. B. second (*d*)	20. Kt. takes Q. P.
21. B. takes Kt.	21. B. takes B.
22. Kt. takes B.	22. Q. takes K. Kt.
23. Kt. takes Kt. (check)	23. Q. takes Kt.
24. Q. to K. R. seventh (check)	24. K. to B. square
25. B. to K. fourth	25. Q. R. to Q. square
26. K. to R. square	26. B. takes Q. Kt. P.
27. Q. R. to Q. Kt. square	27. R. takes R. (chec *k*)

28. R. takes R.	28. Q. takes K. B. P.
29. Q. to R. eighth (check)	29. K. to K. second
30. Q. to R. seventh	30. B. to K. fourth
31. B. to K. B. third	31. Q. to Kt. sixth
32. K. to Kt. square	32. Q. to Kt. third
33. Q. takes Q.	33. P. takes Q.
34. B. to Q. Kt. seventh	34. R. to Q. Kt. square
35. B. takes Q. R. P.	35. P. to Q. B. third
36. K. to B. second	36. B. to Q. third
37. R. to Q. third	37. K. to Q. second
38. K. to K. second	38. R. to Q. R. square
39. B. to Q. Kt. seventh	39. R. takes Q. R. P.
40. B. to Q. B. eighth (check)	40. K. to B. second
41. R. to Q. square	41. R. to Q. R. seventh (check)
42. K. to B. third	42. B. to Q. B. fourth
43. B. to K. sixth	43. R. to K. B. seventh (check)
44. K. to Kt. third	44. R. to K. B. third
45. R. to Q. seventh (check)	45. K. to Kt. third
46. B. to K. Kt. fourth	46. B. to Q. third (check)
47. K. to R. fourth	47. P. to Q. B. fourth
48. B. to K. B. third	48. P. to Q. B. fifth
49. R. takes K. Kt. P.	49. R. to K. B. fifth (check)
50. B. to K. Kt. fourth	50. P. to Q. B. sixth
51. P. to K. Kt. third	51. R. takes B. (check)

And White resigned.

Notes.

(a) Generally the first player in this opening adopts a more attacking style. The move in the text loses time.

(b) If the first player is compelled to obtain an isolated Pawn by the advance of his Queen's Pawn at this juncture, how weak must have been "P. to Q. third" at move fifth.

(c) "P. to Q. fifth" is showy, but "B. to K. fourth" is much sounder, unless we are mistaken.

(d) This seems to be either an oversight or a miscalculation.

GAME V.

White. (Mr. MORPHY.)	*Black.* (Herr ANDERSSEN.)
1. P. to K. fourth	1. P. to Q. fourth
2. P. takes P.	2. K. Kt. to B. third
3. P. to Q. fourth	3. Kt. takes P.
4. P. to Q. B. fourth	4. Kt. to K. B. third
5. Q. Kt. to B. third	5. Q. B. to K. B. fourth
6. K. Kt. to B. third	6. P. to K. third
7. Q. B. to K. third	7. K. B. to Q. Kt. fifth
8. Q. to Q. Kt. third	8. B. takes Kt. (check)
9. P. takes B.	9. B. to K. fifth
10. Kt. to Q. second	10. B. to Q. B. third
11. K. B. to Q. third	11. Q. Kt. to Q. second
12. Q. to Q. B. second	12. P. to K. R. third
13. Castles (K. R.)	13. Castles
14. Q. R. to K. square	14. P. to Q. Kt. third
15. P. to K. R. third	15. Q. to Q. B. square
16. K. to R. second	16. K. to R. square
17. R. to K. Kt. square	17. R. to K. Kt. square
18. P. to K. Kt. fourth	18. P. to K. Kt. fourth
19. P. to K. B. fourth	19. Q. to K. B. square
20. K. R. to K. Kt. third	20. Q. R. to Q. square
21. Kt. to K. B. third	21. B. takes Kt.
22. R. takes B.	22. Q. to Q. third
23. K. to K. Kt. second	23. K. Kt. to K. R. fourth
24. P. takes P.	24. P. takes P.
25. P. takes Kt.	25. P. to K. Kt. fifth
26. P. takes P.	26. R. takes P. (check)
27. K. to K. B. square	27. P. to K. B. fourth
28. Q. to K. B. second	28. Kt. to K. fourth
29. P. takes Kt.	29. Q. takes B. (check)
30. Q. to K. second	30. Q. to K. fifth
31. B. to K. B. second	31. Q. to Q. B. third
32. Q. R. to Q. square	32. R. takes R. (check)
33. Q. takes R.	33. Q. takes P. (check)
34. Q. to Q. third	34. Q. takes Q. R. P.
35. R. to K. Kt. third	35. Q. to Q. B. fifth

36. Q. takes Q.	36. R. takes Q.
37. R. to K. Kt. sixth	37. R. to Q. B. third
38. P. to Q. B. fourth	38. P. to Q. R. fourth
39. K. to K. second	39. R. takes P.
40. R. takes P.	40. R. to Q. B. seventh (check)
41. K. to B. third	41. P. to Q. R. fifth
42. R. to K. Kt. sixth	42. R. to Q. B. fifth
43. R. to K. Kt. square	43. P. to Q. R. sixth
44. P. to K. sixth	44. P. to Q. R. seventh
45. R. to Q. R. square	45. R. to K. fifth
46. R. takes P.	46. R. takes P.
47. K. to K. B. fourth	47. R. to Q. third
48. K. takes P.	48. R. to Q. fourth (check)
49. K. to Kt. fourth	49. P. to Q. Kt. fourth
50. R. to R. eighth (check)	50. K. to R. second
51. R. to R. seventh	51. R. to Q. second
52. B. to K. Kt. third	52. R. to K. Kt. second (check)
53. K. to R. fourth	

And White wins.

GAME VI.

Black. (ANDERSSEN.)	*White.* (MORPHY.)
1. P. to Q. R. third	1. P. to K. fourth
2. P. to Q. B. fourth	2. K. Kt. to B. third
3. Q. Kt. to B. third	3. P. to Q. fourth
4. P. takes P.	4. Kt. takes P.
5. P. to K. third	5. Q. B. to K. third
6. K. Kt. to B. third	6. K. B. to Q. third
7. K. B. to K. second	7. Castles
8. P. to Q. fourth	8. Kt. takes Kt.
9. P. takes Kt.	9. P. to K. fifth
10. Kt. to Q. second	10. P. to K. B. fourth
11. P. to K. B. fourth	11. P. to K. Kt. fourth
12. K. B. to Q. B. fourth	12. B. takes B.
13. Kt. takes B.	13. P. takes P.
14. P. takes P.	14. Q. to K. square
15. Castles	15. Q. to Q. B. third

16. Q. to Q. Kt. third	16. Q. to Q. fourth
17. Q. R. to Kt. square	17. P. to Q. Kt. third
18. Q. to Q. R. second	18. P. to Q. B. third
19. Q. to K. second	19. Kt. to Q. second
20. Kt. to K. third	20. Q. so K. third (a)
21. P. to Q. B. fourth	21. Kt. to K. B. third
22. Q. R. to Q. Kt. third	22. K. to B. second
23. B. to Q. Kt. second	23. Q. R. to Q. B. square
24. K. to R. square	24. K. R. to K. Kt. square
25. P. to Q. fifth	25. P. takes P.
26. P. takes P.	26. Q. to Q. second (b)
27. Kt. to Q. B. fourth	27. K. to K. second (c)
28. B. takes Kt. (check) (d)	28. K. takes B.
29. Q. to Q. Kt. second (check)	29. K. to K. B. second
30. R. to K. R. third	30. K. R. to K. Kt. second
31. Q. to Q. fourth	31. K. to Kt. square
32. K. R. to R. sixth (e)	32. B. to K. B. square
33. P. to Q. sixth	33. R. to K. B. second
34. Q. R. to R. third	34. Q. to Q. R. fifth
35. K. R. to Q. B. square	35. Q. R. to Q. B. fourth
36. Q. R. to K. Kt. third (check)	36. B. to K. Kt. second
37. P. to K. R. third (f)	37. K. to R. square
38. R. takes B.	38. R. takes R.
39. R. to Q. B. third (g)	39. P. to K. sixth
40. R. takes P.	40. R. takes Kt.
41. Q. to K. B. sixth	41. R. to Q. B. eighth (check)
42. K. to R. second	42. Q. takes K. B. P. (check)

And Black resigns.

Notes.

(a) Some of White's moves of the Queen in the first 20 moves appear to give Black time to form a terrible attack.

(b) Clearly he could not take the offered Pawn.

(c) Again he cannot capture the Pawn without loss; for if 27, Kt. takes P., 28, B. to K. fifth, and wins.

(d) "R. to K. R. third" at once would have strengthened Black's already fine game. A Bishop so well posted should not be given up lightly.

(e) He might, with advantage, have brought in his Knight to K. fifth square.

(f) It is now that Black misses the loss of time in not advancing his Knight at move 32.

(g) "Q. to K. B. sixth" is a better resource.

Games between Herr LÖWENTHAL and Herr FALKBEER, played in the St. George's Club.

(*King's Bishop's Opening.**)

(LOPEZ GAMBIT.)

White. (Herr FALKBEER.)	*Black.* (Herr LÖWENTHAL.)
1. P. to K. fourth	1. P. to K. fourth
2. B. to Q. B. fourth	2. B. to Q. B. fourth
3. Q. to K. second	3. Kt. to K. B. third (a)
4. P. to Q. third	4. Kt. to Q. B. third
5. P. to Q. B. third	5. P. to K. R. third
6. P. to Q. Kt. fourth	6. B. to Q. Kt. third
7. P. to Q. R. fourth	7. P. to Q. R. third
8. Kt. to K. B. third	8. P. to Q. third
9. B. to K. third	9. B. takes B.
10. P. takes B.	10. Kt. to K. second
11. Castles	11. Kt. to K. Kt. third
12. Q. Kt. to Q. second	12. Castles
13. P. to K. R. third	13. P. to Q. B. third
14. Q. to K. B. second	14. P. to Q. fourth
15. B. to Q. Kt. third	15. P. takes P.
16. P. takes P.	16. Q. to Q. sixth
17. Q. R. to Q. B.	17. B. to K. third
18. B. takes B.	18. P. takes B.
19. Kt. to K. square	19. Q. to Q. second
20. Kt. from K. to K. B. third	20. Q. R. to Q. square (b)
21. Q. to K. Kt. third	21. K. to R. second (c)
22. Q. takes Kt. (check) (d)	22. K. takes Q.
23. Kt. takes P. (check)	23. K. to R. second
24. Kt. takes Q.	24. R. takes Kt.
25. Kt. to Q. Kt. third (e)	25. P. to K. fourth (f)
26. Kt. to K. B. fifth	26. R. to K. second
27. Q. R. to Q. square (g)	27. P. to Q. Kt. third
28. Kt. to Q. third (h)	28. R. to Q. square
29. Kt. to B. second	29. R. from K. second to Q. second
30. R. takes R.	30. R. takes R.
31. R. to Q. Kt.	31. R. to Q. seventh (i)
32. P. to Q. B. fourth	32. R. to Q. B seventh

2

33. P. to Q. Kt. fifth	33. B. P. takes P.
34. B. P. takes P.	34. P. to Q. R. fourth
35. R. to Q. square	35. R. to Q. R. seventh
36. R. to Q. eighth (*k*)	36. R. takes P.
37. R. to Q. sixth	37. R. to R. eighth (check)
38. K. to R. second	38. R. to K. B. eighth
39. Kt. to K. Kt. fourth (*l*)	39. Kt. takes Kt. (check)
40. P. takes Kt.	40. R. to K. eighth (*m*)
41. R. takes Kt. P.	41. R. takes P.
42. R. to Q. R. sixth	42. R. takes P.
43. R. takes P.	43. R. takes P.
44. P. to Q. Kt. sixth	44. R. to Q. Kt. fifth
45. R. takes P.	45. R. takes P.

And after a few more moves the game was drawn.

Notes.

(*) See Staunton's *Handbook*, second edition, King's Bishop's Opening, Lopez Gambit, p. 210.

(*a*) This defence was played by M'DONNELL against DE LA BOURDONNAIS. See Staunton's *Handbook*, second edition, p. 217.

(*b*) By this move Black evidently loses a Pawn in the long run, if not immediately.

(*c*) Q. to K. would have been far better.

(*d*) This combination has been finely conceived and gives White a winning game.

(*e*) Kt. to Q. B. fourth would have been better.

(*f*) The best move under the circumstances.

(*g*) A very weak move; P. to Q. R. fifth would have ensured the possession of the conquered Pawn.

(*h*) White ought to have taken Q. R. P. with the Kt., or retreated to Kt. third, as the only means of keeping the Pawn.

(*i*) Black begins to recover the lost ground.

(*k*) Why lose a move and not play at once to Q. sixth?

(*l*) In consequence of having lost a move with the Rook, White is now obliged to double another Pawn; and Black could have won the game by playing R. to K. B. third; for if White R. to Q. fifth, Black answers by R. to K. third, and then, by bringing the R. on Q. R. file, Black easily wins.

(*m*) A very weak move, for these two Pawns can do no harm so long as the Black Pawn stops them. As we have said, R. to K. B. sixth was the winning move; for if White plays R. to Q. seventh, Black still plays R. to K. third, and by bringing the King into play, wins.

Between the same Players.

(Queen's Knight's Opening.*)

White. (Herr FALKBEER.)	*Black.* (Herr LÖWENTHAL.)
1. P. to K. fourth	1. P. to K. fourth
2. Kt. to Q. B. third	2. Kt. to K. B. third
3. B. to Q. B. fourth	3. B. to Q. B. fourth
4. P. to Q. third	4. P. to K. R. third
5. P. to K. B. fourth	5. P. to Q. third
6. Kt. to K. B. third	6. Castles (a)
7. Kt. to Q. R. fourth	7. P. to Q. B. third
8. P. takes P.	8. P. takes P.
9. Kt. takes B.	9. Q. to Q. R. fourth (check)
10. B. to Q. second	10. Q. takes Kt.
11. P. to Q. R. third	11. P. to Q. Kt. fourth.
12. B. to Q. Kt. third	12. P. to Q. R. fourth
13. Q. to K. second	13. Kt. to Q. R. third
14. B. to K. third	14. Q. to K. second
15. Castles	15. Kt. to K. Kt. fifth (b)
16. B. to Q. second	16. Kt. to Q. B. fifth
17. B. to Q. R. second	17. Kt. to K. third (c)
18. P. to Q. B. third (d)	18. Q. to Q. third
19. P. to K. R. third (e)	19. Kt. to K. B. third
20. P. to Q. fourth	20. Kt. to Q. second
21. B. to K. third	21. K. to R. second
22. Q. R. to Q. square	22. Q. to Q. B. second (f)
23. Kt. to K. R. fourth	23. Kt. to K. B. third
24. B. takes P. (g)	24. K. takes B.
25. R. takes Kt. (check)	25. P. takes R.
26. Kt. to K. B. fifth (check)	26. K. to Kt. third
27. B. takes Kt.	27. P. takes B.
28. Q. to K. Kt. fourth (check)	28. K. to R. second
29. Q. to R. fifth (check)	29. K. to Kt. square
30. Q. to Kt. sixth (check)	30. K. to R. square
31. Q. to R. sixth (check)	31. K. to Kt. square
32. R. to Q. third	32. P. takes P.
33. P. to K. fifth	33. P. takes Kt.
34. R. to Kt. third (check)	34. K. to B. second

35. Q. to Kt. seventh (check)	35. K. to K. square
36. Q. takes Q.	36. B. to K. third
37. R. to K. Kt. seventh	37. R. to K. B. second
38. R. takes R.	38. B. takes R.
39. Q. takes P. (check)	

And wins.

Notes.

(*) This opening is not to be found in the *Handbook*, nor other chess works, but is quite sound.

(a) Black ought to have pinned the Kt., and thus brought out the Bishop.

(b) Clearly a useless move, as will be seen.

(c) This move loses Black a Pawn, and is therefore bad, for if White plays P. to R. third, he wins a Pawn, thus :—

First—

18. P. to K. R. third	18. Kt. to K. B. third
19. Q. to K. square	19. Q. to K. B. fourth (check) (best)
20. K. to R. square	20. Q. takes Q. B. P. (best)
21. Kt. takes K. P.	21. Q. takes Q. Kt. P.
22. B. to Q. B. third	22. Q. to Q. B. seventh
23. R. to K. B. second	23. Q. to Q. R. fifth
24. Kt. takes Q. B. P.	

With a winning game.

Second—

18. P. to K. R. third	18. Q. to Q. B. fourth (check)
19. P. to Q. fourth	19. Kt. takes P.
20. Kt. takes Kt.	20. Q. takes Kt. (check)
21. K. to R. square	21. Kt. to K. B. third
22. R. takes Kt.	22. P. takes R.
23. B. takes R. P.	

And wins.

(d) P. to K. R. third would have been the stronger move, as we have shown.

(e) From this point of the game White plays admirably to the end.

(f) This is an ill-judged move.

(g) Brilliant as well as sound.

[These two games form part of the match played at the Birmingham tournament between the two above-mentioned champions, and were played on the 16th and 17th September. It is well known that Herr LÖWENTHAL won the 1st, and Herr FALKBEER the 2nd prize.]

The following is the first Game in the match pending between two of the most promising young players, Mr. J. C. CAMPBELL and Mr. R. B. WORMALD. The first has already won a match against so distinguished an amateur as Mr. Barnes; and the second has successfully encountered some of the most eminent players of the day. We shall give the whole of the match, which is to be played at the Philidorian Chess Rooms.

GAME I.

(*Philidor's Defence to King's Knight's Game.*)

White. (Mr. CAMPBELL.)	*Black.* (Mr. WORMALD.)
1. P. to K. fourth	1. P. to K. fourth
2. Kt. to K. B. third	2. P. to Q. third
3. P. to Q. fourth	3. P. takes P.
4. Q. takes P.	4. B. to Q. second
5. B. to K. third	5. Q. Kt. to B. third
6. Q. to Q. second	6. K. Kt. to B. third
7. Q. Kt. to B. third	7. B. to K. second
8. P. to K. R. third	8. Castles
9. Castles	9. P. to Q. R. third
10. P. to K. Kt. fourth	10. P. to Q. Kt. fourth
11. B. to Q. third	11. P. to Q. Kt. fifth
12. Kt. to K. second	12. Kt. to K. fourth
13. Kt. takes Kt.	13. P. takes Kt.
14. Kt. to K. Kt. third	14. B. to K. third (*a*)
15. P. to K. Kt. fifth	15. Kt. to Q. second (*b*)
16. Kt. to K. B. fifth	16. P. to Q. B. fourth
17. P. to K. R. fourth	17. K. R. to K. square
18. Q. to K. second	18. Q. to R. fourth
19. B. to Q. B. fourth	19. Kt. to Q. Kt. third (*c*)
20. B. takes B.	20. P. takes B.
21. Kt. takes B. (check)	21. R. takes Kt.
22. K. to Kt. square	22. R. to Q. B. square (*d*)
23. R. to Q. sixth	23. R. to Q. R. square
24. P. to K. R. fifth	24. Kt. to Q. R. fifth
25. Q. to Q. B. fourth	25. Q. to Q. Kt. fourth
26. Q. takes Q.	26. P. takes Q.
27. P. to K. Kt. sixth	27. P. to K. R. third
28. K. R. to Q. square	28. K. to B. square

29. K. to Q. B. sixth	29. K. R. to Q. R. second
30. R. takes K. P.	30. Kt. to K. B. sixth (check)
31. P. takes Kt.	31. R. takes P.
32. B. takes P. (check)	32. K. to Kt. square
33. R. to K. eighth (check)	33. R. takes R.
34. K. takes R.	

And wins.

Notes.

(*a*) The only move.   (*b*) Why not to K.?
(*c*) It seems to us that B. takes B. would have been better.
(*d*) Evidently a lost move.

Game played some years ago, between the late Mr. DANIELS and Mr. STAUDIGL; Mr. D. giving the move, and engaging to play the Muzio.

(*Muzio Gambit.*)

White. (Mr. STAUDIGL.)	*Black.* (Mr. DANIELS.)
1. P. to K. fourth	1. P. to K. fourth
2. P. to K. B. fourth	2. P. takes P.
3. Kt. to K. B. third	3. P. to K. Kt. fourth
4. B. to Q. B. fourth	4. P. to K. Kt. fifth
5. P. to Q. fourth	5. P. to Q. fourth
6. B. takes P.	6. P. takes Kt.
7. Castles	7. P. to Q. B. third
8. B. to Q. Kt. third	8. B. to K. R. third
9. Q. takes P.	9. Q. to K. Kt. fourth
10. P. to K. Kt. third	10. Q. to K. Kt. fifth
11. Q. to Q. third	11. P. takes P.
12. B. takes P. (check)	12. K. to Q. square
13. B. takes Kt.	13. P. takes P. (check)
14. K. to R. square	14. R. takes B.

And Black checkmated in two moves.

The following games were played December, 1858, in a pool at Mr. STARIE's Philidorian Chess Rooms.

Black. (Mr. CAMPBELL.)	*White.* (Mr. BRIEN.)
1. P. to K. fourth	1. P. to Q. fourth
2. P. takes P.	2. Q. takes P.
3. Kt. to Q. B. third	3. Q. to Q. R. fourth (*a*)
4. P. to Q. fourth	4. B. to K. B. fourth
5. Q. to K. B. third (*b*)	5. P. to Q. B. third
6. B. to Q. third	6. B. takes B.
7. Q. takes B.	7. P. to K. third
8. B. to K. third	8. B. to Q. Kt. fifth
9. K. Kt. to K. second	9. Kt. to K. B. third
10. Castles with K. R.	10. B. takes Kt.
11. Kt. takes B.	11. Q. Kt. to Q. second
12. P. to K. B. fourth	12. P. to K. Kt. third
13. P. to Q. Kt. fourth	13. Q. to K. B. fourth
14. Q. R. to Q. square	14. P. to Q. R. third
15. B. to Q. B. square	15. Q. takes Q.
16. R. takes Q.	16. P. to Q. Kt. fourth
17. R. to K. square	17. Kt. to Q. Kt. third
18. P. to Q. R. third	18. K. to Q. second
19. P. to K. R. third	19. P. to K. R. fourth
20. K. to K. B. second	20. Kt. to Q. B. fifth
21. P. to K. Kt. third	21. P. to Q. R. fourth
22. P. takes P.	22. R. takes P.
23. Kt. to Q. Kt. square	23. Kt. to Q. fourth
24. Kt. to Q. second	24. Kt. takes Kt.
25. B. takes Kt.	25. Q. R. to Q. R. fifth
26. R. to Q. Kt. square	26. K. R. to Q. R. square (*c*)
27. B. to Q. Kt. fourth (*d*)	27. Kt. takes B.
28. P. takes Kt.	28. R. to Q. R. seventh
29. R. to Q. B. third	29. K. R. to Q. R. sixth (*e*)
30. R. takes R.	30. R. takes R.
31. R. to Q. Kt. third	31. R. to Q. R. seventh
32. R. to Q. B. third	32. R. to Q. Kt. seventh
33. K. to K. third	33. R. takes Q. Kt. P.
34. P. to K. Kt. fourth	34. P. takes P.

35. P. takes P.	35. K. to Q. third
36. R. to Q. B. fifth	36. R. to Q. B. fifth (*f*)
37. R. takes R.	37. P. takes R.
38. P. to K. Kt. fifth (*g*)	38. K. to Q. fourth
39. P. to Q. B. third	39. K. to Q. third
40. K. to K. fourth	40. K. to Q. second

And after two or three moves the game was given up as drawn.

Notes.

(*a*) This move, as it supports for a time the Bishop which is posted subsequently at K. B. fourth, is perhaps to be preferred to " Q. to Q. square."

(*b*) If Black, when he made this move, intended to play afterwards " B. to Q. third," he might have noticed that he would lose time by the Queen's sally.

(*c*) This seems to be sounder than " Q. R. to Q. B. fifth."

(*d*) If " B. to Q. B. square," White would gain something by " Q. R. to Q. B. fifth." " K. R. to Q. Kt. third" is perhaps safer than the move in the text ; but White would, even if that move had been made, have retained a strong attack.

(*e*) Threatening, amongst other contingencies, to advance his Pawn to K. B. fourth.

(*f*) This offer of the exchange of Rooks is badly calculated.

(*g*) The correct play. Whether White exchange his K. B. Pawn for the hostile Pawn or not, the game must be drawn if Black play carefully.

Between the same Players.

Black. (Mr. BRIEN.)	*White.* (Mr. CAMPBELL.)
1. P. to K. B. fourth	1. P. to K. B. fourth
2. Kt. to K. B. third	2. Kt. to K. B. third
3. P. to K. third	3. P. to Q. Kt. third
4. P. to K. Kt. third	4. B. to Q. Kt. second
5. B. to K. Kt. second	5. P. to K. third
6. P. to Q. Kt. third	6. P. to K. Kt. third
7. B. to Q. Kt. second	7. B. to K. Kt. second
8. Kt. to Q. R. third	8. Kt. to Q. R. third
9. Castles	9. Castles (*a*)
10. Kt. to K. square	10. B. takes B.
11. K. takes B.	11. Kt. to K. fifth
12. B. takes B.	12. K. takes B.
13. Q. to K. second	13. Kt. to Q. Kt. fifth
14. P. to Q. third	14. Kt. to K. B. third (*b*)

15. P. to Q. B. third (c)	15. Kt. to Q. B. third
16. Kt. to Q. B. fourth	16. P. to Q. third
17. Kt. to K. B. third	17. Q. to Q. second
18. P. to K. fourth (d)	18. Q. R. to K. square
19. P. to K. fifth	19. Kt. to Q. fourth
20. P. takes P.	20. P. takes P.
21. Q. R. to K. square (e)	21. Q. R. to K. second
22. Kt. to K. third	22. Kt. to K. B. third
23. P. to Q. B. fourth	23. P. to K. fourth
24. Kt. to Q. fifth	24. Kt. takes Kt.
25. P. takes Kt.	25. Kt. to Q. Kt. fifth
26. P. takes P.	26. P. takes P.
27. P. to Q. R. third (f)	27. Kt. takes P. at Q. fourth
28. Q. to Q. Kt. second (g)	28. Q. to Q. B. third (h)
29. R. takes P.	29. R. takes R.
30. Q. takes R. (check)	30. Kt. to K. B. third
31. R. to K. B. second	31. R. to K. square
32. Q. to Q. fourth	32. P. to K. Kt. fourth
33. Q. to Q. B. fourth	33. Q. to Q. Kt. second
34. R. to Q. B. second	34. K. to K. Kt. third (i)
35. Q. to Q. B. sixth	35. Q. takes Q.
36. R. takes Q.	36. P. to K. Kt. fifth
37. Kt. to Q. fourth	37. R. to K. second
38. Kt. to K. sixth	38. K. to K. B. second
39. Kt. to K. B. fourth	39. R. to Q. second
40. K. to K. B. second.	40. Kt. to K. square

After a few more moves, the game was declared drawn.

Notes.

(a) The " P. to K. B. fourth " opening is likely to lead to positions of uniformity, and for the most part of little interest.

(b) "Q. to K. B. third," and "Kt. to Q. B. sixth," would be of no avail.

(c) These Pawns are not strongly posted, but it is necessary to drive back the Knights.

(d) This move is hazardous, but it is the only one to impart life to the game.

(e) The threatened move "Q. to Q. Kt. second," always guards the Q. B. Pawn.

(f) To prevent White's Queen from taking the Q. Pawn.

(g) Perhaps more to be relied on than " Kt. takes K. P."

(h) Compelling Black to regain the Pawn by " R. takes P."

(i) Probably " Kt. to Q. fourth " is stronger.

In the first few months of 1856, some consultation games were played at the St. George's Chess Club, London, between various players of eminence. Many of them found their way into the columns of the weekly papers. We have selected two out of the number, and the more so, as the revival of the Magazine, which once owed so much to Mr. Staunton, is with peculiar propriety accompanied by the publication of some of his games. We have not attempted to analyze the ensuing games, but give in a condensed form the notes of the *Illustrated London News*, written doubtless by the players.

Game played in consultation by Messrs. STAUNTON and ALTER against Messrs. LÖWENTHAL and BARNES.

Black. (LÖWENTHAL & BARNES.)	*White*. (STAUNTON and ALTER.)
1. P. to K. fourth	1. P. to K. fourth
2. Kt. to K. B. third	2. P. to Q. third
3. P. to Q. fourth	3. P. takes P.
4. Q. takes P.	4. Kt. to Q. B. third
5. K. B. to Q. Kt. fifth	5. B. to Q. second
6. B. takes Kt.	6. B. takes B.
7. Kt. to Q. B. third	7. Kt. to K. B. third
8. Castles	8. B. to K. second
9. B. to K. third	9. Castles
10. P. to K. R. third	10. Q. to Q. second
11. Q. R. to Q. square (*a*)	11. Q. R. to K. square
12. Kt. to Q. second (*b*)	12. K. B. to Q. square
13. P. to K. B. fourth	13. Kt. to K. R. fourth (*c*)
14. Q. to Q. third (*d*)	14. P. to K. B. fourth (*e*)
15. K. to R. second	15. P. takes P.
16. Q. to K. second (*f*)	16. Kt. to K. B. third
17. Kt. to Q. Kt. third	17. Q. to K. B. second (*g*)
18. Kt. to Q. R. fifth	18. Q. to Q. second
19. B. takes Q. R. P. (*h*)	19. K. to R. square
20. B. to K. third	20. P. to Q. Kt. third
21. Kt. takes B.	21. Q. takes Kt.
22. P. to K. Kt. fourth	22. Q. to Q. second (*i*)
23. P. to K. Kt. fifth	23. Kt. to K. Kt. square
24. R. to Q. fourth	24. Q. to K. B. fourth (*k*)
25. R. to K. Kt. square (*l*)	25. P. to Q. B. third (*m*)
26. R. takes Q. P.	26. B. to Q. B. second

27. R. takes Q. B. P.	27. B. takes P. (check)
28. B. takes B.	28. Q. takes B. (check)
29. K. to R. square	29. Kt. to K. second
30. R. to K. sixth	30. Kt. to K. B. fourth
31. R. takes K. P.	31. Kt. to K. Kt. sixth (check)
32. R. takes Kt.	32. Q. takes R. at Kt. sixth
33. R. takes R. (n)	33. Q. takes K. R. P. (check)
34. K. to Kt. square	34. Q. to K. Kt. sixth (check)
35. K. to R. square	35. Q. to. K. R. fifth (check)
36. Q. to K. R. second	36. Q. takes Q. (check)
37. K. takes Q.	37. R. takes R.
38. K. to Kt. third	38. R. to K. fourth
39. K. to B. fourth	39. R. to Q. B. fourth
40. P. to Q. R. fourth	40. K. to. Kt. square
41. K. to K. Kt. fourth	41. K. to K. B. second
42. K. to K. B. fourth	42. K. to K. Kt. third
43. K. to K. third	43. R. takes P.

The game terminated in favour of White.

Notes.

(a) Not so good a move as it appears.

(b) Apprehending a triple attack upon the King's Pawn, by "K. B. to Q. square."

(c) This impedes the development of Black's game.

(d) To avoid the consequences of White playing their K. Bishop to B. third, and then capturing the adverse Kt. We are not sure, however, that Black played the best move. The general opinion was that they should rather have played their King to R. second.

(e) Threatening, if the Pawn be captured, to move the Kt. to K. Kt. sixth.

(f) They dare not take the Pawn, for the capture would cost them a piece, ex. gr. :—

16. Kt. takes P.	16. Q. to K. third
17. P. to K. Kt. fourth (best)	17. B. takes Kt.
18. Kt. takes B.	18. Q. takes Kt.
	&c. &c.

(g) They should rather have played P. to Q. Kt. third, to prevent "Kt. to Q. R. fifth," which occasions them a good deal of trouble.

(h) It is not often that this Pawn can be taken with impunity; but in the present case White cannot play P. to Q. Kt. third, and imprison the Bishop, without losing a piece through the check of the adverse Queen.

(i) It was necessary to bring the Queen back, or Black would have obtained a strong attack on the K.'s side.

(k) Threatening to take the K. Kt. P. with their Bishop.

(*l*) It would have been better, perhaps, to have moved this Rook to Q. square, or the other to Q. fifth.

(*m*) The correct move.

(*n*) Had they played " Q. to K. Kt. second," White would not have exchanged Queens, but would probably have moved " Q. to Q. third," a winning advantage.

Consultation Game played by Messrs. STAUNTON and BARNES against Messrs. LÖWENTHAL and ALTER.

Black. (Messrs. L. and A.)	*White.* (Messrs. S. and B.)
1. P. to K. fourth	1. P. to K. fourth
2. Q. Kt. to Q. B. third	2. K. Kt. to K. B. third
3. P. to K. B. fourth	3. P. to Q. fourth
4. K. B. P. takes K. P.	4. Kt. takes K. P.
5. K. Kt. to K. B. third	5. Q. B. to K. Kt. fifth
6. K. B. to K. second	6. Q. Kt. to Q. B. third
7. K. B. to Q. Kt. fifth	7. K. B. to Q. Kt. fifth (*a*)
8. Q. to K. second	8. K. Kt. to K. Kt. fourth
9. Q. to K. B. second	9. Q. B. takes K. Kt.
10. K. Kt. P. takes B.	10. Castles
11. B. takes Kt.	11. P. takes B.
12. Kt. to K. second	12. P. to K. B. third
13. P. to K. R. fourth	13. Kt. to K. third
14. P. to Q. B. third	14. B. to Q. R. fourth
15. P. to Q. fourth	15. P. takes K. P.
16. P. takes P.	16. P. to Q. fifth
17. B. to Q. second	17. Q. to Q. fourth
18. K. R. to K. B. square	18. B. to Q. Kt. third
19. Q. to K. Kt. third	19. P. to Q. sixth
20. Kt. to Q. B. square	20. Q. R. to Q. square
21. Kt. to Q. Kt. third	21. P. to Q. R. fourth
22. P. to Q. B. fourth	22. Q. takes Q. B. P.
23. B. to Q. B. third	23. B. to Q. fifth (*b*)
24. Kt. takes B.	24. Kt. takes Kt.
25. K. to Q. second	25. Kt. to K. third
26. P. to K. B. fourth	26. Kt. to Q. B. fourth
27. Q. R. to K. square	27. Kt. to K. fifth (check)
28. R. takes Kt.	28. Q. takes R.
29. R. to K. B. second	29. K. R. to K. B. second
30. Q. to K. third	30. Q. to K. B. fourth

The game was won by White.

Notes.

(a) The *I. L. N.* prefers " K. B. to Q. B. fourth."
(b) This move is condemned by the *I. L. N.*, which recommends "P. to Q. seventh (check)."

A game between Mr. MORPHY, the celebrated American player, and Mr. BARNES, a strong English amateur. Played in 1858.

White. (Mr. MORPHY.)	*Black.* (Mr. BARNES.)
1. P. to K. fourth	1. P. to K. fourth
2. B. to Q. B. fourth	2. Kt. to K. B. third
3. Kt. to K. B. third	3. Kt. takes P.
4. Kt. to Q. B. third	4. Kt. takes Kt.
5. Q. P. takes Kt.	5. P. to K. B. third
6. Castles	6. Kt. to Q. B. third (a)
7. Kt. to K. R. fourth	7. Q. to K. second
8. Kt. to K. B. fifth	8. Q. to Q. B. fourth
9. B. to Q. Kt. third	9. P. to Q. fourth
10. B. to K. third	10. Q. to Q. R. fourth
11. Kt. to K. R. fourth	11. B. to K. third
12. Q. to K. R. fifth (check)	12. P. to K. Kt. third
13. Kt. takes K. Kt. P.	13. B. to K. B. second
14. Q. to K. R. fourth	14. B. takes Kt.
15. Q. takes K. B. P.	15. R. to K. Kt. square
16. Q. R. to Q. square	16. B. to K. second
17. Q. to K. sixth	17. B. to K. B. second
18. Q. to K. R. third	18. Kt. to Q. square
19. P. to K. B. fourth	19. P. to K. fifth
20. R. takes Q. P.	20. B. takes R.
21. Q. to K. R. fifth (check)	21. K. to K. B. square
22. B. takes B.	22. R. to K. Kt. second
23. P. to Q. Kt. fourth	23. Q. to Q. R. third
24. P. to K. B. fifth	24. Kt. to K. B. second (b)
25. P. to K. B. sixth (c)	25. B. takes P.
26. P. to Q. Kt. fifth	26. Q. to Q. third
27. B. takes Kt.	27. P. to Q. Kt. third
28. B. to K. R. sixth	28. K. to K. second

29. B. takes R.	29. B. takes B.
30. B. to Q. Kt. third	30. R. to K. B. square
31. R. to K. B. seventh (check)	31. R. takes R.
32. Q. takes R. (check)	32. K. to Q. square
33. Q. takes B.	33. Q. to Q. eighth (check)
34. K. to K. B. second	34. Q. to Q. seventh (check)
35. K. to K. Kt. third	35. P. to K. sixth
36. Q. to K. B. sixth (check)	36. K. to Q. B. square
37. B. to K. sixth (check)	

And wins.

Notes.

(*a*) "Q. to K. second" is the correct move, and establishes, we believe, the opening in favour of the second player. "P. to Q. third" is of no value, as the following variation from a game between Messrs. CAMPBELL and BRIEN will tend to prove:—

	6. P. to Q. third
7. Kt. to K. R. fourth	7. P. to K. Kt. third
8. P. to K. B. fourth	8. P. to K. B. fourth
9. Kt. takes K. B. P.	9. B. takes Kt.

And Mr. Campbell now won by "Q. to Q. fifth."

In the above variation, if the second player refuse to take the Kt. at move 9, he will get a bad game. We repeat, therefore, that he must destroy this gambit by playing for his 6th move "Q. to K. second."

(*b*) "B. to K. B. third" would have been unavailing.

(*c*) The combined advance of the Pawns on both sides of the board wins more than a piece.

SCORES IN MATCHES ACTUALLY FINISHED.

Mr. MORPHY's Matches :—Morphy, 9 ; Löwenthal, 3 ; drawn, 2.— Morphy, 5 ; Harrwitz, 2 ; drawn, 1.—Morphy, 7 ; Anderssen, 2 ; drawn, 2.

At the Philidorian Chess Rooms :—Campbell, 9 ; Kenny (5+3==) 8. —Wormald, 6 ; Kenny, 0.

Problem by F. HEALEY, Esq.

BLACK.

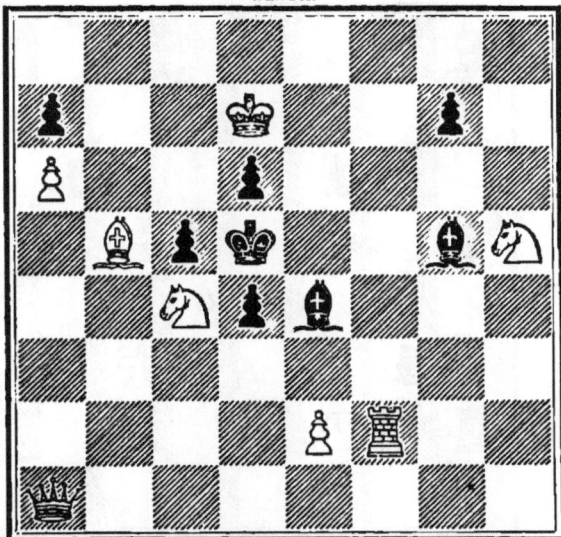

WHITE.

White to play and mate in three moves.

By the same.

BLACK.

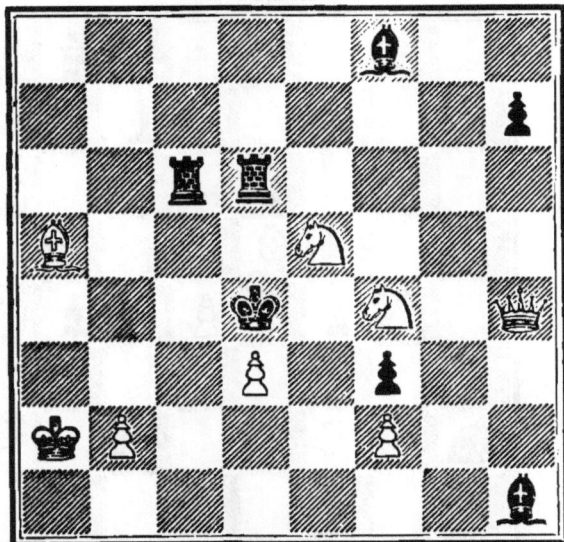

WHITE.

White to play and mate in four moves.

By R. B. Wormald, Esq.

BLACK.

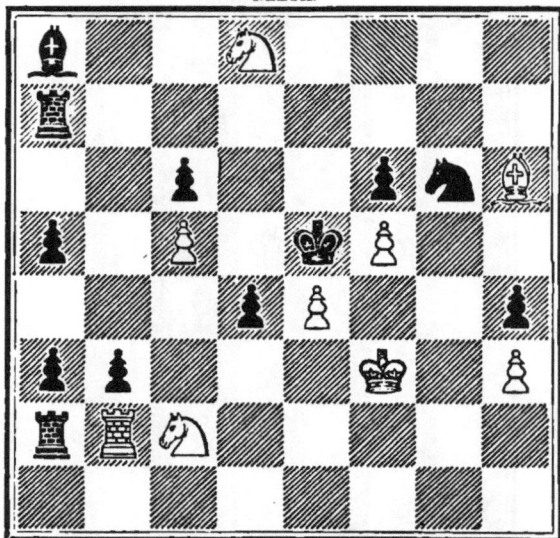

WHITE.

White mates in three moves.

By the same.

BLACK.

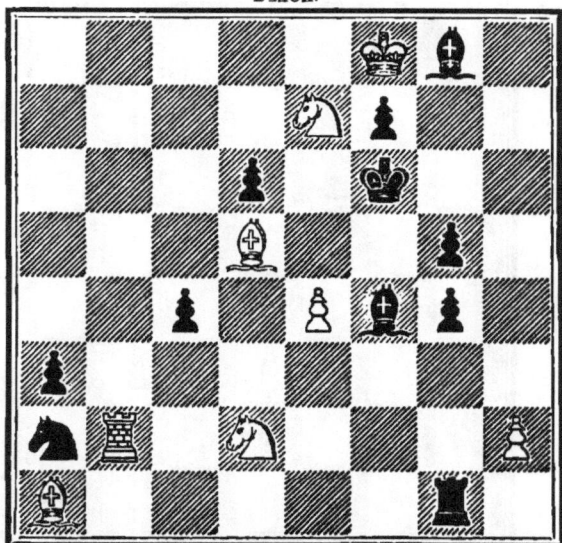

WHITE.

White mates in four moves.

THE PROGRESS OF CHESS.

A QUARTER of a century ago, when the two champions of the rival countries, whose mortal remains now peaceably repose, side by side, in Kensall Green Cemetery, were astonishing the Chess world by their prowess, unrivalled till then, unsurpassed even now, the literary department of Chess was far from being in a flourishing state. The hundred battles, in which, by turns, the high-spirited Frenchman defeated the stern and unyielding Englishman, "who did not know when he was beaten," or he still smarting from the infliction of late and severe punishments, which the son of Albion sometimes administered to him with no sparing hand, was returning to the battle-field with the same unbroken spirit, ready for either victory or defeat, both game to the last, these splendid specimens of Chess strategy scarcely found a chronicler, and a great many of them were entirely lost to posterity. It was then considered an event when a meagre and solitary Chess treatise at distant periods made its appearance. A Chess magazine was a thing as unheard of as an electric telegraph. No weekly paper had as yet opened its columns to regular Chess articles. The Chess editor was destined to be an invention of more recent days. When we now consider that, at the present moment, in the Metropolis alone, we have, besides this magazine, eleven weekly papers with regular Chess columns, we are at once struck by the immense progress Chess literature has made during the last twenty-five years.

Unimportant as this fact may seem to the casual observer, we find therein good reasons to congratulate ourselves upon it. That Chess has found its way into so many periodical publications, in so short a space of time, proves (as the demand is always in the same ratio as the consumption) the rapid increase of Chess players. Now, Chess being a merely intellectual amusement, requiring already a higher and more refined mental standard, the extensive practice of the game shows a more extended civilization. A Chess tournament is a more refined spectacle than a cockfight or a pugilistic encounter, nay, even than a hunt by torch-light. Measuring, therefore, our social progress by our intellectual amusements, we have of late years outstripped all European nations. Even intellectual Germany cannot boast of an equal number of Chess publications, Chess institutions, or Chess players. As to

France, alas! it has remained far behind in the lists; it has, we believe, but one single periodical where Chess occasionally makes a sullen appearance. As to Chess authors, whilst Germany has only its HEYDEBRANDT, VON DER LASA, and Russia its JAENISCH, that have produced works of merit, we have LEWIS, WALKER, and STAUNTON, each of whom has largely contributed to Chess literature. Our transatlantic brethren, although they have as yet no Chess authors, are the only nation that can rival us in periodical Chess literature; they are (and this speaks greatly in their favor) "going ahead" in Chess as well as in other things. Their Chess Monthly, although as yet in its infancy, promises to become, in time, a valuable resource to the Chess student, especially if the country sends forth other knights errant of the same stamp and valor as the one who is now filling Europe with his renown, and whose high deeds they will have the good fortune to chronicle.

It is not an unpleasant consideration, that even in Chess literature, the English nation stands in the foremost ranks—rivalled by few, surpassed by none.

_____

CHESS JOURNALISM.

As we open our eyes on the Chess world after a two years' slumber, we are met on every side by many and great changes.

The victor of 1851 has allowed his sword to rust in its scabbard, and fallen an easy victim to the stripling who has ventured to dispute the championship of Europe. Old veterans have passed away into the dust, or retired upon their laurels, and their place has been filled by a young and rising race of players. The ranks of Problem composers have been recruited by a legion of eager aspirants after fame. Chess has, in fact, undergone a complete transformation. We have had Chess gatherings, Chess quarrels, tournaments, and Problem jousts. The powerful under-current of progress which manifests itself amid all these changes, is unmistakeable; and to our minds, the most satisfactory evidence of this, is the introduction of Chess into the weekly journals.

There are now. in London only, no less than eleven periodicals which devote a column once a week exclusively to Chess. We believe the following will be found to be a complete list of these, which we have arranged in no particular manner, but just in the order they happen to present themselves :—*The Illustrated London News*—*Bell's Life*—*The Era*—*The Field*—*The Sunday Times*—*Cassell's Family Paper*—*The Illustrated News of the World*—*The Review*—*Reynolds's Miscellany*—*The Family Herald*—and *the London Journal.*

It is our intention, as the representative of English Chess players, to exercise our privilege of reviewing the Chess literature of the day. We trust, therefore, that our remarks will be taken in good part, inasmuch as they are influenced by no personal or party feelings; but are dictated solely from a conscientious spirit of fair play, and a desire to promote the true interests of Chess.

Before we proceed further, we will, *in limine*, touch upon a question which the subject naturally suggests. It is a common thing to hear Chess players complain that so large a proportion of the Chess literature of the day should be solely in the hands of foreigners. Now, with all our English prepossessions, we must earnestly protest against their morbid un-English ξενολασία. Chess is essentially cosmopolitan—a vast brotherhood bound together by peculiar ties and sympathies of its own; rivalling even the vaunted union of Freemasonry, and ignoring alike with it, all distinction of birth, profession, or country. And even while we smile at the quaintness of some occasional editorial idiom, we should do well to bear in mind, that, had it not been for the exertions of some of these foreigners, several of our Chess columns would never have existed; and that, moreover, the beauties of German Chess would have been, in many respects, a sealed book to us.

The *Illustrated London News* has certainly the first claim on our attention. Commencing in 1845, it has, for a period of nearly fifteen years, supplied its readers with a weekly game and problem. We feel it will be expected of us to allude to some of the charges which have been brought against its editorial management. We are, however, unwilling to open old sores, or rake up old grievances, which are only calculated to bring Chess into general disrepute. All of us must be aware of the tendency of party spirit to make a man blind to the *good* qualities of an opponent. If we set the good against the evil, there can be little doubt on which side the scales will incline. To say nothing of the intrinsic merits of the column itself, whose list of contributors includes almost every name of note in the Chess world, it is undeniable

3*

that its editor has done more for the cause of Chess than any man living. There are few, we imagine, of our best players, or problem composers, whose earliest and brightest Chess reminiscences are not associated with Mr. STAUNTON.

Bell's Life comes next on our list, and a kindly, gossiping, companionable Chess friend he is! With all his strong party prepossessions, he is still a lover of fair play, and ever willing to give both sides a ready hearing. We must confess, however, to having been considerably startled by the strange *metamorphosis* which has of late come over him. The gallantry and daring of the young novice, who has just entered the ring to dispute the championship of the heavy weights, assuredly must have completely fascinated him. It is only on this supposition that we can account for the high-flown tone of laudation—we almost said adulation—which pervades his annotations on Mr. MORPHY's games. No one who is in the least degree acquainted with the writer's true character, can for a moment doubt the honesty or sincerity of these comments. Yet we would fain remind him, albeit reluctantly, that the great mass of exoteric Chess players, when they find the mildest moves heralded as " Mr. MORPHY's crushing logic "(!) or the modest coup of K. to R. second, hailed with " What, up again, old fellow," will begin to fancy they are on the verge of that narrow boundary where "great wit " becomes undistinguishable from madness, and hero-worship from toadyism.

Herr LÖWENTHAL conducts no less than three columes, viz., the *Era*, the *Illustrated News of the World*, and the *Family Herald ;* the first named, as we are informed every week, "exclusively," whatever that may mean. In one respect the *Era* merits our especial attention. In addition to its other excellent features, it invariably contains the latest Chess intelligence. The other journals are content with supplying a few scraps of information respecting the last new star, or the score of the last match in some favored Chess locality ; but the *Era* is thoroughly cosmopolitan, and gives the sayings and doings of our several metropolitan and provincial Chess centres with a most praiseworthy impartiality.

The *Illustrated News of the World* is conducted on the same principles, and for so young a column seems to enjoy a very considerable share of patronage. The *Family Herald* is mainly devoted to the instruction of young players. To this end it has supplied a series of

" Chess Lessons," illustrated by a selection of carefully annotated games, and some capital two-move problems.

The *Sunday Times* will doubtless he favorably known to the majority of our readers, to whom the name of Mr. FALKBEER will be a sufficient guarantee for the excellence of the editorial arrangements. In the general accuracy and soundness of his Problem department, he may be favorably contrasted with many of his brother editors. Only those who have had a practical experience of this branch of Chess can form any conception of the patient analysis and rigid scrutiny a problem must undergo before it can be pronounced sound. Only a short time ago, no less than five out of twelve weekly Chess problems admitted of a double solution; and yet each of these had probably passed through the hands of several examiners.

The Chess column of the *Field* was originally commenced under the auspices of the late Mr. WILLIAMS. On his death it was for a time discontinued, but was subsequently revived, and is now in the hands of one of our ablest players, whose editorial judgment, good taste, and impartiality, are above all praise. One of the leading features of the *Field* is the prominence it gives to good provincial Chess, though by no means to the exclusion of metropolitan play.

The limits of our paper prevent us saying more than a few words for *Cassell's Family Paper*, and *Reynolds's Miscellany*. The Chess column of the former has been established for some years, and we believe, with the exception of the *Illustrated London News*, has a larger circulation among Chess players than any on our list. In its Problem department, which includes almost every English composer of note, it may challenge comparison with any of its higher priced contemporaries. This, combined with the courtesy of its editor, has rendered *Cassell* a general favorite, more especially in provincial Chess circles.

Reynolds's Miscellany is the latest addition to the ranks of Chess journalism. From the few numbers we have seen, we augur favorably of its success. In fact, judging from its numerous notices to correspondents, it seems to have already established a firm footing among Chess players.

There are now but two left on our list—the *Review*, and *London Journal*. On these silence were the best comment. In no single respect do they merit a favorable criticism. To say nothing of their defects in matter and arrangement, the good taste of parading the utterly unknown editorial names at the head of every column, is, to say the least, questionable.

Hitherto we have hailed the development of Chess in this direction as a matter of congratulation; but the picture has its darker side, and to suppress it, would be only to injure the cause we would serve. We all know what a burlesque of the term is "popular" science. Nor is this remark inapplicable to Chess. There are many dangers attendant on popularizing Chess too much. In the first place, there is every probability of our losing in quality what we gain in quantity. This is borne out by the fact, that whereas at the present day we have a countless host of third and fourth rate players, it is questionable whether we have as many first, or even good second rates, than there were a dozen years ago.

Again, it has a tendency to break up Chess into sects and cliques. One set of players is sunk in a blind state of "hero worship," and pin their faith absolutely on one idolized individual. They make no allowance for the effect of age or other occupations, but fondly imagine that what he once was he must ever be. Others, on the contrary, rush frantically after every new "star" that rises above the Chess horizon, and form around it a halo of fulsome adoration, thus obscuring the very brilliancy they seek to enhance. We cannot condemn too strongly each of these extremes. We are no Chess conservatives. In our eyes the brightness of the new moon is not one whit tarnished by any affectionate regret after the glories of that ancient institution the old one. But, on the other hand, we must most emphatically protest against the prevalent fashion of depreciating a fine player because he has lost this or that match. An old veteran should be neither worshipped as an idol, nor ignored as a nonentity, but reverenced as a relic.

Lastly,—and what is most dangerous of all,—the spread of Chess may cause it to be overrated. Bacon's caution against metaphysical philosophy, is equally applicable to Chess. The danger is, "lest by falsely magnifying and extolling the powers of the mind, we seek not its real helps." Chess can never, either in England or America, become a *profession*. It is but a scientific recreation—the highest, indeed, of all—but still *only* a recreation; and he who would make it more, and propose it as the end and aim of his existence, must inevitably sink into that most contemptible of characters—the man of one idea —the *mere* Chess player.

ANDERSSEN AS A MATCH-PLAYER.

Sic omnia fatis
In pejus ruero, ac retro sublapsa referri.

THE recent encounter at Paris has given rise to a repetition of the opinions which were expressed at the close of the Tournament in 1851. There were then two armies in the field. One of them depreciated, the other too much extolled, the victory of the Prussian conqueror. For our own part, we are neither jealous detracters nor servile admirers of ANDERSSEN. We acknowledge his great merit, we assign to him just limits. Conquest and defeat are relative, not absolute, tests of ability. Even in pursuits wherein bodily strength and good health are considered the chief qualifications, the spoiled favorites of fortune have experienced strange vicissitudes. A maritime nation, attached to aquatic sports, sees the champions of her greatest river beaten by more prosperous opponents. Do good judges, therefore, infer that each successive champion is superior to his predecessor? Or do they weigh in true scales the qualities of form and constant practice? Are, then, the subtler elements of mind to be free from the universal law of decay? Two men of the same period, one the brightest wit, the other the most consummate commander of this country, suffered from the gravest distemper of the intellect. The Chess player is not an exception to the rule. The victor in 1844 may, seven years afterwards, have been unequal to a severe contest; his successor may already be past his prime. Mindful of this gradual deterioration in skill, mindful too that the note of triumph would be sounded after their defeat, the wise LEWIS and the sagacious DES CHAPELLES gave up heavy play before they lost command over their faculties. ANDERSSEN has surpassed those distinguished players in boldness: he has not imitated their discretion. His late campaign has not been crowned by those laurels which encircled his brow in 1851. Indeed, on this occasion he has not only not commanded, but has not even deserved, success. We did not over-rate his good fortune in the tournament. We did not worship his prowess, because he won four games of STAUNTON, and lost but one, that one, as internal evidence proves, having been snatched out of the fire. Far less did we care for his victory in the little one-game contest at the London Chess Club. Our judgment rested on different canons of criticism. It was founded on two principles: firstly, on the *invariable* success of ANDERSSEN in matches; and, secondly, on the excellence of his play. The Chess Tournament shows us that he encountered in succession, KIESERITZKI, SZEN, STAUNTON, and WYVILL, gaining, if we take the four conjointly, fourteen games, and losing five. What was the cause of this success? In 1851 his play was sound, steady, and earnest. Never tedious, he was always patient. Not unwilling to advance, he did not build his combinations on imaginary attack, he kept in view a true line of defence. In a word, he never calculated loosely. But what is the value of his recent play? The games show on his part a want of steadiness, perseverance, and self-possession. Once eminently self-conscious, he seems to have lost the main attribute of a great Chess player. This strikes us as the reason why (to speak technically), in the match before us, he rashly sacrifices Pawns, Knights, and Rooks. This is the true cause why, when the attack is in his hands, he is unable to bring it to a successful issue. The career of ANDERSSEN furnishes instruction to Chess players of all countries. A careful examination of his games shows that his present play finds an exact parallel in that of his opponent's, or, at least, the most distinguished of them, at the time at which he earned the championship of Chess. Then *they* were unsound, *they* failed in their assaults, *his* aim was unerring. We put out of sight entirely the question, whether his late antagonist was a player of higher, or so high, an order. No such question can affect an argument addressed exclusively to the discussion of ANDERSSEN's style of play. A word, however, about his conqueror. MORPHY has shown several qualities which ought to adorn a match player. He has proved himself a skilful general by his prudence and accuracy, not unattended by a promptness in taking advantage of his adversary's mistakes in calculation. Such gifts, so rare in a player of his age, added, as they are, to an extraordinary memory (and that memory already provided with its choicest food—prodigious learning in openings, and unexampled acquaintance with published games) may well make the youthful champion dangerous to any competitor. His power will be better tested hereafter. We would not do injustice to his high-spirited opponent. The games of the match, decidedly inferior as they are to those of M'DONNELL and DE LA BOURDONNAIS, and of STAUNTON and ST. AMANT, are also far below ANDERSSEN's previous match play. We will not, therefore, undertake to say that ANDERSSEN cannot resume his pristine vigour and correctness. His other labours upon mental subjects, perhaps, may not exclude him entirely from the practice of Chess. We remember how M'DONNELL rallied after his first defeat by DE LA BOURDONNAIS. A similar lot may be reserved for the gallant Prussian. Be that as it may, Chess players owe him not a little gratitude for his public spirit, and for his valuable contributions to the literature of our game. Chess would willingly get rid of some of its mere players and professors; it gladly enters upon its muster-roll the names of scholars and mathematicians.

The following five Games form the conclusion of the Match between Mr. MORPHY and Professor ANDERSSEN.

GAME VII.

White. (MORPHY.)	*Black.* (ANDERSSEN.)
1. P. to K. fourth	1. P. to Q. fourth
2. P. takes P.	2. Q. takes P.
3. Q. Kt. to B. third	3. Q. to Q. R. fourth
4. P. to Q. fourth	4. P. to K. fourth (a)
5. P. takes P.	5. Q. takes P. (check)
6. K. B. to K. second	6. K. B. to Q. Kt. fifth
7. K. Kt. to B. third (b)	7. B. takes Kt. (check)
8. P. takes B.	8. Q. takes Q. B. P. (check)
9. Q. B. to Q. second	9. Q. to Q. B. fourth
10. Q. R. to Q. Kt. square	10. Q. Kt. to Q. B. third (a)
11. Castles	11. K. Kt. to K. B. third
12. Q. B. to K. B. fourth	12. Castles (c)
13. Q. B. takes Q. B. P.	13. Q. Kt. to Q. fifth
14. Q. takes Kt.	14. Q. takes B.
15. B. to Q. third	15. Q. B. to K. Kt. fifth (b)
16. Kt. to K. Kt. fifth	16. K. R. to Q. square (c)
17. Q. to Q. Kt. fourth	17. B. to B. square
18. K. R. to K. square	18. P. to Q. R. fourth
19. Q. to K. seventh	19. Q. takes Q.
20. R. takes Q.	20. Kt. to Q. fourth
21. B. takes K. R. P. (check)	21. K. to R. square
22. R. takes K. B. P.	22. Kt. to Q. B. sixth
23. Q. R. to K. square	23. Kt. takes Q. R. P.
24. K. R. to K. B. fourth	24. Q. R. to Q. R. third
25. B. to Q. third	

And Black resigns.

Notes.

(a) This is a very inconsiderate move, as Black must lose Q. B. P. by it. Q. to Q. third, would have been better.

(b) Another weak move, which considerably weakens Black's game.

(c) This last move seals Black's fate. We are at a loss to understand the object of it. Why not play P. to K. R. third, attacking the Kt. ? This is simply throwing a game away, and does not resemble Anderssen's ordinary play.

GAME VIII.

White. (ANDERSSEN.)	*Black.* (MORPHY.)
1. P. to Q. R. third (*a*)	1. P. to K. fourth
2. P. to Q. B. fourth	2. Kt. to K. B. third
3. Kt. to Q. B. third	3. P. to Q. fourth
4. P. takes P.	4. K. Kt. takes P.
5. P. to K. third	5. Q. B. to K. third
6. Kt. to K. B. third	6. B. to Q. third
7. B. to K. second	7. Castles
8. P. to Q. fourth	8. Kt. takes Kt.
9. P. takes Kt.	9. P. to K. fifth
10. Kt. to Q. second	10. P. to K. B. fourth
11. P. to K. B. fourth	11. Q. to K. R. fifth (check)
12. P. to K. Kt. third	12. Q. to K. R. sixth
13. B. to K. B. square	13. Q. to K. R. third
14. P. to Q. B. fourth	14. P. to Q. B. third
15. P. to Q. B. fifth	15. B. to Q. B. second
16. B. to Q. B. fourth (*b*)	16. Kt. to Q. second
17. Castles	17. P. to Q. Kt. fourth
18. P. takes P. (*en passant*)	18. P. takes P.
19. Q. to Q. Kt. third	19. K. R. to K. square
20. B. to Q. Kt. second	20. P. to Q. Kt. fourth
21. B. takes B. (check)	21. Q. takes B.
22. Q. to Q. B. second	22. Q. to Q. fourth
23. K. R. to Q. B. square	23. R. to Q. R. third
24. P. to Q. R. fourth	24. K. R. to Q. R. square
25. P. takes P.	25. Q. takes Kt. P.
26. Q. to Q. B. fourth (check) (*c*)	26. Q. takes Q.
27. Kt. takes Q.	27. R. takes R.
28. B. takes R.	28. Kt. to K. B. third
29. B. to Q. B. third (*d*)	29. R. to Q. R. seventh
30. B. to Q. second	30. Kt. to Q. fourth
31. K. to B. square	31. B. to Q. square
32. K. to K. square	32. B. to K. second
33. R. to Q. Kt. square	33. P. to K. R. third
34. Kt. to K. fifth	34. P. to Q. B. fourth
35. P. takes P.	35. B. takes P.

36. R. to Q. Kt. fifth	36. Kt. takes K. P.
37. R. takes B.	37. Kt. to Kt. seventh (check)
38. K. to K. second	38. P. to K. sixth
39. Kt. to K. B. third	39. P. to K. Kt. third
40. R. to Q. fifth	40. K. to B. second
41. R. to Q. sixth	41. K. to Kt. second
42. P. to K. R. fourth	42. P. takes B.
43. R. takes Q. P.	43. R. to Q. R. fifth
44. K. to B. second	44. Kt. takes K. B. P.
45. P. takes Kt.	45. R. takes P.
46. R. to Q. fourth	46. R. takes R.
47. Kt. takes R.	47. K. to B. third
48. K. to K. third	48. P. to K. Kt. fourth
49. P. to R. fifth	49. K. to K. fourth
50. Kt. to K. B. third (check)	50. K. to B. third

And the game was abandoned as drawn, after a few more moves.

Notes.

(a) This is giving the advantage of the attack away. Morphy's knowledge of the openings must have told upon Anderssen, to reduce him to a defensive move.

(b) Kt. to Q. B. fourth, would have been stronger, as he is quite useless in his present place.

(c) This seems to us a most unnecessary exchange of Queens. Kt. to Q. B. fourth, would have been much stronger.

(d) B. to Q. Kt. second, would have been better.

GAME IX.

(Sicilian Defence.)

White. (MORPHY.)	Black. (ANDERSSEN.)
1. P. to K. fourth	1. P. to Q. B. fourth
2. P. to Q. fourth	2. P. takes P.
3. Kt. to K. B. third	3. Kt. to Q. B. third
4. Kt. takes P.	4. P. to K. third
5. Kt. to Q. Kt. fifth	5. P. to Q. third
6. B. to K. B. fourth	6. P. to K. fourth
7. B. to K. third	7. P. to K. B. fourth (a)
8. Q. Kt. to Q. B. third	8. P. to K. B. fifth (b)

9. Kt. to Q. fifth (b)	9. P. takes B.
10. K. Kt. to Q.B.seventh (check)	10. K. to B. second
11. Q. to K. B. third (check)	11. Kt. to K. B. third
12. B. to Q. B. fourth	12. Kt. to Q. fifth
13. Kt. takes Kt. (discover check)	13. P. to Q. fourth
14. B. takes Q. P. (check)	14. K. to Kt. third
15. Q. to K. R. fifth (check)	15. K. takes Kt.
16. P. takes P.	16. Kt. takes Q. B. P. (check)
17. K. to K. second	

And Black resigned.

Notes.

(a) It is difficult to account for the occurrence of such a move in a match game, for it can neither be called a blunder nor an oversight, but is one of those careless moves which are only pardoned in skittling games. A moment's reflection would have shown that Pawn to Q. R. third was the move.

(b) P. to Q. R. third, could have still saved the game. After the move in the text, the game was beyond redemption.

GAME X.

Black. (ANDERSSEN.)	White. (MORPHY.)
1. P. to Q. R. third	1. P. to K. fourth
2. P. to Q. B. fourth	2. Kt. to K. B. third
3. Kt. to Q. B. third	3. P. to Q. fourth
4. P. takes P.	4. Kt. takes P.
5. P. to K. third	5. Q. B. to K. third
6. Kt. to K. B. third	6. B. to Q. third
7. B. to K. second	7. Castles
8. Castles.	8. Kt. takes Kt.
9. Kt. P. takes Kt.	9. P. to K. B. fourth
10. P. to Q. fourth	10. P. to K. fifth
11. Kt. to Q. second	11. R. to K. B. third
12. P. to K. B. fourth (a)	12. R. to K. R. third
13. P. to K. Kt. third	13. Kt. to Q. second
14. Kt. to Q. B. fourth	14. B. takes Kt.
15. B. takes B. (check)	15. K. to R. square

16. R. to Q. R. second	16. Q. to K. second
17. P. to Q. R. fourth	17. Kt. to K. B. third
18. Q. to Q. Kt. third	18. P. to Q. B. third
19. B. to K. sixth	19. R. to K. square (b)
20. B. to Q. B. fourth (c)	20. Kt. to K. Kt. fifth
21. R. to K. Kt. second	21. R. to Q. Kt. square
22. B. to K. second	22. Kt. to K. B. third
23. P. to Q. B. fourth	23. P. to Q. Kt. third
24. B. to Q. Kt. second	24. Q. to K. B. second
25. Q. to Q. B. second (d)	25. B. to Q. B. second (d)
26. B. to Q. B. third	26. R. to K. Kt. square
27. P. to Q. R. fifth	27. B. to Q. third
28. P. takes P.	28. P. takes P.
29. R. to Q. R. square (e)	29. P. to K. Kt. fourth
30. P. takes P.	30. Q. R. takes P.
31. R. to Q. R. eighth (check) (f)	31. R. to K. Kt. square (f)
32. Q. to Q. R. fourth	32. R. takes R.
33. Q. takes R. (check)	33. Q. to K. square
34. Q. takes Q. (check)	34. Kt. takes Q. (g)
35. P. to Q. B. fifth	35. B. to Q. B. second (h)
36. B. to Q. B. fourth	36. K. to Kt. second
37. P. takes P.	37. K. B. takes Q. Kt. P. (i)
38. R. to Q. Kt. second	38. B. to Q. B. second
39. R. to Q. Kt. seventh	39. K. to B. third
40. B. to Q. Kt. fourth	40. R. to K. Kt. third
41. B. to K. B. eighth	41. P. to K. R. fourth
42. K. to B. second	42. P. to K. R. fifth
43. P. takes P.	43. R. to K. Kt. fifth
44. P. to K. R. fifth	44. R. to K. R. fifth
45. P. to K. R. sixth	45. R. takes P. at K. R. second (check)
46. K. to Kt. square	46. R. to K. R. sixth
47. B. to K. B. square	47. R. to Kt. sixth (check)
48. K. to B. second	48. R. to K. Kt. fifth
49. B. to Q. B. fourth	49. R. to K. R. fifth
50. B. to K. Kt. eighth	50. B. to Q. third
51. B. takes R.	51. Kt. takes B.
52. R. to Q. seventh	52. Kt. to K. square

53. P. to K. R. seventh	53. K. to Kt. fourth
54. R. to. K. seventh	54. Kt. to Q. third
55. R. to K. sixth	55. Kt. to Q. B. fifth
56. R. takes Q. B. P.	56. Kt. to Q. seventh
57. K. to K. second	57. R. to K. R. seventh (check)
58. K. to Q. square	58. Kt. to K. B. sixth
59. R. to Q. B. seventh	59. K. to Kt. third
60. P. to Q. fifth	60. P. to K. B. fifth
61. P. takes P.	61. P. to K. sixth
62. R. to K. seventh	62. P. to K. seventh (check)
63. R. takes P.	63. R. to R. eighth (check)
64. K. to Q. B. second	64. Kt. to Q. fifth (check)
65. K. to Q. second	65. Kt. takes R.
66. K. takes Kt.	66. K. to Kt. second
67. K. to K. third	67. R. to K. eighth (check)
68. K. to Q. fourth	68. R. to K. B. eighth
69. K. to K. fifth	69. R. to K. eighth (check)
70. K. to K. B. fifth	70. R. to Q. eighth
71. B. to K. sixth	71. R. to Q. fifth
72. K. to K. fifth	72. R. to Q. eighth
73. P. to K. B. fifth	73. R. to K. R. eighth
74. P. to B. sixth (check)	74. K. takes R. P.
75. K. to Q. sixth	75. R. to Q. R. eighth
76. K. to K. seventh	76. R. to Q. R. second (check)
77. B. to Q. seventh	

And White resigns.

———

Notes.

(*a*) This is one of the very few instances in which we have seen Mr. Morphy make a weak move; the Rook is now quite powerless, after White shuts out the action of the Black B. by moving P. to Q. B. fourth. Having played the R. to B. third, Black, in order to sustain the attack, ought to have taken the Pawn in passing. Mr. Morphy, however, was so many games ahead, that he could safely take these liberties.

(*b*) Clearly a lost move. White's game, however, is already so strong, that he can afford to lose a move or two.

(*c*) Here the general of the Black forces returns the compliment by also losing a move; for it is evident that the Bishop, when he stops the advance of the Pawn, must retire to K. second, and thereby disturb the tranquillity of the Knight.

(d) This seems to us also a lost move ; P. to Q. R. third, would have been, to all appearances, more effectual.

(e) Black tries now by all means to liberate the K. R., which has been a useless prisoner all the while.

(f) White, as we have said, has so strong a game, that he can afford to lose a few moves, and so he does. Instead of rapidly terminating the game, as was his wont, he plays it on to the 77th move. Why give that now useless check with the Rook, and exchange Rooks, whilst R. to R. sixth wins much more easily? Thus, if Black answers by playing Q. to Q. Kt. second—

White.	*Black.*
Q. to Q. R. second	B. to Q. Kt. (best)
P. to Q. B. fifth	P. takes P. (best)
P. takes P.	

With a winning game.

If Black answers with B. to Q. B. second—

P. to Q. fifth	P. takes P. (best)
P. takes P.	Q. takes P.
B. to Q. B. fourth	

And wins.

If Black makes any other move, White wins the most important Pawn, and has an easy game.

(g) If, instead of Q. takes Q., White had played Q. to Q. Kt. seventh, how could Black have saved his Pawn ?

(h) R. to K. B. second, would have won the game much sooner.

(i) P. to Q. fifth (check) would have spared more than twenty moves; for if the Kt. cover, P. takes B. P. and wins; and if K. to Kt. third, P. to Q. sixth; and if then B. to Q., P. to K. Kt. fourth wins again.

GAME XI.

White. (MORPHY.)	*Black.* (ANDERSSEN.)
1. P. to K. fourth	1. P. to K. third
2. P. to Q. fourth	2. P. to K. Kt. third
3. B. to Q. third	3. B. to K. Kt. second
4. B. to K. third	4. P. to Q. B. fourth
5. P. to Q. B. third	5. P. takes P.
6. P. takes P.	6. Kt. to Q. B. third
7. Kt. to K. second	7. K. Kt. to K. second
8. Castles	8. Castles
9. Q. Kt. to Q. B. third	9. P. to Q. fourth
10. P. to K. fifth	10. P. to K. B. third
11. P. to K. B. fourth	11. P. takes P.
12. B. P. takes P.	12. P. to Q. R. third
13. Q. to Q. second	13. Kt. to Q. Kt. fifth (a)

14. B. to K. Kt. fifth	14. Kt. takes B.
15. Q. takes Kt.	15. B. to Q. second
16. Q. to K. R. third	16. Q. to K. square
17. Kt. to K. Kt. third	17. R. to Q. B. square (b)
18. R. takes R. (check)	18. Q. takes R.
19. R. to K. B. square	19. Q. to K. square
20. Q. to R. fourth	20. Kt. to K. B. fourth
21. Kt. takes Kt.	21. Kt. P. takes Kt.
22. R. to K. B. third	22. B. to Q. Kt. fourth (c)
23. R. to K. Kt. third	23. R. to Q. B. second
24. B. to K. B. sixth	24. P. to K. B. fifth (d)
25. Q. takes K. B. P.	25. Q. to K. B. square
26. Kt. takes B.	26. P. takes Kt.
27. Q. to K. R. sixth	27. K. to R. square (e)
28. R. takes B.	28. R. takes R.
29. K. to B. second	29. K. to Kt. square
30. Q. takes R. (check)	30. Q. takes Q.
31. B. takes Q.	31. K. takes B.
32. K. to B. third	32. P. to Q. Kt. fifth
33. P. to K. Kt. fourth	33. K. to Kt. third
34. P. to K. R. fourth	34. P. to Q. Kt. fourth
35. K. to K. third	

And Black resigns the game and the match.

Notes.

(a) A rash move.

(b) What was the object of this useless move?

(c) Why court a doubled Pawn?

(d) We have looked in vain to find out the reason of this sacrifice; if, instead of giving the Pawn up, Black had played K. to R. square, the game would not have been so desperate.

(e) This move comes too late now, for the Pawn which Black threw away loses him the game.

Game between Messrs. ZYTOGORSKI and FALKBEER, played at the Philidorian Chess Rooms.

White. (Mr. ZYTOGORSKI.)	*Black.* (Mr. FALKBEER.)
1. P. to K. fourth	1. P. to K. fourth
2. Kt. to K. B. third	2. P. to Q. fourth
3. Kt. takes P.	3. P. takes P.
4. P. to Q. fourth	4. Q. B. to K. third
5. K. B. to Q. B. fourth	5. B. takes B.
6. Kt. takes B.	6. P. to K. B. fourth
7. Castles	7. Kt. to K. B. third
8. Q. B. to K. Kt. fifth	8. B. to K. second
9. Kt. to K. third	9. Q. to Q. second
10. P. to Q. B. third	10. P. to Q. B. third
11. Q. Kt. to Q. second	11. Castles
12. P. to K. B. fourth	12. Kt. to Q. R. third
13. B. takes Kt.	13. B. takes B.
14. P. to K. Kt. fourth	14. P. to K. Kt. third
15. P. takes P.	15. P. takes P.
16. Q. to K. R. fifth	16. B. to Kt. second
17. R. to K. B. second	17. Q. R. to K. square
18. K. to R. square	18. Q. to K. B. second
19. Q. to K. R. third	19. R. to K. third
20. Q. R. to K. Kt. square	20. K. to R. square
21. K. R. to Kt. second	21. R. to K. R. third (*a*)
22. Q. takes P.	22. Q. takes Q.
23. Kt. takes Q.	23. R. takes Kt.
24. R. takes B.	24. R. to K. Kt. third
25. K. R. takes R.	25. P. takes R.
26. Kt. takes P.	26. R. takes P.
27. R. to K. square	27. Kt. to Q. B. second
28. K. to Kt. second	28. Kt. to Q. fourth
29. K. to Kt. third	29. R. to K. B. second
30. Kt. to Q. sixth	30. R. to Q. second
31. R. to K. eighth (check)	31. K. to Kt. second
32. Kt. to Q. B. fourth	32. Kt. to K. B. third
33. R. to Q. R. eighth	33. P. to Q. Kt. fourth
34. Kt. to K. fifth	34. R. to Q. B. second

4

35. K. to B. third	35. Kt. to Q. fourth
36. R. to Q. eighth	36. P. to Q. R. fourth
37. R. to Q. seventh (check)	37. R. takes R.
38. Kt. takes R.	38. P. to Q. Kt. fifth
39. P. to Q. B. fourth	39. Kt. to K. second
40. P. to Q. Kt. third	40. K. to B. second
41. K. to K. fourth	41. K. to K. third
42. Kt. to Q. B. fifth (check)	42. K. to K. B. third
43. Kt. to Q. Kt. seventh	

And wins.

Notes.

(*a*) Black played, to this point, the defence with great skill; this move, however, was a rash one, as it loses a Pawn, and gives him an inferior position, which, in spite of his brilliant efforts afterwards, he could not retrieve. "B to K. R. third," would have enabled Black to regain White King's Bishop's Pawn.

Games in the Match between Messrs. CAMPBELL and WORMALD.

GAME II.

White. (WORMALD.)	*Black.* (CAMPBELL.)
1. P. to K. fourth	1. P. to K. fourth
2. K. Kt. to B. third	2. K. Kt. to B. third
3. Kt. takes K. P.	3. P. to Q. third
4. Kt. to K. B. third	4. Kt. takes K. P.
5. P. to Q. fourth	5. P. to Q. fourth
6. B. to Q. third	6. B. to K. second
7. Q. B. to K. third	7. Q. Kt. to B. third
8. Castles	8. Castles
9. P. to Q. R. third	9. P. to K. B. fourth
10. P. to Q. B. fourth	10. P. to K. B. fifth
11. B. to Q. second	11. B. to K. Kt. fifth
12. B. to Q. B. third	12. B. to K. B. third
13. P. takes P.	13. Q. takes P.
14. B. takes Kt.	14. Q. takes B.
15. Q. to Q. Kt. third (check)	15. B. to K. third
16. Q. takes Q. Kt. P.	16. Q. R. to Kt. square

17. Q. to Q. R. sixth	17. B. to Q. fourth
18. Q. Kt. to Q. second	18. Q. to K. Kt. third
19. Q. to Q. R. fourth	19. P. to K. R. fourth
20. Q. R. to B. square	20. Q. to K. Kt. fifth
21. P. to K. R. third	21. Q. to Q. second
22. Q. to Q. B. second	22. K. R. to K. square
23. Q. to Q. third	23. Q. R. to Q. square
24. K. R. to Q. square	24. Q. to K. B. second
25. Q. to K. B. fifth (a)	25. B. takes Q. P.
26. Kt. takes B.	26. Kt. takes Kt.
27. Q. takes Q.	27. B. takes Q.
28. B. takes Kt.	28. R. takes B.
29. Kt. to K. B. third	29. R. takes R. (check)
30. R. takes R.	30. P. to Q. B. third
31. R. to Q. seventh	31. P. to Q. R. third
32. Kt. to Q. fourth	32. B. to Q. fourth
33. Kt. to K. B. fifth	33. R. checks
34. K. to R. second	34. K. to B. square
35. Kt. takes K. Kt. P. (b)	35. R. to K. fourth
36. P. to K. R. fourth	36. B. to K. B. second
37. R. to Q. R. seventh	37. K. takes Kt.
38. R. takes Q. R. P.	38. R. to K. seventh
39. P. to K. B. third	39. B. to Q. fourth
40. K. to R. third	40. R. takes Q. Kt. P.

And wins.

Notes.

(a) This loses a Pawn without necessity.
(b) An inconsiderate move, which loses White the game.

GAME III.

White. (CAMPBELL.)	*Black.* (WORMALD.)
1. P. to K. fourth	1. P. to K. fourth
2. K. Kt. to B. third	2. P. to Q. third
3. P. to Q. fourth	3. P. takes P.
4. Q. takes P.	4. Q. Kt. to B. third

5. B. to Q. Kt. fifth	5. B. to Q. second
6. B. takes Kt.	6. B takes B.
7. B. to K. Kt. fifth	7. P. to K. B. third
8. B. to K. third	8. Kt. to K. second
9. Q. Kt. to B. third	9. Kt. to K. Kt. third
10. Castles (Q. R.)	10. B. to K. second
11. P. to K. R. fourth	11. Kt to K. fourth
12. Kt. to R. second	12. Q. to Q. B. square
13. P. to K. Kt. fourth	13. Q. to K. third
14. Kt. to Q. fifth	14. B. takes Kt.
15. P. takes B.	15. Q. to Q. second
16. P. to K. B. fourth	16. Kt. to K. B. second
17. K. R. to K. Kt. square	17. P. to Q. B. fourth
18. Q. to Q. B. third	18. Castles (Q. R.)
19. Q. to Q. R. fifth	19. K. to Kt. square
20. R. to Q. third	20. R. to Q. B. square
21. R. to Q. R. third	21. P. to Q. Kt. third
22. Q. to Q. R. sixth	22. P. to K. Kt. fourth
23. Kt. to K. B. third	23. P. takes B. P.
24. B. takes P.	24. Kt. to K. fourth
25. R. to K. square	25. R. to Q. B. second
26. Kt. takes Kt.	26. K. B. P. takes Kt.
27. R. takes K. P.	27. Q. takes K. Kt. P.
28. R. to K. fourth	28. Q. takes K. R. P.
29. Q. R. to K. third	29. B. to K. Kt. fourth
30. K. to Kt. square	30. Q. to K. R. fourth (a)
31. Q. to Q. third	31. B. takes B.
32. R. takes B.	32. P. to Q. B. fifth
33. Q. to Q. second	33. K. R. to K. Kt. square
34. P. to Q. R. fourth	34. R. to K. Kt. eighth (check)
35. K. to R. second	35. Q. to K. R. eighth
36. R. to K. eighth (check)	36. K. to Kt. second
37. K. to Q. R. third	37. R. to Q. R. eighth (check)
38. K. to Kt. fourth	38. R. takes P. (check)
39. K. takes R.	39. Q. to Q. R. eighth (check)

And Black mates in two moves.

Note.

(a) The only move to save the game. All these moves were finely played by Black.

Game IV. was not preserved.   It resulted in a draw.

GAME V.

White. (CAMPBELL.)	*Black*. (WORMALD.)
1. P. to K. fourth	1. P. to K. fourth
2. K. Kt. to B. third	2. Q. Kt. to B. third
3. P. to Q. fourth	3. P. takes P.
4. B. to Q. B. fourth	4. B. to Q. B. fourth
5. Castles	5. P. to Q. third
6. P. to Q. B. third	6. P. takes P.
7. Q. Kt. takes P.	7. K. Kt. to K. second
8. Kt. to K. Kt. fifth ♠	8. Q. Kt. to K. fourth
9. B. to K. B. fourth	9. Kt takes B.
10. Q. to Q. R. fourth (check)	10. B. to Q. second
11. Q. takes Kt.	11. Castles
12. Q. R. to Q. square	12. P. to K. R. third
13. Kt. to K. B. third	13. Kt. to K. Kt. third
14. B. to his square	14. B. to K. Kt. fifth
15. Q. to Q. third (a)	15. Kt. to K. fourth
16. Kt. takes Kt.	16. B. takes R.
17. R. takes B.	17. P. takes Kt.
18. Q. to K. Kt. third	18. Q. to K. B. third
19. Kt. to Q. fifth	19. Q. to K. Kt. third
20. Q. takes K. P.	20. K. R. to K. square
21. Q. takes Q. B. P.	21. Q. takes K. P.
22. Q. B. to K. third	22. Q. R. to Q. B. square
23. Q. to K. Kt. third	23. K. to R. square
24. P. to K. R. third	24. K. R. to Q. square
25. B. takes B.	25. Q. R. takes B.
26. Kt. to K. third	26. R. takes R. (check)
27. Kt. takes R.	27. Q. to K. eighth (check)

And wins.

Note.

(a) With the intention of giving up the exchange; which, however, seems to us a mistaken idea.

The following Games were lately played in Paris, between Herr ANDERSSEN, the well-known Prussian master, and M. DE RIVIERE, a French amateur, of considerable skill.

(Scotch Opening.)

Black. (Herr ANDERSSEN.)	White. (M. DE RIVIERE.)
1. P. to K. fourth	1. P. to K. fourth
2. Kt. to K. B. third	2. Kt. to Q. B. third
3. P. to Q. fourth	3. P. takes P.
4. B. to Q. B. fourth	4. Kt. to K. B. third
5. Kt. to K. Kt. fifth (*a*)	5. Kt. to K. fourth
6. B. to Q. Kt. third	6. P. to K. R. third
7. P. to K. B. fourth	7. P. takes Kt.
8. P. takes Kt.	8. Kt. takes P.
9. Castles	9. P. to Q. fourth
10. P. takes P. in passing	10. P. to K. B. fourth
11. Kt. to Q. second	11. Q. takes P.
12. Kt. takes Kt.	12. Q. takes K. R. P. (check)
13. K. to K. B. second	13. P. takes Kt.
14. Q. takes P.	14. B. to K. second (*b*)
15. Q. takes K. P.	15. B. to Q. B. fourth (*c*)
16. B. to K. B. seventh (check)	16. K. takes B.
17. Q. takes Q. B. (check)	17. K. to K. Kt. square
18. Q. to Q. fifth (check)	18. K. to K. R. second
19. Q. to K. fourth (check)	19. K. to K. R. third
20. B. to K. third	20. K. R. to K. B. square (check)
21. K. to K. second	21. Q. to K. R. fourth (check)
22. P. to K. Kt. fourth	22. Q. to K. R. seventh (check)
23. R. to K. B. second	23. R. takes R. (check)
24. B. takes R.	24. R. to K. B. square
25. R. to K. R. square	25. R. takes B. (check)
26. K. to Q. third	26. R. to Q. seventh (check)
27. K. to Q. B. fourth	27. R. takes Q. B. P. (check)
28. K. to Q. fifth	28. B. to K. B. third
29. K. to K. sixth	29. B. takes Q. Kt. P.
30. K. to K. B. seventh	30. R. to K. B. seventh (check)
31. K. to K. Kt. eighth	31. P. to K. Kt. third
32. Q. to K. seventh	

And wins.

Notes.

(a) This move is not given in the *English Handbook*, 1847, p. 162. That manual, following its German predecessor, suggests " Kt. takes P.," or " P. to K. fifth."

(b) " B. to Q. B. fourth " looks promising, but is not so effective as at first sight it appears to be ; for Black may avoid capturing the offered Bishop at his next move, and may play " B. to K. B. seventh (check)," preventing for some time the terrible consequences that would ensue from " R. to K. B. square," if he were at once to make the capture.

(c) Instead of this somewhat showy move, " R. to K. B. square (check) " might have been played with evident advantage.

Between the same Players.
(*King's Knight's Opening.*)

White. (M. DE RIVIERE.)	Black. (Herr ANDERSSEN.)
1. P. to K. fourth	1. P. to K. fourth
2. Kt. to K. B. third	2. Kt. to Q. B. third
3. B. to Q. B. fourth	3. P. to K. B. fourth
4. P. to Q. fourth	4. P. to Q. third
5. P. takes K. P.	5. K. B. P. takes P.
6. Q. to Q. fifth	6. Q. to K. second
7. B. to K. Kt. fifth	7. B. to K. third
8. Q. takes K. P.	8. P. to Q. fourth
9. B. takes P.	9. B. takes B.
10. Q. takes B.	10. Kt. to K. B. third
11. B. takes Kt.	11. P. takes B.
12. Castles	12. P. takes P.
13. Kt. to Q. B. third	13. Q. to Q. third
14. Kt. to Q. Kt. fifth	14. Q. takes Q.
15. Kt. takes Q. B. P. (check)	15. K. to Q. second
16. Kt. takes Q.	16. B. to Q. third
17. Q. R. to Q. square	17. Q. R. to K. B. square
18. Kt. to Q. second	18. K. to Q. B. square
19. P. to Q. B. third	19. B. to Q. Kt. square
20. P. to Q. Kt. fourth	20. R. to K. B. second
21. P. to Q. Kt. fifth	21. Kt. to Q. square
22. K. R. to K. square	22. K. R. to K. B. square
23. P. to K. B. third	23. R. to K. Kt. second
24. R. to K. fourth	24. P. to Q. Kt. third

25. P. to Q. R. fourth	25. Kt. to K. third
26. P. to Q. R. fifth	26. K. to Q. Kt. second
27. P. takes P. (a)	27. P. takes P.
28. R. to Q. B. fourth	28. R. to Q. square
29. Kt. to K. fourth	29. Kt. to K. B. fifth
30. K. Kt. to K. B. sixth (b)	30. R. takes P. (check)
31. K. to K. R. square	31. R. to Q. Kt. seventh
32. R. to K. Kt. square	32. Kt. takes Kt. (c)
33. Kt. takes Kt.	33. R. to Q. second (d)
34. Kt. to K. B. sixth	34. P. to K. fifth (e)
35. R. to K. square	35. R. takes K. R. P. (check)
36. K. to K. Kt. square	36. R. to K. Kt. second (check)
37. K. to K. B. square	37. R. to K. R. eighth (check)
38. K. to K. second	38. P. takes P. (check)
39. K. to Q. square	39. K. R. to K. Kt. seventh (ch.)

And wins.

Notes.

(a) "P. to Q. R. sixth (check)" would cramp Black's game At the present moment, White has two Pawns ahead, with a good position.

(b) White's preceding moves occasion him the difficulty into which he now falls.

(c) He could not take the Q. Kt. Pawn without disaster.

(d) Again, he cannot capture the Pawn. The Knight also is free from danger.

(e) A capital stroke of counter-play, which White seems to have overlooked.

Between the same Players.

(Evans Gambit.)

Black. (Herr ANDERSSEN.)	*White.* (M. DE RIVIERE.)
1. P. to K. fourth	1. P. to K. fourth
2. Kt. to K. B. third	2. Kt. to Q. B. third
3. B. to Q. B. fourth	3. B. to Q. B. fourth
4. P. to Q. Kt. fourth	4. B. takes P.
5. P. to Q. B. third	5. B. to Q. R. fourth
6. P. to Q. fourth	6. P. takes P.
7. Castles	7. Kt. to K. B. third
8. P. to K. fifth	8. P. to Q. fourth

9. P. takes Kt.	9. P. takes B.
10. R. to K. square (check)	10. B. to K. third
11. P. takes K. Kt. P.	11. R. to K. Kt. square
12. B. to K. Kt. fifth	12. Q. to Q. fourth
13. Q. Kt. to Q. second	13. R. takes P.
14. Q. Kt. to K. fourth	14. K. to K. B. square
15. B. to K. R. sixth	15. P. to Q. sixth
16. K. Kt. to K. Kt. fifth	16. Q. to K. B. fourth
17. Q. Kt. to K. B. sixth	17. B. takes P.
18. K. Kt. takes K. R. P. (check)	18. K. to K. second
19. B. takes R.	19. B. takes Kt.
20. Kt. takes B.	20. Q. to K. Kt. third
21. Q. to K. Kt. fourth	21. Q. takes Q.
22. Kt. takes Q.	22. R. to K. Kt. square
23. B. to K. B. sixth (check)	23. K. to Q. third
24. Kt. to K. fifth	24. Kt. takes Kt.
25. B. takes Kt. (check)	25. K. to Q. B. third
26. B. to Q. B. third	26. P. to Q. Kt. fourth
27. P. to K. B. third	27. K. to Q. B. fourth
28. P. to Q. R. third	28. P. to Q. R. third
29. P. to K. Kt. fourth	29. K. to Q. third
30. R. to Q. R. second	30. P. to Q. B. fourth
31. R. to Q. Kt. second	31. K. to Q. B. third
32. K. to K. B. second	32. P. to Q. R. fourth
33. P. to K. R. fourth	33. P. to Q. Kt. fifth
34. B. to K. B. sixth	34. P. to Q. B. sixth
35. Q. R. to Q. Kt. square	35. P. to Q. seventh
36. R. to K. R. square	36. P. to Q. B. seventh
37. P. to K. R. fifth	37. B. to Q. B. fifth
38. P. to K. R. sixth	38. B. to Q. sixth

And our copy states that White eventually won.

The five following Games, all of them Gambits, were played between MORPHY and ANDERSSEN after the termination of their Match in Paris.

GAME I.

(*King's Knight's Gambit.*)

White. (ANDERSSEN.)	*Black.* (MORPHY.)
1. P. to K. fourth	1. P. to K. fourth
2. P. to K. B. fourth	2. P. takes P.
3. Kt. to K. B. third	3. P. to K. Kt. fourth
4. P. to K. R. fourth	4. P. to K. Kt. fifth
5. Kt. to K. fifth	5. Kt. to K. B. third
6. Kt. takes K. Kt. P.	6. P. to Q. fourth
7. Kt. takes Kt. (check)	7. Q. takes Kt.
8. Kt. to Q. B. third	8. Q. to K. Kt. third
9. Q. to K. B. third (*a*)	9. B. to Q. third
10. B. to Q. third	10. B. to K. Kt. fifth
11. Q. to K. B. second	11. Kt. to Q. second
12. P. takes P. (*b*)	12. P. to K. B. fourth
13. B. to Q. Kt. fifth	13. P. to Q. R. third
14. B. takes Kt. (check)	14. K. takes B.
15. P. to Q. third	15. Q. R. to K. square (check)
16. K. to B. square	16. K. R. to Kt. square
17. R. to R. second	17. P. to K. B. sixth
18. P. to K. Kt. third	18. B. to K. R. fourth
19. B. to K. Kt. fifth	19. P. to K. R. third
20. Q. to Q. R. seventh	20. P. takes B.
21. Kt. to Q. R. fourth	21. P. takes P.
22. Q. takes Q. Kt. P.	22. P. takes P.

And White resigns.

Notes.

(*a*) Evidently he could not have taken P. with Kt. for Black's answer Q. to K. Kt. sixth (check).

(*b*) P. to K. fifth would be replied with Q. to K. third.

GAME II.

(*Same Opening.*)

White. (MORPHY.)	*Black.* (ANDERSSEN.)
1. P. to K. fourth	1. P. to K. fourth
2. P. to K. B. fourth	2. P. takes P.
3. Kt. to K. B. third	3. P. to K. Kt. fourth

4. P. to K. R. fourth	4. P. to K. Kt. fifth
5. Kt. to K. fifth	5. Kt. to K. B. third
6. Kt. takes K. Kt. P.	6. Kt. takes K. P.
7. P. to Q. third	7. Kt. to Kt. sixth
8. Q. B. takes P.	8. Kt. takes R.
9. Q. to K. second (check)	9. Q. to K. second
10. Kt. to B. sixth (check)	10. K. to Q. square
11. B. takes Q. B. P. (check) (a)	11. K. takes B.
12. Kt. to Q. fifth (check)	12. K. to Q. square
13. Kt. takes Q.	13. B. takes Kt.
14. Q. to K. Kt. fourth	14. P. to Q. third
15. Q. to K. B. fourth	15. R. to K. Kt. square
16. Q. takes K. B. P.	16. B. takes P. (check)
17. K. to Q. second	17. R. to K. square
18. Kt. to Q. R. third	18. Kt. to Q. R. third (b)
19. Q. to K. R. fifth	19. B. to K. B. third
20. Q. takes Kt.	20. B. takes Q. Kt. P.
21. Q. to K. R. fourth (check)	21. K. to Q. second
22. R. to Q. Kt. square	

And Black resigns.

Notes.

(a) This variation of the King's Knight's Gambit has been analysed, some years ago, by the Berlin *Schachzeitung*, and is supposed to turn in favor of the second player.

(b) Kt. to K. Kt. sixth would have been a better move.

GAME III.

(Same Opening.)

White. (ANDERSSEN.)	*Black.* (MORPHY.)
1. P. to K. fourth	1. P. to K. fourth
2. P. to K. B. fourth	2. P. takes P.
3. Kt. to K. B. third	3. P. to K. Kt. fourth
4. P. to K. R. fourth	4. P. to K. Kt. fifth
5. Kt. to K. fifth	5. Kt. to K. B. third
6. Kt. takes K. Kt. P.	6. P. to Q. fourth
7. Kt. takes Kt. (check)	7. Q. takes Kt.

8. Q. to K. second	8. B. to Q. third
9. Kt. to Q. B. third	9. P. to Q. B. third
10. P. to Q. fourth	10. Q. takes Q. P.
11. B. to Q. second	11. R. to K. Kt. square
12. P. takes P. (dis. check)	12. K. to Q. square
13. Castles	13. B. to K. Kt. fifth
14. Q. to K. fourth	14. Q. takes Q.
15. Kt. takes Q.	15. B. takes R.
16. Kt. takes B.	16. B. to K. R. fourth
17. Q. B. takes P.	17. P. takes P.
18. Kt. takes Kt. P. (check)	18. K. to K. second
19. B. to Q. Kt. fifth	19. R. takes K. Kt. P.
20. R. to K. square (check)	20. K. to B. third
21. R. to K. eighth	21. B. to K. Kt. third
22. Kt. to Q. sixth	22. Kt. to Q. B. third
23. R. takes R.	23. R. takes P. (check)
24. K. to Q. square	24. Kt. to Q. fifth
25. R. to K. eighth	25. B. to R. fourth (check)
26. K. to K. square	26. Kt. to B. sixth (check)
27. K. to B. square	27. R. takes Kt. P.
28. B. to K. second	28. R. takes P.
29. B. to Kt. fifth (check)	29. Kt. takes B.
30. P. takes Kt. (check)	30. K. takes P.
31. R. to K. fifth (check)	31. K. to B. third
32. R. takes B.	

And White won the game.

GAME IV.

White. (ANDERSSEN.)	*Black*. (MORPHY.)
1. P. to K. fourth	1. P. to K. fourth
2. P. to K. B. fourth	2. P. takes P.
3. B. to Q. B. fourth	3. Kt. to K. B. third
4. P. to K. fifth	4. P. to Q. fourth
5. B. to Q. Kt. third	5. Kt. to K. fifth
6. Kt. to K. B. third	6. B. to K. Kt. fifth
7. Castles	7. Kt. to Q. B. third
8. B. to R. fourth	8. P. to K. Kt. fourth

9. B. takes Kt. (check)	9. P. takes B.
10. P. to Q. fourth	10. P. to Q. B. fourth
11. P. to Q. B. third	11. B. to K. second
12. P. to Q. Kt. fourth	12. P. takes Kt. P.
13. P. takes P.	13. Castles
14. Q. to Q. Kt. third	14. R. to Q. Kt.
15. P. to Q. R. third	15. P. to Q. B. fourth
16. Kt. to Q. B. third	16. Kt. takes Kt.'
17. Q. takes Kt.	17. P. takes Kt. P.
18. P. takes P.	18. K. B. takes P.
19. Q. to Q. third	19. P. to Q. R. fourth
20. P. to K. R. fourth	20. P. to K. R. third
21. P. takes P.	21. P. takes P.
22. P. to K. Kt. third	22. R. to Q. Kt. third
23. R. to Q. R. second	23. R. to K. Kt. third
24. R. to K. Kt. second	24. B. to K. R. sixth
25. P. to K. sixth	25. B. takes R.
26. P. takes P. (check)	26. K. to Kt. second
27. K. takes B.	27. Q. to Q. B. square
28. Kt. to K. fifth	28. R. to K. R. third
29. P. takes P.	29. K. R. home
30. P. takes P.	30. R. to R. seventh (check)
31. K. to Kt. square	31. R. to R. eighth (check)
32. K. to B. second	32. K. R. to R. seventh (check)
33. K. to K. third	33. R. to R. sixth (check)
34. Kt. to K. B. third	34. R. takes Kt. (check)
35. R. takes R.	35. Q. takes B. (check)

And White resigns.

Game V.

White. (Morphy.)	*Black.* (Anderssen.)
1. P. to K. fourth	1. P. to K. fourth
2. P. to K. B. fourth	2. P. takes P.
3. Kt. to K. B. third	3. P. to K. Kt. fourth
4. B. to Q. B. fourth	4. B. to K. Kt. second
5. Castles	5. P. to Q. third
6. P. to Q. B. third	6. Kt. to Q. B. third

7. Q. to Q. Kt. third	7. Q. to K. second
8. P. to Q. fourth	8. Kt. to K. B. third
9. Kt. takes K. Kt. P.	9. Kt. takes K. P.
10. B. takes K. B. P. (check)	10. K. to Q. square
11. Kt. takes Kt.	11. Q. takes Kt.
12. Q. B. takes P.	12. B. to K. R. sixth
13. P. takes B.	13. Kt. takes Q. P.
14. Kt. to Q. second	14. Kt. to K. seventh (check)
15. K. to B. second	15. Q. takes B. (check)
16. K. takes Kt.	16. Q. to K. Kt. fourth
17. Q. R. to K. square	17. B. to K. R. third
18. Q. to Q. fifth	18. R. to K. square (check)
19. K. to Q. square	

And Black resigns.

SOLUTIONS TO PROBLEMS.

No. 1.   *Page* 31.

White.

1. Q. to K. R. square
2. R. to K. B. third
3. Mates

Black.

1. P. to K. Kt. third or (A.)
2. Any move

(A.)

1. B. takes Q. or
P. to Q. sixth

2. R. to B. fifth (check)
And mates.

No. 2.   *Page* 31.

1. B. to Q. Kt. sixth (check)
2. Q. to Q. eighth
3. Q. to K. Kt. fifth (check)
4. Q. mates

1. K. to B. fourth (best)
2. K. takes Kt. (best)
3. K. moves.

No. 3.   *Page* 32.

1. B. to Q. second
2. Kt. to K. third
3. B. or Kt. mates.

1. R. takes R. or (A.)
2. Anything.

(A.)

1. P. takes Kt.
2. Anything.

2. R. to Q. Kt. seventh
3. Kt. mates.

No. 4.   *Page* 32.

1. P. to K. fifth (check)
2. Kt. to K. B. third (check)
3. Kt. to K. fifth
4. R. or Kt. mates.

1. K. takes P. (best)
2. K. to B. third (best)
3. Anything.

No. 5.   By Mr. GREENWOOD.

BLACK.

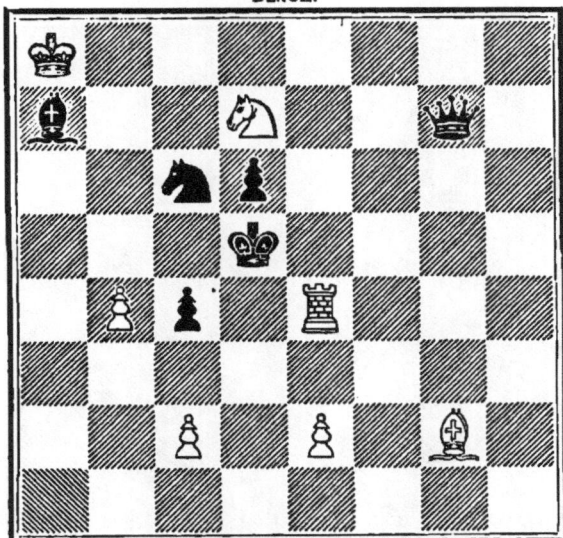

WHITE.

White to play and mate in four moves.

No. 6.   Chess Study by F. HEALEY, Esq.

BLACK.

WHITE.

The game is drawn, whether Black or White have the first move.

No. 7. By Herr KLING (this position occurred in actual play).

BLACK.

WHITE.

White to move and win.

No. 8. By R. B. WORMALD, Esq.

BLACK.

WHITE.

No. 5. By Mr. GREENWOOD.
BLACK.

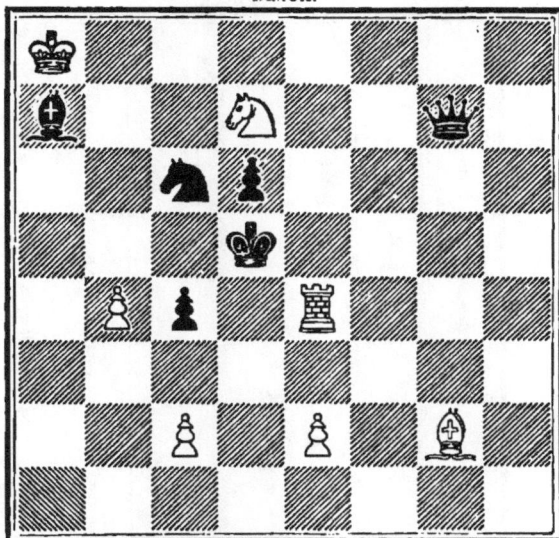

WHITE.
White to play and mate in four moves.

No. 6. Chess Study by F. HEALEY, Esq.
WHITE.

BLACK.
The game is drawn, whether Black or White have the first move.

No. 7. By Herr KLING (this position occurred in actual play).

BLACK.

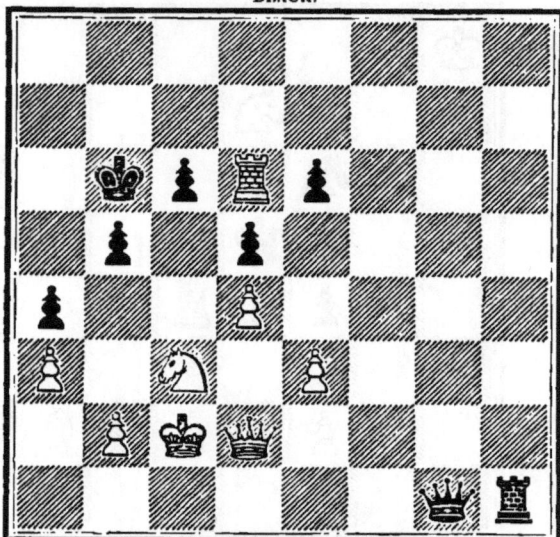

WHITE.

White to move and win.

No. 8. By R. B. WORMALD, Esq.

BLACK.

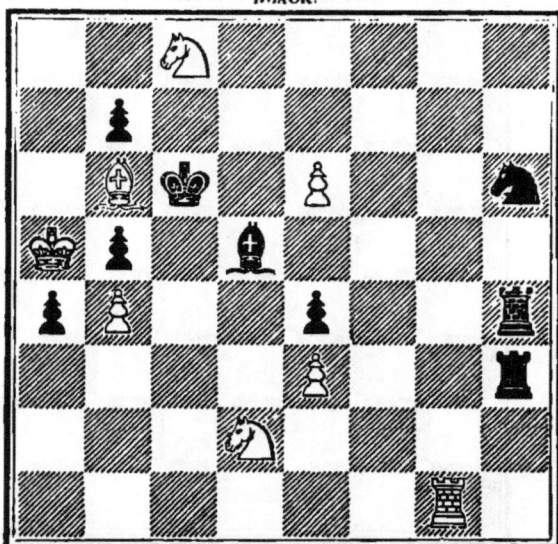

WHITE.

White to move and mate in three moves.

THE LANGUAGES OF CHESS.

THE languages in which the theory and practice of Chess are expressed have not formed a subject of much interest to the general reader. Such a result, is to be attributed partly to an eagerness to avoid everything that is dry in the study of a favorite, not to say popular, game and partly to the essential composition of the very languages. A good game, now examined analytically, at another time viewed synthetically, possesses more attraction for a mind when unbent in the sportive mood of art, than does a consideration of the structure of Chess language, that language which is termed technically notation. The elements of which systems of notation are compounded, furnish also a grave cause for want of interest in the subject. All literature exists in some rudimentary form before it is committed to writing in manuscripts, or to, their more powerful substitute, typography. At a still later period, an attention to the mode of expression, rather than to the thoughts expressed thereby, becomes prevalent. The literature of Chess is still young. Its virgin ore, glad to escape from the thraldom of the mine that confined it, has poured itself with alacrity through any channel by which it can reach the light. Chess, unless we can suppose a nation of blindfold players, has no spoken language ; it could not therefore, like the poems of rhapsodists, have an existence in the traditions of memory. Hence, as the practice of recording games is comparatively one of late birth, it has ensued that the games have been given under several forms of notation. There is no single system of so comprehensive a character, or, to speak more exactly, there is no system generally acknowledged to be so comprehensive, that it has ever been likely to be adopted by the whole of Europe, far less by the world. Indeed, we suspect that this want of uniformity is made a greater cause for complaint than is necessary.

The interests of literature have not been materially injured by the number of languages under which it has appeared. Its progress may have been rendered slower, but perhaps, by the impediment, trifling as it is to those who have the courage to overcome difficulties, it has been compelled to rest upon a more solid and enduring basis. So the Chess player, who has fairly mastered one system of notation, will find it a very easy task to attain the knowledge of another. There are in fact but two principles on which a system of the kind can be founded—one of an expressive or historical, the other of a symbolical or algebraic, cha-

5

racter. These principles can, however, be mixed; but there seems to be no advantage in such a fusion, as it entails upon us an absence of simplicity and good sense. The Anglo-French system has always looked to the meaning of the names by which the officers and foot-soldiers of the game of Chess are called. In a word, it has aimed at *connotation*, not at mere notation. With a lively recollection of the military origin of Chess, it views the board as a field of battle on which the hostile armies are actually engaged. The names also of the capital Pieces and Pawns (with the exception of the unfortunate nomenclature of the Bishop in France) are not inconsistent with the mimicry of war. Perhaps one alteration which we have made, although it has done away with much that is cumbrous, may appear not to carry out the old warlike principle so well. We mean the change of the enemy's side of the board into our own. Thus, instead of using the terms "adverse Kt. fourth," "adverse R. third," as our predecessors used them, we speak of "Kt. fifth" and "R. sixth," applying the language to the whole of the board as belonging to each army in its turn. This change does not, however, impair the military character of our notation. A soldier ought to consider the ground, which he occupies in battle to be his own, or that of his country. We very properly, in the English notation, always name the square to which a piece is moved, save in the cases of capture and of Castling. The author of the *English Handbook* introduced also, in consonance with the principles of reason, a similar description of the moves of the Pawns. This alteration, good as it is, has not, however, been adopted universally in this kingdom. Those who oppose it have argued (*a*) that, there being an essential difference in the moves of Pawns and Pieces, Pawns should be said to move two steps or one step, but that Pieces should have the name of the square, to which they are moved, mentioned. It has been successfully answered to this, that any difference between the moves of Pawns and Pieces does not create a difference in the squares to which they go; and that the squares, being always the same, should always be called squares. To this irrefragable reasoning it may be added, that the difference between the moves of Pawns and Pieces is not greater than that between the moves of such Pieces as the Knight and Rook. Mr. STAUNTON's alteration, or, to speak accurately, recurrence to a still older system of notation, will, it is easy to see,

(*a*) The reader may peruse the last volume of the first series of this magazine, if he wish to carry the subject further.

entirely supersede the antiquated method of noting the moves of Pawns in England. In cases of capture we do not name the square subsequently occupied by the Piece or the Pawn that makes the capture, save by implication. We do, however, imply the name of the square, as, independently of the fact that the previous position of the vanquished points with exactness to the square on which the captor will be posted, the word "takes" may be reckoned one of double meaning, and may refer not only to capture, but position, as standing for "takes the place of." In the process of Castling we do not name the squares to which the King and Rook are moved, as the process is described in the technical phraseology which is given in all elementary treatises on the game.

These being the distinctive features of the historical system of notation, the symbolical languages of Chess adopt a different method. They, or some of them, name the squares from which Pieces and Pawns are moved, as well as the squares to which they proceed. We direct attention to the name of the Piece to be moved, as being pregnant with meaning; the colder and more arbitrary systems, with greater precision, dwell upon the post which he quits. There are, however, amongst them, those who give the name of the Piece moved, either under the first letter of the name by which he is generally known, or by some equivalent symbol.

Of the foreign systems, we are disposed to prefer that which, if not suggested by KIESERITZKI, has been rendered illustrious through his advocacy. Let it once be determined that symbols shall be adopted; and we prefer that system which carries out the principle with consistency and uniformity. Perhaps, however, some will think that, if his system, so far as his symbolical letters are concerned, becomes more fashionable, the numbers of KOCH may be substituted with advantage. These great authorities give an arithmetical symbol for every square in each of the eight files into which the Chess board is divided; and another for the files themselves: they differ, however, in their application. KOCH gives the number of the file before that of the square; KIESERITZKI yields priority to the square. Thus "Q. R. second," would in KOCH's notation be 1.2., or "first file," "second square;" with KIESERITZKI it would be 2.1, or "second square" in the first file. (a) " We purposely place the dot between 1.2, and 2.1, as this modification should be

(a) Koch's numbers may be more popular, but Kieseritzki's seem to be expressed more grammatically.

made in both systems. For the want of it, we have heard English players read the above moves, " twelve " and " twenty-one." The names of the Pieces KIESERITZKI expresses by the capital letters A to H ; the Pawns by the small letters a to h. Of course A represents the first file, or the Queen's Rook's file ; and the move that we should term " R. to Q. R. eighth " (we suppose the White Rook to be on his own square) would be printed "A 81," or, if modified, as proposed by us, " A 8.1," " A," or " Rook," to the eighth square in the first file.   In the case of capture he adds a symbolical letter.   Thus, if the hostile Queen's Rook were captured by the move given above, it could be expressed by " A 8.1, A," or " A to the eighth square in the first file, taking, or taking the place of, hostile A."   The main difference in this mode of expression from that adopted by us, besides its symbolism, is that every square has its definite name ; but that as with us the names of the squares are changed, just as White or Black have the move.

We see much that is excellent in this system of KEISERITZKI ; it is better than that adopted by the Prussian players, as it provides a symbol for Pawns, and omits the names of the squares *from which* Pieces and Pawns are moved.   Thus, both in exactness and simplicity, it is entitled to superiority.   We do not, however, infer from this, that it is necessary to give up the English system of notation.   With its expressive nature, our own Chess language will ever be a favorite with the main portion of our players.   As to the adoption of one uniform system, we believe that it will never take place, and that we shall not be much the losers by its absence.   The project is more splendid than practical.   An educated player should, notwithstanding, have sufficient acquaintance with the foreign systems, in order that he may be able to peruse the able games of Germany ; and this acquaintance he can obtain in less than half an hour.   We have called attention to the subject, to show the simplicity of that which is generally thought dry and uninteresting.   Upon one question connected with English nota-tion we have purposely made no comment : it is whether the Pieces should be named by a single symbol.   Thus, to get rid of the double symbol, " K. R.," " Q. R.," " K. Kt.," " Q. Kt.," &c., ought one of the Rooks, one of the Knights, and one of the Bishops, to receive a new name ?   Much may be said for such a change ; on the whole, however, arguments preponderate against it.   We should have two Pieces of the same power known by different names, and perhaps represented differently by the maker. We should in this way lose the expressive character of our system. Wishing to retain this fundamental principle, we must declare ourselves to be opposed in no small measure to innovation.

CHESS CHARADES. No. I.

I went one night to Number *Nine*,
In something *Terrace Upper*,
To spend an hour with Dr. Rook,
And stay to tea and supper.
At tea, of course, the ladies talked
Incessant pretty prattle,
Diversified by scraps of news,
And charming gems of tattle.

But after tea, when hushed was all
The chatter, noise, and rattle,
The Doctor and myself sat down
To wage a silent battle.
To fight a stern and earnest fight,
In silence, seldom broken;
For *my first!* My first, was the only word,
By either of us spoken.

Well, so we fought for full two hours,
And, though disdaining quarter,
We had a twenty minutes' truce
For bread and cheese and porter;
For serious talk with Mrs. Rook,
For whispers to her daughter;
For pretty smiles, by way of thanks,
For a bouquet I had brought her.

But, supper over, once again
We bid adieu to prattle,
And sat us down in solemn state
To wage our silent battle.
But I soon lost, for the Doctor gave
A regular thumping trouncer;
"Ah! ah! cried he, "my whole is yours,
I believe I've done you brown, sir."

" *My whol*e you give," I said (no doubt,
Grown spooney o'er the porter);
" *My whole* you give, so give as well
My second in your daughter."
He shook my hand : " 'Tis yours, my boy ;
And what will perhaps be reckoned
A better thing, I 'll give *my first*
At the same time with *my second.*"

THE CHESS BOARD.

(From the *Wanderer*, by OWEN MEREDITH.)

My little love, do you remember
   Ere we were grown so sadly wise,
Those evenings in the bleak December,
Curtain'd warm from the snowy weather,
When you and I played Chess together,
   Checkmated by each other's eyes ?
Ah, still I see your soft white hand
Hovering warm o'er Queen and Knight.
   Brave Pawns in valiant battle stand :
The double Castles guard the wings ;
The Bishop, bent on distant things,
   Moves, sidling, through the fight.
   Our fingers touch ; our glances meet,
   And falter ; falls your golden hair
   Against my cheek ; your bosom sweet
Is heaving.   Down the field, your Queen
Rides slow her soldiery all between,
   And checks me unaware.
   Ah me ! the little battle 's done,
Disperst is all its chivalry ;
Full many a move, since then, have we
'Mid Life's perplexing chequers made,
And many a game with Fortune play'd—
   What is it we have won ?
   This, this at least—if this alone :—
That never, never, never more,
As in those old still nights of yore
   (Ere we were grown so sadly wise),
   Can you and I shut out the skies,
Shut out the world, and wintry weather,
   And, eyes exchanging warmth with eyes,
Play Chess, as then we play'd, together !

SOLUTIONS TO PROBLEMS.

No. 5. Page 63.

White.	*Black.*
1. P. to Q. B. third	1. Q. takes P.

If Q. checks, White covers with Rook, &c.

2. P. to K. third	2. B. takes P.
3. R. to K. fifth (double check)	3. K. moves.
4. R. mates.	

No. 6. Page 63.

If White have the move and play "P. to K. R. fourth," Black replies with "K. to Q. fourth," drawing the game; for if White then play "K. to K. B. fifth," Black brings his K. to Q. third; White must then play "P. to K. R. fifth," as the advance of his King to K. B. sixth would lose the game, on account of Black's K. R. Pawn. If Black have the move, he will push his Pawn forward. White will then play "P. to K. R. fourth," compelling Black to bring his King back as before.

No. 7. Page 63.

1. Kt. takes Q. R. P. (check)	1. P. takes Kt. (or A.)
2. Q. to Q. Kt. fourth (check)	2. K. to Q. B. second
3. Q. to Q. R. fifth (check)	3. K. takes R.
4. Q. mates	

(A.)

	1. K. to Q. R. third
	or to Q. Kt. second

If to Q. B. second, the Queen checks, &c.

2. Kt. to Q. B. fifth (check)	2. Kt. moves
3. Q. or R. checks, and forces mate.	

No. 8. Page 64.

1. R. to Q. square	1. Any move.
2. Kt. to Q. B. fourth	2. Any move.
3. One of the Knights mates.	

BLINDFOLD CHESS IN GERMANY.

In Germany a new star has also appeared on the Chess horizon, which threatens to dim the light of the MORPHY star. Herr BERTHOLD SUHLE, in Bonn, twenty-one years of age, has completely defeated several of the German Chess celebrities, amongst others the well-known player Captain BOTHE in Cologne, and the strongest player of Venice, Signor TORLIKO. In blindfold play he has successfully rivalled the performances of MORPHY and HARRWITZ, having, on the 20th of December last, played eight players at the same time, without seeing the board, and, in a series of 295 moves, having won six games and drawn two.

The following is one of the blindfold games played on that occasion, in which the young hero announced a checkmate in ten moves.

White. (Herr B. SUHLE.) (Blindfold).	Black. (Herr KB.) (Over the Board).
1. P. to K. fourth	1. P. to K. fourth
2. P. to K. B. fourth	2. P. takes P.
3. Kt. to K. B. third	3. P. to K. Kt. fourth
4. P. to K. R. fourth	4. P. to K. Kt. fifth
5. Kt. to K. fifth	5. P. to K. R. fourth
6. B. to Q. B. fourth	6. R. to K. R. second
7. P. to Q. fourth	7. B. to K. R. third
8. Kt. to Q. B. third	8. P. to Q. B. third
9. Kt. to Q. third	9. Q. to K. B. third
10. P. to K. fifth	10. Q. to K. B. fourth
11. Kt. to Q. B. fifth	11. Q. to K. Kt. third
12. B. to Q. third	12. Q. to K. Kt. second
13. B. takes R.	13. Q. takes B.
14. Q. Kt. to K. fourth	14. P. to Q. Kt. third
15. Kt. to Q. sixth (check)	15. K. to Q. square
16. Kt. to Q. third	16. P. to K. B. third
17. B. takes P.	17. B. to Q. R. third
18. Q. to Q. second	18. B. to K. B. square
19. R. to K. B. square	19. K. B. takes Kt.
20. P. takes B.	20. Q. to K. fifth (check)
21. Q. to K. third	21. P. to K. B. fourth
22. Q. takes Q.	22. P. takes Q.
23. B. to K. Kt. fifth (check)	23. K. to K. square

Here White announced checkmate in ten moves.

24. Castles on Q. side	24. P. to Q. B. fourth
25. R. to K. square	25. B. to Q. Kt. second
26. Kt. to K. fifth	26. B. to Q. fourth
27. Kt. to K. Kt. sixth	27. B. to K. B. second
28. R. takes P. (check)	28. Kt. to K. second
29. B. takes Kt.	29. Kt. to Q. B. third
30. B. to K. Kt. fifth (check)	30. Kt. to K. second
31. B. takes Kt.	31. any move
32. B. to K. Kt. fifth (check)	32. B. to K. third
33. R. to K.B. eighth (checkmate)	

[We, in common with our readers, have waited patiently for the pamphlet containing the games played in the Chess Tournament at Birmingham. No notice, however, of their publication having reached us, or any one else, as we have reason to believe, we here present our readers with two games played between the winners of the prizes. We hope that the wishes of the Chess community may soon be realized by the appearance of the long-promised pamphlet.]

GAME III.

In the Tournament at Birmingham, between Herren LÖWENTHAL and FALKBEER.

White. (Herr LÖWENTHAL.)	*Black.* (Herr FALKBEER.)
1. P. to K. fourth	1. P. to K. fourth
2. Kt. to K. B. third	2. P. to Q. third
3. P. to Q. fourth	3. P. takes P.
4. Q. takes P.	4. B. to Q. second
5. Q. B. to K. third	5. Kt. to Q. B. third
6. Q. to Q. second	6. Kt. to K. B. third
7. Kt. to Q. B. third	7. Kt. to K. Kt. fifth
8. Castles on Q. side	8. Kt. takes Q. B.
9. Q. takes Kt.	9. B. to K. second
10. B. to Q. Kt. fifth	10. P. to Q. R. third (a)
11. B. to Q. R. fourth	11. P. to Q. Kt. fourth
12. B. to Q. Kt. third	12. Castles on K. side (b)
13. B. to Q. fifth	13. Q. R. to Kt. square
14. B. takes Kt.	14. B. takes B.
15. Kt. to Q. fourth	15. B. to Q. second
16. Q. Kt. to Q. fifth	16. P. to Q. B. third (c)
17. Kt. takes B. (check)	17. Q. takes Kt.
18. K. R. to K. square	18. P. to Q. R. fourth (d)
19. Q. to K. Kt. third	19. K. R. to Q. square (e)
20. P. to K. fifth	20. P. to Q. fourth
21. P. to K. sixth	21. P. takes P.
22. R. to K. fifth	22. P. to Q. B. fourth (f)
23. Kt. to K. B. fifth	23. Q. to K. B. third (g)
24. Kt. takes K. Kt. P.	24. K. to R. square
25. Kt. to K. R. fifth	25. Q. to K. B. second
26. R. to K. Kt. fifth	

And Black resigned.

Notes.

(a) This is a lost move, as it is clearly the intention of White to exchange the B. for the Kt. Castling instead would have been better.

(*b*) Castling now was not the move, as it enables White to gain several moves. "Kt. to R. fourth" would have been the wiser move.

(*c*) Another lost move, as the Kt. does not wish to remain there, but to take the B. If play the P. at all, why not to "Q. B. fourth," to dislodge the other and more dangerous Kt.?

(*d*) A third lost move, which seems to us without meaning at all, as Black can gain nothing whatever by advancing now the Pawns on Queen's side. Why not play K. B. P. one or two?

(*e*) Q. R. would have been preferable; but "P. to K. B. third" seems to us the proper move.

(*f*) The fourth move which Black loses in this game. He is evidently driving the Kt. upon the square he wants to occupy.

(*g*) This move takes away the last chance of saving the game from Black. By playing the "Q. to K. B. square" there might have been some chance left for Black, as if "Kt. takes P.," Black answers by "K. to R. square," and the game is by no means so desperate.

GAME IV.
Between the same opponents.

White. (Herr FALKBEER.)	*Black.* (Herr LÖWENTHAL.)
1. P. to K. fourth	1. P. to K. third
2. Kt. to K. B. third	2. P. to Q. fourth
3. P. takes P.	3. P. takes P.
4. P. to Q. fourth	4. Kt. to K. B. third
5. B. to K. Kt. fifth	5. B. to K. second
6. Kt. to Q. B. third	6. Castles
7. B. to Q. third	7. P. to K. R. third
8. B. to K. third	8. Kt. to Q. B. third
9. P. to Q. R. third	9. Kt. to K. Kt. fifth
10. Q. to her second	10. Kt. takes B.
11. P. takes Kt.	11. P. to K. B. fourth
12. Castles on Q. side	12. P. to Q. R. third
13. Q. Kt. to K. second	13. P. to Q. Kt. fourth
14. Kt. to K. B. fourth	14. P. to Q. Kt. fifth
15. P. to Q. Kt. third	15. R. to K. B. second (*a*)
16. P. to Q. R. fourth	16. Q. to her third
17. Q. to K. second (*b*)	17. B. to K. B. third
18. K. R. to K. B. square	18. Kt. to Q. R. fourth
19. K. to Q. Kt. square	19. B. to Q. second
20. Kt. to K. R. fifth	20. P. to K. Kt. third
21. Kt. takes B. (check)	21. R. takes Kt.
22. Kt. to K. fifth	22. Kt. to Q. B. third
23. Kt. takes B.	23. Q. takes Kt.

24. P. to K. Kt. fourth	24. Kt. to K. second
25. P. takes P.	25. Kt. takes P.
26. Q. to K. Kt. fourth	26. Q. to K. third
27. B. takes Kt.	27. R. takes B.
28. R. takes R. (c)	28. Q. takes R.
29. Q. takes Q.	29. P. takes Q.
30. R. to K. B. square	30. R. to K. B. square
31. P. to Q. R. fifth (d)	31. K. to K. Kt. second
32. P. to Q. B. third	32. P. takes P.
33. K. to Q. B. second	33. K. to K. B. third
34. K. takes P.	34. K. to K. third
35. R. to K. Kt. square	35. K. to K. B. third
36. P. to K. R. fourth	36. R. to K. square
37. K. to Q. third	37. R. to K. third
38. R. to K. Kt. eighth (e)	38. R. to Q. B. third
39. R. to Q. eighth	39. K. to K. third
40. R. to K. eighth (check) (f)	40. K. to K. B. third
41. R. to K. fifth (g)	41. R. to Q. third
42. K. to Q. B. third (h)	42. R. to K. third
43. P. to Q. Kt. fourth	43. P. to Q. B. third
44. R. takes R. (check)	44. K. takes R.
45. K. to Q. third	45. K. to B. third
46. K. to K. second	46. P. to K. B. fifth
47. P. takes P.	47. K. to B. fourth
48. K. to B. third	48. P. to K. R. fourth
49. K. to Kt. third	49. K. to K. fifth
50. P. to K. B. fifth	50. K. takes B. P.
51. K. to R. third	

And the game was given up as drawn.

Notes.

(a) We are at a loss to find out why, instead of this move, Black did not play "P. takes P.;" as we can see no objection to it; we believe that, by taking the P., Black would have won the game.

(b) Rather a weak move; we do not see clearly the aim of it.

(c) "Q. to K. R. third" would have been more effectual than exchanging all the pieces when White had a winning position.

(d) "P. to K. R. fourth" would have been the move, in order to prevent the King coming at all into White's regions.

(e) This is a very bad move at this juncture, as "Pawn to K.R. fifth" would have given White an enormous advantage, and, we have no doubt, won him the game.

(*f*) Quite a useless check; "P. to K. R. fifth" would have still kept White in the advantage.

(*g*) The worst square to choose for the Rook.

(*h*) Again a weak move; it is evident that the general of the White force was worn out by the many marches and counter-marches, and did not play with his usual energy; whilst the Black commander, having the worse position, tries to draw the game by tiring his adversary's patience out, in which he finally succeeded.

A Game played in 1856, Herr LöWENTHAL and Mr. CUNNINGHAM consulting together against Messrs. STAUNTON and BARNES. We do not know whether this game has appeared in the columns of any of our weekly newspapers; we are indebted for our copy to our Prussian contemporary, the *Berliner Schachzeitung*.

(*French Game.*)

White. (Messrs. L. and C.)	*Black.* (Messrs. S. and B.)
1. P. to K. fourth	1. P. to K. third
2. P. to Q. fourth	2. P. to Q. fourth
3. P. takes P.	3. P. takes P.
4. Kt. to K. B. third	4. Kt. to K. B. third
5. B. to K. third	, 5. B. to Q. third
6. B. to Q. third	6. Castles
7. Castles	7. B. to K. third
8. Kt. to K. Kt. fifth	8. B. to K. Kt. fifth
9. P. to K. B. third	9. B. to K. R. fourth
10. Q. to Q. second	10. P. to Q. Kt. third
11. Q. to K. B. second	11. Q. Kt. to Q. second
12. Kt. to Q. second	12. P. to Q. B. fourth
13. P. to Q. B. third	13. Q. to Q. B. second
14. P. to K. Kt. fourth	14. B. to K. Kt. third
15. B. takes B.	15. K. R. P. takes B.
16. Q. R. to Q. B. square (*a*)	16. Q. R. to K. square
17. K. R. to K. square	17. R. takes B.
18. R. takes R.	18. P. takes P. (*b*)
19. R. to Q. third (*c*)	19. Kt. to K. fourth
20. R. takes P.	20. B. to Q. B. fourth
21. Q. to K. B. square (*d*)	21. Kt. to Q. B. third
22. Kt. to Q. Kt. third	22. Kt. takes R.

23. P. takes Kt.	23. B. takes P. (check)
24. Kt. takes B.	24. Q. to K. B. fifth (*e*)
25. Kt. to Q. B. sixth	25. Q. takes Kt.
26. Kt. to K. seventh (check)	26. K. to K. R. square
27. R. to K. square	27. Q. to K. R. fifth
28. R. to K. fifth	28. R. to Q. square
29. Q. to Q. third (*f*)	29. Q. to K. R. sixth
30. P. to K. Kt. fifth	30. Kt. to K. Kt. fifth
31. R. to K. second	31. P. to Q. fifth
32. R. to K. Kt. second	32. Kt. to K. sixth (*g*)
33. R. to K. Kt. third	33. Q. to K. third
34. Q. to K. fourth (*h*)	34. Kt. to K. B. fourth
35. R. to K. R. third (check)	35. Kt. to K. R. third
36. Q. takes Q.	36. P. takes Q.
37. K. to K. B. second	37. K. to K. R. second
38. K. to K. square	38. R. to Q. second
39. Kt. to Q. B. sixth	39. R. to Q. B. second
40. Kt. to K. fifth	40. R. to Q. B. seventh
41. Kt. to Q. third	41. P. to Q. R. fourth
42. P. to K. B. fourth	42. P. to Q. Kt. fourth
43. K. to Q. square	43. R. to K. Kt. seventh
44. K. to Q. B. square	44. P. to Q. Kt. fifth
45. P. takes Kt.	45. P. takes P.
46. Kt. to Q. B. fifth	46. R. to K. seventh
47. R. to Q. third	47. P. to K. fourth
48. P. takes P.	48. R. takes K. R. P.
49. R. takes P.	49. R. to K. seventh
50. Kt. to Q. third	50. P. to K. Kt. fourth
51. K. to Q. square	51. R. to K. Kt. seventh
52. P. to K. sixth	52. K. to K. Kt. second
53. R. to K. fourth	53. K. to K. B. square
54. Kt. to K. fifth	54. P. to Q. Kt. sixth
55. P. takes P.	55. R. takes P.
56. Kt. to K. Kt. sixth (check)	56. K. to K. square
57. R. to Q. B. fourth	57. K. to Q. square
58. P. to K. seventh (check)	

And Black resigned.

Notes.

(*a*) Our Prussian contemporary here notices " K. to K. Kt. second."
(*b*) This seems to be stronger than " B. to K. B. fifth."
(*c*) Here the Berlin critic remarks, " If ' K. R. to K. square,' then ' P. takes P.' followed by ' B. to Q. B. fourth.' "
(*d*) The move in the text has the advantage of preventing " Kt. to Q. sixth," a move which could have been made, if White had played " K. to K. Kt. second."
(*e*) This move, besides attacking the two Knights, threatens " Q. to K. sixth (check)," which prevents the resource of " Kt. to K. sixth," &c.
(*f*) Menacing, presently, " Q. takes K. Kt. P." &c.
(*g*) " Kt. to K. fourth " is noticed by the *Berliner Schachzeitung.*
(*h*) The Knight being at K. sixth, and not at K. fourth, this move can be made advantageously.

Game played December, 1858, in a Pool, at the Philidorian Chess Rooms.

Black. (Mr. BRIEN.)	White. (Mr. CAMPBELL.)
1. P. to K. fourth	1. P. to Q. fourth
2. P. takes P.	2. Q. takes P.
3. Kt. to Q. B. third	3. Q. to Q. R. fourth
4. Kt. to K. B. third	4. B. to K. Kt. fifth
5. P. to K. R. third	5. B. takes Kt.
6. Q. takes B.	6. P. to Q. B. third
7. P. to Q. Kt. fourth	7. Q. to K. fourth (check)
8. B. to K. second	8. P. to K. third
9. R. to Q. Kt. square	9. Kt. to Q. second
10. P. to Q. Kt. fifth	10. R. to Q. B. square
11. P. takes P.	11. P. takes P.
12. Castles	12. K. Kt. to K. B. third
13. R. to Q. Kt. seventh	13. R. to Q. B. second
14. P. to Q. fourth	14. Q. to Q. R. fourth
15. R. takes R.	15. Q. takes R.
16. B. to Q. third	16. B. to Q. third
17. Kt. to K. fourth	17. Castles
18. Kt. takes B.	18. Q. takes Kt.
19. B. to Q. R. third (*a*)	19. P. to Q. B. fourth
20. P. takes P.	20. Kt. takes P.
21. Q. to K. third	21. R. to Q. B. square
22. R. to Q. Kt. square	22. K. Kt. to Q. second
23. R. to Q. Kt. seventh	23. Q. to Q. fourth
24. R. takes P.	24. Kt. takes B.

25. Q. takes Kt.	25. Q. takes Q.
26. P. takes Q.	26. Kt. to K. fourth
27. P. to Q. fourth	27. Kt. to Q. sixth
28. R. to Q. R. fifth	28. P. to K. R. third
29. P. to Q. fifth	29. P. takes P.
30. R. takes P.	30. R. to Q. B. sixth
31. R. to Q. sixth	31. R. to Q. B. eighth (check)
32. K. to K. R. second	32. Kt. takes P.
33. P. to Q. R. fourth	33. R. to K. R. eighth (check)
34. K. to K. Kt. third	34. Kt. to K. fifth (check)
35. K. to K. B. fourth	35. Kt. to Q. B. sixth (*b*)
36. R. to Q. R. fifth	36. R. to Q. R. eighth
37. R. to Q. R. eighth (check)	37. K. to K. R. second
38. B. to K. fifth (*c*)	38. R. takes P. (check)
39. R. takes R.	39. Kt. takes R.
40. B. to Q. fourth	40. K. to K. Kt. third

Drawn eventually. (*d*)

Notes.

(*a*) The legitimate result of the second player's 17th move. Of course this Bishop cannot be taken.

(*b*) "Kt. takes B." would perhaps be equally good.

(*c*) Whether the game would be drawn or not, if Black retained his passed Pawn instead of imprisoning the Knight, may be a subject of discussion. We are inclined to think that it would.

(*d*) This position may be commended to the careful examination of our readers. Its true result we believe to be a drawn game.

The following Game, played between Mr. MEDLEY, the Hon. Sec. of the London Chess Club, and Mr. MORPHY, has already appeared in print. The Games between Mr. MORPHY and English Players being very scarce, we present it again to our readers.

White. (Mr. MEDLEY.)	*Black.* (Mr. MORPHY.)
1. P. to K. fourth	1. P. to K. fourth
2. Kt. to K. B. third	2. Kt to Q. B. third
3. B. to Q. Kt. fifth	3. K. Kt. to K. second
4. P. to Q. B. third	4. P. to Q. R. third
5. B. to Q. R. fourth	5. P. to Q. Kt. fourth
6. B. to Kt. third	6. P. to Q. fourth

7. P. takes P.	7. Kt. takes P.
8. P. to Q. fourth	8. P. takes P.
9. Kt. takes P.	9. Kt. takes Kt.
10. Q. takes Kt.	10. B. to K. third
11. Castles	11. P. to Q. B. fourth
12. Q. to K. fifth	12. P. to Q. B. fifth
13. B. to Q. B. second	13. B. to Q. third
14. Q. to Q. fourth	14. Castles
15. Q. to K. fourth	15. P. to K. Kt. third
16. Q. to K. B. third	16. Q. to K. R. fifth
17. P. to K. Kt. third	17. Q. to R. sixth
18. B. to K. fourth	18. Kt. to Q. B. second
19. B. to K. B. fourth	19. Q. R. to Q. square
20. B. takes B.	20. R. takes B.
21. Q. to B. fourth	21. K. R. to Q. square
22. B. to K. Kt. second	22. Q. to R. fourth
23. B. to B. third	23. Q. to Q. B. fourth
24. Kt. to R. third	24. Kt. to Q. fourth
25. Q. to K. fifth	25. P. to K. B. third
26. Q. to K. second (a)	26. Kt takes P.
27. P. takes Kt.	27. Q. takes Kt
28. Q. to K. third	28. B. to K. R. sixth
29. K. R. to Q. square	29. Q. takes R. P.
30. Q. to K. seventh	30. Q. to Kt. seventh
31. Q. takes R. (check)	31. R. takes Q.
32. R. takes R. (check)	32. K. to Kt. second
33. Q. R. to K. square	33. Q. takes B. P.
34. Q. R. to K. seventh (check)	34. K. to R. third
35. Q. R. to K. third	35. Q. to Kt. seventh
36. K. R. to Q. square	36. P. to B. sixth
37. Q. R. to K. square	37. P. to B. seventh
38. K. R. to Q. B. square	38. P. to Q. Kt. fifth
39. B. to K. fourth	39. P. to Kt. sixth, wins

Note.

(a) This loses a Pawn; but if he had played " Q. to Q. fourth," he would have done so equally, as Black would have exchanged Queens. " Q. to K." seems a better move, though even that would not have much improved White's position.—*Era.*

GAMES BETWEEN THE GREAT PRUSSIAN PLAYERS.

At the commencement of the CHESS PLAYER'S CHRONICLE, and indeed throughout its progress, it was favoured from time to time with friendly contributions from the distinguished amateurs of Prussia. An important addition to these valuable games has lately been made by the publication of DER LASA'S *Erinnerungen aus dem früheren Berliner Schachleben.* Our contemporary the *Berliner Schachzeitung* has already given its readers much of this important matter. Some of the games, however, we find in English books, such as Walker's *Chess Studies*, and the *Chess Player's Chronicle*, doubtless contributed by the eminent leaders of German Chess. We have extracted three games hitherto, we believe, not to be found in an English volume, and have ventured to append to them original notes and variations. They were played between DER LASA and the lamented HANSTEIN. In all of them the Scotch opening is adopted, both the attack and the defence receiving some modification. The Chess literature of England being peculiarly rich in specimens of play at the same opening, our readers will be able to put these games of the great Prussians by the side of the parties of COCHRANE, POPERT, and STAUNTON.

Played September 13, 1841.

White. (V. D. LASA.)	*Black.* (HANSTEIN.)
1. P. to K. fourth	1. P. to K. fourth
2. Kt. to K. B. third	2. Kt. to Q. B. third
3. P. to Q. fourth	3. P. takes P.
4. B. to Q. B. fourth	4. B. to Q. B. fourth
5. P. to Q. B. third	5. P. to Q. sixth (*a*)
6. P. to Q. Kt. fourth	6. B. to Q. Kt. third
7. P. to Q. R. fourth (*b*)	7. P. to Q. R. third
8. Q. to Q. Kt. third	8. Q. to K. second
9. Castles	9. P. to Q. third
10. B. to K. Kt. fifth	10. Kt. to K. B. third
11. Q. Kt. to Q second	11. Castles
12. B. takes P. at Q. third	12. B. to K. third
13. Q. to Q. B. second	13. P. to K. R. third
14. B. to K. R. fourth	14. P. to K. Kt. fourth
15. B. to K. Kt. third	15. Kt. to K. R. fourth

6

16. K. to K. R. square	16. K. to K. Kt. second
17. Q. R. to K. square	17. R. to K. R. square
18. P. to K. fifth	18. P. to Q. fourth
19. Kt. to Q. Kt. third	19. Q. R. to Q. B. square
20. P. to Q. R. fifth	20. B. to Q. R. second
21. Q. Kt. to Q. fourth	21. B. takes Q. Kt.
22. Kt. takes B.	22. Kt. takes Kt.
23. P. takes Kt.	23. Q. takes P.
24. P. to K. B. fourth	24. Kt. takes B. (check) (c)
25. P. takes Kt.	25. Q. takes Q. P. (d)
26. P. to K. B. fifth	26. B. to Q. second·
27. P. to K. sixth	27. B. to Q. R. fifth (e)
28. P. to K. B. sixth (check)	28. K. to K. B. square
29. Q. to Q. Kt. square	29. P. to Q. Kt. fourth
30. B. to K. B. fifth	30. R. to Q. Kt. square
31. B. to K. Kt. sixth	31. P. to K. R. fourth
32. B. takes K. B. P.	32. R. to K. R. third
33. B. to K. Kt. sixth	33. P. to Q. Kt. fifth
34. P. to K. seventh (check)	34. K. to K. Kt. square
35. P. to K. B. seventh (check)	

And wins.

———

Notes.

(*a*) " Kt. to K. B. third," suggested by Jaenisch, in order to reduce the opening to that of an ordinary Giuoco Piano, is now considered a better move.

(*b*) Upon " P. to Q. Kt. fifth," a move occurring in a match between Harrwitz and Staunton, the reader may consult the *English Handbook*, 1847, p. 159.

(*c*) Although this move doubles Pawns, and also uncovers the hostile King, yet, as the Black King is at the moment exposed to a powerful attack, it would, we suspect, be sounder play to capture K. B. Pawn with Knight. In the case supposed White could not, we fancy, play " R. takes Kt." with the view of afterwards moving his Bishop to K. R. fourth, as Black would just have time to extricate himself by " P. to Q. B. fourth." White could, however, still cramp Black a little by taking Knight with Bishop, and then playing " Q. to K. B. second ;" but perhaps the confinement would be temporary rather than permanent, as " Q. to K. second," followed by " P. to Q. B. fourth," would yield him resource.

(*d*) " P. takes P.," with the view of taking the Q. Pawn afterwards, and, by this means, of either obtaining perpetual check or gaining some little breathing-time, would not have been efficacious, as the following variations will prove :—

We give a diagram of the position after White's 25th move.

BLACK.

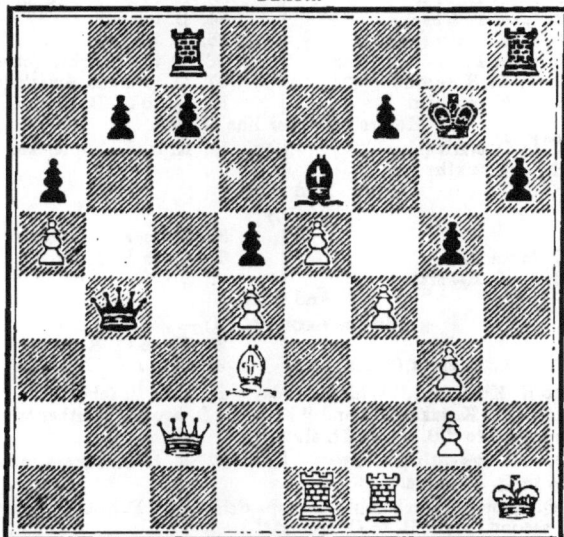

WHITE.

Suppose

	25. P. takes P.
26. P. takes P.	26. Q. takes Q. P.
27. P. to K. B. fifth	27. Q. to K. R. fifth (check)
28. K. to K. Kt. square	28. Q. to Q. fifth (check)
29. R. to K. B. second	

To prevent perpetual check.

29. B. to Q. second

30. P. to K. sixth

There are now five methods of defence, four of which spring from the advance or retreat of the Bishop, and the fifth from the capture of K. Pawn with Pawn. We will notice these moves in their order, commencing with the most defensive line of play.

In the first place :—

	30. B. to K. square
31. P. to K. B. sixth (check)	31. K. to K. B. square (or A.)
32. P. to K. seventh (check)	32. K. to K. Kt. square
33. B. to K. B. fifth	33. R. to Q. R. square
34. Q. takes P.	34. Q. to K. R. fifth (best)
35. Q. takes P.	

And wins.

(A.)

	31. K. to K. Kt. square
32. P. takes P. (check)	32. B. takes P.

"Q. to K. second" would be a satisfactory answer to "K. takes P."

33. B. to K. B. fifth	33. R. to K. square (or B.)
34. R. takes R. (check)	34. B. takes R.
35. B. to K. sixth (check)	35. K. to K. B. square
36. Q. takes P.	36. Q. to Q. eighth (check)
37. K. to K. R. second	37. Q. to K. R. fourth (check)
38. B. to K. R. third	38. Q. to K. B. second

He has no better line of play.

39. Q. to Q. sixth (check)	39. K. to K. Kt. square
40. B. to K. sixth	

And wins.

(B.)

	33. R. to K. B. square
34. Q. takes P.	34. Q. to K. R. fifth
35. B. to K. Kt. sixth	

And wins.

In the second place :—

	30. B. to Q. R. fifth
31. P. to K. B. sixth (check)	31. K. to K. B. square

If "K. to K. Kt. square," White can play "P. takes P. (check)." Black has then two moves, "K. takes P.," and "K. to K. B. square," neither of which can be safely opposed to "B. to K. Kt. sixth."

32. P. to K. seventh (check)	32. K. to K. square (or G.)
33. Q. to Q. Kt. square	

"Q. to Q. second" Black could perhaps defeat by "P. to Q. B. fourth," and "Q. to K. second" by "B. to Q. second."

	33. B. to Q. second (or D. or F.)

"B. to Q. B. third" is examined under the next head.

34. B. to K. B. fifth	34. B. takes B. (or C.)
35. Q. takes B.	35. R. to Q. Kt. square
36. R. to Q. Kt. square	36. P. to Q. Kt. fourth

"Q. to K. fifth" is worthless.

37. P. takes P. in passing	37. P. takes P.

If "Q. to K. fifth," White captures Q., and then plays "R. to Q. second."

38. R. to Q. B. square	

And wins.

(C.)

	34. P. to Q. B. third
35. B. takes B. (check)	35. K. takes B.
36. Q. takes P. (check)	36. R. to Q. B. second
	or K. to Q. third
37. Q. takes Q. R. P.	

And, as White threatens to play "Q. to K. second," which will attack the right, the left, and also the centre of Black's position, we believe that this variation, although not fully developed, must be successful.

(D.)

	33. P. to Q. Kt. fourth
34. B. to K. B. fifth	34. R. to Q. R square

"R. to Q. Kt. square" would be worse.

35. Q. to Q. B. square	35. P. to Q. B. fourth

If " Q. to Q. B. fifth," then " Q. to K. third," with a capital game.

36. Q. to Q. R. third	36. R. to K. Kt. square (or E.)
37. Q. to K. R. third	37. P. to Q. Kt. fifth
38. B. to K. sixth	

And wins.

(E.)

	36. Q. to Q. Kt. fifth

If " Q. to K. R. fifth," then " Q. takes Q. B. P." •

37. Q. to K. Kt. third	37. Q. takes R. (check)
38. K. to K. R. second	

And must win.

Black's best resource seems to be " Q. takes K. R." White then captures Q., attacking Q. B. P., and threatening to return to K. Kt. third.

(F.)

	33. P. to Q. Kt. third
34. B. takes Q. R. P.	34. R. to Q. Kt. square
	or to Q. R. square
35. B. to Q. Kt. fifth (check)	35. P. to Q. B. third (best)
36. Q. R. to Q. square	36. Q. to K. Kt. fifth

He can neither take Rook, nor move " Q. to K. R. fifth ;" for, if he were to adopt the latter mode of play, White, at move 38 in this variation, could win by " R. takes B."

37. R. takes P.	37. B. takes B.

If " P. takes B.," White will post his three surviving officers on the Q. file.

38. R. to Q. sixth	

And will win by placing another piece on the same file. In the above variation, White has, at move 38, two daring methods of prosecuting his attack: " Q. takes B," and " R. takes B." Neither of them is critically sound; but " Q. takes B." would lead to a very interesting mode of play, e.g. :—

38. Q. takes B.	38. P. takes Q.
39. K. R. to Q. second.	39. Q. to Q. B. square
40. P. takes P.	40. K. R. to K. Kt. square

" Q. to Q. B. eighth (check)," followed by " Q. takes R.," would lose the game, as White always threatens to advance his Pawn to Q. Kt. seventh.

41. P to Q. Kt. seventh	41. R. takes P. (check)

It is this resource which renders " Q. takes B." unsound. White's attack will now be exhausted.

(G.)

	32. K. to K. Kt. square
33. R. to K. third	33. Q. takes R.

If " Q. to K. R. fifth," White takes B. with Q., threatening, if Q. takes Q., to mate with his Rook.

34. Q. takes B.	34. Q. to K. eighth (check)
	or to Q. B. eighth (check)

It would be bad to move the Q. Rook, as White would check with his Queen at K. Kt. fourth, driving the hostile Queen to K. Kt. fourth, and afterwards play " Q. to Q. seventh." Again, if Black play " Q. takes R.," White will win both Rooks, giving up his old Queen, but obtaining a new one.

35. R. to K. B. square |
"B. to K. B. square" is also good.

| 35. Q. checks
And White wins by "K. to K. R. square."

In the third place:—

| | 30. B. to Q. B. third
31. P. to K. B. sixth (check) | 31. K. to K. B. square
"K. to K. Kt. square" may be traced in the preceding variations.

32. P. to K. seventh (check) | 32. K. to K. square
If "K. to K. Kt. square," then "Q. takes B." and wins.

33. B. to K. B. fifth | 33. B. to Q. second (or K.)
If "B. to Q. R. fifth," then "Q. to Q. Kt. square," threatening either to bring about the variations analyzed above, or to move afterwards "B. to K. sixth."

34. Q. R. to Q. square | 34. B. takes B. (or I.)
35. R. takes Q. | 35. B. takes Q.
36. R. takes P. | 36. B. to K. fifth

If "P. to Q. B. third," White takes the Bishop; but, if "B. to Q. Kt. sixth," he plays "R. to Q. third" (for "R. to Q. fourth" at once would not be good), and, when the Bishop occupies Q. B. fifth, "R. to Q. fourth," moving afterwards his other Rook to Q. second.

37. R. to Q. fourth | 37. R. to K. Kt. square (or H.)
38. R. takes B. | 38. P. to Q. B. fourth (a)

If "R. to K. Kt. third," White brings back his Rook to Q. fourth, and must win a Rook in exchange for his Pawns; but, if "K. to Q. second," the K. R. checks at Q. second, &c.

39. R. to Q. second | 39. R. to K. Kt. third
He has no better move.

40. R. to Q. sixth | 40. R. to K. Kt. fourth
"R. to K. Kt. sixth" leads to the same result.

41. R. to K. second | 41. R. to K. Kt. fifth
The advance of the Pawn would be of no avail.

42. R. to Q. B. second | 42. P. to Q. B. fifth
| or R. to K. Kt. fourth

43. R. from Q. B. second to Q. second
And wins.

(H.)

| 37. P. to Q. B. third
38. R. takes B. | 38. K. to Q. second

If "R. to Q. B. second," White places one of his Rooks on the Q. file; and, on that piece being attacked by the hostile Rook at Q. second, supports him with the other Rook.

39. K. R. to Q. second (check) | 39. K. to Q. B. second
40. Q. R. to Q. fourth | 40. Q. R. to K. square (best)
41. Q. R. to Q. seventh (check) | 41. K. to Q. B. square

And White can now win, by bringing his King to Q. Kt. sixth, taking care not to cut off the communication of his Rooks, but occupying the head of every file in succession, until he reaches Q. file, when he can advance more rapidly.

(a) "P. to Q. B. third," with the view of bringing "K. R. to K. Kt. fourth" would be unavailing, as White would double Rooks on the Q. file, giving one of his own Rooks in exchange for the hostile Rook when that piece reaches Q. fourth, and would afterwards move the King up on his right wing.

(I.)

| | 34. Q. to K. fourth |

"Q. to Q. R. fifth" would be answered by "R. takes P."

| 35. B. takes B. (check) | 35. K. takes B. |
| 36. R. to K. B. fifth | |

This, perhaps, is better than the exchange of two Rooks for Q. and P., &c.

| | 36. Q. to K. sixth (check) (best) |
| 37. K. to K. B. square | 37. P. to Q. B. third |

Should he play "Q. R. to K. square," the answer must be, "K. R. takes P. (check)," followed by "Q. to K. B. fifth (check)," with a winning game.

| 38. K. R. takes P. (check) | 38. K. to Q. B. second |

If he take R. with P., he must be mated.

| 39. R. to Q. seventh (check) | 39. K. to Q. Kt. square |
| 40. Q. to Q. Kt. second | 40. Q. to K. B. fifth (check) |

"Q. to Q. R. second" could be defeated by "Q. to K. fifth (check)," followed by "R. to Q. eighth." Again, "P. to Q. Kt. fourth" could be rendered unavailing, by "P. takes P. in passing."

| 41. K. to K. Kt. square | 41. Q. to K. sixth (check) |
| 42. Q. to K. B. second | 42. Q. takes Q. (check) |

If he does not exchange Queens, the reply is "Q. to Q. Kt. sixth."

| 43. K. takes Q. | |

And wins.

(K.)

| | 33. R. to Q. R. square |
| 34. B. to K. sixth | |

Threatening "Q. to K. B. fifth."

| | 34. P. takes B. |

He seems to have no resource.

| 35. Q. to K. Kt. sixth (check) | 35. K. to Q. second |
| 36. P. to K. B. seventh | 36. K. takes P. |

"P. to K. fourth," and "K. to Q. third," are equally fatal.

| 37. Q. takes K. P. (check) | |

And wins.

In the fourth place:—

| | 30. B. to Q. Kt. fourth |

The positions arising from this defence can be found in the foregoing analysis.

In the fifth place:—

| | 30. P. takes P. |

Most of the positions that would occur under this head being similar to those examined in the next note, we shall leave our readers the opportunity of drawing their own inference in such cases. As, however, in one variation, namely, L., there would arise an essential difference, we must substitute another line of play for the present emergency.

31. P. to K. B. sixth (check)	31. K. to K. Kt. square
	(or L.)
32. B. to Q. Kt. fifth	32. R. to K. R. second
33. Q. to K. Kt. sixth (check)	33. K. to K. R. square
34. B. to Q. third	

And wins.

(L.)

	31. K. to K. B. second
32. B. to K. Kt. sixth (check)	32. K. to K. B. square
33. B. to K. R. seventh	33. B. to K. square
34. R. takes P.	34. Q. to Q. B. fifth
35. P. to K. B. seventh	35. B. to Q. second
36. R. to K. eighth (check)	36. B. takes R.

"R. takes R." is also of no avail.

37. P. takes B.

Becoming a Q. (double check).

37. K. takes Q.

38. Q. to K. Kt. sixth (check)

And wins.

(*e*) Variations.

	27. P. takes P.
28. P. to K. B. sixth (check)	28. K. to K. B. square

If to K. Kt. square, White may play "B. to Q. Kt. fifth," winning easily; but if to K. B. second, White may rejoin with "B. to K. Kt. sixth (check)," placing his Bishop on K. R. fifth, if Black then play "K. to K. Kt. square," and following the variation given below if the King retreat to K. B. square.

29. B. to K. R. seventh	29. B. to K. square

Apparently as good a move as he has.

30. R. takes P.	30. B. to K. B. second
	(or M.)
31. R. to K. seventh	31. Q. to Q. B. fifth
32. Q. to K. B. fifth	32. R. to Q. square
33. K. R. to K. square	33. P. to Q. fifth
34. B. to K. Kt. sixth	34. B. takes B.
35. Q. takes B.	

And wins.

(M.)

	30. Q. to Q. B. fifth
31. Q. to K. B. fifth	31. B. to Q. second

"B. to K. B. second" would lead to the position examined above.

32. Q. to K. Kt. sixth)	32. Q. takes R. (check)

He has no better move.

33. K. to R. second

And must win.

Between the same Combatants.

Played September 16, 1841.

White. (Hanstein.)	*Black.* (V. D. Lasa.)
1. P. to K. fourth	1. P. to K. fourth
2. Kt. to K. B. third	2. Kt. to Q. B. third
3. P. to Q. fourth	3. P. takes P.
4. B. to Q. B. fourth	4. B. to Q. B. fourth
5. P. to Q. B. third	5. P. to Q. sixth
6. P. to Q. Kt. fourth	6. B. to Q. Kt. third

7. P. to Q. R. fourth	7. P. to Q. R. third
8. Castles	8. P. to Q. third
9. Q. to Q. Kt. third	9. Q. to K. second
10. B. to K. Kt. fifth	10. Kt. to K. B. third
11. Q. Kt. to Q. second	11. Castles
12. B. takes P. at Q. third	12. B. to K. third
13. Q. to Q. B. second	13. P. to K. R. third
14. B. to K. R. fourth (a)	14. Kt. to K. fourth
15. Kt. takes Kt.	15. P. takes Kt.
16. K. to K. R. square	16. P. to K. Kt. fourth
17. B. to K. Kt. third	17. Kt. to Q. second
18. Kt. to Q. B. fourth	18. B. to K. Kt. fifth
19. P. to K. B. third	19. B. to K. R. fourth
20. Q. R. to Q. square	20. P. to K. B. third
21. P. to Q. R. fifth	21. B. to Q. R. second
22. B. to K. B. second	22. B. takes B.
23. R. takes B.	23. Q. R. to Q. square
24. Kt. to K. third	24. B. to K. Kt. third
25. Q. to Q. Kt. third (check)	25. K. to K. Kt. second
26. Kt. to Q. fifth	26. B. to K. B. second
27. Q. to Q. B. second	27. B. takes Kt.
28. P. takes B. (b)	28. R. to K. R. square
29. B. to K. Kt. sixth	29. P. to K. R. fourth
30. K. R. to Q. second	30. Q. to Q. third
31. B. to K. B. fifth	31. Kt. to K. B. square
32. Q. to Q. Kt. square	32. P. to Q. Kt. fourth
33. P. takes P. in passing	33. P. takes P.
34. P. to Q. B. fourth	34. Kt. to Q. second
35. R. to Q. R. second	35. Kt. to Q. Kt. square
36. P. to Q. B. fifth	36. P. takes P.
37. P. takes P.	37. Q. takes Q. B. P.
38. Q. to Q. Kt. seventh (check)	38. K. to K. R. third (c)
39. Q. to K. B. seventh	

And wins.

Notes.

(a) So far, the opening is the same as that adopted in the last game, the combatants, however, being reversed. After this move the games cease to be identical.

(b) White seems now to have obtained a twofold advantage in position. Firstly, he has given scope for action to his Bishop; and, secondly, will be superior at the point of attack, when he assails the right wing of the Black army.

(c) He has now no resource.

Between the same Combatants

Played October 21, 1841.

White. (HANSTEIN.)	Black. (V. D. LASA.)
1. P. to K. fourth	1. P. to K. fourth
2. Kt. to K. B. third	2. Kt. to Q. B. third
3. P. to Q. fourth	3. P. takes P.
4. B. to Q. B. fourth	4. B. to Q. B fourth
5. P. to Q. B. third	5. P. to Q. sixth
6. P. to Q. Kt. fourth	6. B. to Q. Kt. third
7. P. to Q. R. fourth	7. P. to Q. R. third
8. Q. takes P.	8. P. to Q. third
9. Castles	9. K. Kt. to K. second
10. B. to K. B. fourth	10. Castles
11. Q. Kt. to Q. second	11. Kt. to K. Kt. third
12. B. to K. Kt. third	12. K. to K. R. square
13. Q. to Q. B. second	13. P. to K. B. fourth
14. P. takes P.	14. Q. B. takes P.
15. B. to Q. third	15. Q. to Q. second
16. Q. R. to K. square	16. Kt. to K. B. fifth
17. B. takes B.	17. Q. takes B.
18. Q. takes Q.	18. R. takes Q.
19. Kt. to K. R. fourth	19. R. to K. B. second
20. Kt. to K. fourth	20. Kt. to K. fourth
21. P. to Q. R. fifth	21. B. to Q. R. second
22. Kt. to K. Kt. fifth	22. R. to K. B. third
23. B. takes Kt.	23. R. takes B.
24. P. to K. Kt. third	24. R. to Q. B. fifth
25. Kt. to K. fourth	25. R. to K. B. square (a)
26. R. to K. second	26. P. to K. R. third
27. K. to K. R. square	27. P. to K. Kt. fourth
28. Kt. to K. Kt. second	28. Kt. to K. B. sixth
29. R. to Q. square	29. R. to K. square
30. Kt. takes Q. P.	30. R. takes R.

31. Kt. takes R.	31. R. takes P.
32. Kt. to Q. R. third (b)	32. P. to K. Kt. fifth
33. R. to Q. R. square	33. B. to K. sixth
34. P. to Q. Kt. fifth	34. P. takes P.
35. Kt. takes P.	35. B. to Q. seventh
36. Kt. takes P.	36. B. takes P.
37. R. to Q. square	37. B. to K. eighth (c)
38. R. takes B.	38. Kt. takes R.
39. Kt. takes Kt.	39. R. to K. B. eighth (check)
40. K. to K. Kt. second	40. R. takes Kt.
41. P. to Q. R. sixth	41. P. takes P.
42. Kt. takes P.	42. R. to K. seventh (check) (d)
43. K. to K. Kt square	43. R. to Q. R. seventh
44. Kt. to Q. B. fifth	44. R. to Q. B. seventh
45. Kt. to Q. third	45. K. to K. R. second
46. Kt. to K. B. fourth	46. K. to K. Kt. second
47. P. to K. R. third	47. P. takes P.
48. Kt. takes P.	48. K. to K. Kt. third
49. Kt. to K. B. second	49. K. to K. B. fourth
50. K. to K. Kt. second	50. P. to K. R. fourth
51. K. to K. B. third	51. R. to Q. B. sixth (check)
52. K. to K. Kt. second	52. K. to K. fourth

Drawn game (e)

Notes.

(a) Clearly "P. to Q. fourth" would lose, at least, the exchange.

(b) This Knight is now most unfortunately posted, as he cannot, for some time, lend succour to his besieged sovereign.

(c) He could also take Pawn with Bishop, and win through his passed Pawn.

(d) He might, we believe, have brought up his King with advantage.

(e) Perhaps, with the most careful manœuvres on the part of his King, Black ought to win.

Games in the Match between Messrs. CAMPBELL and WORMALD.

GAME VI.

White. (Mr. WORMALD.)	Black. (Mr. CAMPBELL.)
1. P. to K. fourth	1. P. to K. fourth
2. K. Kt. to B. third	2. K. Kt. to B. third
3. Kt. takes K. P.	3. P. to Q. third

4. Kt. to K. B. third	4. Kt. takes P.
5. Q. Kt. to B. third	5. Kt. takes Kt.
6. Q. P. takes Kt.	6. B. to K. second
7. B. to Q. third	7. P. to Q. B. fourth
8. B. to K. B. fourth	8. Q. Kt. to B. third
9. P. to K. R. third	9. Castles
10. B. to K. fourth	10. B. to K. third
11. B. to Q. fifth	11. Q. to Q. second
12. P. to Q. B. fourth	12. B. takes B.
13. P. takes B.	13. Kt. to Q. Kt. fifth
14. P. to K. Kt. fourth (a)	14. Q. to Q. R. fifth
15. Castles	15. Q. takes P.
16. P. to Q. R. third	16. Q. takes Q.
17. Q. R. takes Q.	17. Kt. to Q. R. third
18. K. R. to K. square	18. K. R. to K. square
19. K. R. to K. third	19. B. to K. B square
20. Kt. to Q. second	20. R. takes R.
21. P. takes R.	21. Kt. to Q. B. second
22. Kt. to K. fourth	22. Kt. to K. square
23. K. to B. second	23. P. to Q. Kt. fourth
24. P. to Q. Kt. third	24. P. to Q. R. fourth
25. K. to K. second	25. P. to K. B. third
26. K. to Q. third	26. K. to K. B. second
27. K. to Q. B. second	27. K. to K. second
28. B. to K. Kt. third	28. K. to Q. second
29. B. to K. square	29. P. to Q. R. fifth
30. P. to Q. Kt. fourth	30. Kt to Q. B. second
31. K. to Q. Kt. second (b)	31. R. to K. square
32. Kt. to Q. B. third	32. P. takes P.
33. P. takes P.	33. R. takes K. P.
34. P. to K. R. fourth	34. P. to K. Kt. third
35. B. to K. B. second	35. R. to R. sixth
36. B. to Q. Kt. sixth	36. R. takes R. P.
37. B. takes Kt.	37. K. takes B.
38. Kt. takes P. (check)	38. K. to Kt. third
39. Kt. to Q. B. third	39. R. takes P.
40. K. to Q. R. third	40. R. to K. Kt. sixth
41. R. to Q. B. square	41. P. to K. B. fourth

42. K. takes P.	42. R. to Q. sixth
43. Kt. to Kt. fifth	43. R. takes Q. P.
44. R. to B. eighth	44. B. to Q. R. third
45. R. to Kt. eighth (check)	45. K. to B. third
46. R. to B. eighth (check)	46. K. to Kt. second
47. R. to B. seventh (check)	47. K. to Kt. third
48. R. takes K. R. P.	48. B. to K. B. fifth
49. Kt. to Q. B. seventh	49. R. to Q. eighth
50. Kt. to R. eighth (check)	50. K. to B. third
51. P. to Kt. fifth (check)	51. K. to Q. fourth
52. Kt. to B. seventh (check)	52. K. to B. fifth
53. K. to R. fifth	53. P. to K. fourth
54. Kt. to K. sixth	54. R. (check)
55. K. to Kt. sixth	55. B. to K. sixth (check
56. K. to B. sixth	56. P. to K. Kt. fourth
57. R. to K. B. seventh	57. P. to K. Kt. fifth
58. R. takes B. P.	58. P. to K. Kt. sixth
59. Kt. to K. B. fourth	59. R. to K. B. eighth
60. Kt. takes K. P.	60. R. takes R.
61. Kt. takes B. (check)	61. K. to Kt. fifth
62. P. to Kt. sixth	62. R. to B. third (check)
63. K. to Kt. seventh (c)	63. K. to Kt. fourth

And wins.

Notes.

(a) "P. to Q. Kt. third," seems the only move to avoid the loss of a Pawn.
(b) A blunder, which loses a second Pawn.
(c) "K. to B. seventh," and the game is drawn!

Game VII.

White. (Mr. Campbell.)	*Black.* (Mr. Wormald.)
1. P. to K. fourth	1. P. to K. third
2. P. to Q. fourth	2. P. to Q. fourth
3. P. takes P.	3. P. takes P.
4. K. Kt. to B. third	4. B. to Q. third
5. P. to Q. B. fourth	5. P. to Q. B. third (a)
6. Q. Kt. to B. third	6. B. to K. third

7. Q. to Q. Kt. third	7. Q. to K. second (b)
8. B. to K. third	8. P. takes P.
9. B. takes P.	9. B. takes B.
10. Q. takes B.	10. K. Kt. to B. third
11. Castles (K.)	11. Castles
12. K. R. to K. square	12. Q. to B. second (c)
13. Q. R. to B. square	13. P. to Q. R. third
14. P. to Q. fifth	14. P. takes P.
15. Kt. takes P.	15. Kt takes Kt.
16. Q. takes Kt.	16. Q. Kt. to B. third
17. Q. to K. R. fifth (d)	17. B. to K. B. fifth
18. Q. R. to B. fourth	18. B. takes B.
19. R. takes B.	19. Q. R. to Q. square
20. Kt. to K. Kt. fifth	20. P. to K. R. third
21. Kt. to K. fourth (e)	21. Q. to K. fourth (f)
22. P. to K. Kt. fourth	22. Q. takes Q.
23. P. takes Q.	23. P. to K. B. fourth
24. Kt. to Q. B. fifth	24. P. to K. B. fifth
25. R. to Q. third	25. Q. R. to K. square
26. R. to K. fourth	26. R. takes R.
27. Kt. takes R.	27. R. to K. square
28. Kt. to Q. B. third	28. Kt. to K. fourth
29. R. to Q. fifth	29. K. to B. second
30. K. to Kt. second	30. K. to K. third
31. R. to Q. fourth	31. K. to K. B. fourth
32. P. to K. B. third	

Drawn game.

Notes.

(a) Perhaps "P. takes P." would have been better.
(b) The only move to avoid loss.
(c) To prevent the advance of K. Kt. to his fifth.
(d) Better, perhaps, to K. B. fifth.
(e) Threatening to check at B. sixth; and, on Black's capturing the Kt., to mate in three moves.
(f) With this move the attack changes hands. Had White replied with "Q. to K. second," Black would have captured Q. Kt. P. with Q. &c.

No. 9.   Problem by Mr. SILAS ANGAS.

BLACK.

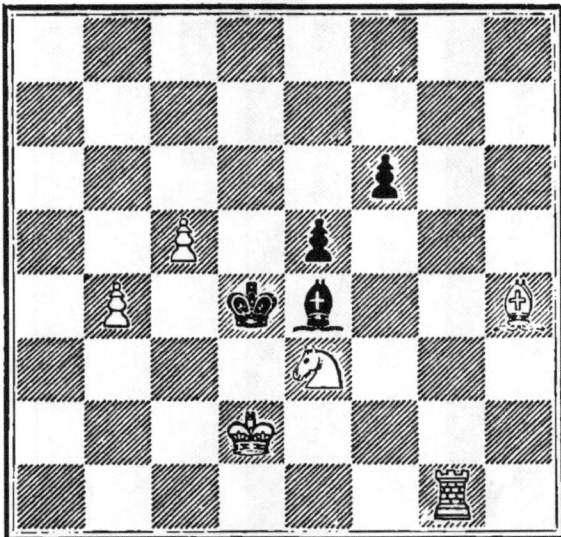

WHITE.

White to play, and mate in three moves.

No. 10.   Problem by Mr. S. CRAWSHAY.

BLACK.

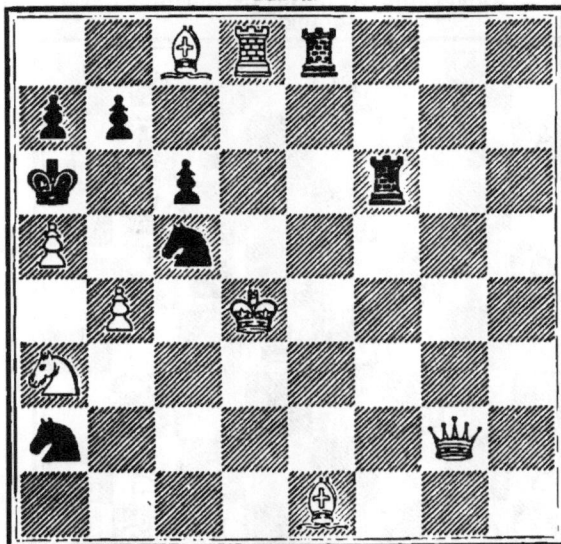

WHITE.

White to play, and force Black to checkmate in three moves.

No. 11.   Problem by Mr. S. CRAWSHAY.

BLACK.

WHITE.

White to move, and mate in two moves.

No. 12.   Problem which occurred in actual play, in a game between Messrs. MARACHE and MORPHY during the American Chess Congress.

BLACK.

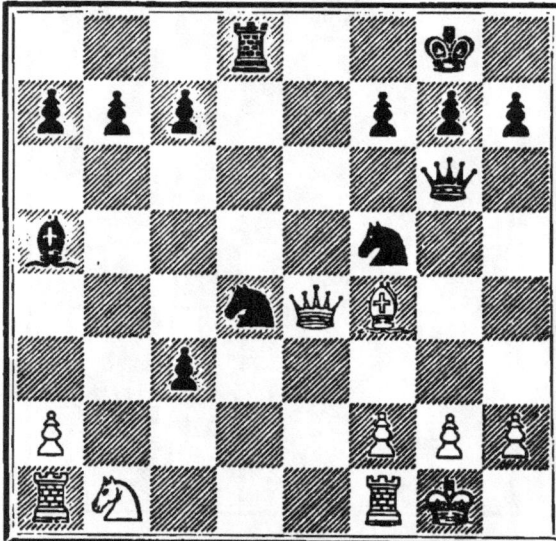

WHITE.

Black (MORPHY) made a move which at once decided the game.

MATCH-PLAY FROM 1856 TO 1859.

THE second series of the CHESS PLAYER'S CHRONICLE introduced to public notice a plan, which, being founded on the spirit of impartiality, tended to assign to every individual player his due rank in the management of matches. For the first time in the history of Chess, the exact scores of matches were given. Attention to every match was of course out of the question, care therefore was taken to select for insertion all matches in which one of the two combatants was *at least* up to the standard of *a good* "Pawn and two moves" player. By such data an opportunity was afforded for writing the history of a Chess period. To supply the void occasioned by the temporary cessation of our magazine, the brief sketch in the present number proposes to give the scores of the chief matches contested in the last two years. In 1856, which was rather a dull year for Chess, the main event was a series of games played by consultation, in which players of the rank of ALTER, BARNES, BIRD, FALKBEER, LÖWENTHAL, RANKEN, and STAUNTON, took part. Some good games were played by these artists, their skill inducing many to expect the recovery by Mr. STAUNTON of his old play. That expectation has not, however, been as yet realized. The ensuing year opened with a more interesting contest. FALKBEER, an eminent disciple of the German school, and BIRD, one of the most attacking amongst English amateurs, were pitted against one another in a couple of short matches. In the first battle, a little affair of three games, Mr. BIRD won two and lost one. In a longer contest of thirteen games, FALKBEER redeemed his laurels, scoring five, whilst his opponent won four games, and four were drawn. Thus each player in sixteen games won six, and drew four, showing no great disparity in play.

The merit of Mr. BIRD in these combats was, that after losing the first game in his primary skirmish he gained the victory; and that after losing three games in succession in the second campaign, he all but staved off defeat. In these matches Mr. BIRD showed more soundness than opponents to his style of play gave him credit for, and perhaps a little less vigour than is usually the case with our somewhat dashing amateur. FALKBEER, on the contrary, did not exhibit the patience that he had shown in his match with BRIEN in 1855, and again in his victory over JANSSENS in a Tournament in the spring of 1856. Fond of attack, he produces games of a higher order, when opposed to cool and defensive tacticians, than when facing antagonists of a style similar to his own. On the subject of this contest we must here deprecate the practice of fixing a small number of games for the decision of a doubtful question. If two really good players of nearly equal pretensions wish to decide the question of superiority, they should

7

play a comparatively long series of important games. Should the time at their disposal prevent the adoption of this plan, then that want of time will equally preclude them from doing justice to their merits. In matches of Chess, men must be cool and must have sufficient leisure; they must not steal, as it were, their time from other business. Unfortunately for the public, the games between BIRD and FALKBEER were not taken down as a series. A few found their way into the columns of the weekly newspapers of the time: three of the games which were gained by FALKBEER, were published in the *Berliner Schachzeitung*.

The next event of the year was the meeting of the Chess Association at Manchester. It was well attended; but we need say the less of this, as a pamphlet edited by Herr LÖWENTHAL, under the auspices of the Association, has given an accurate account of the proceedings. The usual practice at meetings of this description is to promote the general interests of Chess, by the institution of little contests between skilful players. It may, however, be reasonably made a matter of question, whether the practice alluded to is as useful in result as in design it is meritorious. A body of games, to a certain extent valuable, is got together beyond doubt, but the quality of such games is rarely equal to that of set matches. Limited time indeed has caused the adoption of the practice; but perhaps for it might be substituted with advantage the inauguration of *bonâ fide* matches between strong players. True it is that many members of the Association could not stay to see the result, but the *commencement* of such contests would interest them far more than do short Tournaments, which are skirmishes, rather than pitched battles. At Manchester several Tournaments were set on foot, defeat following the loss of one game. In one of these, eight players took part, ANDERSSEN, BODEN, BRIEN, HARRWITZ, HORWITZ, LÖWENTHAL, PINDAR, and SOUL. Victory fell to LÖWENTHAL, and no one will grudge the veteran his laurels on this occasion. He has not been so fortunate in his set matches as his Chess career would seem to deserve, but then he has played against really good men. BODEN was not a loser here, time preventing him from playing more than one drawn game with LÖWENTHAL; but it must be remembered that LÖWENTHAL had won *his* games from ANDERSSEN and HORWITZ. There is, however, no disparagement of the losers to be made, as a contest of one game the veteran winner would doubtless agree with us in terming "a feather thrown into the air." In another little Tournament, wherein the combatants were ALTER, Rev. C. BLACKSTONE, COHEN, FRANCIS, HAGUE, HUGHES, E. JEPHCOTT, T. JEPHCOTT, KLING, M'DONNELL, G. MEDLEY, Rev. H. O'DONNELL, Rev. T. KIRKMAN, ROGERS, SIMPSON, and G. A. OWEN, who, when well up, could not stay to finish the contest; the ultimate winner was ALTER, Mr. FRANCIS coming in second.

Some consultation matches took place. Ashton met Chester with no decisive result, whilst Scotland got. the best of a game with Ireland ; but the contest was not finished. In one consultation game between ANDERSSEN, HORWITZ, and KLING, on one side, and BODEN, KIPPING, and STAUNTON, on the other, victory fell to the latter.

The match between Manchester and Oxford University, which was adjourned at the last meeting of the Association, was resumed. Oxford being represented by one Birmingham, one Manchester, and one Oxford player. After a struggle, the " scratch crew " lost : Manchester thus won two games against one, one being drawn. All the four games were, in our opinion, up to match-play ; three of them were published in the second series of the CHRONICLE, the fourth in Herr LÖWENTHAL's pamphlet.

A far more satisfactory contest than any of the encounters which we have mentioned was projected. The intended combatants were the old opponents, HARRWITZ and LÖWENTHAL. They played an elaborate game of 100 moves. Several interesting alternations took place, now one, now the other, leading, but always pressed by his adversary. At length the crafty veterans of the art made a drawn game. This really great match, much to our regret, was never resumed. The style of these eminent players is not the same. LÖWENTHAL is laborious, learned, and analytical; HARRWITZ is full of resource, practical, and dexterous. If Chess-players be divided into three schools, as they fairly may be, viz., one of analysis, a second of theory, and the third of practice, LÖWENTHAL is pre-eminently a theorist, and HARRWITZ belongs essentially to the school of practice. Let it, however, be borne in mind, that this division, although true in nature, does not deny the fact that every good player enters more or less into the spirit of rival schools. At the end of 1857, we had another contest between a skilful German player and one of our own countrymen. This match was very properly made for a large number of games. Twenty-one games were played, of which Mr. HANNAH won eleven, Mr. LOWE won six, and four were drawn. Mr. LOWE is no longer a young man, and must not wonder at the success of opponents who can afford more time to the study of moves than the veteran's want of patience or of inclination, or perhaps of both, will allow him. By this performance, Mr. HANNAH, previously known as a good player at Brighton, at once forced an entrance into the ranks of strong metropolitan amateurs. In 1858, we were favored with some interesting contests between ALTER and BODEN. The advantage rested with the latter player. We believe that we are correct in stating the scores of two matches to be BODEN 5, ALTER 2, drawn 1; and BODEN 5, ALTER 1. Mr. BODEN is a very ingenious player, and, unless we are mistaken, would be considered a representative of the school of theory. ALTER is a harder, not to say colder, player. Ex-

tremely painstaking, he displays a good deal of breadth in his play.
Of his analytical power, and of the extent of his knowledge, we cannot
very well judge. A better match was played in the same year between
two other English players, Messrs. BARNES and CAMPBELL. Mr.
BARNES is eminently practical, and has a very quick perception.
CAMPBELL is defensive, and when in difficulty, conducts an uphill
game with unflinching courage and determination. Upon this occasion
he scored 7 games against 6, having been five games behind in the first
part of the match.

The American Chess Congress of the same year was far too important
a meeting to be treated here in a cursory manner. When the book of
the Congress reaches us, we shall give a detailed notice. We shall now
content ourselves with observing that, as in England in 1851, the mistake of choosing short matches was made. In America, however, the
mistake was of little consequence, as the chief honors fell to MORPHY.
In a contest between 16 players, MORPHY was first, PAULSEN second,
LICHTENHEIN third, and RAPHAEL fourth. In a minor contest, the result
was, HORNER 1, SOLOMONS 2, SEEBACH 3, and MANTIN 4. Soon after
his victory, Mr. MORPHY started for Europe, to gain fresh laurels in set
matches, the true test of skill in Chess. A collection of his games,
with elaborate notes attached thereto, will shortly appear. Of this important book, which will be edited by Herr LÖWENTHAL, we shall give
an account at the proper time. The meeting of the Chess Association
at Birmingham stands much on the same footing. The pamphlet,
which will contain a detailed account of its proceedings, has not yet
appeared. It will be edited by Mr. STAUNTON. Reserving remarks
upon it until after the appearance of the pamphlet, we may state that
the meeting was successful. In one of the usual short Tournaments,
LÖWENTHAL, who was in good form after his match with MORPHY,
came in first, the second place being secured by FALKBEER, who, in
short matches, is an excellent beginner. The several scores we shall
give in our notice of the pamphlet. Besides these contests in 1858, a
pool was played at the Philidorian Rooms, Rathbone Place. The *Era*
observes, " A pool differs from a tournament at Chess. In a tournament, the players are paired off, and the loser retires. The best pair
may be matched at once, and the player who ought to gain the second
honours is dismissed from the contest. But in a pool the players are
compelled to encounter in turn every one whose name is put down for
the combat. In the pool now under consideration, each player was
given seven lives; with the understanding, that when seven games
were lost by any one, he retired immediately from the contest, and the
necessary condition that drawn games not counting, two players must
play on in every round until one of them won a game." Seven players
took part in this pool. The result was, that BRIEN won. Playing 29

games, he won 14, lost 5, and drew 10. CAMPBELL was second. He played 24 games, winning 11, losing 7, and drawing 6. ZYTOGORSKI, who was third, played 19 games, winning 8, losing 7, and drawing 4. FALKBEER, the fourth, played 17 games, winning 8, losing 7, and drawing 2. HEALEY, the well-known problem-maker, played 10 games, gaining 3, and losing 7. KENNY played also 10 games, losing 7, and drawing 3. The seventh, Mr. MÜLLER, resigned, when he had lost 5 games. In this pool Mr. CAMPBELL showed the same qualities that he had previously displayed in his match with Mr. BARNES. Getting the worst of the contest at first, and also opposed to match-players, he made up at the close a great deal of ground, and finished a very good second. Mr. ZYTOGORSKI commenced very well, but appeared to relax in his efforts as he went on. FALKBEER, who shines most in little matches, showed the same want of patience that we had noticed in his play against BIRD. The winner, who is one of the worst beginners in matches that we know, or have known, doubtless was successful through the number of games played. It was, we heard, his last match. A short match then ensued between HEALEY and KENNY, in which the latter reversed their respective positions in the pool, scoring five games against his opponent's four. We believe, that in the above account we have given exact scores. To ascertain them, we have searched the files of papers which have been published since the suspension of the *Chronicle*, and are especially indebted to the careful columns of the *Era*. We need hardly assure our readers that we shall continue the same accurate supervision in giving future scores. We invite Clubs to transmit them to us in the most exact manner possible. We repeat also, that we shall hereafter publish a detailed notice of the American and Birmingham meetings, but are necessarily obliged to await the appearance of the official documents. Scores in matches are absolutely required, in order to mete out to every one justice.

CHESS IN THE PROVINCES.

BIRMINGHAM AND EDGBASTON CHESS CLUB.

THE Annual Meeting of the Subscribers to the Birmingham and Edgbaston Chess Club was held on the 10th of February last at Evans's Library in Birmingham. Mr. Thomas Avery, the President, in the chair. The Annual Report having been read by the Secretary, Mr. W. R. Wills, the Committee for the next year was then elected, consisting of, Mr. T. Avery, President; Mr. W. B. Wills, Secretary and Treasurer; Messrs. B. Chesshire, J. Deykins, T. S. Hill, C. T. Saunders, and Dr. Freeman, Members. The Club meet at Evans's Library on Tuesday and Thursday evenings, at seven o'Clock. We need not further allude to the services this Club has rendered to the Chess community, for the General Meeting of the Chess Association, which was held last year in Birmingham, is still fresh in the memory of our readers, who, we doubt not, duly appreciate the efforts then made by the President, Secretary, and Members of that Club.

THE MATCH AND PROBLEM CHESS BOARD.—DAY AND SON, *Gate Street, Lincoln's Inn.*—The chief peculiarity of this useful production consists in the different squares being prominently designated according to the usual notation of the day, thus facilitating the playing over published Games and Solutions to Problems, and making what has hitherto, to young players, been found tedious and difficult, easy and pleasant. The squares are surrounded with an illuminated border, strongly framed and glazed, and forming altogether, in addition to its utility, an elegant ornament for the drawing-room or boudoir.

POCKET CHESS AND DRAUGHTS.—BEAL, *Grove Terrace, West Ham.* A cheap and simple combination of these two games, affording facilities for play at times when a better but more cumbersome set of men would be inconvenient. It consists of a flat box, four inches square, containing a folding board, with the proper squares ; also, flat chessmen, about the size of a farthing, their characters stamped in gold on dark purple and white grounds ; the reverse form draughts. All goes easily into the pocket, and can be transmitted per book post.

THE SEVEN AGES OF CHESS.

INTRODUCTION.

From youth to age how dear the game of Chess !
How kind a comforter in our distress !
How sweet a solace, weaning one from pain,
Giving fresh impulse to the wearied brain.
How pleasant an amusement after toil !
A quiet recreation, and a foil
To the wild mirth of more ecstatic pleasures,
To the glad music of swift dancing measures,
To the mad gallop o'er the breezy plain,
To the swift sailing on the joyous main,
To summer plunges in refreshing fountains,
To all the full emotions born on mountains.
Oh, many a time have I had cause to bless
The quiet pleasures of the game of Chess.

I. CHESS IN CHILDHOOD.

When quite a child, before I knew
 Anything, except the name
 Of the ancient royal game;
When I dreamt that all was true;
When the wizard tales of yore,
And all their legendary lore
Of countless wonders, were to me
Truer than reality :
When, with interest and amaze,
 I listened to wild stories
Of enchanters, giants, fays,
 And all their fabled glories ;
O then the game of Chess to me
Was a magic mystery.
I thought the men were really men
 Transformed to Bishop, King, and Knight,
And doomed by powers beyond our ken,
 To strive on chequers, black and white.
And when I saw grave men, who scorned
 All trinkets, toys, and baubles ;
Who never played at whipping-tops,
 And didn't care for marbles ;
Oh when I saw them playing Chess,
 For hour after hour,
I marvelled at their quietness,
 And at the Chessmen's power ;
Till a yearning seized my spirit
 To know more than the mere name ;
To be worthy to inherit
 The secret of the game.

II. CHESS IN BOYHOOD.

I had been very ill : night after night,
In a delirium of wild dreams,
I roused the startled sleepers with affright,
At the fierce terror of my screams.

But I grew better, and was wont to lie,
When it was warm, for many hours
Where the breeze, with full melodious sigh,
Came laden with the breath of flowers.

I had a nurse, a fair young girl,
With deep blue eyes of love and truth,
Shaded by many a clustered curl,
Rich with the golden light of youth.

And often would she sit with me,
And while I held her fairy hands,
Would tell me tales of mystery,
And stories of far distant lands.

But sometimes I would tire of these,
Sick and ill for weariness,
Till once, when nothing else would please,
She taught to me the game of Chess.

And I, with boyish eagerness,
Would play all day and never stir,
Part for the love I bore to Chess,
Part for the love I bore to her.

For in the pauses of our game
She used to kiss me if I won,
And if I lost, 'twas all the same,
I had the kisses every one.

But she is gone! regret is wrong,
For those blue eyes another owns,
And all her kisses now belong,
They tell me, to a Mr. Jones.

Ah! happy Jones—those eyes are thine,
And I perhaps may see them never;
But Chess, that intellectual mine,
Thy wooing cannot from me sever.

(*To be continued.*)

CHESS ENIGMA.

The monarch Charles, yclept " the merry "
(Some of whose ways were shocking, very),
Went out one night with his favourite minister
(Whose dress was gay, whose deeds were sinister);
Their " little game " was not monarchical,
But most decidedly sky-lark-ical;
For, truth to tell, I must confess,
Though state affairs were in a mess,

Charles and the Earl incognito,
Went where they didn't ought to go ;
Left all the royal convocation,
And sallied forth for a jollification.
At a snug tavern by the river,
Charles (who was always a free liver,
Had sprats for two, then mutton chops,
Which they washed down with sundry drops
Of something much more strong than water,
Brought them by the landlord's daughter.
The wine was good, the damsel fair ;
(Good teeth, bright eyes, and rich brown hair ;
And she spoke in a silvery, winsome tone
That thousands of ladies might covet to own).
Rochester and the monarch gay
At tippling proved themselves *au fait*,
Nor thought of what they'd have to pay,
While wine and time ran fast away,
Till pretty nearly break of day.
At length the Earl to Charley said,
" I think it 's time to be off to bed."
And the King thought it needless longer to stay,
When he saw what a bill he 'd got to pay
For victuals and drink, aud Havannah cigars ;
For wine out of bottles, and whisky from jars;
For " negus " and " cobblers," for port and for sherry,
With which these roysterers made themselves merry.
" By Gad ! " says the King," now what 's to be done ?
The whole of my cash is one pound one !"
" Indeed," says Rochester, " I've got none."
" I 'll send you the money," said Charles to the maid ;
Says she, " You can't go till the bill is paid."
So Charles, when he found that fork out he must,
Left his gold watch with the girl as a trust ;
And then, with a good many stumblings and dodgings,
They blundered their way to Rochester's lodgings ;
And there in a state which the vulgar call " tight,"
The King and the Earl turned in for the night.
Next day went a courtier to " pay off the shot,"
And safe in his pocket he brought back the—what ?
Cunning reader, rack your brains to guess
What piece this story indicates in *Chess*.

T. H. C., *Hereford.*

THE MATCH BETWEEN MESSRS. MORPHY AND
MONGREDIEN.

IN presenting to our readers the games played in this match, we feel
bound to make a few observations upon the players engaged in it, and
their respective strength, especially as the former player won every
game, after drawing the first. Of all the victories which the American
champion has obtained since his arrival in Europe, this was the most
complete, but by no means the most glorious; his opponent in that
struggle being of inferior strength to his former adversaries, and entering
into the contest with less ardour and energy than might have been expected in an encounter with so strong and illustrious a foe. The proof
of this will be found in the games, of which only two or three have the
criterions of a hard-contested fight. Mr. MONGREDIEN is the only
Englishman who has played a match with Mr. MORPHY, and his defeat
was complete; but it must not be therefrom concluded that others would
share a similar fate, for, with all deference to Mr. MONGREDIEN's fine
play, there are players in this country with whom he would have
scarcely stood a better chance, if he had encountered them in a serious
match. We have read carefully through all the games which Mr.
MORPHY has played since his arrival in Europe, and we have invariably
found a want of nerve and a deficiency of pluck in the play of his adversaries, which makes us wish that he might yet encounter a player of
more stamina, to make the games of more intrinsic value; and it is only
when Greek meets Greek that really fine games can be produced. Up
to the present time, if we were asked to choose amongst all the games
he has played, one we should call a standard game, we would be at a
loss to do so. But let us be well understood: we do not mean by this
to throw any blame upon Mr. MORPHY's play, far from it; he has invariably won, and what more can we ask of him? His adversaries have
perhaps given him no chance of bringing out his finest and best play,
which may yet happen if he encounters sterner stuff. Nor has Mr.
MORPHY had occasion to test his own abilities in a heavy match, which
means, *at least*, the best out of 21 games. LA BOURDONNAIS and MAC-
DONNELL have played a hundred games in order to test their respective
abilities; and their games are a glorious legacy—there is play of the
highest order in them. Mr. MORPHY's games are chiefly remarkable on
account of his knowledge of openings, and the deficiency of blunders on
his side; which gap, however, his adversaries take good care to fill out.

GAME I.
(*Double Gambit.*)

White. (Mr. MONGREDIEN,)	*Black.* (Mr. MORPHY.)
1. P. to K. fourth	1. P. to K. fourth
2. B. to B. fourth	2. B. to B. fourth
3. P. to Q. Kt. fourth	3. B. takes P.
4. P. to K. B. fourth	4. P. to Q. fourth (*a*)
5. P. takes Q. P.	5. P. to K. fifth
6. Kt. to K. second	6. Kt. to K. B. third
7. P. to B. third	7. B. to Q. B. fourth
8. P. to Q. fourth	8. P. takes P. (*en pas.*)
9. Q. takes P.	9. Castles
10. B. to Q. R. third	10. B. takes B.
11. Kt. takes B.	11. B. to Kt. fifth
12. Castles	12. B. takes Kt.
13. Q. takes B.	13. Kt. takes P.
14. Q. to B. third	14. P. to Q. B. third
15. Q. R. to Kt. square	15. Q. to K. second (*b*)
16. B. takes Kt.	16. P. takes B.
17. P. to B. fourth	17. P. takes P.
18. R. takes P.	18. Kt. to Q. second
19. K. to R. square (*c*)	19. K. R. to K. square
20. Kt. takes P.	20. Q. to K. third
21. Kt. to K. fifth	21. Kt. takes Kt.
22. P. takes Kt.	22. R. to K. B. square
23. Q. to Q. Kt. third	23. Q. takes Q.
24. P. takes Q.	24. Q. R. to Kt. square
25. R. takes R. P.	25. R. takes P.

And the game was by mutual consent given up as drawn.

Notes.

(*a*) This move was invented by La Bourdonnais in his match with M'Donnell.

(*b*) "Q. to her R. fourth" would, it seems to us, have saved the Pawn, which now must fall.

(*c*) Why not "Kt. take P.," which would give the advantage to White? for even if the Q. checks on Q. Kt. fourth, White still remains with the better game by interposing the Q. on K. B. second.

GAME II.

(*Evans' Gambit.*)

White. (Mr. MORPHY.)	Black (Mr. MONGREDIEN.)
1. P. to K. fourth	1. P. to K. fourth
2. Kt. to K. B. third	2. Kt. to Q. B. third
3. B. to B. fourth	3. B. to B. fourth
4. P. to Q. Kt. fourth	4. B. takes P.
5. P. to Q. B. third	5. B. to B. fourth
6. Castles	6. P. to Q. third
7. P. to Q. fourth	7. P. takes P.
8. P. takes P.	8. B. to Kt. third
9. B. to Q. Kt. second	9. Kt. to B. third
10. Q. Kt. to Q. second	10. Castles
11. P. to Q. fifth	11. Kt. to K. fourth (*a*)
12. Kt. takes Kt.	12. P. takes Kt.
13. B. takes P.	13. R. to K. square
14. B. takes Kt.	14. Q. takes B.
15. K. to R. square	15. B. to R. fourth (*b*)
16. Q. to R. fourth	16. P. to Q. Kt. fourth
17. Q. takes P.	17. B. to Q. R. third
18. Q. takes K. B.	18. B. takes B.
19. Kt. takes B.	19. R. takes P.
20. Q. takes B. P.	20. Q. R. to K. square
21. Kt. to Q. sixth	21. Q. takes R.
22. Q. takes P. (check)	

And wins.

Notes.

(*a*) "Kt. to Q. R. fourth" is the proper move at this stage of the game ; for by the above move, Black loses, uselessly, a Pawn.

(*b*) This evident oversight loses a piece and the game.

GAME III.

White. (Mr. MONGREDIEN.)	Black. (Mr. MORPHY.)
1. P. to Q. fourth	1. P. to K. third
2. P. to Q. B. fourth	2. P. to K. B. fourth
3. P. to K. B. fourth	3. Kt. to K. B. third

4. Kt. to K. B. third	4. P. to Q. Kt. third
5. P. to Q. R. third	5. P. to Q. R. fourth
6. Kt. to Q. B. third	6. B. to Kt. second
7. P. to K. third	7. B. to K. second
8. B. to K. second	8. Castles
9. Castles	9. P. to K. R. third
10. P. to Q. Kt. third	10. P. to Q. third
11. B. to Kt. second	11. Q. Kt. to Q. second
12. R. to Q. B. square	12. K. to R. second
13. B. to Q. third	13. P. to K. Kt. third
14. P. to K. R. third	14. Q. to K. square
15. Q. to K. square	15. Kt. to K. fifth
16. B. takes Kt.	16. P. takes B.
17. Kt. to Q. second	17. Kt. to B. third
18. K. to R. second	18. Q. to Q. second
19. R. to K. Kt. square	19. P. to Q. fourth
20. R. to B. second	20. P. to K. Kt. fourth
21. Kt. to K. B. square	21. P. takes K. B. P.
22. P. takes K. B. P.	22. B. to Q. third
23. P. to K. Kt. third	23. P. to Q. B. third
24. Kt. to K. third (a)	24. R. to K. Kt. square
25. Q. R. to K. Kt. second	25. Q. R. to K. B. square
26. Kt. to K. second	26. B. to B. square
27. P. to K. Kt. fourth (b)	27. Q. to Q. B. second
28. R. to K. B. second	28. Kt. to K. square
29. Q. to K. B. square	29. R. to B. second
30. K. to R. square	30. K. R. to B. square
31. Kt. to Kt. second	31. B. to R. third
32. Q. to Q. B. square (c)	32. Q. to K. second (d)
33. Kt. to Kt. third	33. Kt. to Kt. second
34. R. to K. square	34. P. to B. fourth
35. Kt. to K. second	35. B. to Kt. second
36. P. takes Q. P.	36. K. P. takes P.
37. P. to B. fifth	37. Kt. to K. third
38. K. Kt. to B. fourth	38. Kt. takes Kt.
39. Kt. takes Kt.	39. R. to Q. B. square
40. Q. to K. third	40. P. takes P.
41. B. takes P.	41. B. takes P.

42. B. takes P. (*e*)	42. B. to Kt. fifth
43. R. to Q. square	43. R. to B. sixth
44. Q. to Q. fourth	44. Q. to R. fifth
45. R. to K. Kt. square	45. R. to Kt. second
46. Q. to K. fifth	46. R. to K. second
47. Q. to Q. fourth	47. B. to Q. third
48. Q. takes R.	48. P. to Q. fifth
49. Q. takes Q. P.	49. B. takes Kt.
50. K. to Kt. second	50. P. to K. sixth

Discovering check, and winning.

Notes.

(*a*) To this point of the game White has very carefully played, but begins to lose ground from this move, and does not seem to have a fixed plan of attack or defence. "B. to his square" would have been much stronger, as it effectually keeps both Black's Bishops out of play.

(*b*) A *bad* provision against the threatened advance of the adversary's King's Pawn, which ought to have been foreseen and cared for, some moves before.

(*c*) The best move, as it renders the last move of Black null and void.

(*d*) We should have preferred "P. takes P.," and then "P. to Q. B. fourth," to keep the attack on.

(*e*) "Kt. to K. sixth" instead, would have given White a decided advantage, and would, *at least*, have prevented Black from winning the game.

GAME IV.

(*Two Knights' Opening.*)

White. (Mr. MORPHY.)	*Black.* (Mr. MONGREDIEN.)
1. P. to K. fourth	1. P. to K. fourth
2. Kt. to K. B. third	2. Kt. to Q. B. third
3. B. to B. fourth	3. Kt. to B. third
4. Kt. to K. Kt. fifth	4. P. to Q. fourth
5. P. takes P.	5. Kt. to Q. R. fourth
6. P. to Q. third	6. P. to K. R. third
7. Kt. to K. B. third	7. B. to K. Kt. fifth (*a*)
8. P. to K. R. third	8. B. takes Kt.
9. Q. takes B.	9. B. to Q. third (*b*)
10. B. to Kt. fifth (check)	10. P. to Q. B. third
11. P. takes P.	11. P. takes P.
12. B. takes P. (check)	12. Kt. takes B.

13. Q. takes Kt. (check)	13. K. to K. second
14. Kt. to B. third	14. R. to Q. B. square
15. Q. to K. B. third	15. R. to K. square
16. Castles	16. K. to B. square
17. B. to Q. second	17. P. to K. Kt. fourth
18. P. to K. R. fourth	18. Kt. to R. second
19. Q. to B. fifth	19. K. to Kt. second
20. P. takes P.	20. P. takes P.
21. P. to K. Kt. third	21. P. to K. B. third
22. K. to Kt. second	22. K. R. to R. square
23. K. R. to R. square	23. R. to B. second
24. R. to R. second	24. Q. to Q. B. square
25. Q. takes Q.	25. K. R. takes Q.
26. Q. R. to R. square	26. Kt. to K. B. square
27. Kt. to Q. Kt. fifth	27. R. to Q. second
28. Kt. takes B.	28. R. takes Kt.
29. B. to Q. Kt. fourth	

And Black resigns.

Notes.

(a) "P. to K. fifth" instead, is a better defence, as it forces the Queen to King's second and then "Kt. takes B." followed by "B. to Q. third," gives Black, although he has lost a Pawn, a strong attack.

(b) "P. to K. fifth" would have been far better, although with an opponent of Mr. Morphy's strength there is but little chance of retrieving a game with two Pawns minus.

GAME V.

White. (Mr. MONGREDIEN.)	*Black.* (Mr. MORPHY.)
1. P. to K. fourth	1. P. to K. fourth
2. P. to K. B. fourth	2. P. takes P.
3. B. to B. fourth	3. P. to Q. fourth
4. B. takes P.	4. Kt. to K. B. third
5. P. to Q. third (a)	5. Kt. takes B.
6. P. takes Kt.	6. Q. takes P.
7. Q. to K. second (check)	7. B. to K. third
8. B. takes P.	8. Kt. to Q. B. third
9. Kt. to K. B. third	9. Castles

10. Kt. to Q. B. third	10. B. to Q. Kt. fifth
11. Castles K. R.	11. Q. to K. R. fourth
12. P. to Q. R. third (b)	12. B. to B. fourth (check)
13. K. to R. square	13. B. to K. Kt. fifth
14. Q. to Q. second	14. K. R. to K. square
15. Q. R. to K. square	15. B. takes Kt.
16. R. takes B.	16. R. takes R. (check)
17. Q. takes R.	17. Kt. to Q. fifth
18. R. to K. B. square (c)	18. Kt. takes P.
19. Q. to B. square	19. Kt. to Q. fifth
20. P. to Q. Kt. fourth (d)	20. B. to Q. third
21. B. takes B.	21. R. takes B.
22. Q. to K. third	22. Kt. to B. fourth
23. Q. to B. third	23. Q. takes Q.
24. R. takes Q.	24. R. to Q. B. third
25. Kt. to K. second	25. Kt. to Q. fifth

And wins.

Notes.

(a) " Q. Kt. to B. third " would have been better, as it brings at once another piece into play, and prevents the loss of a Pawn, which only players of first-rate strength seem to appreciate.

(b) A very weak move.

(c) " R. to K. R. third " could have yet saved the game.

(d) Another weak move, for " B. takes Q. B. P." would have won the Pawn back, and most likely have drawn the game; for "B. takes P." "Black K. takes B." best.

White.	Black.
Kt. to K. fourth	P. to K. Kt. third (best)
P. to Q. Kt. fourth	Kt. to K. seventh (best)
Q. to Q. B. fourth	

And the game is even.

GAME VI.

(Irregular Opening.)

White. (Mr. MORPHY.)	Black. (Mr. MONGREDIEN.)
1. P. to K. fourth	1. P. to K. fourth
2. Kt. to K. B. third	2. P. to Q. fourth
3. P. takes P.	3. P. to K. fifth
4. Q. to K. second	4. Q. to K. second (a)

5. Kt. to Q. fourth	5. Q. to K. fourth
6. Kt. to Kt. fifth	6 B. to Q. third (b)
7. P. to Q. fourth	7. Q. to K. second
8. P. to Q. B. fourth	8. B. to Kt. fifth (check)
9. B. to Q. second	9. B. takes B. (check)
10. Kt. takes B.	10. P. to Q. R. third
11. Kt. to Q. B. third	11. P. to K. B. fourth
12. Castles	12. Kt. to K. B. third
13. R. to K. square	13. Castles
14. P. to K. B. third	14. P. to Q. Kt. fourth
15. P. takes K. P.	15. P. takes K. P.
16. Q. Kt. takes K. P.	16. P. takes P.
17. Q. takes P.	17. K. to R. square
18. B. to Q. third	18. B. to Kt. second
19. Kt. takes Kt.	19. Q. takes Kt.
20. K. R. to B. square	20. Q. to Q. square
21. R. takes R. (check)	21. Q. takes R.
22. Q. to Q. Kt. fourth	

And wins.

Notes.

(a) "P. to K. B. fourth," would have been better; for what is the use of giving up a Pawn, if you don't open your game by it?

(b) "P. to Q. sixth," would have answered as well; in fact Black is already doomed.

GAME VII.

(Evans' Gambit.)

White. (Mr. MONGREDIEN.)	Black. (Mr. MORPHY.)
1. P. to K. fourth	1. P. to K. fourth
2. Kt. to K. B. third	2. Kt. to Q. B. third
3. B. to B. fourth	3. B. to B. fourth
4. P. to Q. Kt. fourth	4. B. takes P.
5. P. to Q. B. third	5. B. to R. fourth
6. Castles (a)	6. Kt. to B. third
7. P. to Q. fourth	7. Castles
8. P. to Q. fifth	8. Kt. to K. second

8

9. Q. to Q. third	9. P. to Q. third
10. P. to K. R. third (*b*)	10. Kt. to Kt. third
11. Kt. to R. second	11. Kt. to R. fourth
12. B. to Kt. third (*c*)	12. Kt. to K. B. fifth
13. B. takes Kt.	13. Kt. takes B.
14. Q. to B. third	14. P. to K. B. fourth
15. P. takes P.	15. Q. B. takes P.
16. P. to K. Kt. fourth	16. B. to Q. sixth
17. Q. to K. third	17. B. to Q. Kt. third
18. Q. to Q. second	18. Q. to K. R. fifth

And wins.

Notes.

(*a*) " P. to Q. fourth " would have been better.
(*b*) Why not bring the pieces out, instead of losing this move?
(*c*) Another lost move, which enables Black to crush his adversary in a few moves.

GAME VIII.
(*Philidor's Defence.*)

White. (Mr. MORPHY.)	*Black.* (Mr. MONGREDIEN.
1. P. to K. fourth	1. P. to K. fourth
2. Kt. to K. B. third	2. P. to Q. third
3. P. to Q. fourth	3. P. takes P.
4. Q. takes P.	4. P. to Q. R. third (*a*)
5. B. to K. Kt. fifth	5. P. to K. B. third
6. B. to K. third	6. B. to K. third
7. Kt. to B. third	7. Kt. to K. second
8. B. to K. second	8. K. Kt. to Q. B. third
9. Q. to Q. second	9. B. to K. second
10. Castles K. R.	10. Castles
11. Q. R. to Q. square	11. Kt. to Q. second
12. Kt. to Q. fourth	12. Kt. takes Kt.
13. B. takes Kt.	13. P. to K. B. fourth
14. P. takes P.	14. B. takes B. P.
15. B. to Q. B. fourth (check)	15. K. to R. square
16. Kt. to Q. fifth	16. Kt. to K. B. third
17. Kt. takes B.	17. Q. takes Kt.
18. K. R. to K. square	18. Q. to Q. second

19. Q. to K. Kt. fifth	19. P. to K. R. third
20. Q. to R. fourth	20. Q. R. to K. square
21. P. to Q. B. third	21. R. to K. fifth (*b*)
22. R. takes R.	22. Kt. takes R.
23. Q. takes P. (check)	23. B. to R. second
24. R. to K. square	24. P. to B. fourth
25. R. takes Kt.	25. P. takes B.
26. Q. to R. fifth	26. P. to K, Kt. third
27. Q. to R. sixth	27. R. to K. square
28. Q. to K. B. fourth	28. K. to Kt. second
29. R. takes R.	29. Q takes R.
30. Q. takes P. (check)	Resigns.

This game concluded the match.

Notes.

(*a*) " B. to Q. second " would have been better, bringing a piece into play.
(*b*) This is a great blunder, and gives the game away.

Games between the great PRUSSIAN PLAYERS.
(*Philidor's Defence in the King's Knight's Opening.*)
Played August 28th, 1839.

White. (V. D. LASA.)	*Black.* (HANSTEIN.)
1. P. to K. fourth	1. P. to K. fourth
2. Kt. to K. B. third	2. P. to Q. third (*a*)
3. P. to Q. fourth	3. P. to K. B. fourth (*b*)
4. Q. P. takes P.	4. K. B. P. takes P.
5. Kt. to K. Kt. fifth	5. P. to Q. fourth
6. P. to K. sixth (*c*)	6. Kt. to K. R. third
7. P. to Q. B. fourth (*d*)	7. B. to Q. Kt. fifth (check) (*e*)
8. Kt. to Q. B. third	8. P. to Q. fifth
9. P. to Q. R. third	9. P. to K. sixth
10. Q. to K. R. fifth (check) (*f*)	10. P. to K. Kt. third
11. Q. takes Kt.	11. P. takes P. (check) (*g*)
12. K. takes P.	12. B. to K. B. square
13. Q. to K. R. third	13. Q. to K. B. third (check)
14. Q. to K. B. third	14. Q. takes Q. (check)
15. P. takes Q.	15. P. takes Kt.
16. B. to K. R. third	16. B. to Q. B. fourth (check)

17. K. to K. Kt. second	17. Kt. to Q. B. third
18. P. takes P.	18. Kt. to K. fourth
19. B. to K. B. fourth	19. Kt. takes P. at Q. B. fifth
20. B. takes P.	20. Kt. to K. sixth (check)
21. K. to K. Kt. third	21. P. to K. R. fourth (*h*)
22. P. to K. B. fourth	22. P. to Q. Kt. third (*i*)
23. Kt. to K. fourth	23. P. to K. R. fifth (check)
24. K. to K. B. second	24. Kt. to Q. fourth (discovering check)
25. Kt. takes B.	25. P. takes Kt.
26. B. to K. fifth	26. R. to K. B. square
27. B. to K. Kt. second	27. B. takes P.
28. P. to Q. B. fourth	28. Kt. takes P.
29. B. takes Kt.	29. R. to Q. square
30. B. to Q. B. sixth (check)	30. K. to K. second
31. K. to K. third	31. R. to Q. fifth
32. B. to K. Kt. fifth (check)	32. K. to Q. third
33. B. to K. fourth	33. K. to K. fourth
34. B. to Q. third	34. B. takes P.
35. B. takes B.	35. R. takes B.
36. K. R. to K. square	36. R. to Q. fifth
37. Q. R. to Q. square	37. K. to K. B. fourth (*k*)
38. B. to K. R. sixth	38. R. to K. square (check)
39. K. to K. B. third	39. R. takes R. at K. eighth
40. R. takes R. at K. square	40. P. to K. Kt. fourth
41. B. to K. Kt. seventh	41. P. to K. Kt. fifth (check)
42. K. to K. B. second	42. R. to Q. seventh (check)
43. R. to K. second	43. P. to K. Kt. sixth (check)
44. P. takes P.	44. P. takes P. (check)
45. K. to K. B. square	45. R. takes R.

The game was drawn. (*l*)

Notes.

(*a*) Lopez maintained this defence to be better than that of " Q. Kt. to Q. B. third," a move which had received the sanction of Damiano. Amongst the players who have supported the opinion of Lopez, the most distinguished, up to the present time, are Philidor and Boncourt. These, however, have been opposed by the great Italian authors, and by the celebrated La Bourdonnais; by men, in short, who excelled them in analytical power, and were fully their equals in practical knowledge of the game. Many of our recent analysts have a tendency to agree with Lopez; but we cannot pronounce their case to be established on decisive evidence.

(b) Philidor so thoroughly believed this counter-gambit to be sound, that he went so far as to declare the first player's attack with the "K. Kt." to be radically bad. This opinion was denounced in the strongest manner by the most eminent of the Italian critics. The French master does not appear to have shaped his *début* after the reigning fashion, which rejects the counter-gambit. This game, with the accompanying one, will form specimens of the manner in which the chief players of Prussia managed Philidor's defence at the date assigned.

(c) Philidor here played "P. to K. B. fourth." His French contemporaries, the best players amongst whom were Bernard, Carlier, Leger, and Verdeni, recommended the move in the text. The title of their work is—"Traité Theorique et Pratique du Jeu des Echecs, par une Société des Amateurs." Paris, Stoupe, 1775; and, again, 1786. 12mo, pp. 412. For a translation of part of this useful volume, by Mr. G. Walker, the English reader may refer to the *Chess Player's Chronicle*, 1846.

(d) Several modes of continuing the attack are given by the authors, viz., "Q. to K. R. fifth (check)," recommended by Lewis; "P. to K. B. third," a suggestion of V. Der Lasa; "Q. Kt. to Q. B. third," which, occurring in the games of Mr. Attwood, one of Philidor's contemporaries, has been noticed elaborately in the *English Handbook;* and "K. Kt. to K. R. third," a move adopted by previous players. Of the move in the text, but very little notice has been taken in England. One specimen between two Berlin players will be found in Walker's *Chess Studies*, No. 957, p. 161; but this attack is not mentioned, even by implication, in the *Art of Chess-play*, nor in the *English Handbook*.

(e) In the game given by Mr. Walker, the second player here moves "P. to Q. B. third."

(f) The next game gives an important variation upon this move, the combatants changing places.

(g) A winning series of moves from Bilguer is here supplied by the Prussian players. Suppose—

	11. P. takes Kt.
12. P. takes B.	12. P. takes Q. Kt. P. &c.

As a supplement to this, we may remark, that White would gain no resource by playing for his 12th move, "Q. to K. Kt. seventh."

(h) Threatening to win the Queen's Bishop.

(i) Again threatening to win a piece.

(k) This is quite safe, as, if the King were now checked, Black could simply take the Bishop.

(l) The Bishop cannot command the square on which White's Pawn must become a Queen.

Between the same combatants, at the same opening.

Played September 4, 1839.

White. (HANSTEIN.)	*Black.* (V. D. LASA.)
1. P. to K. fourth	1. P. to K. fourth
2. Kt. to K. B. third	2. P. to Q. third

3. P. to Q. fourth		3. P. to K. B. fourth	
4. Q. P. takes P.		4. K. B. P. takes P.	
5. Kt. to K. Kt. fifth		5. P. to Q. fourth	
6. P. to K. sixth		6. Kt. to K. R. third	
7. P. to Q. B. fourth		7. B. to Q. Kt. fifth (check)	
8. Kt. to Q. B. third		8. P. to Q. fifth	
9. P. to Q. R. third		9. P. to K. sixth	
10. P. takes B.		10. Q. takes Kt.	
11. Q. takes P.		11. P. takes P. (check) (a)	
12. Q. takes P. at K. B. second		12. Q. to K. fourth (check)	
13. B. to K. second		13. R. to K. B. square	
14. Q. to K. R. fourth		14. Kt. to Q. B. third	
15. Kt. to Q. Kt. fifth (b)		15. B. takes P.	
16. Q. to K. R. fifth (check)		16. Q. takes Q.	
17. B. takes Q. (check)		17. K. to Q. second	
18. P. to Q. Kt. third		18. Kt. to K. Kt. fifth	
19. B. to K. Kt. fifth		19. Kt. to K. B. seventh	
20. R. to K. B. square		20. Kt. to Q. sixth (check)	
21. K. to K. second		21. R. takes R.	
22. R. takes R.		22. K. Kt. takes P.	
23. R. to Q. square (check)		23. K. to Q. B. square (c)	
24. B. to K. B. fourth		24. Kt. to Q. R. third	
25. B. to K. B. third (d)		25. P. to K. R. third	
26. P. to K. R. fourth		26. Kt. to K. second	
27. B. to K. fifth		27. Kt. to K. B. fourth	
28. P. to K. Kt. fourth		28. Kt. takes P.	
29. B. takes K. Kt. P.		29. Kt. takes B.	
30. K. takes Kt.		30. P. to Q. Kt. third	
31. Kt. to Q. fourth		31. B. to Q. second	
32. B. takes P.		32. Kt. to Q. B. fourth	
33. P. to K. Kt. fifth		33. Kt. to K. third	
34. Kt. takes Kt.		34. B. takes Kt.	
35. R. to K. square		35. B. to K. Kt. square	
36. P. to K. Kt. sixth		36. K. to Q. Kt. second	
37. R. to K. seventh		37. P. to Q. Kt. fourth	
38. B. to K. B. fourth		38. P. takes P. (e)	
39. R. takes P. (check)		39. K. to Q. Kt. third	
40. P. takes P.		40. R. to K. B. square	

41. P. to Q. B. fifth (check)	41. K. to Q. Kt. fourth
42. K. to K. fourth	42. P. to Q. R. fourth
43. B. to Q. sixth	43. R. to K. square (check)
44. K. to Q. fourth	44. P. to Q. R. fifth
45. R. to Q. Kt. seventh (check)	45. K. to Q. B. third
46. R. to Q. Kt. sixth (check)	46. K. to Q. second
47. R. to Q. R. sixth	47. R. to K. third
48. P. to K. Kt. seventh	48. R. to K. Kt. third
49. P. to Q. B. sixth (check)	49. K. to K. square (*f*)
50. R. to Q. R. eighth (check)	50. K. to K. B. second
51. R. to K. B. eighth (check)	51. K. takes P.
52. R. takes B. (check)	52. K. takes R.
53. P. to Q. B. seventh	53. R. takes B. (check)
54. K. to Q. B. fifth	54. R. to K. Kt. third
55. P. to Q. B. eighth	55. K. to K. R. second
(becoming a Q.) (check)	
56. Q. to Q. seventh (check)	56. R. to K. Kt. second
57. Q. takes P.	57. R. to K. Kt. fourth (check)
58. K. to Q. sixth	58. R. to K. Kt. third (check)
59. K. to K. fifth	59. R. to K. Kt. fourth (check)
60. K. to K. B. sixth	60. R. to K. Kt. third (check)
61. K. to K. B. fifth	61. R. to K. Kt. second
62. Q. to K. eighth	

And wins. (*g*.)

Notes.

(*a*) Bilguer's *Handbook* continues the game thus:—

	11. Kt. to K. B. fifth
12. Q. to K. fifth	12. P. takes P. (check)
13. K. takes P.	13. Q. to K. R. fifth (check)
14. P. to K. Kt. third	14. Q. to Q. fifth (check)
15. Q. takes Q.	15. Kt. takes Q.
16. P. to K. seventh, &c.	

(*b*) This is menacing ; "B. takes K. Kt.," seems also to be good play.

(*c*) The imprisonment of the Rook materially deranges Black's game.

(*d*) Preventing the release of Black's pieces for several moves.

(*e*) This seems to be a very perilous mode of play ; "R. to Q. B.," unless we are mistaken, would be safer.

(*f*) If K. takes B., White plays "P. to Q. B. seventh" (dis. ch.) capturing the Rook afterwards, and winning easily.

(*g*) We must refer those amongst our readers who wish to be acquainted with the manner of playing the end-game of Q. against R., to the Chess Studies of Horwitz and Kling. London: C. J. Skeet, 21, King William Street, Charing Cross, 1851, p. 170.

Our next game is a specimen of Mr. MORPHY's play in the Philidor counter-gambit—the opening already illustrated in the games of the Prussian players which we have given above. Mr. MORPHY's competitor, in the lively game that follows, was Mr. BIRD, an English amateur of more than ordinary talent.

Played in 1858.

White. (Mr. BIRD.)	*Black.* (Mr. MORPHY.)
1. P. to K. fourth	1. P. to K. fourth
2. Kt. to K. B. third	2. P. to Q. third
3. P. to Q. fourth	3. P. to K. B. fourth
4. Kt. to Q. B. third	4. K. B. P. takes P.
5. Q. Kt. takes P.	5. P. to Q. fourth
6. Kt. to K. Kt. third (*a*)	6. P. to K. fifth
7. Kt. to K. fifth	7. Kt. to K. B. third
8. B. to K. Kt. fifth	8. B. to Q. third
9. Kt. to K. R. fifth (*b*)	9. Castles
10. Q. to Q. second	10. Q. to K. square (*c*)
11. P. to K. Kt. fourth (*d*)	11. Kt. takes K. Kt. P.
12. Kt. takes Kt.	12. Q. takes Kt.
13. Kt. to K. fifth	13. Kt. to Q. B. third
14. B. to K. second	14. Q. to K. R. sixth
15. Kt. takes Kt.	15. P. takes Kt.
16. B. to K. third	16. R. to Q. Kt. square
17. Castles on the Q. side	17. R. takes K. B. P.
18. B. takes R.	18. Q. to Q. R. sixth
19. P. to Q. B. third	19. Q. takes Q. R. P.
20. P. to Q. Kt. fourth	20. Q. to Q. R. eighth (check)
21. K. to Q. B. second	21. Q. to Q. R. fifth (check)
22. K. to Q. Kt. second	22. B. takes Q. Kt. P.
23. P. takes B.	23. R. takes P. (check)
24. Q. takes R.	24. Q. takes Q. (check)
25. K. to Q. B. second (*e*)	25. P. to K. sixth
26. B. takes P.	26. B. to K. B. fourth (check)
27. R. to Q. third	27. Q. to Q. B. fifth (check)
28. K. to Q. second	28. Q. to Q. R. seventh (check)
9. K. to Q. square	29. Q. to Q. Kt. eighth (check)

And wins.

Notes.

(*a*) An ingenious variation may be played here. It occurred in practice to Mr. S. R. Calthrop, an English amateur, now residing in America. Suppose

6. Kt. takes P.	6. P. takes Kt.
7. Q. to K. R. fifth (check)	7. P. to K. Kt. third
8. Kt. takes K. Kt. P.	

With a fine game.

(*b*) This seems to be a good move, but is the real cause of White's subsequent embarrassment.

(*c*) This move, we are of opinion, wins a Pawn by force.

(*d*) Firstly,

11. B. takes Kt.	11. Q. takes Kt. (best)

if "P. takes B.," "Q. to K. R. sixth" would be an effective reply.

12. Whether White play B. or Q. to K. Kt. fifth, he must lose a Pawn ultimately.

Secondly,

11. Kt. to K. B. fourth	11. B. takes Kt.
12. P. takes B.	12. Q. takes P.
13. B. takes Kt.	13. Q. takes B.

and whether White capture Q. Pawn with Knight or Queen, he must have a bad game.

(*e*) "K. to Q. R. second," is a better resource.

In 1857, the Chess Association held its annual meeting at Manchester. Upon that occasion several distinguished players, not only of this country, but also from foreign parts, attended the meeting. Many good games were played, and some little one-game tournaments set on foot, of which an account has been given in the pamphlet published by the Association in 1857, under the superintendence of Herr LÖWENTHAL. The game given below was not included in Herr LÖWENTHAL'S selection. In reference to its result, and also to similar contingencies, we must remind our readers that these *short* tournaments are not intended to establish the absolute superiority of any player, but rather to call into existence a body of games in which every combatant sacrifices personal reputation for the common cause. Experience has proved that the best tournament-players are not the best managers of set matches, and *vice versâ*.

Between ALTER and Mr. G. MEDLEY.

(*Philidor's Defence in the King's Knight's Opening.*)

White. (ALTER.)	Black. (Mr. MEDLEY.)
1. P. to K. fourth	1. P. to K. fourth
2. Kt. to K. B. third	2. P. to Q. third
3. B. to Q. B. fourth	3. B. to K. second (*a*)

4. P. to K. R. third	4. Kt. to K. B. third
5. Kt. to Q. B. third	5. Castles
6. Castles	6. Kt. to Q. B. third
7. P. to Q. fourth	7. P. to Q. R. third
8. B. to Q. Kt. third	8. P. to K. R. third
9. B. to K. third	9. B. to Q. second
10. Q. to Q. second	10. K. to K. R. second
11. Q. R. to Q. square	11. Q. to K. square
12. K. R. to K. square	12. B. to Q. B. square
13. Q. to K. second	13. B. to Q. square
14. P. to Q. R. third	14. K. to K. R. square
15. B. to Q. fifth	15. Kt. to K. R. second (b)
16. B. takes Kt.	16. P. takes B.
17. P. takes P.	17. P. takes P.
18. B. to Q. B. fifth	18. R. to K. Kt. square
19. Q. to Q. third	19. P. to K. Kt. fourth
20. Kt. takes K. P. (c)	20. P. to K. B. third
21. Q. takes B.	21. Q. takes Kt.
22. Q. to Q. fourth	22. P. to K. Kt. fifth
23. Q. takes Q.	23. P. takes Q.
24. P. to K. R. fourth	24. B. to K. third
25. Kt. to K. second	25. K. to K. Kt. second
26. Kt. to K. Kt. third	26. K. to K. Kt. third
27. R. to Q. second	27. R. to K. Kt. second
28. P. to K. R. fifth (check)	28. K. to K. B. second
29. Kt. to K. B. fifth	29. B. takes Kt.
30. P. takes B.	30. K. to K. B. third
31. R. takes K. P.	31. K. takes R.
32. B. to Q. fourth (check)	32. K. takes P.
33. B. takes R.	33. K. to K. Kt. fourth
34. R. to K. second	34. K. takes P.
35. R. to K. sixth	35. Kt. to K. B. square
36. R. takes R. P. (check)	36. K. to K. Kt. fourth
37. R. to K. R. eighth	

And wins.

Notes.

(a) This modern move is now considered safer than Philidor's counter-gambit, and perhaps, also, is more to be relied on than "P. to Q. B. third."

(b) Black loses time.
(c) This is perfectly safe, as the Q. fourth square can at any time be occupied by the Bishop.

Game in the Match between Messrs. CAMPBELL and WORMALD.

GAME VIII.

White. (Mr. WORMALD.)	*Black.* (Mr. CAMPBELL.)
1. P. to K. fourth	1. P. to K. fourth
2. K. Kt. to B. third	2. K. Kt. to B. third
3. Kt. takes P.	3. P. to Q. third
4. Kt. to K. B. third	4. Kt. takes P.
5. P. to Q. fourth	5. P. to Q. fourth
6. B. to Q. third	6. B. to K. second (a)
7. Castles	7. B. to K. Kt. fifth (b)
8. P. to Q. B. fourth	8. Castles
9. Kt. to Q. B. third	9. Kt. takes Kt.
10. P. takes Kt.	10. Kt. to Q. B. third
11. B. to K. B. fourth	11. P. takes P.
12. B. takes P.	12. Kt. to Q. R. fourth (c)
13. B. to Q. third	13. B. to Q. third
14. B. takes B.	14. P. takes B.
15. K. R. to K. square	15. P. to K. B. fourth
16. P. to K. R. third	16. B. to R. fourth
17. Q. R. to B. square	17. Q. to K. B. third
18. P. to Q. fifth	18. Q. R. to Q. B. square (d)
19. P. to Q. B. fourth	19. Q. R. to K. square
20. R. takes R.	20. R. takes R.
21. Q. to Q. R. fourth	21. P. to Q. Kt. third
22. Q. to Q. seventh	22. R. to K. second
23. Q. to Q. B. eighth (check)	23. K. to B. second
24. Kt. to Q. fourth	24. Q. takes Kt.
25. Q. takes B. P. (check)	25. K. to K. square
26. Q. takes B. (check)	26. P. to K. Kt. third
27. Q. to K. B. third	27. Q. to Q. Kt. seventh
28. Q. to K. B. fourth	28. Q. takes R. P.
29. P. to Q. B. fifth (e)	29. Q. takes Q. P.
30. B. to Kt. fifth (check)	30. Kt. to Q. B. third
31. B. takes Kt. (check) (f)	31. Q. takes B.

32. P. takes P.	32. R. to K. fifth
33. P. to Q. seventh (check)	33. K. takes P.
34. Q. to K. B. seventh (check)	34. R. to K. second
35. Q. takes R. (check)	35. K. takes Q.
36. R. takes Q.	

Notes.

(a) The Petroff defence to the K. Kt. game, as here played, is generally classed amongst *open débûts;* the French game, on the contrary, is designated a *close débût.* They are, however, strictly similar in principle, and mainly so in practice; but in the French game the second player has decidedly greater scope for action.

(b) This Bishop should act on the defensive.

(c) This sally of the Knight, for the most part, turns out badly. The present game supports our remark.

(d) Black should have released his Knight at any cost.

(e) After this move we see no resource for his opponent.

(f) "Q. to Q. R. fourth" is also a good move.

Game between Mr. LUMBLEY, the blind player of Manchester, and Mr. RAINGER, an amateur of Norwich.

White. (Mr. LUMBLEY.)	*Black.* (Mr. F. G. RAINGER.)
1. P. to K. fourth	1. P. to K. fourth
2. K. Kt. to B. third	2. Q. Kt. to B. third
3. K. B. to Q. B. fourth	3. K. B. to Q. B. fourth
4. P. to Q. Kt. fourth	4. B. takes P.
5. P. to Q. B. third	5. B. to Q. R. fourth
6. Q. to Q. Kt. third	6. Q. to K. second
7. B. to Q. R. third	7. P. to Q. third
8. Castles	8. P. to K. R. third
9. P. to Q. fourth	9. B. to Q. Kt. third
10. P. takes K. P.	10. Kt. takes P.
11. Kt. takes Kt.	11. Q. takes Kt.
12. B. takes K. B. P. (check)	12. K. to K. B. square
13. Kt. to Q. second	13. Q. to K. B. fifth
14. B. to K. R. fifth	14. Kt. to K. second
15. Q. R. to Q. square	15. P. to K. Kt. third
16. B. to K. B. third	16. K. to Kt. second
17. P. to Q. B. fourth	17. K. to K. R. second

18. P. to K. Kt. third	18. Q. to K. B. second
19. P. to K. fifth	19. Kt. to K. B. fourth
20. B. to Q. fifth	20. B. to K. third
21. B. to Q. Kt. second	21. K. R. to K. B. square
22. Kt. to K. fourth	22. P. takes P.
23. B. takes K. P.	23. Q. to K. second
24. P. to Q. B. fifth	24. B. takes B.
25. Q. takes B.	25. P. to Q. B. third
26. Q. to Q. seventh	26. R. to K. B. second
27. Q. takes Q.	27. R. takes Q.
28. Kt. to K. B. sixth (check)	28. K. to K. R. square
29. R. to Q. seventh	29. B. takes P.
30. K. R. to Q. square	30. Q. R. to K. B. square
31. R. takes R.	31. B. takes R.
32. Kt. to Q. seventh (dis. check)	32. K. to K. Kt. square
33. Kt. takes R.	33. K. takes Kt.
34. R. to Q. seventh	34. K. to K. B. second
35. R. takes Q. Kt. P.	35. K. to K. third
36. B. to Q. B. third	36. B. to Q. B. fourth
37. B. to Q. Kt. fourth	37. B. to Q. fifth
38. R. to Q. B. seventh	38. K. to Q. fourth
39. P. to K. Kt. fourth	39. Kt. to Q. third
40. B. takes Kt.	40. K. takes B.
41. R. to K. R. seventh	41. P. to K. R. fourth
42. P. takes P.	42. P. takes P.
43. R. takes K. R. P.	43. P. to Q. B. fourth
44. K. to K. B. square	44. P. to B. fifth
45. K. to K. second	45. P. to B. sixth
46. P. to K. B. fourth	46. K. to K. third
47. R. to Q. R. fifth	47. P. to Q. B. seventh
48. R. to Q. R. sixth (check)	48. K. to K. B. fourth
49. K. to Q. second	49. P. queens (check)
50. K. takes Q.	50. K. takes P.
51. R. to Q. R. fourth	51. K. to K. fourth
52. R. takes B.	52. K. takes R.
53. K. to B. second	53. K. to Q. fourth
54. K. to B. third	

Resigns.

PROBLEMS FOR YOUNG PLAYERS.

No 1.　By E. A., *Hereford*.

White to play, and mate in three moves.

White.	*Black.*
K. at Q. B. eighth	K. at Q. B. third
R. at Q. second	R. at Q. B. fifth
B. at Q. square	Kt. at K. Kt. square
B. at Q. B. seventh	Kt. at K. R. fifth
Kt. at K. B. fifth	P. at Q. fourth
P. at Q. Kt. fourth	P. at Q. fifth
	P. at Q. Kt. fourth

No. 2.　By W. Abbot.

White to play, and mate in three moves.

White.	*Black.*
K. at Q. eighth	K. at Q. third
Kt. at Q. seventh	Kt. at Q. fourth
Kt. at Q. fourth	B. at Q. B. third
B. at Q. Kt. second	R. at K. B. second
R. at K. B. square	P. at K. third
P. at Q. R. fifth	P. at K. B. fourth
P. at Q. Kt. fourth	
P. at K. B. fourth	
P. at K. R. fourth	

SOLUTIONS TO PROBLEMS.

No. 9.　*Page* 95.

White.	*Black.*
R. to K. Kt. fourth	P. to K. B. fourth
R. to K. B. fourth	P. takes R.
B. mates	

No. 10.　*Page* 95.

P. to Q. Kt. fifth (check)	P. takes P.
Q. takes Q. Kt. P. (check)	Kt. takes Q.
R. to Q. sixth (check)	R. takes R. (mate)

No. 11.　*Page* 96.

. Q. to Q. Kt. sixth, and white mates next move.

No. 12.　*Page* 96.

. Kt. to K. Kt. sixth

No. 13.   Chess Study by KLING and HORWITZ.

BLACK.

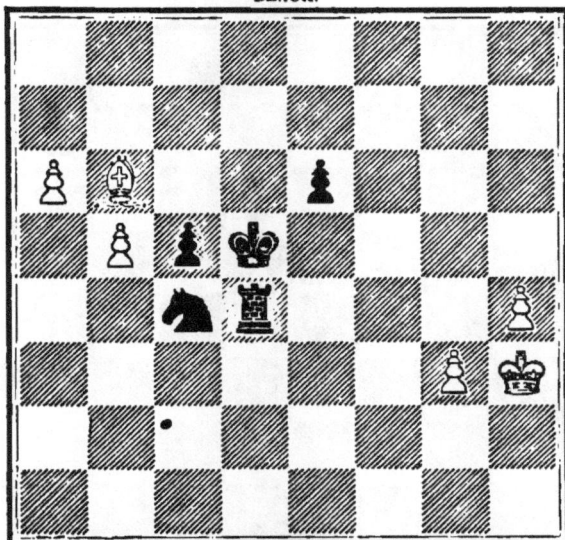

WHITE.

White moves first and wins.

No. 14.   Study by Mr. ZYTOGORSKI.

BLACK.

WHITE.

White, even without the move, can draw.

No. 15.   Problem by Mr. S. CRAWSHAY.

BLACK.

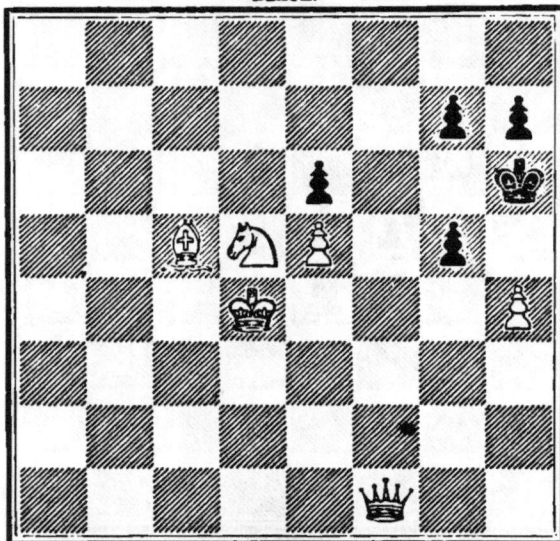

WHITE.

White to mate in three moves.

No. 16.   Problem by A. GREEN, Esq.

WHITE.

BLACK.

White compels Black to checkmate in eight moves.

BLINDFOLD PLAY.

WE have recently been favored with some of the most admirable specimens that have ever been exhibited in a peculiar department of Chess.
We allude to Blindfold Play. MORPHY—rivalling BUZECCA, PHILI-
DOR, and LA BOURDONNAIS; excelling M'DONNELL, KIESERITZKI,
and HARRWITZ—has given us a true notion of blindfold Chess. He has
maintained his proud position, without sight of board and men, against
good, nay, against distinguished players of all countries. His natural-
ized countryman, PAULSEN, by birth a German, has attempted the same
splendid feat, and has also succeeded. What, then, is the inherent
principle in blindfold Chess? What are its merits? Has it any disadvantages? Blindfold play, if we may speak of it experimentally,
does not demand so much memory, learning, or invention, as is generally imagined. It is, however, a strain, and no common strain on
the intellect. Above all things it requires capacity for match-play, and
that capacity bound up in coolness, courage, and endurance. In the
beginning of a game the able player, when blindfolded, may, unless
learned, feel more than ordinary difficulty; in the middle, he warms
to his work, although intricate variations he *knows* (and knowledge is
an acquisition) to be beyond his reach; at the end, he finds to his
surprise that he can manage the subtle combinations of Pawns and
Pieces almost as well as with the board. The merits of blindfold Chess
may be put in a very clear light. There are some men who, in games
played with the assistance of the board, aspire to brilliancy; more
moderate men content themselves with soundness and accuracy; a
more phlegmatic set, positively against all inspirations of what is called
Chess genius—against the rules of cautious prudence, have the audacity
to win. But without the board, LA BOURDONNAIS was brilliant,
PHILIDOR safe, and MORPHY wins. Did, or do, however, such players
bestow upon us even a tithe of their genius in such unnatural struggles?
Was blindfold play a cause of the death of LA BOURDONNAIS, that
illustrious man, who moved pieces made of wood and ivory, simply to
show that the grandest creations of the imagination, the well-poised
balance of a mature and not over-learned judgment, the elaborate
diligence of a life devoted to practice, could give even a Chess-player
reputation? Was blindfold play the cause of M'DONNELL's premature
decline? MORPHY and PAULSEN, we cannot spare you. The intel-

9

ligent amateur, M'DONNELL, who studied Chess, who fought for Chess, aye, and who fought for it against one whom you will own to be a valorous Champion, played blindfold Chess. The same cemetery contains the bones of LA BOURDONNAIS and M'DONNELL. Both, we unhesitatingly say, were sacrificed to the love of the public for blindfold Chess. For ourselves, we must acquit our conscience in the matter. Let blindfold play be left to those who have been deprived of sight; to them an effort of memory is not so unnatural, as they deal not with the world of every day; we wish, however, to preserve the lives of such Chess-players as MORPHY. To him we will say, on his departure from this country, "Macte tuâ virtute, puer;" but must remind him that Ascanius took the advice of Apollo, and therefore reigned *thirty* years.

THE SEVEN AGES OF CHESS.—*(Continued from p. 104.)*

III. CHESS IN YOUTH.

Escaped from " durance vile," as boys are fain .
To call their school-life : whirl'd to town,
Not less by eager hope than by the train ;
Proudly we don the College cap and gown.

Engaged henceforth in honorable strife,
Eager for knowledge, thirsting after Fame,
We still find leisure in our student life,
For many a brave exhilarating game ;

For many a hardy pull against the stream ;
For many a contest in the cricket-field ;
For many a fight in which no weapons gleam,
But English fists and limbs the victory yield.

And when the leaping, wrestling, rowing 's o'er,
When we sit still for very weariness,
And vote all further exercise a bore,
How welcome then the quiet game of Chess !

At first we yawn and stretch our length of limb
In cushioned ease beside the marshalled ranks,
Heedless of dusky foe in phalanx grim,
Taking the swift checkmate almost with thanks.

But emulative wishes soon imbue
Our minds with energy to do and dare ;
Gathering our scattered faculties anew,
We fight with greater patience, skill, and care.

Deep in the subtle scheming of the game,
. Wary of purpose, watchful of our foe;
New vigour animates our weary frame,
New life and interest in our features glow.

Caution and forethought, combinations rare,
Close calculation, and refined finesse,
At length for us the victory declare,
And fix our liking for the Game of Chess.

III.   CHESS IN YOUTH.—THE SCHOLAR'S PRIZE.

Keen was the contest for the Scholar's prize :
  Our strength consumed we with the midnight oil,
  And slow-paced dawn surprised us at our toil,
Ere slumbers coy would rest our weary eyes.
But still we grudged not of the time for Chess :
  We knew that who excelled in tactics fine,
  Was he who best the sense of Latin line,
Or Greek in classic English could express :
That he who found in algebraic maze
  A path to others dark ; who clearly saw
The purpose which the analyst displays,
  And loved the mind which showed the latent law :
Such was the man who played the deepest game,
And won the Scholar's prize—all honour to his name.

THE MATCH BETWEEN HARRWITZ AND MORPHY.

IN presenting our readers with the games played in this match, we feel
bound to make a few observations upon the respective players and their
performances, in order to enable those who are but indifferently
acquainted with the Chess biography of the two champions, to arrive
at a just appreciation of their merits.

Herr HARRWITZ, after having during the space of nearly two years
played in Paris with considerable success, came, we believe, in 1846
to England, to try his skill against Mr. STAUNTON; but, having seen
that master's play, he found that he was not as yet able to cope with
him upon equal terms; a match was therefore arranged, in which Mr.
STAUNTON gave him in seven games the odds of Pawn and two moves,
in seven games the odds of Pawn and move, and in seven games played
upon even terms. The result of that match was unfavourable to
HARRWITZ, for he lost all the even games, won six games with Pawn
and move, but only three with Pawn and two. Soon after, he played
a match with Herr HORWITZ, which he won six to five. A match

which he played about that time in Germany with ANDERSSEN was left unfinished, the players leaving off even. On his return to England he played another match with HORWITZ at Brighton, which he won seven to six. Also another match with the late Mr. WILLIAMS, who won the third prize in the great tournament of 1851. (We did not mention here the first match with Mr. WILLIAMS, which was played in 1847, and which Mr. WILLIAMS gave up after losing three games, and drawing two.) In this match Herr HARRWITZ won seven games, and Mr. WILLIAMS none. In a third match with Mr. WILLIAMS, Herr HARRWITZ scored seven to Mr. WILLIAMS's two. Finally, HERR HARRWITZ won the great match with Herr LÖWENTHAL in 1853— eleven games to eight, and twelve drawn. In that match the nominal score was eleven to ten: Herr HARRWITZ by the conditions, having been obliged to give up two games on account of illness. It may not be amiss to mention also a match at odds which Herr HARRWITZ has played, as the strength of his opponent, Mr. G. MEDLEY, entitles it to notice. Herr HARRWITZ won eleven games to Mr. MEDLEY's nine.

From the above enumeration it may be seen that Herr HARRWITZ has not been surpassed by any living player in match-play, either by the number of matches, or by the results: having beaten all his opponents except Mr. STAUNTON, against whom he broke his maiden lance.

In the discussion of Herr HARRWITZ's merits it would be unjust to omit one very important point: that is to say, blindfold play, of which, though by no means great admirers, we must confess that he has been the most distinguished representative for a series of years. We use the words *a series of years* advisedly; for although we have had the splendid performances of KIESERITZKI, MORPHY, and PAULSEN, we must remember that they have not travelled through the whole of England and Scotland, with their nerves likely to be shaken by railway, and then played with a WITHERS, a GORDON, and other distinguished amateurs.

Such was the opponent Mr. MORPHY had to overcome in order to establish his renown. Mr. MORPHY, still young in glory as well as in years—his achievements yet few, though by no means inconsiderable,— may have well been nervous in meeting an opponent with so many laurels. His first great success was the winning of the first prize in the tournament at New York, where he had to encounter such players as PAULSEN, LICHTENHEIN, STANLEY, S. R. CALTHROP, &c.; his second, the match with Herr LÖWENTHAL in London, of which we have given an account. A preliminary game played before the match, which we shall give in another number, was won by Herr HARRWITZ. The match was then arranged, the winner of the first seven games to be the conqueror. Herr HARRWITZ won the first two games, Mr. MORPHY five, one was drawn, and the match was then given up by Herr HARRWITZ on account of ill health.

GAME I.
(*Irregular Opening.*)

White. (HARRWITZ.).	*Black.* (MORPHY.)
1. P. to Q. fourth	1. P. to K. third
2. P. to Q. B. fourth	2. P. to Q. fourth
3. Kt. to Q. B. third	3. Kt. to K. B. third
4. B. to K. B. fourth	4. P. to Q. R. third
5. P. to K. third	5. P. to Q. B. fourth
6. Kt. to K. B. third	6. Kt. to Q. B. third
7. P. to Q. R. third	7. P. takes Q. P.
8. K. P. takes P.	8. P. takes P.
9. K. B. takes P.	9. P. to Q. Kt. fourth
10. B. to Q. third	10. B. to Q. Kt. second
11. Castles	11. B. to K. second
12. B. to K. fifth	12. Castles
13. Q. to K. second	13. Kt. to Q. fourth
14. B. to K. Kt. third	14. K. to R. square (*a*)
15. K. R. to K. square	15. B. to K. B. third
16. Q. to K. fourth	16. P. to K. Kt. third
17. Kt. takes Kt.	17. Q. takes Kt.
18. Q. takes Q.	18. P. takes Q.
19. Kt. to K. fifth	19. Q. R. to Q. square
20. Kt. takes Kt.	20. B. takes Kt.
21. Q. R. to Q. B. square	21. Q. R. to Q. B. square
22. B. to Q. sixth	22. R. to K. Kt. square
23. B. to K. fifth	23. K. to Kt. second
24. P. to K. B. fourth	24. B. to Q. second
25. K. to B. second	25. P. to K. R. third
26. K. to K. third	26. R. takes R.
27. R. takes R.	27. R. to Q. B. square
28. R. to Q. B. fifth	28. B. takes B.
29. B. P. takes P.	29. B. to K. third
30. P. to Q. R. fourth	30. P. takes P.
31. B. takes R. P.	31. R. to Q. Kt. square
32. R. to Q. Kt. fifth	32. R. to Q. square
33. R. to Q. Kt. sixth	33. R. to Q. R. square
34. K. to Q. second	34. B. to Q. B. square
35. B. takes B.	35. R. takes B.

36. R. to Q. Kt. fifth	36. R. to Q. R. square
37. R. takes Q. P.	37. P. to Q. R. sixth
38. P. takes P.	38. R. takes P.
39. R. to Q. B. fifth	39. K. to B. square
40. K. to K. second	40. K. to K. second
41. P. to Q. fifth	41. K. to Q. second
42. R. to Q. B. sixth	42. P. to K. R. fourth
43. R. to K. B. sixth	43. K. to K. second
44. P. to Q. sixth (check)	44. K. to K. square
45. P. to K. sixth	45. P. takes P.
46. R. takes P. (check)	46. K. to K. B. second
47. P. to Q. seventh	47. R. to Q. R. square
48. R. to Q. sixth	48. K. to K. second
49. R. takes P.	49. K. takes P.
50. R. to K. Kt. fifth	50. R. to K. R. square
51. R. to K. B. third	51. R. to K. third
52. K. to K. Kt. third	52. P. to K. R. fifth (check)
53. K. to Kt. fourth.	53. P. to K. R. sixth
54. P. to K. Kt. third	54. K. to K. B. third
55. R. to K. R. fifth	

And White wins.

Notes.

(a) We do not see the purport of this move; it seems to us clearly a lost move as the White King is too well defended to admit of a successful attack.

White played this game throughout very carefully, and with great skill.

GAME II.
(*Philidor's Defence.*)

White. (MORPHY.)	Black. (HARRWITZ).
1. P. to K. fourth	1. P. to K. fourth
2. Kt. to K. B. third	2. P. to Q. third
3. P. to Q. fourth	3. P. takes P.
4. Q. takes P.	4. Kt. to Q. B. third
5. K. B. to Q. Kt. fifth	5. B. to Q. second
6. B. takes Kt.	6. B. takes B.
7. B. to K. Kt. fifth	7. Kt. to K. B. third

8. Kt. to Q. B. third		8. B. to K. second
9. Castles (with Q. R.)		9. Castles
10. K. R. to K. square		10. P. to K. R. third
11. B. to K. R. fourth		11. Kt. to K. square
12. B. takes B.		12. Q. takes B.
13. P. to K. fifth		13. B. takes Kt.
14. P. takes B.		14. Q. to K. Kt. fourth (check)
15. K. to Kt. square		15. P. takes P.
16. R. takes P.		16. Q. to K. Kt. seventh
17. Kt. to Q. fifth		17. Q. takes K. R. P.
18. K. R. to K. square		18. Q. to Q. third
19. R. to K. Kt. square		19. K. to R. second
20. Q. to K. third		20. P. to K. B. fourth
21. Kt. to K. B. fourth		21. Q. to Q. Kt. third
22. Q. to K. second		22. R. to K. B. second
23. Q. to Q. B. fourth		23. Q. to K. B. third
24. Kt. to K. R. fifth		24. Q. to K. second
25. Q. R. to K. square		25. Q. to Q. second
26. P. to Q. R. third		26. Kt. to Q. third
27. Q. to Q. fourth		27. R. to K. Kt. square
28. R. to K. Kt. second		28. Kt. to K. square
29. Q. to Q. B. third		29. P. to K. B. fifth
30. R. to K. R. square		30. P. to K. Kt. third
31. Q. R. to K. Kt. square		31. Q. to Q. fourth
32. Q. to K. square		32. Q. takes Kt.
33. R. to K. Kt. fifth		33. Q. takes K. B. P.
34. Q. to K. sixth		34. R. to K. B. third
35. Q. to K. seventh (check)		35. R. to K. Kt. second
36. Q. takes Kt.		36. P. takes R.
37. Q. to K. square		37. Q. to Q. B. third

And Black wins.

Note.

This game was admirably played by Herr Harrwitz, and is one of the best of his games on record.

GAME III.

(Irregular Opening.)

White. (HABRWITZ.)	Black. (MORPHY.)
1. P. to Q. fourth	1. P. to K. B. fourth
2. P. to Q. B. fourth	2. P. to K. third
3. Q. Kt. to Q. B. third	3. K. Kt. to K. B. third
4. Q. B. to K. Kt. fifth	4. K. B. to Q. Kt. fifth
5. Q. to Q. Kt. third	5. P. to Q. B. fourth
6. P. to Q. fifth	6. P. to K. fourth
7. P. to K. third	7. Castles
8. K. B. to Q. third	8. P. to Q. third
9. K. Kt. to K. second	9. P. to K. R. third
10. B. takes K. Kt.	10. Q. takes B.
11. P. to Q. R. third	11. B. takes Kt. (check)
12. Q. takes B.	12. Kt. to Q. second
13. Castles on K side	13. Q. to K. Kt. third
14. P. to Q. Kt. fourth	14. P. to Q. Kt. third
15. P. to K. B. third	15. P. to K. R. fourth
16. B. to Q. B. second	16. B. to Q. Kt. second
17. B. to Q. R. fourth	17. Q. to K. B. second
18. B. takes Kt. (a)	18. Q. takes B.
19. P. takes P.	19. Q. Kt. P. takes P.
20. P. to K. B. fourth	20. P. to K. fifth
21. Q. R. to Q. Kt. square	21. B. to Q. R. third
22. K. R. to Q. B. square	22. Q. to Q. R. fifth
23. Kt. to K. Kt. third	23. P. to K. R. fifth
24. Kt. to K. B. square	24. Q. R. to Q. Kt. square
25. Kt. to Q. second	25. Q. R. to Q. Kt. third
26. R. takes R.	26. P. takes R.
27. Q. to Q. Kt. third	27. Q. takes Q.
28. Kt. takes Q.	28. P. to Q. Kt. fourth
29. P. takes P. (b)	29. B. takes P.
30. Kt. to Q. R. fifth	30. R. to Q. R. square
31. Kt. to Q. Kt. seventh	31. R. to Q. R. third
32. R. to Q. B. third	32. K. to K. B. square
33. Kt. to Q. eighth	33. B. to Q. second
34. R. to Q. Kt. third	34. K. to K. second
35. R. to Q. Kt. eighth	35. P. to Q. B. fifth

36. K. to K. B. second	36. P. to Q. B. sixth
37. K. to K. second	37. R. takes Q. R. P.
38. Kt. to Q. B. sixth (check)	38. B. takes Kt.
39. P. takes B.	39. P. to Q. B. seventh
40. K. to Q. second	40. R. to Q. B. sixth
41. K. to Q. B. square	41. R. takes Q. B. P.
42. R. to Q. Kt. third	42. K. to K. B. third
43. R. to Q. R. third	43. P. to K. Kt. fourth
44. P. to K. Kt. third	44. K. R. P. takes P.
45. K. R. P. takes P.	45. K. Kt. P. takes P.
46. K. Kt. P. takes P.	46. K. to K. Kt. third
47. R. to Q. R. fifth	47. R. to Q. B. fourth
48. R. to Q. R. sixth	48. R. to Q. B. sixth
49. R. takes Q. P. (check)	49. K. to K. R. fourth
50. R. to Q. second	50. K. to K. Kt. fifth
51. R. to K. Kt. second (check)	51. K. to K. B. sixth
52. R. to K. Kt. fifth	52. R. to Q. B. fourth
53. R. to K. R. fifth	53. K. takes K. P.
54. R. to K. R. fourth	54. K. to K. B. sixth

And White gave up the game.

Notes.

(a) This is a very weak move; "B. to Q. B. sixth" would have given White at once the best of the game.

(b) "Kt. to Q. second" was the proper move; the above move gives Black the best of the game.

GAME IV.
(*Philidor's Defence.*)

White. (MORPHY.)	*Black.* (HARRWITZ.)
1. P. to K. fourth	1. P. to K. fourth
2. Kt. to K. B. third	2. P. to Q. third
3. P. to Q. fourth	3. P. takes P.
4. Q. takes P.	4. Kt. to Q. B. third
5. K. B. to Q. Kt. fifth	5. B. to Q. second
6. B. takes Kt.	6. B. takes B.
7. B. to K. Kt. fifth	7. P. to K. B. third (a)
8. B. to K. R. fourth	8. Kt. to K. R. third

9. Kt. to Q. B. third	9. Q. to Q. second
10. Castles (with K. R.)	10. B. to K. second
11. Q. R. to Q. square	11. Castles (with K. R.)
12. Q. to Q. B. fourth (check)	12. R. to K. B. second
13. Kt. to Q. fourth (b)	13. Kt. to K. Kt. fifth
14. P. to K. R. third	14. Kt. to K. fourth
15. Q. to K. second	15. P. to K. Kt. fourth
16. B. to K. Kt. third	16. R. to K. Kt. second
17. Kt. to K. B. fifth	17. R. to K. Kt. third
18. P. to K. B. fourth	18. P. takes P.
19. R. takes P.	19. K. to R. square
20. R. to K. R. fourth	20. B. to K. B. square
21. B. takes Kt.	21. B. P. takes B.
22. R. to K. B. square	22. Q. to K. third
23. Kt. to Q. Kt. fifth	23. Q. to K. Kt. square
24. R. to K. B. second	24. P. to Q. R. third (c)
25. Kt. takes B. P.	25. R. to Q. B. square
26. Kt. to Q. fifth	26. B. takes Kt.
27. P. takes B.	27. R. to Q. B. second
28. P. to Q. B. fourth	28. B. to K. second
29. R. to K. R. fifth	29. Q. to K. square
30. P. to Q. B. fifth	30. Q. R. takes P.
31. R. takes K. R. P. (check)	31. K. takes R.
32. Q. to K. R. fifth	32. K. to Kt. square
33. Kt. takes B. (check)	33. K. to Kt. second
34. Kt. to B. fifth (check)	34. K. to Kt. square
35. Kt. takes Q. P.	

And White wins.

Notes.

(a) We should like to know on what principle Herr Harrwitz played "P. to K. B. third," instead of bringing the Kt. there, as in the second game of the match, which he won. Why try to improve a good move, and not leave well alone?

(b) " P. to K. fifth " seems to us a stronger move, although in a note in the *Chess Monthly*, it is stated that "P. to K. fifth" would not be well played.

(c) A very weak move, which has no object, and loses the game.

GAME V.

(Queen's Pawn's Opening Irregular).

White. (HARRWITZ.)	*Black.* (MORPHY.)
1. P. to Q. fourth	1. P. to K. B. fourth
2. P. to Q. B. fourth	2. P. to K. third
3. Kt. to Q. B. third	3. Kt. to K. B. third
4. Q. B. to K. Kt. fifth	4. B. to K. second
5. P. to K. third	5. Castles
6. K. B. to Q. third	6. P. to Q. Kt. third
7. K. Kt. to K. second	7. Q. B. to Q. Kt. second
8. Castles	8. Kt. to K. R. fourth
9. B. takes B.	9. Q. takes B.
10. Kt. to K. Kt. third	10. Kt. takes Kt.
11. R. P. takes Kt.	11. P. to Q. third
12. P. to K. B. fourth	12. Kt. to Q. B. third
13. P. to K. Kt. fourth	13. Kt. to Q. Kt. fifth
14. P. takes P.	14. P. takes P.
15. Q. to Q. second	15. Q. R. to K. square
16. Q. R. to K. square	16. Q. to K. R. fifth
17. K. B. to Q. Kt. square	17. R. to K. third
18. Q. to K. B. second	18. Q. to K. R. fourth
19. P. to Q. fifth	19. R. to K. R. third
20. Q. to K. B. third	20. Q. to K. R. fifth
21. P. to Q. R. third	21. Kt. to Q. R. third
22. P. to Q. Kt. fourth	22. Kt. to Q. Kt. square
23. Kt. to K. second	23. Kt. to Q. second
24. Kt. to K. Kt. third (*a*)	24. P. to K. Kt. third
25. K. to B. second	25. Kt. to K. B. third
26. R. to K. R. square	26. Kt. to Kt. fifth (check)
27. K. to Kt. square	27. Q. to K. B. third
28. R. takes R.	28. Kt. takes R.
29. Q. to Q. square	29. Kt. to Kt. fifth
30. Q. to Q. second	30. Q. to K. R. fifth
31. Kt. to K. B. square	31. R. to K. square
32. P. to K. Kt. third	32. Q. to K. R. sixth
33. P. to Q. Kt. fifth	33. Kt. to K. B. third
34. Q. to K. Kt. second	34. Q. takes Q. (check)
35. K. takes Q.	35. P. to Q. R. third

36. P. to Q. R. fourth	36. P. takes P.
37. R. P. takes P.	37. R. to Q. R. square
38. Kt to Q. second (*b*)	38. R. to Q. R. sixth
39. P. to K. fourth	39. P. takes P.
40. Kt. takes P.	40. Kt. takes Kt.
41. B. takes Kt. (*c*)	41. R. to Q. B. sixth
42. B. to K. B. third (*d*)	42. K. to B. second
43. R. to K. fourth	43. B. to B. square
44. B. to K. second	44. B. to K. B. fourth
45. R. to Q. fourth	45. P. to K. R. fourth
46. K. to B. second	46. K. to B. third
47. R. to Q. second	47. B. to Q. B. seventh
48. K. to K. square	48. B. to K. fifth
49. K. to B. second	49. K. to B. fourth
50. R. to Q. R. second	50. P. to K. R. fifth
51. P. takes P.	51. K. takes P.
52. R. to Q. R. seventh	52. R. to K. R. sixth
53. R. takes P.	53. R. to R. seventh (check)
54. K. to K. square	54. K. to K. sixth

And wins.

Notes by *Herr* FALKBEER.

(*a*) Up to this point, and a few moves further, the game was exceedingly well conducted by the German player. In the latter part of the game, however, he faltered in his defence.

(*b*) This, we believe, was the turning point of the game. The King's Pawn being rather weak, Mr. Harrwitz ought to have advanced it at that moment, threatening to get either a passed Pawn, or, eventually, to open the Rook's line, and thus to free his pieces. It is true that Mr. Harrwitz pushed the same Pawn on the following move, but then the position was altered in favour of Mr. Morphy.

(*c*) It strikes us that " R. takes Kt " would have forced the draw. Thus:—

White.	*Black.*
41. R. takes Kt.	41. K. to B. second (best)

(In answer to " R. to Q. Kt. sixth," White can safely play " B. to Q. B. second.")

42. P. to K. B. fifth	42. P. takes P. (best)
43. R. to K. B. fourth, &c.	

(*d*) Threatening to win the Bishop.

Game VI.

(*Philidor's Defence.*)

White. (Morphy.)	*Black.* (Harrwitz.)
1. P. to K. fourth	1. P. to K. fourth
2. K. Kt. to B. third	2. P. to Q. third
3. P. to Q. fourth	3. P. takes P.
4. Q. takes P.	4. K. Kt. to B. third (*a*)
5. P. to K. fifth	5. P. takes P.
6. Q. takes Q. (check)	6. K. takes Q.
7. Kt. takes K. P.	7. B. to K. third
8. Kt. to Q. B. third	8. B. to Q. third
9. Kt. to Q. B. fourth	9. B. takes Kt. (*b*)
10. B. takes B.	10. R. to K. square (check)
11. B. to K. third	11. K. to K. second
12. Castles (Q. R.)	12. P. to Q. R. third
13. B. to K. Kt. fifth	13. Q. Kt. to Q. second
14. Kt. to K. fourth	14. P. to K. R. third
15. B. takes Kt. (check)	15. Kt takes B.
16. Kt. takes B.	16. P. takes Kt.
17. K. R. to K. square (check)	17. Q. to B. square
18. R. takes R. (check)	18. Kt. takes R.
19. B. to Q. fifth	19. R. to Q. Kt. square
20. B. to K. B. third	20. P. to K. Kt. third
21. P. to Q. B. third	21. K. to K. second
22. R. to K. square (check)	22. K. to B. square
23. K. to B. second	23. Kt. to Q. B. second
24. K. to Q. Kt. third	24. Kt. to K. third
25. K. to R. fourth	25. P. to Q. Kt. third (*c*)
26. P. to Q. Kt. fourth	26. P. to K. R. fourth
27. P. to K. R. fourth	27. K. to K. second
28. R. to K. third	28. K. to Q. second
29. B. to Q. fifth	29. R. to K. square
30. K. to Q. Kt. third	30. R. to K. Kt. square
31. R. to K. B. third	31. K. to K. second
32. P. to Q. R. fourth	32. P. to Q. R. fourth
33. B. takes Kt.	33. K. takes B.
34. K. to B. fourth	34. P. to K. Kt. fourth
35. K. to Kt. fifth	35. Q. R. P. takes P.

36 P. takes Q. R. P.	36 P. takes P.
37. K. takes P.	37. R. to Q. Kt. square (check)
38. K. to R. fifth	38. K. to Q. fourth
39. R. to Q. third (check)	39. K. to B. fifth
40. R. takes Q. P.	40. R. takes P.
41. R. to Q. fourth (check)	41. K. takes R.
42. K. takes R.	42. P. to K. B. fourth
43. P. to K. B. fourth	43. K. to K. sixth
44. P. to Q. R. fifth	44. K. to B. seventh
45. P. to R. sixth	45. K. takes P.
46. P. to R. seventh	46. P. to R. sixth
47. P. queens (check)	47. K. to Kt. eighth
48. Q. to K. B. third	

And Black resigns.

Notes.

(a) "B. to Q. second," or "Kt. to Q. B. third," would have been the move ; as it is, White has the advantage of getting immediately an attack with an advantageous position.

(b) "B. to Q. Kt. fifth" instead, seems to us by far better.

(c) Why not check with the Kt., thus preventing the White King from entering Black's game?   The whole of this end game is weakly played by Black.

GAME VII.

(Irregular Opening.)

White. (HARRWITZ.)	Black. (MORPHY.)
1. P. to Q. fourth	1. P. to K. B. fourth
2. P. to Q. B. fourth	2. P. to K. third
3. Kt. to Q. B. third	3. Kt. to K. B. third
4. B. to K. Kt. fifth	4. B. to K. second
5. P. to K. third	5. Castles
6. B. to Q. third	6. P. to Q. Kt. third
7. K. Kt. to K. second	7. B. to Q. Kt. second
8. B. takes Kt.	8. B. takes B.
9. Castles	9. Q. to K. second
10. Q. to Q. second	10. P. to Q. third
11. P. to K. B. fourth (a)	11. P. to Q. B. fourth
12. P. to Q. fifth	12. Kt. to Q. R. third
13. P. takes P.	13. Q. takes P.

14. Q. R. to K. square	14. B. to K. R. fifth
15. Kt. to K. Kt. third (*b*)	15. Q. to K. Kt. third
16. Kt. to Q. fifth (*c*)	16. Q. B. takes Kt.
17. P. takes B.	17. B. takes Kt.
18. P. takes B.	18. Kt. to Q. B. second
19. K. to B. second	19. Q. R. to K. square
20. R. to K. R. square	20. R. to K. second
21. R. to K. R. fourth	21. Q. to K. B. second
22. B. to K. second (*d*)	22. Kt. to K. square
23. Q. to Q. third	23. Kt. to K. B. third
24. B. to K. B. third (*e*)	24. P. to K. Kt. third
25. R. to K. second (*f*)	25. K. R. to K. square
26. P. to Q. Kt. third	26. Q. to K. Kt. second
27. R. to K. R. square	27. P. to K. R. third
28. K. to Kt. square (*g*)	28. P. to K. Kt. fourth
29. P. takes P.	29. P. takes P.
30. B. to K. R. fifth	30. Kt. to K. fifth (*h*)
31. R. to K. square (*i*),	31. R. to K. B. square
32. B. to B. third (*k*)	32. Kt. takes P.
33. R. to K. R. third	33. Q. to K. fourth
34. R. to K. R. sixth	34. P. to K. Kt. fifth
35. B. to Q. square	35. K. to Kt. second
36. R. to K. R. fourth	36. R. to K. R. square
37. R. takes R.	37. K. takes R.
38. B. to Q. B. second	38. R. to K. R. second
39. Q. to Q. second	39. Q. to Q. Kt. seventh
40. R. to Q. square	40. R. to R. eighth (check)
41. K. to B. second	41. R. to K. B. eighth (check) (*l*)
42. K. takes Kt.	42. Q. to K. fourth (check)
43. K. to R. fourth	43. Q. to K. B. third (check)
44. K. to Kt. third	44. Q. to K. fourth (check)

Perpetual check.

Notes by Herr FALKBEER.

(*a*) A move which generally renders the King's Pawn weak, and therefore ought to be made with great care, and not without pressure.

(*b*) The correct move. "P. to K. Kt. third" would have been "heaping wood to one's own stake."

(*c*) A clever device. It secures the Pawn for the moment, as evidently the King's Knight could not be taken with impunity.

(*d*) Whether this move, or perhaps "Q. to Q. B. second" instead, with the view of advancing afterwards the King's Knight's Pawn, would have better answered the purpose, may be left as an open question. At any rate, the move in the text was safe enough, as obviously the Queen's Pawn could not well be taken on this or on the preceding move.

(*e*) " P. to K. Kt. fourth," although being a showy move, would have given Black the advantage. *Ex. gr.*:—

White.	Black.
24. P. to K. Kt. fourth	24. P. takes P.
25. B. takes P.	25. Kt. to K. fifth (check)
26. K. to Kt. square (best)	26. Q. to K. B. third
27. R. to R. third	27. Q. takes Q. Kt. P.
28. R. to K. second (best) ·	28. Q. to Q. B. third, with the best game.

(*f*) For this move we can assign no other reason than that White intended to advance his King's Pawn, which, however, at this point he could not conveniently do, on account of Black's taking the Pawn and doubling his Rooks afterwards.

(*g*) " K. R. to K. square," doubling the Rooks, which at this juncture seems the most obvious move, has probably been rejected by Mr. Harrwitz, on account of the more pressing necessity of covering both flanks in case of attack.

(*h*) An admirable move; quite in Morphy's style.

(*i*) " B. takes R." would have been suicidal.   Thus—

White.	Black.
31. B. takes R.	31. Kt. takes P.
32. B. to Q. Kt. fifth	32. Q. to Q. R. eighth (check)

(32. " B. to K. R. fifth," would be answered by " Q. to Q. R. eighth (check)," &c.)

White.	Black.
33. K. to R. second (best)	33. Q. takes R. (check)
34. K. takes Kt.	34. Q. to K. R. fifth (check)
35. K. to B. third	35. P. to Kt. fifth (check)
36. K. to B. fourth	36. P. to Kt. sixth (discov. check) and wins.

(*k*) We do not see any sufficient reason for this uncalled-for sacrifice of a Pawn.   " P. to K. Kt. fourth," instead, could have been made with great propriety.

(*l*) This, although brilliant, yet inconsiderate ꞌmove (a case very scarce with Mr. Morphy), throws a won game away.   " R. takes R." instead, would have secured the victory.   Suppose—

White	Black.
	41. R. takes R.
42. Q. takes R.	42. Kt. to K. fifth (check)
43. K. to Kt. square (best)	43. Kt. to Q. B. sixth
44. Q. to Q. third (best)	44. Q. to Q. R. eighth (check)
45. K. to R. second	45. Kt. to K. fifth
46. P. to K. Kt. third (best)	46. K. to Kt. square, and must win

GAME VIII.
(*Philidorian Defence.*)

White. (MORPHY.)	*Black.* (HARRWITZ)
1. P. to K. fourth	1. P. to K. fourth
2. Kt. to K. B. third	2. P. to Q. third
3. P. to Q. fourth	3. B. to K. Kt. fifth (*a*)
4. P. takes P.	4. B. takes Kt.
5. Q. takes B.	5. P. takes P.
6. B. to Q. B. fourth	6. Kt. to K. B. third (*b*)
7. Q. to Q. Kt. third	7. B. to Q. third
8. B. takes P. (check)	8. K. to B. square
9. B. to K. Kt. fifth	9. Q. Kt. to Q. second
10. K. B. to K. R. fifth	10. P. to K. Kt. third
11. B. to K. R. sixth (check)	11. K. to K. second (*c*)
12. B. to K. B. third	12. Kt. to Q. B. fourth
13. Q. to Q. B. fourth	13. P. to Q. Kt. fourth
14. Q. to K. second	14. Kt. to K. third
15. B. to K. third (*d*)	15. P. to Q. R. third
16. Kt. to Q. second	16. K. to B. second
17. Castles (Q. R.)	17. Q. to K. second
18. P. to K. Kt. third	18. K. R. to Q. Kt. square
19. B. to K. Kt. second	19. P. to Q. R. fourth
20. K. R. to K. B. square	20. P. to Q. R. fifth
21. P. to K. B. fourth	21. P. to Q. R. sixth
22. P. to Q. Kt. third	22. K. to Kt. second
23. P. to K. B. fifth	23. Kt. to K. B. square
24. P. to K. Kt. fourth	24. Q. to K. square
25. B. to K. B. third	25. Q. to Q. B. third
26. Kt. to Q. Kt. square	26. P. to Q. Kt. fifth
27. Q. to K. B. second	27. Q. Kt. to Q. second
28. P. to K. Kt. fifth	28. Kt. to K. Kt. square
29. P. to K. B. sixth (check)	29. K. to R. square
30. P. to K. B. seventh	30. Kt. to Q. B. fourth (*e*)
31. P. takes Kt. (check)	31. K. takes P.
32. B. takes Kt.	32. B. takes B.
33. Q. to K. second	33. Q. to K. third
34. Kt. to Q. second	34. K. to R. square
35. B. to K. Kt. fourth	35. Q. to K. second

10

36. Kt. to K. B. third	36. R. to Q. square
37. P. to K. R. fourth	37. R. to Q. third
38. R. takes R.	38. P. takes R.
39. Q. to B. fourth	39. R. to K. B. square
40. Q. to K. sixth	40. B. to K. sixth (check)
41. K. to Q. square	41. Q. to Q. B. second
42. Kt. to Q. second	42. B. to K. B. fifth
43. Kt. to Q. B. fourth	43. Q. to Q. B. fourth
44. Q. to Q. fifth	44. Q. takes Q. (check)
45. P. takes Q.	45. R. to Q. square
46. R. to K. B. third	46. K. to Kt. second
47. P. to Q. B. third	47. R. to Q. Kt. square
48. P. takes P.	48. R. takes P.
49. K. to B. second	49. K. to B. square
50. K. to B. third	50. R. to Q. Kt. fourth
51. B. to K. sixth	51. R. to Q. B. fourth
52. P. to Q. Kt. fourth	52. R. to Q. B. second
53. P. to Q. Kt. fifth	53. K. to K. second
54. P. to Q. Kt. sixth	54. R. to Q. Kt. second
55. B. to Q. B. eighth	55. R. to Q. Kt. square
56. P. to Q. Kt. seventh	56. K. to Q. square
57. Kt. takes Q. P.	57. K. to K. second
58. Kt. to Q. Kt. fifth	58. P. to K. R. third
59. P. to K. sixth (check)	

And Black resigned.

Notes by Herr FALKBEER.

(a) Perhaps for the sake of novelty. The usual move, " P. takes P.," is better play.

(b) Losing a Pawn at the seventh move! Mr. Harrwitz, we learn, has resigned the match on the plea of ill health, and the present game, the last in the contest, is certainly what lawyers would call good evidence of the truth of his statement. At all events, it is almost beyond comprehension that a player of Mr. Harrwitz's strength should have overlooked the proper move in this position—viz., " Q. to Q. second."

(c) This is decidedly anything but a desirable position at so early a stage of an important match game.

(d) Compulsory, for Black's threatened advance of " P. to K. Kt. fourth."

(e) A desperate effort.

Game in the Match between Messrs CAMPBELL and WORMALD.

GAME IX.

Black. (Mr. CAMPBELL.)	*White.* (Mr. WORMALD.)
1. P. to K. fourth	1. P. to K. fourth
2. Kt. to K. B. third	2. Kt. to Q. B. third
3. B. to Q. Kt. fifth	3. P. to Q. R. third
4. B. to Q. R. fourth	4. Kt. to K. B. third
5. Castles	5. B. to K. second
6. P. to Q. B. third	6. Castles
7. R. to K. square	7. P. to Q. Kt. fourth
8. B. to Q. B. second	8. P. to Q. fourth
9. P. takes P.	9. Q. takes P.
10. P. to Q. fourth	10. P. to K. fifth
11. P. to Q. B. fourth (*a*)	11. Q. to K. R. fourth
12. B. takes P.	12. Kt. takes B.
13. R. takes Kt.	13. B. to K. B. fourth
14. R. to K. square	14. B. to Q. Kt. fifth (*b*)
15. B. to Q. second	15. P. takes P.
16. Q. to Q. R. fourth (*c*)	16. B. takes Q. Kt.
17. Q. takes Kt.	17. B. takes B.
18. Kt. takes B.	18. Q. to Q. R. fourth (*d*)
19. Q. R. takes B.	19. Q. takes Kt.
20. Q. takes P. at B. fifth	20. Q. R. to Q. square
21. K. R. to Q. square	21. Q. to K. B. fifth
22. P. to K. Kt. third	22. Q. to K. fifth
23. Q. R. to Q. B. square	23. K. R. to K. square
24. R. to Q. B. third	24. Q. to K. seventh
25. Q. takes Q.	25. R. takes Q.
26. R. takes P.	26. R. takes Q. Kt. P.
27. R. to K. square	27. R. to Q. Kt. fourth
28. R. to Q. seventh	28. K. R. to Q. Kt. square
29. K. R. to K. seventh	29. R. takes R.
30. R. takes R.	30. K. to B. square
31. P. to Q. fifth	31. K. to K. square
32. R. to Q. R. seventh	32. R. to Q. square
33. R. takes R. P.	33. R. takes Q. P.
34. R. to R. seventh	34. P. to K. Kt. third
35. K. to Kt. second	35. R. to Q. sixth

36. P. to Kt. fourth	36. K. to B. square
37. P. to B. third	37. P. to R. third
38. P. to R. fourth	38. K. to Kt. second
39. P. to Kt. fifth	39. P. takes P.
40. P. takes P.	40. R. to Q. fourth
41. P. to B. fourth	41. R. to Q. sixth
42. P. to R. fourth	42. R. to Q. B. sixth
43. P. to R. fifth	43. R. to Q. sixth
44. P. to R. sixth	44. R. to Q. R. sixth
45. K. to B. second	45. K. to B. square
46. R. to Q. R. eighth (check)	46. K. to K. second
47. P. to Q. R. seventh	47. R. to Q. R. fifth
48. K. to B. third	48. R. to R. eighth
49. P. to K. B. fifth (e)	49. P. takes P.
50. P. to Kt. sixth	50. R. to R. sixth (check)
51. K. to B. fourth	51. R. to R. fifth (check)
52. K. takes P.	52. R. to R. fourth (check)
53. K. to Kt. fourth	53. R. to R. fifth (check)
54. K. to Kt. fifth	54. R. to R. fourth (check)
55. K. to R. sixth	55. R. to R. third
56. K. to R. seventh	56. R. to R. eighth
57. P. to Kt. seventh	

And wins.

Notes.

(a) Well played; by retiring the Knight he would have had an embarrassed game.

(b) "Bishop to King's Knight's fifth" we think would have been better.

(c) A good move, winning a Pawn by force.

(d) This is also a good move, getting the Knight in exchange for the Bishop

(e) It is a very finely conceived idea to sacrifice the two Pawns, as it is the only way to win; even the advanced Chess Player will do well to study this end game.

Game between Mr. BIRD and Mr. M——.

White. (Mr. M——.)	*Black.* (Mr. BIRD.)
1. P. to K. fourth	
2. P. to Q. fourth	2. P. to Q. B. fourth
3. Q. to R. fifth (check)	3. P. to K. Kt. third
4. Q. takes Q. B. P.	4. Q. Kt. to B. third

5. K. Kt. to B. third	5. K. Kt. to B. third
6. B. to Q. third	6. P. to K. fourth
7. Q. to her B. fourth	7. P. to Q. Kt. fourth
8. Q. to her Kt. third (*a*)	8. P. takes Q. P.
9. P. to K. fifth	9. Kt. to Q. R. fourth
10. Q. takes Q. Kt. P.	10. Kt. to K. R. fourth
11. Castles	11. Kt. to Q. B. third
12. P. to K. sixth	12. B. to K. second
13. B. to K. R. sixth	13. R. to Q. Kt. square
14. P. takes P. (check)	14. B. takes P.
15. Q. to Q. fifth	15. Kt. to K. B. third
16. Q. to K. Kt. fifth	16. Q. to her B. second
17. Q. to K. Kt. third	17. Q. takes Q.
18. B. P. takes Q.	18. R. takes Q. Kt. P.
19. Q. Kt. to Q. second	19. Kt. to K. Kt. fifth
20. B. to K. Kt. seventh	20. R. to K. Kt square
21. B. takes P.	21. Kt. takes B.
22. Kt. takes Kt.	22. B. to Q. B. fourth
23. K. R. check	23. K. to Q. square
24. Q. Kt. to K. B. third	24. R. to K. B. square
25. P. to K. R. third	25. R. takes Kt.
26. P. takes R. (*b*)	26. B. takes Kt. (check)
27. K. to Kt. second	27. Kt. to K. sixth (check)
28. K. to R. second	28. Kt. takes Q. B. P.

And White resigns after a few moves.

Notes.

(*a*) If Black's Queen takes the Pawn, "R. to Kt. square" would give White a very strong game.

(*b*) Black ought to have played the King.

The following interesting game was played between Herren FALK-BEER and HAMPE, two of the strongest players of Vienna.

White. (FALKBEER.)	*Black.* (HAMPE.)
1. P. to K. fourth	1. P. to K. fourth
2. Kt. to K. B. third	2. P. to Q. third
3. P. to Q. fourth	3. P. takes P.
4. B. to Q. B. fourth	4. Kt. to Q. B. third

5.	P. to Q. B. third	5.	P. to Q. sixth
6.	Q. takes P.	6.	B. to K. second
7.	B. to K. B. fourth	7.	B. to K. third
8.	Q. Kt. to Q. second	8.	B. to K. B. third
9.	K. Kt. to Q. fourth	9.	B. takes B.
10.	Kt. takes B.	10.	K. Kt. to K. second
11.	Kt. to K. third	11.	Castles
12.	P. to K. Kt. fourth	12.	Kt. to K. Kt. third
13.	B. to K. Kt. third	13.	B. to K. fourth
14.	Kt. to K. second	14.	B. takes B.
15.	R. P. takes B.	15.	Q. Kt. to K. fourth
16.	Q. to her B. second .	16.	Kt. to K. B. sixth (check)
17.	K. to K. B. square	17.	K. Kt. to K. fourth
18.	Kt. to Q. fourth	18.	Q. to K. square
19.	K. to K. Kt. second	19.	Kt. takes Kt.
20.	P. takes Kt.	20.	Kt. to Q. B. third
21.	P. to Q. fifth (a)	21.	Kt. to Q. Kt. fifth
22.	Q. to her B. fourth	22.	P. to Q. R. fourth
23.	Kt. to K. B. fifth	23.	P. to Q. Kt. fourth
24.	Q. to Q. fourth	24.	P. to K. B. third
25.	Q. R. to Q. B. square	25.	R. to K. B. second
26.	P. to Q. R. third	26.	Kt. to Q. R. third
27.	Q. to K. third	27.	Kt. to Q. B. fourth
28.	P. to K. B. third	28.	P. to Q. Kt. fifth
29.	R. to K. R. fourth	29.	Q. to K. fourth
30.	Q. to K. second	30.	P. takes P.
31.	Q. R. to K. R. square	31.	P. to K. Kt. fourth
32.	Kt. to B. sixth (check)	32.	K. to B. square
33.	Kt. takes B.	33.	Q. takes Q. Kt. P. (check)
34.	Q. takes Q.	34.	P. takes Q.
35.	R. takes P.	35.	R. to K. square
36.	Kt. to K. R. sixth	36.	R. to K. fourth
37.	Kt. to K. B. fifth		

And wins.

Note.

(a) Had he played "P. to K. fifth," the best reply seems to be "P. to K. R. third," as "P. to K. Kt. third" would be very bad play.

A lively game played some little time ago in a Tournament at Paris, between M. JOURNOUD, a French amateur of eminence, and Colonel SZABO, who recently distinguished himself in the contest of Liverpool against Manchester.

(*Centre Gambit.*)

White. (SZABO.)	*Black.* (JOURNOUD.)
1. P. to K. fourth	1. P. to K. fourth
2. P. to Q. fourth	2. P. takes P.
3. K. Kt. to K. B. third	3. P. to Q. B. fourth
4. K. B. to Q. B. fourth	4. P. to Q. Kt. fourth
5. K. B. to Q. fifth	5. Q. Kt. to Q. B. third
6. Kt. to K. fifth	6. Kt. takes Kt.
7. K. B. takes Q. R.	7. Q. B. to Q. R. third
8. K. B. to Q. fifth	8. Q. to K. R. fifth
9. Q. to Q. second	9. K. Kt. to K. B. third
10. Q. to K. B. fourth	10. Q. takes Q.
11. B. takes Q.	11. K. B. to Q. third
12. B. takes Kt.	12. B. takes B.
13. Castles	13. Kt. takes B.
14. P. takes Kt.	14. P. to Q. third
15. K. R. to K. square	15. K. to Q. second
16. Kt. to Q. second	16. Q. B. to Q. Kt. second
17. P. to Q. R. fourth	17. P. to Q. Kt. fifth
18. Kt. to K. fourth	18. Q. B. takes P.
19. Kt. takes Q. B. P. (check)	19. P. takes Kt.
20. R. takes B.	20. K. to Q. third
21. Q. R. to K. square	21. B. to K. third
22. P. to K. B. fourth	22. P. to K. Kt. third
23. P. to Q. B. third	23. Q. P. takes P.
24. P. takes P.	24. P. to Q. Kt. sixth
25. Q. R. to Q. square (check)	25. K. to Q. B. third
26. Q. R. to Q. Kt. square	26. P. to Q. B. fifth
27. K. to K. B. second	27. R. to Q. square
28. Q. R. to Q. Kt. second	28. R. to Q. sixth
29. K. R. to K. third	29. R. takes R.
30. K. takes R.	30. K. to Q. Kt. third
31. P. to K. R. third	31. P. to K. R. fourth
32. K. to Q. fourth	32. K. to Q. R. fourth

33. R. to Q. Kt. square	33. B. to K. B. fourth
34. R. to Q. Kt. second	34. B. to Q. sixth
35. R. takes P.	35. P. takes R.
36. K. takes B.	36. K. takes P.
37. P. to Q. B. fourth	37. K. to Q. R. sixth

And wins.

A game played by ANDERSSEN during his last visit to the Leipsig Chess Club.

(Gambit Declined.)

White. (Herr POLLMAECHER.)	*Black.* (Herr ANDERSSEN.)
1. P. to K. fourth	1. P. to K. fourth
2. P. to K. B. fourth	2. B. to Q. B. fourth
3. Kt. to K. B. third	3. P. to Q. third
4. B. to Q. B. fourth (a)	4. Kt. to K. B. third
5. P. to Q. third	5. Q. B. to K. Kt. fifth
6. P. takes P.	6. B. takes Kt. (b)
7. Q. takes B.	7. P. takes P.
8. B. to K. third	8. B. takes B.
9. Q. takes B.	9. Q. Kt. to Q. second
10. Q. Kt. to Q. second	10. Q. to K. second
11. Castles (K. R.)	11. Q. Kt. to K. B. square
12. Kt. to K. B. third	12. Q. Kt. to K. Kt. third
13. Kt. to K. Kt. fifth	13. Castles (K. R.)
14. P. to K. Kt. third	14. P. to K. R. third
15. Kt. to B. third	15. P. to Q. Kt. fourth
16. B. to Kt. third (c)	16. P. to Q. B. fourth
17. K. to R. square	17. Q. R. to Q. B. square
18. Q. to K. second	18. Q. to Q. B. second
19. Kt. to Q. second	19. K. to R. second
20. K. R. to B. second	20. Kt. to K. square
21. Q. R. to K. B. square	21. Kt. to Q. third
22. B. to Q. fifth	22. P. to Q. B. fifth
23. Q. to K. R. fifth	23. P. to K. B. third
24. Kt. to B. third	24. Q. to Q. second
25. P. to Q. fourth	25. K. R. to K. square
26. P. takes P.	26. Kt. takes P.

27. Kt. to R. fourth	27. Q. to K. Kt. fifth
28. Q. takes Q.	28. Kt. takes Q.
29. R. to K. second	29. R. to Q. B. fourth
30. R. to Q. square	30. Kt. takes K. P. (d)
31. B. to K. B. seventh	31. Kt. from K. Kt. fifth to K. B. seventh (check)
32. K. to Kt. second	32. Kt. takes R.
33. B. takes R.	33. Kt. to Q. third
34. B. to Kt. sixth (check)	34. K. to Kt. square
35. R. to K. sixth	35. R. to Q. fourth
36. Kt. to K. B. fifth	36. R. takes Kt.
37. R. takes Kt.	37. R. to Q. fourth (e)
38. R. to K. sixth	38. R. to Q. square
39. P. to Q. Kt. third	39. P. takes P.
40. R. P. takes P.	40. P. to Q. R. fourth
41. K. to B. third	41. Kt. to B. sixth
42. R. to Q. R. sixth	42. P. to Q. R. fifth
43. P. takes P.	43. P. takes P.
44. R. to Q. B. sixth	44. Kt. to Q. fourth
45. R. to Q. R. sixth	45. Kt. to Q. B. third
46. R. to Q. B. sixth	

Drawn game.

Notes by Herr FALKBEER.

(a) "P. to Q. B. third" has been recommended by strong players, and successfully carried out by Morphy, in the match with Löwenthal. Still we prefer the move in the text.

(b) It is evident he could not retake P. with P. for White's reply "B. takes P. (check)."

(c) White could not have taken the Pawn without exposing himself to a powerful attack.

(d) This brilliant move, and White's clever answer to it, are very well conceived.

(e) Capital play on both sides. Anderssen's defence is most brilliant, forming a very spirited end game.

Game played simultaneously by MR. MORPHY, without seeing the board, in Paris.

(*Philidorian Defence.*)

White. (Mr. MORPHY.)	*Black.* (Mr. SEGUIN.)
1. P. to K. fourth	1. P. to K. fourth
2. Kt. to K. B. third	2. P. to Q. third

3. P. to Q. fourth	3. P. takes P.
4. Kt. takes P.	4. Kt. to K. B. third
5. Kt. to Q. B. third	5. B. to K. second
6. B. to Q. third	6. Castles
7. P. to K. B. fourth	7. P. to Q. B. fourth
8. Kt. to K. B. third	8. Kt. to Q. B. third
9. Castles	9. Q. B. to K. Kt. fifth
10. B. to K. third	10. P. to Q. R. third
11. P. to Q. R. fourth	11. P. to K. R. third
12. P. to K. R. third	12. B. takes Kt.
13. Q. takes B.	13. Kt. to Q. Kt. fifth
14. Q. R. to Q. square	14. Q. to Q. B. second
15. P. to Q. Kt. third	15. Kt. takes B.
16. P. takes Kt.	16. K. R. to K. square
17. P. to Q. fourth	17. Q. to Q. B. third
18. P. takes P.	18. P. takes P.
19. P. to K. fifth	19. Q. takes Q.
20. R. takes Q.	20. Kt. to K. R. second
21. R. to Q. seventh	21. Q. R. to Q. Kt. square
22. Kt. to Q. fifth	22. B. to B. square
23. B. to B. second	23. K. R. to Q. square
24. Kt. to Q. Kt. sixth	24. R. takes R.
25. Kt. takes R.	25. R. to Q. B. square
26. R. to Q. B. third	26. R. to Q. B. second
27. Kt. takes B.	27. Kt. takes Kt.
28. R. takes P.	28. R. takes R.
29. B. takes R.	29. Kt. to K. third
30. B. to K. third	30. P. to K. Kt. third
31. P. to K. Kt. fourth	31. Kt. to Q. square
32. K. to B. second	32. Kt. to Q. B. third
33. K. to K. second	33. P. to Q. Kt. fourth
34. P. takes P.	34. P. takes P.
35. K. to Q. third	35. K. to B. square
36. B. to Q. B. fifth (check)	36. K. to K. square
37. K. to K. fourth	37. K. to Q. second
38. K. to Q. fifth	38. Kt. to Q. square
39. P. to K. B. fifth	39. P. takes P.
40. P. takes P.	40. P. to K. R. fourth

41. P. to Q. Kt. sixth	41. Kt. to Q. Kt. second
42. P. to K. sixth (check)	42. P. takes P.
43. P. takes P. (check)	43. K. to K. second
44. K. to Q. B. sixth	44. Kt. to Q. square (check)
45. B. takes Kt. (check)	45. K. takes B.
46. K. to Q. sixth	46. K. to K. square
47. P. to K. seventh	

And Black resigned.

We extract from our transatlantic contemporary the following neat little skirmish, played by Mr. MORPHY, without the sight of the board and men, at the late Chess Congress, held at New York, before his departure to Europe.

(Evans' Gambit.)

White. (MR. MORPHY.)	Black. (MR. —.)
1. P. to K. fourth	1. P. to K. fourth
2. Kt. to K. B. third	2. Kt. to Q. B. third
3. B. to Q. B. fourth	3. B. to Q. B. fourth
4. P. to Q. Kt. fourth	4. B. takes Kt. P.
5. P. to Q. B. third	5. B. to Q. B. fourth
6. Castles	6. P. to Q. third
7. P. to Q. fourth	7. P. takes P.
8. P. takes P.	8. B. to Kt. third
9. Q. Kt. to B. third	9. Q. Kt. to R. fourth
10. Kt. to K. Kt. fifth	10. Kt. takes B.
11. Q. to Q. K. fourth (check)	11. P. to Q. B. third
12. Q. takes Kt.	12. Kt. to K. R. third (a)
13. K. to R. square	13. Castles
14. P. to K. B. fourth	14. K. to R. square
15. P. to K. B. fifth	15. P. to K. B. third (b)
16. Kt. to K. sixth	16. B. takes Kt.
17. P. takes B.	17. Q. to K. second (c)
18. B. takes Kt.	18. P. takes B.
19. R. to K. B. third	19. R. to K. Kt. square
20. Q. R. to K. B. square	20. R. to K. Kt. third
21. Kt. to K. second	21. R. to K. B. square
22. Kt. to B. fourth	22. R. to Kt. fourth
23. P. to Q. fifth	23. P. to Q. B. fourth

24. Q. to Q. B. third	24. B. to Q. square
25. Kt. to K. second	25. Q. to Kt. second
26. Kt. to Kt. third	26. Q. to Q. B. second .
27. R. takes P.	27. B. takes R.
28. R. takes B.	28. R. takes R.
29. Q. takes R. (check)	29. Q. to Kt. second
30. Q. to Q. eighth (check)	30. Q. interposes
31. P. to K. seventh	·31. R. to K. fourth
32. Kt. to K. R. fifth	32. R. takes K. P.

White mated in five moves.

Notes.

(a) This is a bad defence. "Q. to K. second" would have afforded more liberty of action.

(b) Fatal, as will be seen by White's spirited reply.

(c) Another error. He ought to have played the Queen on the twelfth move. At this juncture "Kt. to K. Kt. square" was Black's only plausible reply.

On Tuesday evening, the 26th of April, Mr. MORPHY undertook the difficult task of playing five games, simultaneously, with five strong players; his antagonists were Messrs. BARNES, BIRD, BODEN, RIVIERE, and LÖWENTHAL; the play commenced at the St. James's Hall about 6 P.M., and terminated a little after 12 with the following result: the games with Messrs. BIRD and RIVIERE, Mr. MORPHY won; those with Messrs. BODEN and LÖWENTHAL were drawn, and the game with Mr. BARNES he lost. The following game, one of the two drawn, we have been favored with for publication.

(Rui Lopez Knight's Gambit.)

White. (LÖWENTHAL.)	Black. (MORPHY).
1. P. to K. fourth	1. P. to K. fourth
2. Kt. to K. B. third	2. Kt. to Q. B. third
3. B. to Kt. fifth	3. P. to Q. R. third
4. B. to R. fourth	4. Kt. to B. third
5. Castles	5. B. to K. second
6. P. to Q. fourth	6. P. takes P.
7. P. to K. fifth	7. Kt. to K. fifth
8. B. takes Kt.	8. Q. P. takes B.
9. Q. takes P.	9. B. to K. B. fourth
10. Kt. to B. third	10. B. to Q. B. fourth

11. Q. takes Q. (check)	11. R. takes Q.
12. Kt. to R. fourth	12. Kt. takes Q. Kt.
13. Kt. takes B.	13. Kt. to K. seventh (check)
14. K. to R. square	14. P. to K. Kt. third
15. Kt. to K. Kt. third	15. Kt. takes Kt. (check)
16. R. P. takes Kt.	16. P. to R. third
17. R. to Q. Kt. square	17. K. to K. second
18. P. to Q. Kt. fourth	18. B. to Q. fifth
19. P. to K. B. fourth	19. K. to K. third
20. R. to Kt. third	20. P. to K. R. fourth
21. R. to Q. third	21. B. to Q. Kt. third
22. K. R. to Q. square	22. R. takes R.
23. R. takes R.	23. K. to B. fourth
24. B. to Q. Kt. second	24. R. to K. R. second
25. B. to Q. fourth	25. P. to K. R. fifth
26. B. takes B.	26. P. takes P. (check)
27. K. to Kt. square	27. P. takes B.
28. R. to Q. seventh	28. K. to K. third
29. R. takes P.	29. R. to R. fifth
30. R. takes P.	30. R. takes P.
31. R. takes P. (check)	31. K. takes P.
32. R. to Q. B. fifth (check)	32. K. to Q. third
33. R. to K. Kt. fifth	33. R. takes P.
34. R. takes P.	34. R. to Q. R. fifth
35. P. to Q. R. third	35. R. to Q. B. fifth
36. R. to Q. third (check)	36. K. to K. third
37. R. to Q. Kt. third	37. R. takes P.
38. R. to Kt. sixth (check)	38. K. to B. fourth
39. R. takes P.	39. P. to Kt. fourth
40. R. to Kt. sixth	40. R. to R. seventh
41. R. to Kt. third	41. P. to Kt. fifth
42. R. to Kt. fifth (check)	42. K. to B. fifth
43. R. to Kt. third	43. P. to B. fourth
44. P. to Kt. third (check)	44. K. to K. fifth
45. K. to B. square	45. K. to K. fourth
46. K. to Kt. square	46. P. to B. fifth

Drawn game.

SOLUTIONS TO PROBLEMS.

No. 13.　*Page* 127.

White.	*Black.*
1. B. to Q. R. fifth	1. Kt. to Q. Kt. third (or A.)
2. B. takes Kt.	2. R. to Q. R. fourth
3. B. to Q. eighth	3. P. to Q. B. fifth
4. P. to Q. Kt. sixth	4. K. to Q. B. third
5. P. to Q. Kt. seventh	5. R. to Q. Kt. fifth
6. B. to Q. R. fifth	6. R. to Q. Kt. fourth
7. P. to K. Kt. fourth	7. P. to Q. B. sixth
8. B. takes P.	8. K. to Q. B. second
9. K. to K. R. fourth	

And wins.

(A.)

1.	1. Kt. takes B.
2. P. to R. seventh	2. K. to Q. B. fifth
3. P. queens	3. K. takes P.
4. Q. to K. eighth (check)	4. K. to Q. Kt. fifth
5. Q. takes P.	

And with careful play, wins.

No. 14.　*Page* 127.

Black.	*White.*
1. R. to Q. B. third (*a*)	1. P. to Q. seventh
2. R. to Q. third	2. Kt. to K. sixth
3. R. takes P.	3. Kt. to Q. B. fifth (check)

And draws.

(*a*) Were Black to play "K. to K. sixth," with the intention of giving check-mate, White would win by checking with Kt. on Q. fifth.

No. 15.　*Page* 128.

White.	*Black.*
1. Q. to K. B. fourth	1. P. takes Q.
2. Kt. takes P.	2. P. moves
3. B. mates	

No. 16.　*Page* 128.

White.	*Black.*
1. Kt. to R. sixth (check)	1. K. to B. square
2. R. to B. seventh (check)	2. K. to his square
3. Kt. to B. fifth	3. P. moves
4. Kt. to Kt. seventh (check)	4. K. to Q. square
5. B. to B. seventh (check)	5. K. to B. square
6. Kt. to K. sixth	6. P. moves
7. B. to R. fifth	7. P. moves
8. R. to Q. Kt. seventh	8. P. takes R. and mates

No. 17. Problem by Mr. S. CRAWSHAY.

BLACK.

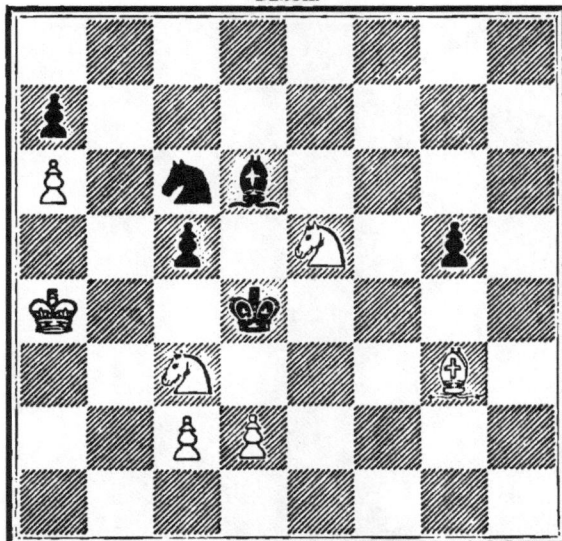

WHITE.

White to mate in two moves.

No. 18. Problem by J. C. ROLL, Esq.

BLACK.

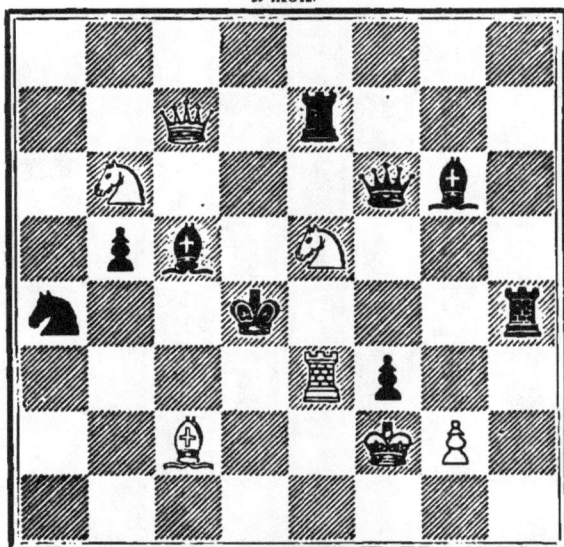

WHITE.

White to mate in two moves.

No. 19. Problem by J. C. ROLL, Esq.
BLACK.

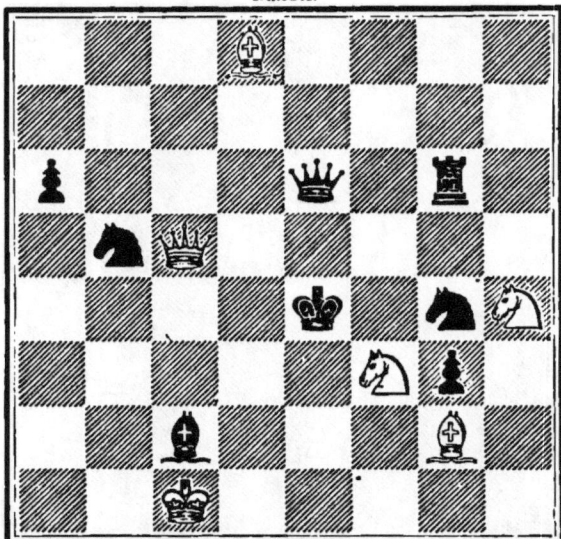

WHITE.
White to mate in three moves.

No. 20. Problem by Mr. W. GREENWOOD,
BLACK.

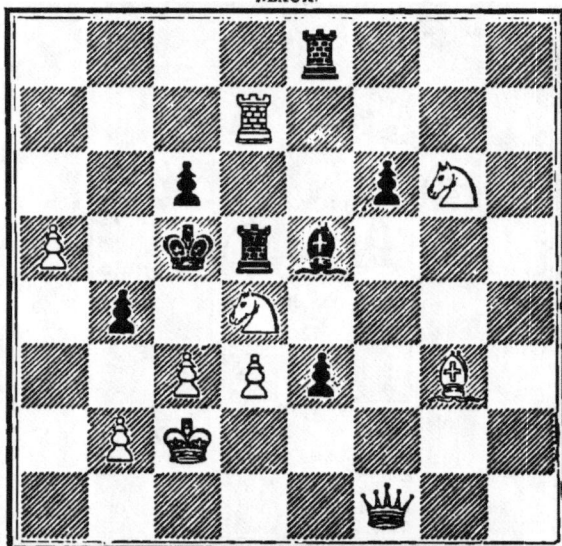

WHITE.
White to mate in four moves.

OUR POLITICAL CREED.

THOSE who may ask why we have delayed till now to lay down the principles of our policy, we must refer to our first number, where, in the introductory chapter, we have said everything we thought it behoved our readers to know, in that respect. We, therefore, believed the matter settled, and said and thought no more about it. But great was our mistake; we were not left long to enjoy the editorial *dolce farniente*. With stoical indifference we at first perused the numerous letters addressed to us, mostly by persons unknown to fame, and reproaching us for not stating to what party we belonged, and what were our opinions about the great living Chess Masters. This indifference insensibly changed, in spite of the increasing number of letters, into a sort of satisfaction, not by reason of their contents, but simply on account of their number, which clearly demonstrated that the CHESS PLAYER'S CHRONICLE was extensively read; yet there is no unalloyed happiness in this world, and so it proved with our satisfaction, which was somewhat dimmed by the consciousness that the principles of our policy were not well understood by the public at large. This most uncomfortable feeling was still heightened by open attacks and covert insinuations, mostly originating with American weekly papers, in which we were accused of not being impartial, and of not rendering justice to Mr. MORPHY's play. Although our answer to all and every one may have been, "Read the CHRONICLE and judge for yourself," we have decided to make a clear and distinct statement of our political creed, so that the public may fully know what they have to expect of us.

The CHESS PLAYER'S CHRONICLE is devoted to the interest of Chess in general, and to that of British Chess in particular. From this may easily be inferred that, *cæteris paribus*, we always give the preference in our columns to English players and English play. If we are arraigned by any one on that account, we at once plead guilty. Nay, we frankly admit that we think several of our leading clubs blameable for having, in preference to native genius, encouraged foreign talent. The CHESS PLAYER'S CHRONICLE is impartial in its judgments, admits no authority, it judges not the players but the games, and calls a bad move bad if made by MORPHY or by DE LA BOURDONNAIS. It cannot be, therefore, expected that the CHRONICLE will use those phrases, so often reiterated by the weekly Chess papers, in the notes to MORPHY's games, as "finely played," "quite a MORPHY," "wonderful combina-

11

tion," &c. &c., which are generally annexed to quite commonplace moves or combinations. Those phrases may be usefully employed in encouraging young players; but when applied to a master like MORPHY they sound like the exclamations of a gaping crowd at a juggler's tricks.

The CHESS PLAYER'S CHRONICLE accepts contributions in the shape of Articles, Games, Problems, from every living player, if suited to its columns, but will always carefully exclude party polemics.

The CHESS PLAYER'S CHRONICLE, as to its foreign relations—that is, foreign periodicals and Chess players—will always keep a strict neutrality: that is, select the best games of the best players, without reference to Town or Country. But, in order that our pages should not be altogether invaded by the foreigner, we shall always take care to have the full amount of good English Games and Problems, and thus keep, as the phrase now goes, a strict but *armed neutrality*.

BLINDFOLD PLAY.

SIR,—As Blindfold Play has attracted so much attention in this country since the arrival of Mr. MORPHY, perhaps it may interest some of your readers to receive an old Arabian author's instructions for the acquisition of that art. In the British Museum there is a Persian MS. on Chess (No. 16,856), which devotes a whole chapter to the subject. The people of Arabia and Persia have been not only cunning players over the board, but they have also excelled in playing without seeing the board, ever since they received the game from India in the sixth century of our era. The author of the above-mentioned MS. lived in Northern India upwards of three hundred years ago, as his work is dedicated to the Emperor Humāyūn, who reigned between A.D. 1531 and 1554. He tells us in his preface, that it is a translation of an old Arabic work on Chess, entitled, the *Chess Player's Guide and Monitor*. (a)

In order to follow the author's instructions, the reader must always bear in mind the peculiarities in which the Persi-Arabian as well as

(a) The name of the author of the orignal Arabic work was "Abū Muhammad Bin Umar Kājīna," of whom I never heard except here. It is highly probable that his lucubrations have long been lost, like many others, in countries where the art of printing is still in its infancy. Now, talking of the art of printing, is it not a curious fact that the work of Caxton on Chess—the *first book* printed by our *first printer*, is all but non-existent in our land?

medieval European game differed from ours of the present day. They are the following, viz.:—1. The Queen moved only one square diagonally, consequently she could move on no more than one half the squares of the board, being those of her own color (*a*), as we should say. 2. The Bishops moved only two squares diagonally, and had no influence over the intermediate squares; hence a Bishop, as may be seen on trial, could touch only seven squares of the board besides that on which he originally stood. 3. The Pawns were never allowed to move more than one square at the beginning; and castling was unknown. 4. Lastly, to save time, and to avoid frivolous exchanges, the first player made fifteen moves, more or less, at once, without, however, being allowed to cross the middle line of the board. This was called the *battle-array*; and then the opponent was allowed the same number of moves on his side of the board, as a *counter-battle-array*. Then came "the tug of war," each of the forces being posted upon the middle line, which we may imagine to be the Ticino of the bloodless combatants. I now proceed to condense the precepts of the Arabian sage on the art of Blindfold Play, and for simplicity's sake I will address myself to the player of the White.

" In the first place you are to bear in mind that the board is divided into two equal portions by the middle line, from left to right. The half next to you is White's ground, and the other half is Black's.(*b*) Again, imagine the board to be divided by a line from top to bottom, thus forming four equal portions of sixteen squares each. The right-hand quarter is your King's; and the quarter on the left, your Queen's. In like manner the quarter opposite your King's belongs to the adversary's King, and the quarter opposite to your Queen's, that of the adverse Queen. The various squares are reckoned from either extremity, and are named after the King or Queen in whose quarter they are. Thus, the square before your King's is called W. K.'s second square; next to that W. K.'s third square; then W. K.'s fourth square.

(*a*) The Orientals never used a checkered board till a comparatively recent period.

(*b*) This is precisely the mode of describing the moves, &c., used by the early Italian masters, and by all our own writers on the subject till some twenty-five years ago, more or less, when our present method was introduced by Mr. Lewis. The last work on the old system is perhaps Walker's *Phillidor*, London, 1832. I confess I am myself partial to the old or Arabian system, being that which was in vogue when I began to read books on Chess. I think it is decidedly better adapted to the art of Blindfold Play than the new.

Proceeding beyond the middle line, the next square is Black King's fourth square, next to that his third square, &c.; and a similar rule holds with regard to all the other squares. With regard to the Pieces and Pawns, those originally standing in your King's quarter are styled King's Pieces and Pawns, and the others Queen's.

" The adversary's Pieces and Pawns are similarly styled, and the squares in front of each are named descendingly. Thus the Knight on your right hand is White King's Knight; the square in front of him is White King's Knight's second square, and so on of all the rest. All these things you must thoroughly master and carry in your head, so that you may readily know the precise locality, (b) as well as the name and designation of every square on the board.

PRECEPTS AND MAXIMS.

" 1. Before you begin the game, fix firmly in your memory the exact state of your battle array, as well as that of your adversary. Bear in mind what pieces of your own occupy each of your quarters, and also how your adversary's pieces are stationed in his quarters. Never lose sight of the relative changes and modifications which are being constantly effected by each successive move that is made. Never allow your attention to be withdrawn from the board and pieces which you are contemplating in your mind.

" 2. The pieces that require most watching are the Knights, owing to the obliquity of their moves. The Rooks, though the more powerful pieces, are much more easily followed in their movements. The Queen and Bishops can attack only a certain number of well-known squares; and it is good play, when possible, to keep your King out of their reach.

" 3. Do not at first attempt Blindfold Play except with inferior players; nor would I advise you to attempt it at all, unless you possess strong powers of memory and mental abstraction, and unless you can play well with your eyes open."

The author concludes by stating, "that some men, from long practice, have arrived at such a degree of perfection in this art, as to have

(b) I consider this same *locality* as a great help to the memory ; and I cannot help thinking that the Oriental player would have further profited by having the board colored black and white, as with us. He could thus more easily foollw the movements of the Queens and Bishops, all of which kept to their original colors.

played blindfold at four or five boards at one and the same time, and never to have committed a mistake in any of the games. Nay, further, some have been known to have recited poetry, or told amusing stories, or conversed with the company present during the progress of the contest. I have seen it written in a book, that one person played blindfold in this manner at ten boards at once; and gained all the games, and even corrected many errors in describing the moves made by his opponents."

Such are the instructions of Abū Muhammad to those who are ambitious to excel in Blindfold Play; and if slightly modified, so as to suit our board, you will find that they are precisely those given by Damiano, 350 years ago. Now, the Arabian author could not have borrowed his from Damiano; then arises a query—are Damiano's original? If we suppose that the two authors have, independent of each other, hit upon precisely the same thing, it amounts to a tolerable proof that the principles of the art are founded on a sound basis. I am inclined to think, however, that Damiano's notions on this subject reached him either directly or indirectly from the Arabs, who ruled in Spain during several centuries before that in which he was born. But I must stop short at present, though I have much more to say. Perhaps I may resume the subject at some future period.

Yours, &c.,   D. FORBES.

To the Editor of
THE CHESS PLAYER'S CHRONICLE.

SCIENCE AND ART OF CHESS, BY J. MONROE, B.C.L.—*New York*, C. SCRIBNER.—A new work under this title has just reached us from America; although not so full of instructive matter as Staunton's *Hand Book*, it still has the merit of imparting the knowledge of this noble game in a novel and ingenious way, and learners may study it with advantage. The chief fault of the book is, that it contains so meagre an analysis of the various openings, that it can only be considered as an elementary book. As such we can recommend it to those who are beginning to study the game; it is full of capital problems, excellently printed, and can be obtained of the London Agents, Messrs. LOW, SON, and Co., *Ludgate Hill.*

THE SEVEN AGES OF CHESS.—(*Continued from p.* 131.)

IV. CHESS IN MANHOOD.

In manhood's prime, when from my native shore
A stately vessel bore me proudly on,
Baffling the winds, braving the tempest's roar,
Dimming the memories of pleasures gone,

And leaving me, the weary night and day,
To lay out plans for my maturer life;
To build up towers of hope, or cast away
The futile schemes with which my brain was rife;

I walked in fancy then o'er untrod ground,
Hasting to push my fortune in new lands;
Heedless meanwhile of all my shipmates round,
Failing to mark their skill of head or hands.

But oh! the weary sameness of each day,
The fettered dulness of that mimic world,
In which I held my solitary way
Self-isolated; all my thoughts close-furled

And pressing on my heart; until I burned
To spread them out before my fellow-men,
To catch the breeze for which my spirit yearned,
And meet the sunshine of their smiles again.

But how should I the chain of silence break,
Which I had formed by mine own moodiness?
How from my cold stern character awake?
The means were furnished by the game of Chess.

Inviting to the conflict of the game,
A fellow-passenger of courteous air,
I heard him whisper, " Can this be the same?
The man whose confidence we never share? "

Chess, in its close-absorbing manly strife,
Its plots and counterplots, its deep-laid schemes,
Its likeness to the battle of my life,
Redeemed me from my vague and empty dreams.

Chess reconciled me to my fellows then;
Chess made me happy in my ocean home;
And ever since, a Travelling-Board and Men
Have been my solace, when condemned to roam.

The eight following Games were played at Paris by Mr. MORPHY, simultaneously, without sight of board or men; the eight gentlemen, his antagonists, are considered strong players of the Café de la Régence, to whom first-class players could scarcely give any odds.

GAME I.
(*Philidor's Defence.*)

White. (Mr. MORPHY.)	Black. (Mr. BOUCHER.)
1. P. to K. fourth	1. P. to K. fourth
2. K. Kt. to K. B. third	2. P. to Q. third
3. P. to Q. fourth	3. P. takes P.
4. Q. takes P.	4. Q. Kt. to Q. B. third
5. K. B. to Q. Kt. fifth	5. Q. B. to Q. second
6. B. takes Kt.	6. B. takes B.
7. B. to K. Kt. fifth	7. P. to K. B. third (*a*)
8. B. to K. R. fourth	8. Kt. to K. R. third
9. Q. Kt. to Q. B. third	9. K. B. to K. second
10. Castles on K. side	10. Castles
11. Q. to Q. B. fourth (check)	11. K. to R. square (*b*)
12. K. Kt. to Q. fourth	12. Q. to her second
13. Q. R. to Q. square	13. K. R. to K. B. second (*c*)
14. P. to K. B. fourth	14. P. to Q. R. fourth
15. P. to K. B. fifth	15. K. R. to K. B. square (*d*)
16. K. Kt. to K. sixth	16. K. R. to K. Kt. square
17. P. to Q. R. fourth	17. Kt. to Kt. fifth
18. Q. to K. second	18. Kt. to K. fourth
19. B. to K. Kt. third	19. Q. to Q. B. square (*e*)
20. B. takes Kt.	20. Q. P. takes B.
21. K. R. to K. B. third	21. Q. B. to Q. second (*f*)
22. K. R. to K. R. third	22. P. to K. R. third
23. Q. to Q. second	23. K. to R. second
24. Q. takes Q. B.	24. B. to Q. third
25. K. R. takes K. R. P. (check)	25. K. takes R.
26. R. to Q. third	26. K. to R. fourth
27. Q. to K. B. seventh (check)	

And wins; the battle having lasted about seven hours.

Notes.

(*a*) "Kt. to K. B. third" is safer, as it allows Black to draw the game, if, by exchanging Queens, White doubles Black's Pawns.

(b) "Kt. to K. B. second" would have been much better, as the Kt. is badly placed, and has here an occasion of changing his bad position for a much better one.

(c) A very weak move; why not "Kt. to K. Kt. fifth"?

(d) This move evidently shows the unsoundness of the 13th move.

(e) This was done to enable Black to take the Bishop, if he takes Kt. with Queen's P.; we should, however, have preferred "Q. Kt. P. first," and take the B. with K. B. P.

(f) Black has already a lost game, and no move could save it.

GAME II.
(*French Opening.*)

White. (Mr. MORPHY.)	Black. (Mr. BIERWIRTH.)
1. P. to K. fourth	1. P. to K. third
2. P. to Q. fourth	2. P. to. Q. B. third
3. K. B. to Q. third	3. P. to Q. fourth
4. P. takes P.	4. K. P. takes P.
5. K. Kt. to K. B. third	5. Q. B. to K. Kt. fifth
6. Castles	6. K. B. to Q. third
7. P. to K. R. third	7. Q. B. to K. R. fourth
8. Q. B. to K. third	8. Q. Kt. to Q. second
9. K. R. to K. square	9. K. Kt. to K. second
10. Q. Kt. to Q. second	10. Q. B. takes Kt.
11. Kt. takes B.	11. P. to K. R. third
12. Q. to Q. second	12. Q. to Q. B. second
13. P. to Q. B. fourth	13. P. takes P.
14. K. B. takes P.	14. P. to K. B. fourth
15. Kt. to K. fifth	15. Castles on Q.'s side
16. K. B. to K. sixth	16. B. takes Kt.
17. P. takes B.	17. K. to Q. Kt. square
18. Q. to B. third	18. Q. Kt. to Q. Kt. third (a)
19. Q. to Q. R. third	19. Q. Kt. to Q. B. square
20. Q. R. to Q. B. square	20. P. to K. Kt. fourth
21. P. to K. B. fourth	21. P. takes. P.
22. Q. B. takes P.	22. Q. R. to Q. fifth
23. Q. to K. third	23. Q. R. to K. fifth
24. Q. to K. B. third	24. Q. to Q. Kt. third (check)
25. K. to K. R. second	25. Q. R. takes R.
26. R. takes R.	26. Q. to Q. Kt. fifth

27. R. to K. second	27. K. Kt. to K. Kt. third
28. Q. B. to Q. second	28. Q. to Q. Kt. fourth
29. K. B. takes Kt.	29. R. takes B.
30. B. takes K. R. P.	30. R. to K. R. square
31. B. to K. Kt. seventh	31. R. to K. R second
32. B. to K. B. sixth	32. R. to K. B. second
33. Q. to K. R. fifth	33. Kt. to K. B. fifth
34. Q. takes R.	

And Black surrenders, after a struggle of nearly nine hours.

Note.

(*a*) If, instead of this move, he takes P. with Q., he loses her by " B. takes Q. R. (check) ;" and if he takes P. with the Kt., he loses at least a piece.

GAME III.
(King's Gambit declined.)

White. (Mr. MORPHY.)	*Black.* (Mr. BORNEMANN.)
1. P. to K. fourth	1. P. to K. fourth
2. P. to K. B. fourth	2. K. B. to Q. B. fourth
3. K. Kt. to K. B. third	3. P. to Q. third
4. P. to Q. B. third	4. Q. B. to K. Kt. fifth
5. K. B. to Q. B. fourth	5. K. Kt. to K. B. third
6. P. takes P.	6. B. takes Kt.
7. Q. takes B.	7. Q. P. takes P.
8. P. to Q. third	8. Q. Kt. to Q. B. third
9. Q. B. to K. Kt. fifth	9. P. to Q. R. third
10. Q. Kt. to Q. second	10. B. to K. second
11. Castles on Q. side	11. Q. to Q. second
12. Kt. to K. B. square	12. Castles on Q. side
13. Kt. to K. third	13. P. to K. R. third
14. Q. B. to K. R. fourth	14. P. to K. Kt. fourth
15. Q. B. to K. Kt. third	15. Q. R. to K. B. square
16. Kt. to Q. fifth	16. K. Kt. to K. square
17. P. to Q. fourth	17. P. takes Q. P.
18. P. takes P.	18. K. Kt. to Q. third
19. K. B. to Q. Kt. third	19. B. to Q. square
20. K. R. to K. B. square	20. K. Kt. to Q. Kt. fourth
21. Q. to K. third	21. P. to K. B. fourth

22. P. takes P.	22. Q. R. takes P.
23. Kt. to Q. Kt. sixth (check) (a)	23. P. takes Kt.
24. K. B. to K. sixth	24. Q. R. to Q. fourth
25. K. R. to K. B. seventh	25. Q. Kt. to K. second
26. K. to Q. Kt. square	26. K. R. to K. square (b)
27. Q. R. to Q. B. square (check)	27. K. Kt. to Q. B. second
28. K. B. takes Q. (check)	28. Q. R. takes B.
29. P. to Q. fifth (c)	29. Q. Kt. to Q. B. third
30. P. takes Kt.	30. K. R. takes Q.
31. P. takes Q. R. (check)	

And Black gives up the battle, after fighting for above nine hours.

Notes.

(a) This manœuvre was evidently not foreseen by Black.
(b) The game is at this point completely lost for Black.
(c) Black cannot take P. without losing a piece.

GAME IV.
(*Irregular Opening.*)

White. (Mr. MORPHY.)	*Black.* (Mr. GUIBERT.)
1. P. to K. fourth	1. P. to Q. fourth
2. P. takes P.	2. Q. takes P.
3. Q. Kt. to Q. B. third	3. Q. to her square
4. P. to Q. fourth	4. P. to K. third
5. K. Kt. to K. B. third	5. K. B. to Q. third
6. K. B. to Q. third	6. K. Kt. to K. second
7. Castles	7. P. to K. R. third
8. Q. B. to K. third	8. P. to Q. B. third
9. K. Kt. to K. fifth	9. Q. Kt. to Q. second
10. P. to K. B. fourth	10. Q. Kt. to K. B. third
11. Q. Kt. to K. fourth	11. K. Kt. to K. B. fourth
12. Q. B. to K. B. second	12. K. B. to Q. B. second
13. P. to Q. B. third	13. Q. Kt. to Q. fourth
14. Q. to K. B. third	14. Q. to K. second
15. Q. R. to K. square	15. K. B. takes Kt.
16. Q. P. takes B.	16. P. to K. R. fourth (a)
17. Q. B. to Q. B. fifth	17. Q. to her square
18. Kt. to Q. sixth (check)	18. Kt. takes B.

19. Q. B. takes Kt. (*b*)	19. P. to K. Kt. third
20. Q. to K. Kt. third	20. Kt. to K. second
21. Q. R. to Q. square	21. B. to Q. second
22. Q. R. to Q. second	22. P. to K. R. fifth
23. Q. to K. Kt. fourth	23. Kt. to K. B. fourth
24. K. B. takes Kt.	24. K. P. takes Kt.
25. Q. to K. B. third	25. Q. to Q. Kt. third (check)
26. K. to R. square	26. Castles on Q. side
27. P. to Q. B. fourth	27. P. to K. R. sixth
28. P. to K. Kt. third	28. B. to K. third
29. Q. to Q. B. third	29. Q. R. to Q. second
30. K. R. to Q. square (*c*)	30. P. to Q. B. fourth
31. K. to K. Kt. square	31. K. R. to Q. square
32. Q. to Q. R. third	32. P. to Q. R. third
33. B. takes Q. B. P.	33. Q. to Q. B. third (*d*)
34. B. to Q. sixth	34. P. to K. B. third
35. Q. R. to Q. fifth	35. B. takes R.
36. R. takes B.	36. R. takes B.
37. P. takes R.	37. K. to Kt. square
38. Q. to Q. third	38. R. takes P.
39. Q. to Q. second	39. R. takes R.
40. P. takes R.	40. Q. to Q. B. fourth (check)
41. K. to B. square	41. Q. to Q. B. fifth (check)
42. K. to B. second	42. Q. to Q. B. fourth (check)

And the game was declared drawn, having lasted about nine hours.

Notes.

(*a*) It is evident Black cannot castle; White's game is already far superior; his pieces are all in play, whilst Black's are out of play

(*b*) A very strong position for the Bishop.

(*c*) Threatens to win at once by taking K. Kt. P. with K. B.

(*d*) The best move; it saves Black's game, as his adversary, on account of the threatened mate, cannot exchange Rooks.

GAME V.
(*Irregular Opening.*)

White. (Mr. MORPHY.)	*Black.* (Mr. LEQUESNE.)
1. P. to K. fourth	1. P. to Q. Kt. third
2. P. to Q. fourth	2. Q. B. to Q. Kt. second

3. K. B. to Q. third	3. P. to K. third
4. K. Kt. to K. R. third	4. K. Kt. to K. second
5. Castles	5. P. to Q. fourth
6. P. to K. fifth	6. K. Kt. to Q. B. third (a)
7. P. to Q. B. third	7. K. B. to K. second
8. P. to K. B. fourth	8. P. to K. Kt. third
9. P. to K. Kt. fourth	9. P. to K, R. fourth
10. P. takes P.	10. K. R. takes P.
11. Q. to K. Kt. fourth	11. K. R. to his fifth
12. Q. to K. Kt. third	12. K. to Q. second
13. Q. Kt. to Q. second	13. Q. to K. R. square
14. K. Kt. to K. Kt. fifth	14. K. Kt. to Q. square (b)
15. Q. Kt. to K. B. third	15. K. B. takes K. Kt
16. P. takes B.	16. K. R. to K. R. sixth
17. Q. to K. Kt. second	17. Q. Kt. to Q. B. third
18. Q. B. to Q. second	18. Q. Kt. to K. second (c)
19. Q. R. to Q. B. square	19. Q. R. to Q. B. square
20. P. to Q. Kt. fourth	20. P. to Q. R. third
21. P. to Q. R. fourth	21. Q. to K. R. fourth
22. Kt. to K. square	22. Kt. to K. B. fourth
23. K. R. to K. B. third	23. K. R. to his fifth
24. K. R. to K. B. fourth	24. K. R. takes R.
25. Q. B. takes R.	25. P. to Q. B. fourth
26. Q. Kt. P. takes P.	26. P. takes P.
27. R. to Q. Kt. square	27. P. to Q. B. fifth
28. K. B. takes Kt.	28. K. Kt. P. takes B.
29. Kt. to Q. B. second	29. B. to Q. B. third
30. P. to Q. R. fifth	30. Q. to K. R. fifth
31. Q. to K. Kt. third	31. Q. to K. R. fourth
32. Q. to K. Kt. second	32. Q. to K. R. fifth

At this point, neither party being disposed to vary his moves, the game was resigned as a DRAWN BATTLE.

Notes.

(a) Why not " Q. Kt. to Q. B. third," and form at once an attack upon the King's side?

(b) We do not see the object of that move, unless it is to defend the P., which could have been played two squares; Black's pieces are now all crammed together.

(c) All this is very weak play; Black had the best of the opening, and ought to have won. However, Mr. Morphy's clever play enabled him to draw the game against his weaker opponent.

Game VI.

(*Petroff Defence.*)

White. (Mr. Morphy.)	Black. (Mr. Potier.)
1. P. to K. fourth	1. P. to K. fourth
2. K. Kt. to K. B. third	2. K. Kt. to K. B. third
3. K. B. to Q. B. fourth	3. Kt. takes K. P.
4. Q. Kt. to Q. Kt. third	4. K. Kt. to K. B. third (a)
5. Kt. takes K. P.	5. P. to Q. fourth
6. K. B. to Q. Kt. third	6. K. B. to K. second
7. P. to Q. fourth	7. P. to Q. B. third
8. Castles	8. Q. Kt. to Q. second
9. P. to K. B. fourth	9. Q. Kt. to Q. Kt. third
10. Q. to K. B. third	10. P. to K. R. fourth
11. P. to K. B. fifth	11. Q. to Q. B. second
12. Q. B. to K. B. fourth	12. K. B. to Q. third
13. Q. R. to K. square	13. K. to B. square
14. Q. to K. Kt. third	14. P. to Q. R. fifth
15. K. Kt. to Kt. sixth (check)	15. K. to Kt. square
16. Q. B. takes B.	16. P. takes Q.
17. Q. B. takes Q.	17 P. takes Kt.
18. K. B. P. takes P.	18. P. takes K. R. P. (check)
19. K. to R. square	19. B. to K. Kt. fifth
20. Q. R. to K. seventh	20. Q. Kt. to Q. second
21. Q. B. to K. fifth	21. K. to B. square
22. Q. R. to K. B. seventh (ch.)(b)	22. K. to Kt. square
23. Kt. takes Q. P.	23. P. takes Kt.
24. K. B. takes P.	24. Q. Kt. to Q. Kt. third
25. K. B. to Q. Kt. third	

And Black abandons the game.

Notes.

(*a*) Black's move was "Kt. takes Kt." Mr. Potier is clearly not a strong player, else he would have procured us the pleasure to see how Mr. Morphy would have carried out his attack against Petroff's defence.

(*b*) Finely played without seeing the board, and elegantly finished.

GAME VII.
(Sicilian Opening.)

(*White.* (Mr. MORPHY.)	*Black.* (Mr. PRETI.)
1. P. to K. fourth	1. P. to Q. B. fourth
2. P. to Q. fourth	2. P. takes P.
3. K. Kt. to K. B. third	3. P. to K. fourth
4. K. B. to Q. B. fourth	4. K. B. checks (*a*)
5. P. to Q. B. third	5. P. takes P.
6. P. takes P.	6. K. B. to Q. B. fourth
7. K. Kt. takes K. P.	7. Q. to K. B. third
8. K. B. takes K. B. P. (check)	8. K. to B. square
9. K. Kt. to Q. third	9. K. B. to Q. Kt. third
10. K. B. to Q. Kt. third	10. P. to Q. third
11. Q. B. to Q. R. third	11. Q. Kt. to Q. B. third
12. Castles	12. K. Kt. to K. R. square
13. P. to K. fifth	13. Q. to K. Kt. third
14. K. Kt. to K. B. fourth	14. Q. to K. Kt. fifth
15. K. Kt. to K. sixth (check)(*b*)	15. Q. B. takes Kt.
16. Q. takes Q. P. (check)	16. K. to B. second
17. Q. to Q. seventh (check)	17. K. to K. Kt. third
18. K. B. takes B.	18. Q. to K. Kt. fourth
19. K. B. to Q. fifth	19. Q. Kt. takes K. P.
20. K. B. to K. fourth (check)	20. K. Kt. to K. B. fourth
21. Q. to K. sixth (check)	21. Q. to K. B. third
22. K. B. takes Kt. (check)	22. K. to K. R. fourth
23. P. to K. Kt. fourth (check)	23. Kt. takes P.
24. K. B. takes Kt. (check)	

And Black surrenders.

Notes.

(*a*) A bad move, as it loses K. P. "Q. Kt. to B. third " is the proper move.
(*b*) A better move than to take the Queen's Pawn at once with the Queen.

GAME VIII.
(Philidor's Defence.)

White. (Mr. MORPHY.)	*Black.* (Mr. SEGUIN.)
1. P. to K. fourth	1. P. to K. fourth
2. K. Kt. to K. B. third	2. P. to Q. third

3. P. to Q. fourth
4. K. Kt. takes P.
5. Q. Kt. to Q. B. third
6. K. B. to Q. third
7. P. to K. B. fourth
8. K. Kt. to K. B. third
9. Castles
10. Q. B. to K. third
11. P. to Q. R. fourth
12. P. to K. R. third
13. Q. takes B.
14. Q. R. to Q. square
15. P. to Q. Kt. third
16. P. takes Kt.
17. P. to Q. fourth
18. P. takes Q. B. P.
19. P. to K. fifth
20. K. R. takes Q.
21. Q. R. to Q. seventh
22. Kt. to Q. fifth
23. B. to K. B. second
24. Kt. to Q. Kt. sixth
25. Kt. takes R.
26. R. to Q. B. third
27. Kt. takes B.
28. R. takes P.
29. B. takes R.
30. B. to K. third
31. P. to K. Kt. fourth
32. K. to K. B. second
33. K. to K. second
34. P. takes P.
35. K. to Q. third
36. B. to Q. B. fifth (check)
37. K. to K. fourth
38. K. to Q. fifth
39. P. to K. B. fifth
40. P. takes P.

3. P. takes P.
4. K. Kt. to K. B. third
5. K. B. to K. second
6. Castles
7. P. to Q. B. fourth
8. Q. Kt. to Q. B. third
9. Q. B. to K. Kt. fifth
10. P. to Q. R. third
11. P. to K. R. third
12. Q. B. takes Kt.
13. Q. Kt. to Q. Kt. fifth
14. Q. to Q. B. second
15. Q. Kt. takes B.
16. K. R. to K. square (a)
17. Q. to Q. B. third
18. P. takes P.
19. Q. takes Q.
20. Kt. to K. R. second
21. Q. R. to Q. Kt. square
22. B. to K. B. square (b)
23. K. R. to Q. square
24. R. takes R.
25. R. to Q. B. square
26. R. to Q. B. second (c)
27. Kt. takes Kt.
28. R. takes R.
29. Kt. to K. third
30. P. to K. Kt. third
31. Kt. to Q. square
32. Kt. to Q. B. third
33. P. to Q. Kt. fourth
34. P. takes P.
35. K. to B. square
36. K. to K. square
37. K. to Q. second
38. Kt. to Q. square
39. P. takes P.
40. P. to K. R. fourth

White	Black
41. B. to Q. Kt. sixth	41. Kt. to Q. Kt. second
42. P. to K. sixth (check)	42. P. takes P.
43. P. takes P. (check)	43. K. to K. second
44. K. to Q. B. sixth	44. Kt. to Q. square (check)
45. B. takes Kt. (check)	45. K. takes B.
46. K. to Q. sixth	46. K. to K. square
47. P. to K. seventh	

And Mr. Seguin gave in.

Notes.

(a) To this point the game is very finely played by Black, and if, instead of this move, Black had played "P. to Q. Kt. fourth," we should have decidedly preferred Black's position.

(b) To play the Rook on the Queen's side next move.

(c) Black ought to have played "B. to K. second," and with proper care the game would have been drawn.

Game played in 1853, between Herr FALKBEER and Mr. JANSSENS.

White. (Herr FALKBEER.)	*Black.* (Mr. JANSSENS.)
1. P. to K. fourth	1. P. to Q. B. fourth
2. P. to Q. fourth	2. P. takes P.
3. Kt. to K. B. third	3. P. to K. fourth
4. B. to Q. B. fourth	4. Kt. to Q. B. third
5. P. to Q. B. third	5. Q. to Q. Kt. third
6. Castles	6. B. to K. second
7. P. takes P.	7. P. takes P.
8. P. to K. fifth	8. P. to K. R. third (a)
9. Q. Kt. to Q. second	9. B. to Q. B. fourth
10. Kt. to K. fourth	10. K. Kt. to K. second
11. Kt. to Q. sixth (check)	11. B. takes Kt.
12. P. takes B.	12. Kt. to K. Kt. third
13. Q. to K. second (check)	13. K. to K. B. square
14. R. to K. square	14. Q. to Q. square
15. B. to Q. second	15. K. to Kt. square
16. P. to K. R. fourth	16. Kt. to K. B. square
17. Q. to K. eighth	17. Q. takes Q. (b)
18. R. takes Q.	18. P. to K. Kt. third (c)
19. Q. R. to K. square	19. K. to Kt. second

20. Q. R. to K. seventh	20. Kt. to K. third (d)
21. R. takes R.	21. K. takes R.
22. R. takes P.	22. K. to Kt. square
23. B. takes Kt.	23. P. takes B.
24. R. to Q. B. seventh	

And wins.

Notes.

(a) This is evidently a useless move; "B. to Q. square" would have been better.

(b) This was an inconsiderate move; Black has to this point of the game cleverly defended the skilful attack of his opponent, and could have escaped with loss of a Pawn by playing "Q. to K. B. third."

(c) It would have been better to give up at once the K. B. P.

(d) All efforts are too late now; White's skilful manœuvres have carried the day.

Games played in 1853, in a match between Messrs. KENNY and JANSSENS.

White. (Mr. KENNY.)	*Black.* (Mr. JANSSENS.)
1. P. to K. fourth	1. P. to K. third
2. P. to Q. fourth	2. P. to Q. fourth
3. P. takes P.	3. P. takes P.
4. B. to Q. third	4 P. to Q. B. fourth
5. P. takes P.	5. B. takes P.
6. Kt. to K. B. third	6. Kt. to K. B. third
7. Castles	7. Castles
8. P. to K. R. third	8. Kt. to Q. B. third
9. Kt. to Q. B. third	9. P. to K. R. third
10. P. to Q. R. third	10. B. to K.˙third
11. P. to Q. Kt. fourth	11. B. to Q. third
12. B. to Q. Kt. second	12. R. to Q. B. square
13. Kt. to K. second	13. Kt. to K. fifth
14. Kt. to Q. second	14. P. to K. B. fourth
15. Kt. to Q. fourth	15. Kt. takes Kt.
16. B. takes Kt.	16. Kt. takes Kt. (a)
17. Q. takes Kt.	17. P. to K. B. fifth
18. Q. to K. second	18. B. to Q. second
19. Q. to K. R. fifth	19. Q. to K. Kt. fourth

12

20. Q. takes Q.	20. P. takes Q.
21. B. takes Q. R. P. (b)	21. P. to K. B. sixth
22. B. to K. third (c)	22. P. to K. Kt. fifth
23. R. P. takes P.	23. B. takes P.
24. K. R. to Q. B. square	24. K. to B. second
25. P. takes P. (d)	25. B. takes P.
26. K. to B. square	26. R. to K. R. square
27. K. to K. square	27. B. to K. fourth
28. Q. R. to Kt. square	

And Black mates in three moves.

Notes.

(a) "Q. to K. R. fifth," we believe, would have been a stronger move.

(b) A bad move; as Black could not have obtained so formidable an attack if White had made the obvious move, "P. to K. B. third."

(c) Another weak move; "B. to Q. fourth" would have been better, or "Q. R. to K. square."

(d) This settles White's fate. Why not play "B. to Q. fourth," and then "P. to Q. B. fourth"?

Between the same Players.

White. (Mr. KENNY.)	*Black.* (Mr. JANSSENS.)
1. P. to K. fourth	1. P. to K. fourth
2. Kt. to K. B. third	2. Kt. to Q. B. third
3. P. to Q. B. third	3. Kt. to K. B. third
4. P. to Q. fourth	4. P. to Q. fourth (a)
5. B. to Q. Kt. fifth	5. K. Kt. takes P.
6. Kt. takes P.	6. B. to Q. second
7. B. takes Kt.	7. P. takes B.
8. Q. to K. second	8. B. to K. second
9. Castles	9. Castles
10. Kt. to Q. second	10. P. to K. B. fourth
11. R. to K. square	11. P. to Q. B. fourth (b)
12. P. to K. B. third	12. Kt. takes Kt.
13. Kt. takes B.	13. R. to K. square (c)
14. Q. to K. sixth (check)	14. K. to R. square
15. Kt. to K. fifth	15. Kt. takes P. (check)
16. P. takes Kt.	16. R. to B. square
17. Kt. to K. B. seventh (check)	17. R. takes Kt.
18. Q. takes R.	

And wins.

Notes.

(a) This gives Black at once a disadvantage; Black ought to have played now "P. takes P."

(b) "B. to K. third" was the move.

(c) A very bad move, which loses Black the game at once.

The following well-contested Game was played in 1854, in a match between Messrs. JANSSENS and V. GREEN.

White. (Mr. JANSSENS.)	Black. (Mr. V. GREEN.)
1. P. to K. fourth	1. P. to K. third
2. Kt. to K. B. third	2. P. to Q. fourth
3. P. takes P.	3. P. takes P.
4. P. to Q. fourth	4. Kt. to K. B. third
5. P. to Q. B. fourth	5. B. to Q. Kt. fifth (check)
6. Kt. to Q. B. third	6. Kt. to Q. B. third
7. P. to Q. R. third	7. B. takes Kt. (check)
8. P. takes B.	8. B. to K. third
9. P. takes P.	9. B. takes P.
10. B. to Q. Kt. fifth	10. Castles
11. Castles	11. Kt. to K. second
12. Kt. to K. fifth (a)	12. B. takes K. Kt. P.
13. K. takes B.	13. Q. to Q. fourth (check)
14. Q. to K. B. third	14. Q. takes B.
15. B. to K. Kt. fifth	15. Q. to Q. fourth (b)
16. Q. R. to Q. Kt. square	16. P. to Q. Kt. third
17. B. takes Kt.	17. P. takes B.
18. Kt. to K. Kt. fourth	18. Q. takes Q.
19. K. takes Q.	19. K. to Kt. second
20. R. to K. Kt. square	20. Kt. to K. Kt. third
21. Kt. to K. third	21. K. R. to K. square
22. R. to Q. Kt. fifth	22. R. to K. third
23. P. to K. R. fourth (c)	23. K. to R. square
24. R. to K. Kt. fourth	24. P. to Q. B. third
25. R. to Q. Kt. square	25. P. to K. R. fourth
26. K. R. to K. Kt. square	26. Kt. takes K. R. P. (check)
27. K. to Kt. third	27. R. to K. fifth
28. P. to K. B. fourth	28. R. takes Kt.
29. K. takes Kt.	29. R. takes K. B. P.

30. Q. R. to Q. B. square	30. R. takes R.
31. R. takes R.	31. K. to K. Kt. second
32. R, to K. Kt. square (check)	32. K. to K. R. third
33. R. to K. B. square	33. R. to K. Kt. square
34. R. takes B. P. (check)	34. R. to K. Kt. third
35. R. takes B. P.	

And the game was given up as drawn.

Notes.

(a) "Bishop to Q. third" would have been the proper move.
(b) This was very well played, as it is the only move to keep the Pawn.
(c) "P. to K. R. fifth" would have been a stronger move, as it would have given White the advantage of position.

Game played in 1842, between Mr. BUCKLE and Mr. ZYTOGORSKI.

White. (Mr. ZYTOGORSKI.)   *Black.* (Mr. BUCKLE.)

1. P. to K. fourth	1. P. to K. fourth
2. P. to K. B. fourth	2. P. takes P.
3. Kt. to K. B. third	3. P. to K. Kt. fourth
4. B. to Q. B. fourth	4. B. to K. Kt. second
5. P. to Q. fourth	5. P. to K. R. third
6. P. to Q. B. third	6. P. to Q. third
7. Castles	7. P. to Q. B. third
8. P. to K. Kt. third	8. P. to K. Kt. fifth
9. Kt. to K. R. fourth	9. P. to K. B. sixth
10. Kt. to Q. second	10. Q. to Q. B. second (a)
11. Q. Kt. takes P.	11. P. takes Kt.
12. Q. takes P.	12. Kt. to K. B. third (b)
13. B. takes K. B. P. (check)	13. Q. takes B.
14. P. to K. fifth	14. B. to K. Kt. fifth
15. Q. to K. B. second	15. B. to K. R. sixth
16. Kt. to K. Kt. second	16. B. takes Kt.
17. Q. takes B.	17. P. takes P.
18. P. takes P.	18. Q. to Q. fourth
19. P. takes Kt.	19. Q. takes Q.
20. K. takes Q.	20. B. to K. B. square
21. B. to K. B. fourth	21. K. to K. B. second
22. Q. R. to Q. square	22. P. to Q. Kt. third (c)
23. B. takes Kt.	23. R. takes B.

24. R. to Q. seventh (check)	24. K. to K. Kt. square
25. P. to K. B. seventh (check)	25. K. to K. Kt. second
26. R. takes P. (d)	26. P. to K. R. fourth
27. P. to K. R. third	27. R. to K. R. third
28. R. to K. B. fifth	28. R. to K. B. third
29. P. to K. Kt. fourth	29. P. takes P.
30. P. takes P.	30. K. to K. Kt. third
31. R. to Q. B. second	31. P. to Q. B. fourth
32. R. to K. B. third	32. B. to Q. third
33. R. to Q. seventh	33. B. to K. B. square
34. P. to Q. R. fourth (e)	34. R. to Q. R. square
35. R. to Q. Kt. seventh (f)	35. R. to K. third (g)
36. R. to K. B. fourth	36. B. to K. Kt. second
37. P. to Q. Kt. fourth	37. P. takes P.
38. P. takes P.	38. R. takes Q. R. P. (h)
39. P. to Q. B. eighth	39. B. takes P.
40. R. takes B.	40. R. takes Q. Kt. P.
41. K. to K. Kt. third	

And the game was, after a few moves, given up as drawn.

Notes.

(a) " P. to Q. fourth " would have been, we believe, a safer move.

(b) " B. to K. B. third " would have been preferable ; for if then B. had taken K. B. P., the Q. would have retaken it, and Black would have answered to White's pushing the Queen's Pawn by playing " B. to K. third," with the best game ; whilst, in the way it has been played, White has a formidable attack, and although Black has played the subsequent moves with great skill, and remains with a piece against two Pawns, we believe White, through his position, has, after the 20th move, the best of the game.

(c) It is evident Black could not take the P. without losing a piece. He plays this Pawn to be enabled to bring the Knight out without losing the Knight's Pawn.

(d) Black has evidently, and we think rightly, preferred to lose the Q. R. P. than the Q. Kt. P., having thus still two Pawns united.

(e) " P. to Q. R. third " would have been better ; we think, however, that after this move, the game was drawn by its nature.

(f) To ensure the drawn game ; for if Black R. takes P., White can make a drawn game by " R. takes R."

(g) To prevent the exchange of Rooks, and thus to protect the Kt.'s Pawn.

(h) Preferring to exchange three Pawns for the B., and thus draw the game at once.

Blindfold Game played in Antwerpen by Mr. JANSSENS against a Belgian Amateur.

White. (MR. JANSSENS.)	*Black.* (AMATEUR.)
1. P. to K. fourth	1. P. to K. fourth
2. P. to K. B. fourth	2. P. to Q. third
3. Kt. to K. B. third	3. P. takes P.
4. B. to Q. B. fourth	4. Kt. to K. B. third
5. Kt. to Q. B. third	5. B. to K. third
6. B. takes B.	6. P. takes B.
7. P. to Q. fourth	7. P. to Q. fourth
8. P. takes P.	8. B. takes P.
9. Castles	9. B. to K. second
10. B. takes P.	10. P. to Q. B. fourth
11. P. takes P.	11. B. takes P.
12. K. to R. square	12. Castles
13. B. to K. fifth	13. Q. to Kt. third
14. Kt. to Kt. fifth	14. Q. Kt. to Q. second
15. Q. Kt. takes P.	15. Kt. takes Kt.
16. Q. takes Kt. (check)	16. K. to R. square
17. Kt. to K. B. seventh (check)	17. K. to Kt. square
18. Kt. to R. sixth (check)	18. K. to R. square
19. Q. to K. Kt. eighth (check)	19. R. takes Q.
20. Kt. to B. seventh	

Check mate.

The following Game between Mr. DE RIVIERE and Mr. MORPHY is one of the five played simultaneously by Mr. MORPHY.

(Two Knights' Game.)

White. (MR. DE RIVIERE.)	*Black.* (MR. MORPHY.)
1. P. to K. fourth	1. P. to K. fourth
2. Kt. to K. B. third	2. Kt. to Q. B. third
3. B. to B. fourth	3. Kt. to B. third
4. Kt. to Kt. fifth	4. P. to Q. fourth
5. P. takes P.	5. Kt. to Q. B. fourth
6. P. to Q. third	6. P. to K. R. third
7. Kt. to K. B. third	7. P. to K. fifth
8. Q. to K. second	8. Kt. takes B.
9. P. takes Kt.	9. B. to Q. B. fourth

10. P. to K. R. third	10. Castles
11. Kt. to R. second	11. Kt. to R. second
12. Kt. to Q. B. third	12. P. to K. B. fourth
13. B. to K. third	13. B. to Q. Kt. fifth
14. Q. to Q. second	14. B. to Q. second
15. P. to K. Kt. third	15. Q. to K. second
16. P. to R. third	16. B. to Q. third
17. Kt. to K. second	17. P. to Q. Kt. fourth
18. P. takes P.	18. B. takes P.
19. Kt. to Q. fourth	19. B. to Q. B. fifth
20. Kt. to K. sixth	20. K. R. to K. square
21. Q. to Q. fourth	21. B. to Q. R. third
22. P. to Q. B. fourth	22. P. to B. fourth
23. Q. to B. third	23. B. to Q. B. square
24. Kt. to B. fourth	24. R. to Q. Kt. square
25. R. to Q. Kt. square	25. P. to Kt. fourth
26. Kt. to K. second	26. Kt. to B. square
27. P. to K. R. fourth	27. Kt. to Kt. third
28. P. takes P.	28. P. takes P.
29. Q. to Q. B. square	29. Kt. to K. fourth
30. B. takes Kt. P.	30. Kt. to Q. sixth (check)
31. K. to B. square	31. Q. to K. Kt. second
32. Q. to Q. second	32. Kt. takes Kt. P.
33. Q. to B. second	33. B. to R. third
34. B. to B. square	34. Kt. takes P.
35. Q. to R. fourth	35. Kt. to Q. seventh (check)
36. K. to Kt. second	36. Kt. takes R.
37. Q. takes B.	37. R. to Kt. third
38. Q. to R. fourth	38. K. R. to Kt. square
39. Kt. to K. B. square	39. B. to K. fourth
40. Kt. to K. third	40. P. to K. B. fifth
41. Kt. takes P.	41. B. takes Kt.
42. Kt. to B. fifth	42. Q. to K. B. second
43. B. takes B.	43. Q. takes Kt.
44. B. takes R.	44. R. takes B.
45. Q. takes R. P.	45. R. to K. B. square
46. Q. takes P.	46. Q. to B. sixth (check)
47. K. to Kt. square	47. Kt. to B. sixth

48. R. to R. fourth	48. Kt. to K. seventh (check)
49. K. to R. second	49. Q. takes B. P. (check)
50. Q. takes Q.	50. R. takes Q. (check)
51. K. to R. third	51. Kt. to Kt. eighth (check)
52. K. to Kt. fourth	52. P. to K. sixth
53. K. to R. fifth	53. P. to K. seventh
54. R. to K. fourth	54. R. to B. eighth

And wins.

A game played December, 1858, in a Pool, at the PHILIDORIAN CHESS ROOMS.

(Q. B. P. Game in the K. Kt. Opening.)

White (Mr. ZYTOGORSKI.)	*Black.* (Mr. BRIEN.)
1. P. to K. fourth	1. P. to K. fourth
2. Kt. to K. B. third	2. Kt. to Q. B. third
3. P. to Q. B. third (a)	3. K. Kt. to K. second (b)
4. B. to Q. Kt. fifth (c)	4. P. to Q. R. third
5. B. to Q. R. fourth	5. Kt. to K. Kt. third
6. P. to Q. fourth	6. P. takes P.
7. P. takes P.	7. B. to Q. Kt. fifth (check)
8. Kt. to Q. B. third	8. Kt. to K. R. fifth (d)
9. Kt. takes Kt.	9. Q. takes Kt.
10. Castles	10. B. takes Kt.
11. P. takes B.	11. Castles
12. P. to K. B. fourth	12. P. to K. B. fourth (e)
13. P. to K. fifth	13. P. to Q. Kt. fourth
14. B. to Q. Kt. third (check)	14. K. to K. R. square
15. R. to K. B. third	15. Kt. to Q. R. fourth (f)
16. B. to Q. fifth	16. P. to Q. B. third (g)
17. R. to K. R. third	17. Q. to K. Kt. fifth (h)
18. B. to K. B. third	18. Q. to K. Kt. third
19. B. to Q. R. third	19. R. to K. Kt. square
20. P. to Q. fifth (i)	20. Q. to K. square
21. B. to K. R. fifth	21. P. to K. Kt. third
22. B. to K. B. third	22. Kt. to Q. B. fifth (k)
23. B. to Q. B. fifth	23. Kt. to Q. Kt. seventh
24. Q. to K. square (l)	24. Kt. to Q. sixth
25. Q. to K. R. fourth	25. R. to K. Kt. second (m)

26. B. to Q. fourth (*n*)
27. B. to K. third
28. Q. to K. R. fifth (*p*)
29. R. takes Q.
30. B. to K. second
31. R. takes P. at K. B. fifth
32. B. takes K. B. P.
33. R. to K. B. sixth
34. B. to K. B. third (*r*)
35. B. to K. Kt. fifth
36. P. to K. R. fourth
37. B. to K. R. fifth
38. B. takes Kt.
39. R. to K. B. fourth
40. Q. R. to K. square
41. Q. R. to K. eighth
42. P. to Q. R. fourth
43. K. R. takes P.
44. R. to K. B. fourth
45. R. to K. seventh (check) (*s*)
46. B. takes R.
47. P. to K. Kt. fourth
48. R. takes P. (check)
49. B. to Q. eighth
50. R. to K. B. fourth (check)
51. R. takes R. (check)
52. B. to K. Kt. fifth
53. B. to Q. B. square
54. B. to Q. Kt. second
55. K. to K. B. second
56. K. to K. third
57. K. to Q. second
58. K. to Q. B. square
59. B. to Q. R. square
60. K. to Q. Kt. second
61. K. to Q. B. square
62. B. to Q. Kt. second (*u*)

26. P. to Q. B. fourth
27. P. to K. Kt. fourth (*o*)
28. Q. takes Q.
29. P. takes P.
30. Kt. takes P.
31. Kt. to K. Kt. third (*q*)
32. P. to Q. third
33. R. to K. second
34. K. to K. Kt. second
35. R. to K. fourth
36. P. to K. R. third
37. Kt. takes P.
38. R. takes B.
39. R. takes P.
40. R. to Q. R. second
41. B. to K. B. fourth
42. P. takes P.
43. P. to K. R. fourth
44. P. to Q. R. fourth
45. R. takes R.
46. B. to Q. B. seventh
47. P. takes P.
48. K. to K. B. second
49. P. to Q. R. fifth
50. R. to K. B. fourth (*t*)
51. B. takes R.
52. P. to Q. R. sixth
53. P. to Q. R. seventh
54. P. to Q. B. fifth
55. K. to K. third
56. K. to Q. fourth
57. K. to Q. B. fourth
58. K. to Q. Kt. fourth
59. K. to Q. R. fifth
60. B. to Q. Kt. eighth
61. K. to Q. Kt. sixth
62. P. to Q. R. eighth
    (becoming a Q. (check))

63. B. takes Q.	63. K. to Q. R. seventh
64. B. to Q. Kt. second	64. B. to K. fifth

And wins.

Notes.

(*a*) The best illustrations of this fine attack will be found in the CHESS PLAYER'S CHRONICLE of 1847, 1854, and 1855.

(*b*) "K. Kt. to K. B. third" seems to afford the best defence to the second player. This subject has been discussed previously in the CHESS PLAYER'S CHRONICLE of 1855.

(*c*) This brings about a variation of the Lopez' Knight's Game, the third and fourth moves of White being transposed.

(*d*) The defence invented in this opening will not, we believe, bear the test of analysis; for, although it arrests the progress of some of White's Pieces, it leaves the hostile Pawns in a menacing position.

(*e*) The confinement of Black's Pieces on the Q. side renders it hardly possible for him to forbear from making some dangerous move.

(*f*) White having in reserve his 17th move, this counter-attack is unavailing.

(*g*) "B. to Q. Kt. second" would have been better, but his game would, notwithstanding, have been inferior to that of his adversary.

(*h*) The only move; for, had the Queen retreated, mate would have followed.

(*i*) This is more effective than "B. to K. R. fifth" at once would be.

(*k*) The advance of the Knight is clearly a resource inspired by desperation. No other move could have held Black out even the faintest hopes of extrication.

(*l*) "Q. to Q. second" would have left Black nothing to do but to retreat. The move in the text, however, is not so bad in its merits as the result would appear to prove.

(*m*) He could not have played "Q. to K. B. second" on account of "B. to K. seventh."

(*n*) Not so good as "B. to K. third."

(*o*) The supplementary move to the manœuvres of the Knight. It could however, as we have noticed incidentally in the previous remarks, have been prevented.

(*p*) Having been taken by surprise, White does not here adopt his best line of play. He should have overcome his reluctance to break up his Pawns in the centre, and should have taken Pawn with Pawn. A leading variation thereupon is:—

28. P. takes P.	28. Q. takes P.
29. B. to K. second	29. P. to K. B. fifth
30. B. takes Kt.	30. P. takes B.

31. B. takes K. R. P., with the best game; for, if Black now take K. Kt. Pawn with Queen, White can exchange Queens, and win the advanced Pawn.

(*q*) In order to render the capture of his K. B. Pawn dangerous.

(*r*) "B. to Q. third" would have been stronger.

(*s*) Perhaps "R. to Q. R. fourth" would be safer.

(*t*) This was injudicious. He should have kept his Rook on the board, to make sure of victory.

(*u*) The mistake that loses the game, which would have been drawn if he had played "K. to Q. square"; for White could obtain no advantage by the sacrifice of his Queen's Pawn.

Game played between the late HANSTEIN and HEYDEBRANDT VON DER LASA.

White. (Mr. HANSTEIN.)	Black. (Von der LASA.)
1. P. to K. fourth	1. P. to K. fourth
2. P. to K. B. fourth	2. P. takes P.
3. Kt. to K. B. third	3. P. to K. Kt. fourth
4. B. to Q. B. fourth	4. B. to K. Kt. second
5. P. to K. R. fourth	5. P. to K. R. third
6. P. to Q. fourth	6. P. to Q. third
7. P. to Q. B. third	7. P. to K. Kt. fifth (a)
8. Q. B. takes P. (b)	8. P. takes Kt.
9. Q. takes P.	9. B. to K. third
10. Kt. to Q. second	10. Kt. to K. second
11. P. to Q. fifth (c)	11. B. to Q. B. square
12. Castles on Q. side	12. P. to K. R. fourth
13. Q. R. to K. B. square	13. B. to K. Kt. fifth
14. Q. to K. B. second	14. Castles
15. Kt. to K. B. third	15. Kt. to K. Kt. third
16. B. to K. third	16. Q. Kt. to Q. second
17. Kt. to K. R. second	17. Q. Kt. to K. fourth
18. B. to K. second	18. P. to K. B. fourth
19. B. to K. Kt. fifth	19. Q. to Q. second
20. Q. to K. third	20. Q. R. to K. square
21. B. takes B.	21. Kt. takes B.
22. Kt. takes Kt.	22. R. takes P.
23. Q. to Q. third	23. R. takes Kt.
24. R. to K. B. second	24. Kt. to K. fourth
25. Q. to Q. second	25. Q. to Q. Kt. fourth
26. K. to Q. Kt. square	26. Q. to K. sixth (check)

And wins.

Notes.

(a) Bledow was the first who introduced the advance of the K. Kt. P. at this stage of the game, and it gives the second player a very strong game.

(b) Hanstein generally used to make this move at this juncture, but sometimes he also played " Q. to her Kt. third."

(c) This move was decidedly disadvantageous for White.

PROBLEMS FOR YOUNG PLAYERS.

No. 3.   By J. W. Abbott, *of Southampton.*

White.	*Black.*
K. at K. sixth	K. at Q. B. third
Rs. at Q. fifth and Q. Kt. square	R. at Q. Kt. second
Kt. at K. B. fifth	Kt. at Q. B. sixth
B. at K. R. seventh	B. at Q. third
P. at Q. fourth	Ps. at Q. B. second, and Q. B. fourth

White to mate in four moves.

No. 4.   By Mr. Edwin Geake.

White.	*Black.*
K. at Q. B. fourth	K. at K. fourth
Q. at K. R. square	Q. at K. B. second
B. at Q. Kt. fifth	R. at K. B. third
Kts. at K. eighth and K. B. eighth	Kt. at Q. sixth
Bs. at K. R. fourth and Q. fifth	Bs. at Q. R. sixth and K. Kt. fifth
Ps. at Q. Kt. seventh, K. B. sixth,	Ps. at K. second, K. Kt. second,
K. fourth and K. third	K. R. fourth

White to mate in three moves.

No. 5.   By Mr. Edwin Geake.

White.	*Black.*
K. at Q. R. second	K. at K. Kt. fifth
Q. at K. Kt. fourth	Q. at K. R. third
Kt. at Q. fifth	Kt. at K. Kt. eighth
B. at Q. B. eighth	Ps. at K. B. seventh, Q. B. fourth,
P. at Q. R. third	Q. Kt. third, and Q. R. fourth

White to mate in three moves.

SOLUTIONS TO PROBLEMS.

No. 17.   *Page* 159.

White.

K. to Q. Kt. fifth, and next move B. or Kt. mates.

No. 18.   *Page* 159.

Q. to Q. sixth (check), and next move Q. or Kt. mates.

No. 19. *Page* 160.

White	Black
1. Kt. to K. Kt. sixth, taking R.	1. Q. takes Kt.
2. Kt. to K. Kt. fifth (disc. ch.)	2. K. moves
3. Kt. or B. mates	

(Var. A.)

	1. Q. to K. fourth
2. Kt. takes Q. (disc. check)	2. K. moves
3. Q. mates	

(Var. B.)

	1. Q. to K. B. second
2. Kt. to K square (disc. check)	2. Q. covers
3. B. mates	

(Var. C.)

	1. Kt. to K. fourth
2. Kt. takes Kt. (disc. check)	2. K. moves
3. Q. takes B. mate	

(Var. D.)

	1. Kt. to Q. fifth
2. Q. takes Kt. (check)	2. K. moves
3. Kt. mates	

(Var. E.)

	1. K. moves
2. Q. takes B. (check)	2. K. moves.
3. B. to K. Kt. fifth, mate	

No. 20. *Page* 160.

White.	*Black.*
1. P. takes P.	1. K. takes Kt. best
2. Q. to Q. R. square	2. R. takes R. best
3. Q. to Q. R. second, and next move the Q. or B. mates.	

SOLUTIONS TO PROBLEMS FOR YOUNG PLAYERS.

No. 1. *Page* 126.

White.	*Black.*
1. R. to Q. B. second	1. Kt. takes Kt.
2. R. takes R. (check)	2. P. takes R.
3. B. mates	

No. 2. *Page* 126.

White.	*Black.*
1. Kt. takes K. B. P. (check)	1. R. takes Kt.
2. B. to K. fifth (check)	2. R. takes B.
3. P. mates	

or,

	1. P. takes Kt.
2. B. to K. fifth (check)	2. K. moves
3. Kt. mates	

WEST YORKSHIRE CHESS ASSOCIATION.

The Fourth Annual Meeting of this Association was held at the Imperial Hotel, Huddersfield, on Saturday the 21st of May, and was perhaps the largest and most influential ever held in the county, as the following list of gentlemen who were present will show :—

Huddersfield.—Dr. Scott, vice-president of the West Yorkshire Chess Association. Mr. John Watkinson, secretary of the Association. Messrs. David Marsden, J. B. Wrigley, Louis Löwenthal, J. H. Hebblethwaite, D. Boscovitz, F. Liebreich, John Dodds, William Marriott, C. Atkinson, D. A. Cooper, C. Pritchett, J. Eastwood, T. Parratt, Walter Parratt, G. Brook, jun., J. Burgess, B. Bradley, J. R. Robinson, A. Campbell, M. R. Webb, Richard Hinchliff, J. Gibson, W. G. Dyson, J. Holroyd, E. Barlow, J. Marsden. *Bradford*—Messrs. R. Milligan, jun., M. E. Werner, B. Broughton, C. Noerdlinger, F. Landolphe, J. Smith, Mark Dawson, H. Ammelburg, R. Levig, Andrew Frinichs, G. Leunfert, W. S. Anson, and P. Cheadle. *Halifax*—Dr. Alexander, Messrs. J. Farrar, Jonathan C. Wainhouse, Thomas A. Brierly, F. A. Leyland, W. Fleming, W. H. Scott, D. R. Edgar, and T. D. Swallow. *Leeds*—Rev. W. Thorold, Messrs. R. Cadman, Jerome Reunert, W. Greenwood, E. Stark, Bradley Clay, W. C. Myers, and W. Mann. *Wakefield*—Mr. E. Shepherd, president of the Wakefield Club; Messrs. J. W. Young, W. H. B. Tomlinson, J. Oakes, W. H. Pearson, Arthur Cavy, C. S. Bennett, and W. L. Robinson. *Sheffield*—Messrs. C. Birchall and E. Thorold. *Holmfirth*—Mr. Joshua Moorhouse, J. P.; Messrs. T. Barber, and Brook Beardsell. *Morley*—W. Ellis. *Brighouse*—Dr. Lundy.

A Tournament by the following gentlemen was played—Mr. J. S. Kipping *v.* Mr. Werner; Mr. R. Cadman *v.* Mr. W. Parratt; Mr. E. Thorold *v.* Mr. Young; Mr. Birchall *v.* Mr. Reunert; the winners of the first bout were Messrs. Kipping, Parratt, Thorold, and Birchall; these were again paired—Thorold *v.* Parratt; Kipping *v.* Birchall; in this bout, Messrs. Thorold and Kipping were victorious; these gentlemen had to play to decide who was to be the hero of the day; a fine game—protracted to near midnight, but which ended in a draw by mutual consent—was the result; the deciding game will be played at Manchester, in a few weeks.

Herr Horwitz played six games, simultaneously, with Messrs. Werner, Cadman, Young, Davy, Parratt, and Robinson, winning five out of the six—Mr. Young, of Wakefield, being the winner at the sixth board.

At six P.M. the company, to the number of seventy-six, adjourned to a most substantial tea, served in the usual "imperial style" of Mr. Bradley.

Dr. Scott, in the absence of W. Wyvill, Esq., M.P., took the chair. Bradford was unanimously chosen as the place of meeting for 1860, and a vote of thanks was carried by acclamation to the chairman and the secretary, for the admirable character of the arrangements, and the general success of the gathering. The Association then resumed their play, the interest of the meeting increasing as it proceeded, and the gentlemen separated by the expression of a hope that the Bradford meeting next year may be equally successful.—*Abridged from the Huddersfield Chronicle.*

No. 21. Problem from an Arabic MS. in the Brit. Mus., No. 7515, f. 61 *b*, given to the Editor by Professor DUNCAN FORBES, LL.D.

BLACK.

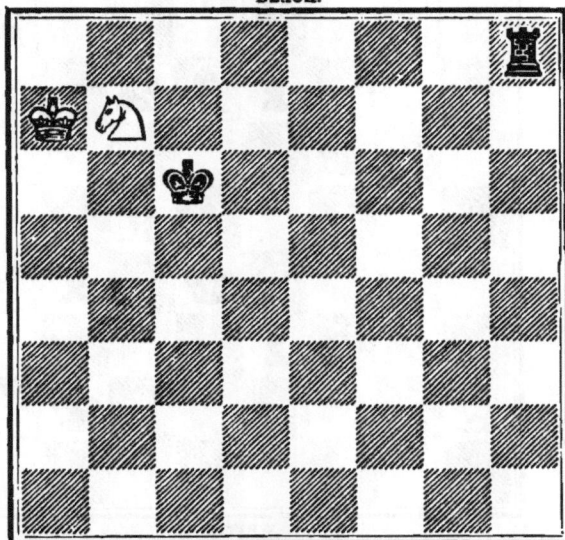

WHITE.

White to move and Black to win.

No. 22. Problem by Mr. EDWIN GEAKE.

BLACK.

WHITE.

White to mate in three moves.

No. 23.   Problem by Mr. EDWIN GEAKE.

BLACK.

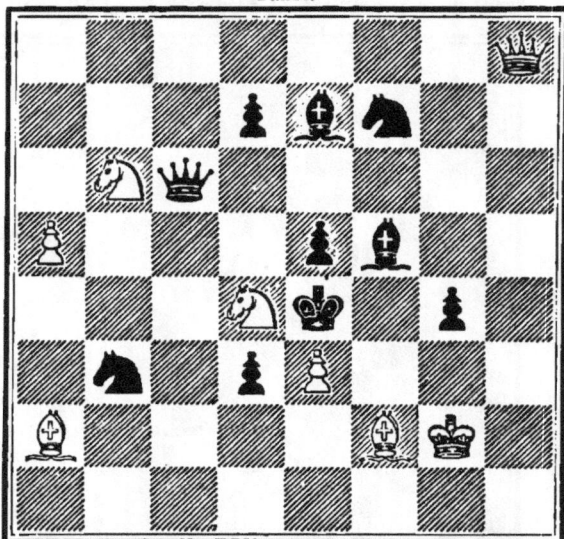

WHITE.

White to mate in three moves.

———

No. 24.   Problem by J. W. ABBOTT, Esq., of Southampton.

BLACK.

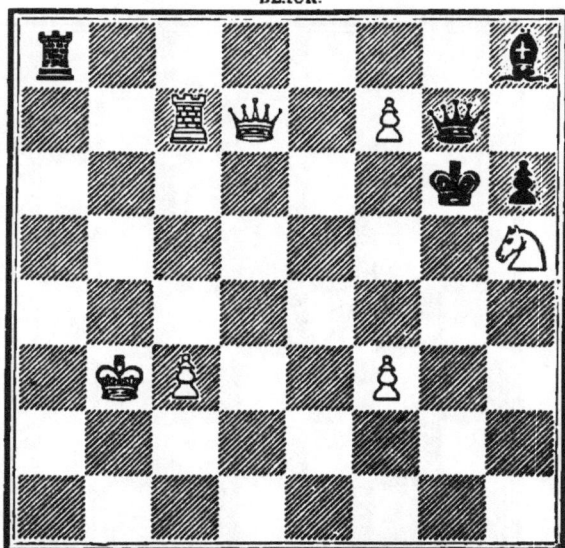

WHITE.

White to play and mate in four moves.

THE CHAMPIONSHIP OF ENGLAND.

THERE is probably not one of our readers to whom the question has not been addressed over and over again, " Who is the strongest player in England?" We, at least, have had this question hundreds of times addressed to us, but of late we found it next to impossible to give a satisfactory answer. And why not? We can only answer with the child, "Because we did not know." Nor do we believe that there is one person in England who does know. For in our capacity of Chess Editor we have had ample occasion to judge of the games that have been played, and, moreover, are personally acquainted and have played with almost all the strong players of the United Kingdom, and still could come to no satisfactory conclusion. Chess players can claim no immunity from the common weaknesses of mankind—nay, it seems that they possess some of them in a more than average degree. It is one of these foibles, which it would be useless to name, that makes our Chess writers so chary on the subject of championship. We, also, had some scruples of treating the question ; but finding ourselves at the present moment in a philosophical mood, we have boldly ventured into the subject, and, at the risk of hurting susceptibilities, shall freely discuss the matter.

England had its more than share of great men in almost every branch, and former centuries could boast of its statesmen, generals, poets, philosophers, historians, &c., but not of Chess players. Italy, Spain, Greece, France, Germany, even Arabia, had their renowned Chess champions, whilst Chess in England was but a blank. Albion's soil was not congenial then to the seed of Chess, which but slowly germinated, and only arrived to full bloom in the nineteenth century.

The history of Chess in England, therefore, begins only with the present century, and so does its Chess literature. But already many pages are chronicled in its history, and its literature has already taken rank amongst the first. It is in the present century only that the unwonted spectacle of an English Chess Champion could be presented to the world. Mr. LEWIS, the well-known Chess writer, was, to all purposes, the first champion of England ; he was acknowledged the best Chess player by all contemporary players, and broke a lance with the then champion of France, the renowned DESCHAPEL ; but his reign was but short, for he abdicated in favour of a younger player, nearly at the same time and in the same way as DESCHAPEL did in France.

13

MACDONNELL succeeded LEWIS in England; DE LA BOURDONNAIS,
DESCHAPEL in France. The champion of France and the champion of
England were now incontestably the two greatest living and practising
players. No third could compete with them; it was natural they should
wish to measure swords with each other, and fight for the championship
of the world. They met, and glorious was the contest: the son of
Britannia, beaten but not conquered, again and again took the field,
and the ultimate victory was still doubtful, when the unrelenting hand
of the great destroyer made an end to the game. The great champion
of France, as if despairing ever again to find a worthy adversary, soon
followed him to the grave.. France and England both, had lost their
champion; in both countries the ex-champions were still alive, and
could therefore resume the belt—but they did not. There was as hort
interregnum.

It is often a thankless task to be the successor of a great man, and
so in this case nobody seemed in a hurry to step into the vacant office.
In England, Mr. POPERT, a German by birth, was considered the best
player; in France St. AMAND, whom LA BOURDONNAIS considered his
most promising pupil, was fighting his way to eminence, and finally
succeeded to the championship. In 1841 a young player, HOWARD
STAUNTON, having encountered many English players with great success,
challenged Mr. POPERT to play a match, the winner of the first eleven
games to be the victor. Mr. POPERT accepted, and after one of the
hardest and best-contested fights on record, Mr. STAUNTON won by the
odd game. There was again a champion of England! It was the third
the country could boast of. Again the rival champions met—but this
time with different success. The Englishman was the conqueror; the
victory was complete; France has not recovered from the blow since.
But alas! it was also the last of England's victories on the chequered
field. Having conquered the French champion, and there being no
other champion in the field at the time, the English champion was considered the champion of the world. His reign was uncontested till
1851, when the great Chess Tournament took place. It was generally
expected that this tournament would proclaim the English champion to
the world as holding the sceptre of Chess, but it turned out differently.
The newly elected German champion, ANDERSSEN, carried all before
him, and the English champion, from causes, which it were useless to
enumerate here, underwent a complete defeat. The defeat of Mr.

STAUNTON by a foreigner did not deprive him of his right to the championship of England—especially as he announced his determination of challenging all the world, and did issue a challenge at the Manchester meeting, which, however, was not responded to at the time. Mr. STAUNTON being still considered the champion of England, was also probably the reason that Mr. MORPHY addressed his challenge exclusively to him. Mr. STAUNTON, after wavering for some time, finally declined the challenge, and thus, by this act, abdicated the championship. Since 1851, Mr. STAUNTON's championship was only nominal : he enjoyed his *otium cum dignitate*, which may do very well for the champion of England, who just twenty-one years ago, made his last official appearance, but will not do for a Chess champion who is daily open to challenge : an inconvenience, certainly, to which every one does not like to submit, and on account of which LEWIS and DESCHAPEL resigned their belts.

The Chess championship of England is therefore vacant. Messrs. LEWIS and STAUNTON are both ex-champions, and fully entitled to the respect and gratitude of all Chess players for the many services they have rendered to the cause of Chess, but neither of them is entitled to claim the actual championship, unless they fight anew for it. Now, the question will obtrude itself to every one, " Why, among so many fine players of which England can justly boast, there is no candidate for the championship ?" The answer is simply this :—It is on account of one of the foibles inherent to English Chess players : Greek does not like to meet Greek ; strong players scarcely ever play together. We do not wish to be personal, but we could mention several of our Chess grandees who systematically shun what they call strong play—that is, meeting a player of equal strength. Thus it was that Mr. MORPHY met with so little resistance in England.

France is in this respect not a bit more fortunate ; for in France, also, the championship is vacant. We wish for our own sake a champion to France, for we are sure that Englishmen would not withstand a challenge from a French champion.

We hope that Mr. MORPHY, should he again visit England, will find her endowed with a champion ready to take the field against any comer ; and to obtain this result, we appeal to all strong Chess players to join in matches and tournaments, and to patronize them on all occasions, and not allow of MORPHY to be said in future,

> Tantum illa inter alias caput extulit urbes
> Quantum lenta solent inter viburna cupressi.

THE SEVEN AGES OF CHESS.—(*Continued from p.* 166.)

V.   CHESS IN MIDDLE AGE.

YEARS have elapsed : their course has brought
The rich rewards of toil-worn life ;
Rewards beyond my utmost thought,
Peace, plenty, and a charming wife.

Here, as I sit in villa'd ease,
With marks of skill and taste around
(Taste, all my wife's—such things as these
I pass to tread on higher ground),

My eye regaled with objects rare
(These wealth may purchase without blame),
I still find nothing half so fair
As Julia, at her favourite game.

For nightly is the Chess-board brought,
A " Staunton," and we play for love ;
·Poor Julia's face is full of thought,
(Of course I give her *pawn and move*).

So sits she now : our eldest boy ;
Bold champion of his mother's fame,
Stands by her side, in fear and joy,
Watching the progress of the game.

And I, how can I view that pair—
So like, so loved—nor feel elated !
Alas ! Tom jumps upon the chair,
To shout HURRAH ! PAPA'S CHECKMATED !

WEST YORKSHIRE CHESS ASSOCIATION.

THE Game between the Rev. W. THOROLD and Mr. KIPPING having
resulted in a draw, as reported in our last Number, these gentlemen
met at Manchester on June 23rd, and agreed that the result should
turn on the best of three Games. The score at the termination was as
follows :—Rev. W. THOROLD, 2 ; Mr. KIPPING, 1 ; Drawn, 1.

ERRATA IN LAST NUMBER.

In Problem No. 22, the Pawn on Black's K. Kt. sixth, should be a Black
Pawn.

In Problem No. 24, the Black Rook should be on King's Bishop's square,
and not on Queen's Rook's square.

Game between Herr HARRWITZ and Mr. F. HEALEY (Herr HARR-
WITZ giving Pawn and Move), played at the PHILIDORIAN CHESS
ROOMS, June 24th, 1859.

(*Remove White's K. B. P.*)

Black. (Mr. F. HEALEY.)	White. (Herr HARRWITZ.)
1. P. to K. fourth	1. Q. Kt. to B. third
2. P. to Q. fourth	2. P. to K. fourth
3. P. to K. B. fourth	3. P. takes Q. P.
4. P. to K. fifth	4. P. to Q. fourth
5. B. to Q. third	5. Kt. to K. R. third
6. Kt. to K. B. third (*a*)	6. B. to K. second
7. Castles	7. Castles
8. P. to Q. B. third	8. P. takes P.
9. Kt. takes P.	9. B. to K. third
10. Q. to Q. B. second	10. B. to K. B. fourth
11. B. takes B.	11. Kt. takes B.
12. P. to K. Kt. fourth	12. B. to Q. B. fourth (check)
13. K. to R. square	13. K. Kt. to Q. fifth
14. Kt. takes Kt.	14. B. takes Kt.
15. Q. to Kt. second	15. Kt. to K. second
16. Kt. to Kt. fifth	16. B. to Kt. third
17. P. to Q. Kt. third	17. Q. to Q. second
18. B. to R. third	18. Q. R. to K. square
19. Kt. to Q. B. third	19. P. to Q. B. fourth
20. P. to Q. Kt. fourth	20. P. to Q. B. fifth
21. P. to Q. Kt. fifth	21. P. to Q. fifth
22. Q. R. to Q. square	22. Q. to K. third
23. Kt. to K. fourth	23. Kt. to Q. fourth
24. Kt. to K. Kt. fifth	24. Q. to Q. second
25. B. takes R.	25. R. takes B.
26. Q. to K. fourth	26. P. to Kt. third
27. P. to B. fifth (*b*)	27. Kt. to B. sixth
28. Q. to Q. B. second	28. Q. to Q. fourth (check)
29. R. covers	29. Kt. takes R.

And after a few moves Black resigned.

Notes.

(*a*) Q. checks was the proper move.
(*b*) "P. to K. sixth" would have won the game.

Game in the Match between Messrs. CAMPBELL and WORMALD.

White. (Mr. WORMALD.)	*Black*. (Mr. CAMPBELL.)
1. P. to K. fourth	1. P. to K. fourth
2. Kt. to K. B. third	2. Kt. to Q. B. third
3. B. to Q. Kt. fifth	3. P. to Q. R. third
4. B. to Q. R. fourth	4. Kt. to K. B. third
5. P. to Q. fourth	5. P. takes P.
6. P. to K. fifth	6. Kt. to K. fifth
7. Castles	7. B. to K. second
8. P. to Q. B. third (*a*)	8. P. takes P.
9. Kt. takes P.	9. Kt. takes Kt.
10. P. takes Kt.	10. Castles
11. R. to Q. third	11. P. to Q. third
12. B. to Q. B. second	12. P. to K. Kt. third
13. Q. to K. third	13. P. takes P.
14. Q. to K. R. sixth	14. B. to B. third
15. B. to K. Kt. fifth	15. B. to K. Kt. second
16. Q. to K. R. fourth	16. Q. to K. square
17. B. to K. third (*b*)	17. Q. to K. second
18. Q. to Kt. third	18. P. to K. B. fourth
19. Kt. to Kt. fifth	19. P. to K. B. fifth
20. B. to Q. Kt. third (check)	20. K. to R. square
21. Q. to K. R. fourth	21. P. to K. R. third
22. Kt. to K. B. third	22. P. takes B.
23. Q. to K. Kt. third	23. P. takes P. (check)
24. R. takes P.	24. B. to B. fourth
25. Kt. to R. fourth	25. Q. to K. Kt. fourth
26. R. takes B.	26. P. takes R.
27. Q. takes Q.	27. P. takes Q.
28. Kt. to Kt. sixth (check)	28. K. to R. second
29. Kt. takes R.	29. R. takes Kt.

And White resigned.

Notes.

(*a*) This must be wrong, for it loses a Pawn without sufficient advantage.

(*b*) Hasty move, which loses the game.

MATCH BETWEEN MR. MORPHY & HERR LOWENTHAL.

As the games of Mr. MORPHY are now the height of fashion in the Chess World, and all must submit more or less to her tyrannical sway, we have decided on publishing in the CHESS PLAYER'S CHRONICLE, all the Match Games, as well as the Blindfold Games, which Mr. MORPHY has played in Europe, so that our readers shall not be obliged to have recourse to other publications to find out the different openings and ways of conducting the attack and managing the defence, which Mr. MORPHY has brought into vogue by making use of them. We should have already, in former numbers, given a general review of Mr. MORPHY's games, but were prevented from doing so by the lack of some of them, and although we have, at the present moment, the entire collection, we have not had time to analyze them all. But in our December Number we shall give a complete review of the games, as well as of Mr. MORPHY's play in general.

The LÖWENTHAL and MORPHY series of games, of which we give the three first in the present number, is perhaps the most interesting; for, besides being the best contested, Herr LÖWENTHAL is, if we except Mr. MORPHY, the best living opening player, and our readers will find, that in the greater part of the parties Herr LÖWENTHAL had the advantage in the earlier part of the contest, nay, some of the games would have been easily won by a pawn-and-two-moves player, though they were lost by Herr LÖWENTHAL. If the Hungarian's nerves had been made of sterner stuff the contest might have been a serious one; as it is, the games are still very instructive on account of the openings, which were generally conducted by both players with the greatest skill.

GAME I.
(*Philidor's Defence.*)

White. (Herr LÖWENTHAL.)	*Black.* (Mr. MORPHY.)
1. P. to K. fourth	1. P. to K. fourth
2. K. Kt. to B. third	2. P. to Q. third (*a*)
3. P. to Q. fourth	3. K. P. takes P.
4. K. Kt. takes P.	4. K. Kt. to B. third
5. Q. Kt. to B. third	5. K. B. to K. second
6. K. B. to K. second (*b*)	6. Castles
7. Castles	7. P. to Q. B. fourth (*c*)
8. Kt. to K. B. third	8. Q. Kt. to B. third
9. Q. B. to K. B. fourth	9. Q. B. to K. third
10. Q. to Q. second	10. P. to Q. fourth
11. P. takes P.	11. K. Kt. takes P.

12. Q. R. to Q. square	12. K. Kt. takes Q. B.
13. Q. takes K. Kt.	13. Q. to Q. R. fourth
14. B. to Q. third	14. Q. R. to Q. square
15. K. Kt. to Kt. fifth	15. K. B. takes K. Kt.
16. Q. takes K. B.	16. P. to K. R. third
17. Q. to K. R. fourth	17. Kt. to Q. fifth
18. P. to Q. R. third	18. K. R. to K. square
19. K. R. to K. square	19. Q. to Kt. third
20. Kt. to Q. R. fourth	20. Q. to Q. R. fourth
21. Kt. to Q. B. third	21. P. to K. B. fourth
22. K. R. to K. fifth	22. B. to K. B. second
23. Q. R. to K. square	23. Q. to Kt. third
24. K. R. takes K. R. (check)	24. Q. R. takes K. R.
25. R. takes R. (check)	25. B. takes R.
26. Q. to K. seventh	26. B. to B. second
27. Kt. to Q. R. fourth	27. Q. to Q. R. fourth
28. Kt. takes Q. B. P.	28. Q. to Q. seventh
29. P. to K. B. third (d)	29. Kt. to Q. B. third
30. Q. to K. second	30. Q. to B. eighth (check)
31. K. to B. second	31. Q. takes Kt. P.
32. B. takes B. P.	32. Q. takes R. P.
33. Q. to Q. Kt. fifth	33. Q. to Q. B. sixth
34. Kt. to Q. Kt. third	34. Q. to K. B. third
35. Q. takes Q. Kt. P.	35. P. to K. Kt. third
36. Q. to Q. B. eighth (check)	36. K. to R. second
37. B. to Q. third	37. Kt. to K. fourth
38. Kt. to Q. second	38. Q. to R. fifth (check)
39. K. to B. square	39. Q. takes R. P.
40. Kt. to K. fourth	40. Q. to R. eighth (check)
41. K. to B. second	41. Q. to Q. B. eighth
42. Q. to Q. B. third	42. Q. to K. B. fifth
43. K. to K. second	43. P. to K. R. fourth
44. Kt. to K. B. second	44. P. to K. R. fifth
45. Q. to Q. second	45. Q. to K. Kt. sixth
46. Q. to K. third	46. P. to Q. R. fourth
47. Q. to K. fourth	47. B. to K. third
48. P. to K. B. fourth	48. Kt. takes B.
49. P. takes Kt.	49. B. to Kt. fifth (check)

50. K. to B. square	50. B. to K. B. fourth
51. Q. to K. seventh (check)	51. K. to R. third

And the game was drawn.

Notes.

(*a*) This is, we believe, the only game in which Mr. Morphy played Philidor's Defence. Fine play and deep combinations are wanting in this game.

(*b*) "B. to K. B. fourth" would have been stronger; the B. is now certainly not on his proper square.

(*c*) This move evidently weakens the Pawns on Queen's side.

(*d*) At this point, Mr. Löwenthal had probably a won game; he is a Pawn ahead, and has by far the best position: we only wonder how he could not see that by playing any of the three Pawns on King's side, the game was necessarily drawn. The move to win the game was "B. to K. B. square." We give here, the position, after the 28th move of Black, in a diagram, to enable our readers to make a study of it. In our next number we shall show how White could have won. Here Herr Löwenthal missed his first victory.

Position of the Game after Black's 28th move.

BLACK.

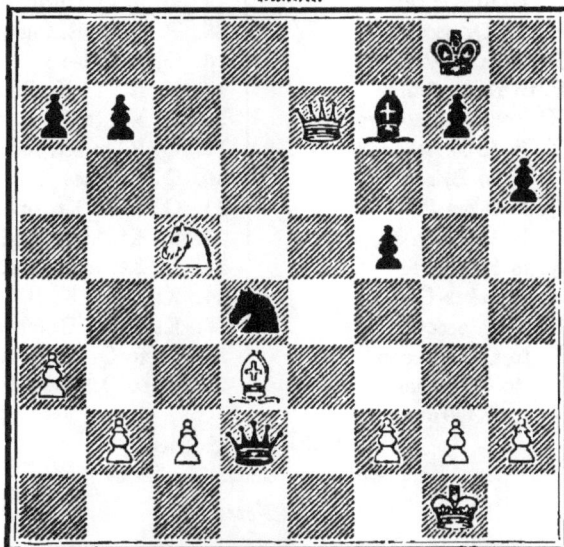

WHITE.
White to move.

13*

GAME II.

(*King's Gambit Refused.*)

White. (Mr. MORPHY.)	Black. (Herr LÖWENTHAL.)
1. P. to K. fourth	1. P. to K. fourth
2. P. to K. B. fourth	2. K. B. to Q. B. fourth
3. K. Kt. to B third	3. P. to Q. third
4. P. to Q. B. third	4. Q. B. to K. Kt. fifth
5. K. B. to Q. B. fourth	5. Q. B. takes Q. Kt.
6. Q. takes B.	6. K. Kt. to B. third
7. P. to Q. Kt. fourth	7. B. to Q. Kt. third
8. P. to Q. third	8. Q. Kt. to Q. second
9. P. to K. B. fifth (*a*)	9. Q. to K. second
10. P. to K. Kt. fourth	10. P. to K. R. third
11. K. to K. second (*b*)	11. P. to Q. B. third
12. P. to K. Kt. fifth	12. R. P. takes P.
13. Q. B. takes P.	13. P. to Q. fourth
14. K. B. to Kt. third (*c*)	14. Q. to Q. third
15. Kt. to Q. second	15. P. to Q. R. fourth
16. P. takes R. P.	16. Q. R. takes P.
17. P. to K. R. fourth	17. K. Kt. to K. R. fourth
18. Kt. to K. B. square	18. Q. Kt. to Q. B. fourth
19. K. R. to B. second	19. Q. R. to Kt. fourth (*d*)
20. Q. B. to B. square	20. Q. P. takes P.
21. Q. P. takes P.	21. Q. R. to Kt. seventh (*e*)
22. Q. B. takes Q. R.	22. K. Kt. to B. fifth (check)
23. K. to K. square	23. Q. Kt. to Q. sixth (check)
24. K. B. takes Q. Kt.	24. Kt. takes K. B. (check)
25. K. to Q. second	25. Kt. takes B. (check)
26. K. to Q. B. second	26. Q. to Q. R. sixth (*f*)
27. Kt. to Q. second	27. B. to Q. B. second (*g*)
28. Kt. to Kt. square	

And Black resigned.

Notes.

(*a*) Evidently a weak move.

(*b*) We do not see the necessity of this move.

(*c*) It is clear, we hope, to our readers, that White could not take the Queen's Pawn, on account of Black advancing the King's Pawn.

(*d*) " R. to Q. R. sixth," we believe would have won the game; we give the position here, in a diagram, after White's 19th move, and shall give in our next number the complete analysis.

(*e*) A false combination.

(*f*) " Kt. to Q. B." would have given Black still a strong attack.

(*g*) This inconsiderate move loses Black a piece, and the game.

Position of the Game after White's 19th move.

BLACK.

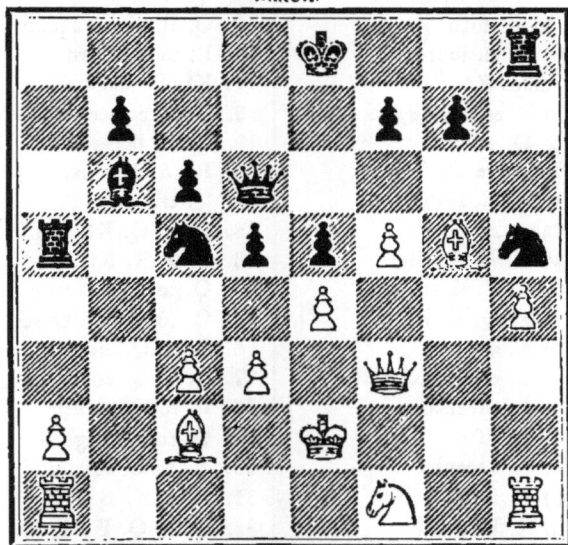

WHITE.

Black to move.

GAME III.
(*Petroff's Defence.*)

White. (Herr Löwenthal.)	Black. (Mr. Morphy.)
1. P. to K. fourth	1. P. to K. fourth
2. K. Kt. to B. third	2. K. Kt. to B. third
3. K. Kt. takes K. P.	3. P. to Q. third
4. K. Kt. to B. third	4. K. Kt. takes P.
5. P. to Q. fourth (*a*)	5. P. to Q. fourth
6. K. B. to Q. third	6. K. B. to K. second

7. Castles	7. Q. Kt. to B. third
8. K. R. to K. square	8. P. to K. B. fourth
9. P. to Q. B. fourth	9. Q. B. to K. third
10. P. takes P. (*b*)	10. Q. B. takes P.
11. Q. Kt. to B. third	11. K. Kt. takes Q. Kt.
12. Kt. P. takes K. Kt.	12. Castles
13. Q. B. to K. B. fourth	13. K. B. to Q. third
14. Q. B. takes K. B. (*c*)	14. Q. takes Q. B.
15. Kt. to K. fifth	15. Q. R. to K. square
16. P. to Q. B. fourth	16. B. to K. third
17. Kt. takes Kt.	17. Kt. P. takes Kt.
18. B. to B. square (*d*)	18. B. to B. second
19. Q. to Q. second	19. Q. R. takes K. R.
20. Q. R. takes Q. R.	20. R. to Q. square
21. Q. to Q. R. fifth	21. Q. takes Q. P.
22. Q. takes B. P.	22. Q. to Q. Kt. third
23. Q. to K. B. fourth	23. P. to K. Kt. third
24. P. to K. R. third	24. Q. to Kt. seventh
25. Q. takes Q. B. P.	25. Q. to Q. Kt. third
26. R. to K. seventh	26. R. to Q. eighth
27. Q. to B. eighth (check)	27. R. to Q. square
28. Q. to B. seventh	28. R. to Q. eighth
29. Q. to K. fifth	29. Q. to Kt. eighth
30. Q. to K. second	30. K. to B. square
31. R. to K. fifth	31. P. to K. B. fifth
32. P. to K. B. third	32. Q. to Q. B. eighth
33. P. to K. R. fourth	33. P. to K. R. third
34. P. to Q. B. fifth	34. K. to Kt. second
35. R. to K. fourth	35. Q. takes B. P. (check)
36. K. to R. second	36. Q. to Q. B. eighth
37. K. to Kt. square	37. R. to Q. seventh
38. Q. to Q. R. sixth	38. R. takes R. P.
39. Q. to Q. third	39. R. to Q. seventh
40. Q. to Q. R. sixth	40. R. to Q. eighth
41. P. to K. Kt. third	41. P. takes Kt. P.
42. K. to Kt. second	42. Q. to Q. B. fourth
43. K. takes Kt. P.	43. Q. to K. Kt. eighth (check)
44. B. to Kt. second	44. R. to Q. seventh

45. Q. to K. B. square	45. Q. takes Q.
46. B. takes Q.	46. K. to B. third
47. B. to Q. B. fourth	47. B. takes B.
48. R. takes B.	48. R. to Q. third
49. K. to B. fourth	49. R. to K. third
50. R. to Q. fourth	50. K. to K. second
51. R. to R. fourth	51. K. to Q. third
52. R. takes R. P.	52. P. to Q. B. fourth
53. R. to R. square	53. P. to Q. B. fifth
54. P. to K. R. fifth	54. Kt. P. takes P.
55. K. to B. fifth	55. R. to K. sixth
56. K. to B. fourth	56. R. to K. square
57. R. to R. sixth (check)	57. K. to Q. fourth
58. R. takes R. P.	58. P. to B. sixth
59. R. takes R. P. (check)	59. K. to Q. fifth
60. R. to K. R. seventh	60. R. to Q. B. square
61. R. to Q. seventh (check)	61. K. to B. fifth
62. K. to K. third	62. R. to K. square (check)
63. K. to B. second	63. P. to B. seventh
64. R. to Q. B. seventh (check)	64. K. to Q. sixth
65. R. to Q. seventh (check)	65. K. to Q. B. sixth
66. R. to Q. B. seventh (check)	66. K. to Q. seventh
67. R. to Q. seventh (check)	67. K. to Q. B. eighth
68. R. to Q. Kt. seventh	68. R. to K. fourth
69. P. to B. fourth	69. R. to K. fifth
70. K. to B. third	70. R. to Q. B. fifth
71. R. to K. R. seventh	71. K. to Q. seventh
72. R. to K. R. square	72. P. to B. eighth
73. R. takes Q.	73. R. takes R.
74. K. to K. fourth	74. R. to K. eighth (check)
75. K. to Q. fourth	75. K. to K. seventh
76. P. to B. fifth	76. K. to B. sixth
77. K. to Q. fifth	77. K. to B. fifth
78. P. to B. sixth	78. K. to Kt. fourth
79. P. to B. seventh	79. R. to K. B. eighth
80. K. to K. sixth	80. K. to Kt. third

And wins.

Notes.

(a) "P. to Q. third," followed by "P. to Q. fourth," clearly wins a move.

(b) We cannot see the reason why White took the Pawn instead of playing Pawn to "Q. Kt. third," which makes White's position very attacking.

(c) Why not "B. to Q. Kt. fifth," which gives White evidently the advantage of position? We give here a diagram after the 13th move of Black, and request our readers to study the position, of which we shall give an analysis in our next number.

(d) How White managed to lose this game is truly astonishing; it took him, however, more than two moves to perform this feat, and this was the first; why not play "B. to K. fifth," which is the obvious and probably best move? The following moves are instructive only because they show how a game can be lost, without any great blunder being committed, simply by making a number of useless moves.

Position of the Game after Black's 13th move.

BLACK.

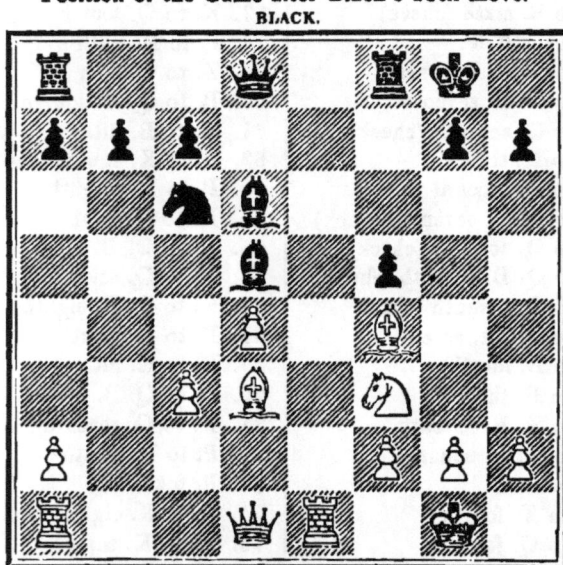

WHITE.

White to move.

Game between Herr KOLISCH and Herr HARRWITZ.

White. (Herr HARRWITZ.)	Black. (Herr KOLISCH.)
1. P. to Q. fourth	1. P. to K. B. fourth
2. P. to Q. B. fourth	2. Kt. to K. B. third ˙
3. Kt. to Q. B. third	3. P. to K. third
4. Kt. to K. B. third	4. B. to K. second
5. P. to K. third	5. P. to Q. fourth
6. Kt. to K. fifth	6. Castles
7. B. to K. second	7. P. to Q. B. third
8. Castles ⸺	8. Kt. to K. fifth
9. P. to K. B. third	9. Kt. to K. B. third
10. B. to Q. second	10. Kt. to Q. second
11. P. takes P.	11. Q. B. P. takes P.
12. Q. R. to Q. B. square	12. B. to Q. third
13. Kt. to Q. third	13. Kt. to K. R. fourth
14. Q. to K. square	14. P. to K. B. fifth
15. P. to K. fourth (a)	15. Kt. to K. Kt. sixth (b)
16. Q. B. takes P.	16. K. Kt. takes B. (check) (c)
17. Q. Kt. takes Kt.	17. B. takes B.
18. Q. Kt. takes B.	18. Q. to Q. Kt. third
19. K. to R. square (d)	19. Q. takes Q. P.
20. Q. to K. Kt. third	20. Kt. to Q. Kt. third
21. Q. R. to Q. B. seventh	21. K. R. to K. B. second
22. K. R. to Q. B. square	22. B. to Q. second
23. K. Kt. to Q. B. fifth (e)	23. Q. takes Q. Kt. P.
24. Q. Kt. to Q. third	24. Q. to Q. seventh
25. P. to K. B. fourth	25. Q. R. to K. B. square
26. P. to K. R. third	26. B. to Q. B. third
27. Kt. to Q. Kt. third	27. Q. takes Q. R. P.
28. R. takes R.	28. R. takes R.
29. Kt. to K. fifth	29. R. to K. B. square
30. Q. Kt. takes B.	30. P. takes Kt.
31. R. to Q. R. square (f)	31. Q. to Q. Kt. seventh
32. R. takes Q. R. P.	32. Kt. to Q. B. fifth
33. Kt. to Q. B. fifth	33. Kt. to Q. seventh
34. Kt. to Q. third	34. Kt. takes K. P.
35. Q. to K. Kt. fourth	35. Q. to K. B. third
36. K. to R. second	36. P. to Q. B. fourth

37. R. to Q. R. sixth	37. R. to K. square
38. Kt. to K. fifth	38. Q. to K. B. fourth
39. K. to K. Kt. square	39. Q. takes Q.
40. P. takes Q.	40. P. to K. Kt. fourth
41. P. takes P.	41. Kt. takes P.
42. K. to K. B. second	42. R. to Q. Kt. square
43. K. to K. third	43. R. to Q. Kt. fifth
44. R. to Q. R. eighth (check)	44. K. to Kt. second
45. R. to Q. R. seventh (check)	45. K. to R. third
46. Kt. to Q. seventh	46. R. to K. fifth (check)
47. K. to K. B. second	47. P. to Q. B. fifth
48. K. to K. Kt. third	48. P. to Q. B. sixth
49. Kt. to K. B. sixth	49. P. to Q. B. seventh
50. R. to Q. R. square	50. P. to Q. fifth
51. Kt. takes R.	51. Kt. takes Kt. (check)
52. K. to K. B. third	52. P. to Q. sixth (*g*)

And Black resigned the game.

Notes.

(*a*) " P. takes P." would have been the simplest and most effectual move.

(*b*) Very well conceived. If White takes Kt., Black by " P. takes P." and then " Q. to K. R. fifth," wins.

(*c*) Black should have taken the B. instead, and thus won the exchange.

(*d*) " Q. to K. B. second " would have preserved the Pawn which White has already won. By playing in the subsequent move, " Q. to K. Kt. third," White obtains a sort of attack, but no equivalent for the loss of a Pawn.

(*e*) Evidently an oversight.

(*f*) " R. takes P." seems to us a better move.

(*g*) This game was not played by Herr Harrwitz with his usual skill, but still some credit is due to his opponent's play.

Two Games played at the PHILIDORIAN CHESS ROOMS, June 3rd, 1859, between Mr. F. HEALEY and Herr SCHULDER.

GAME I.

(*Irregular Opening.*)

Black. (Mr. F. HEALEY.)	*White.* (Herr SCHULDER.)
1. P. to K. fourth	1. P. to K. fourth
2. B. to Q. B. fourth	2. Q. to K. second
3. Kt. to Q. B. third	3. P. to Q. B. third
4. K. Kt. to K. second	4. P. to Q. third
5. Castles	5. B. to K. third

6. B. to Q. Kt. third	6. P. to K. Kt. third
7. P. to Q. fourth	7. B. takes B.
8. R. P. takes B.	8. Kt. to Q. second
9. P. to K. B. fourth	9. B. to Kt. second
10. P. to Q. fifth	10. P. to K. B. third
11. P. to K. B. fifth	11. P. takes K. B. P.
12. R. takes P.	12. Kt. to R. third
13. Kt. to Kt. third (a)	13. Kt. takes R.
14. Kt. takes Kt.	14. Q. to B. square
15. P. takes P.	15. P. takes P.
16. Kt. takes P. (check)	16. K. to Q. square
17. B. to K. third	17. K. to B. second
18. Kt. to K. B. fifth (b)	18. P. to K. R. fourth
19. R. to R. sixth	19. R. to R. second
20. R. takes B. P. (check)	20. K. takes R.
21. Q. to Q. fifth (check)	21. K. to B. second
22. Kt. to Kt. fifth (check)	

And White resigned.

Notes.

(a) Very well played.
(b) "Q. Kt. to Q. Kt. fifth (check)" would have been equally well.

GAME II.

(*Irregular Opening.*)

White. (Herr SCHULDER.)	*Black.* (Mr. F. HEALEY.)
1. P. to K. fourth	1. P. to K. fourth
2. P. to K. Kt. third (a)	2. P. to K. B. fourth
3. P. to Q. fourth	3. P. takes Q. P.
4. B. to Kt. second	4. Kt. to Q. B. third
5. Kt. to K. second	5. P. takes P.
6. B. takes P.	6. B. to Q. B. fourth
7. B. to Q. fifth	7. K. Kt. to B. third
8. P. to Q. B. fourth	8. Kt. to Q. Kt. fifth
9. Kt. to K. B. fourth	9. Q. Kt. takes B.
10. Kt. takes Kt.	10. Castles
11. Castles	11. Kt. takes K.
12. P. takes Kt.	12. P. to Q. third

14

White	Black
13. P. to Q. Kt. fourth	13. B. takes P.
14. Q. takes P.	14. B. to Q. B. fourth
15. Q. to B. third	15. B. to K. R. sixth
16. B. to Kt. second	16. Q. to K. second
17. Kt. to Q. second	17. R. to K. B. second
18. Q. R. to K. square	18. R. takes P. (*b*)
19. R. takes R.	19. Q. takes R. (check)
20. K. to B. square	20. Q. takes Kt. (check mate)

Notes.

(*a*) We cannot approve this way of opening the game.
(*b*) Finely played throughout by Black.

Game between Mr. PAUL MORPHY, and Colonel CHARLES MEAD, President of the New York Chess Club.

White. (Col. MEAD.)	*Black.* (Mr. MORPHY.)
1. P. to K. R. third (*a*)	1. P. to K. fourth
2. P. to K. fourth	2. Kt. to K. B. third
3. Kt. to Q. B. third	3. B. to Q. B. fourth
4. B. to Q. B. fourth	4. P. to Q. Kt. fourth (*b*)
5. K. B. takes Kt. P.	5. P. to Q. B. third
6. K. B. to R. fourth	6. Castles
7. K. Kt. to K. second (*c*)	7. P. to Q. fourth
8. P. takes P.	8. P. takes P.
9. P. to Q. fourth	9. P. takes P.
10. K. Kt. takes P.	10. Q. to Q. Kt. third
11. Q. Kt. to K. second	11. Q. B. to R. third
12. P. to Q. B. third	12. Q. B. takes Q. Kt.
13. K. takes B.	13. B. takes Kt.
14. Q. takes B.	14. Q. to R. third (check)
15. K. to B. third	15. K. R. to Q. B. square
16. P. to Q. Kt. third	16. K. Kt. to K. fifth
17. Q. B. to Kt. second	17. Q. Kt. to B. third
18. K. B. takes Q. Kt.	18. K. R. takes B.
19. K. to K. third	19. Q. R. to K. square
20. K. R. to K. square	20. Kt. takes Q. B. P. (check)
21. K. to B. third	21. K. R. to B. third
22. K. to Kt. third	22. Q. to Q. third (check)

23. P. to K. B., fourth	23. Kt. to K. seventh (check)
24. K. R. takes Kt.	24. Q. R. takes R.
25. R. to K. B. square	25. K. R. to Kt. third (check)
26. K. to B. third	26. Q. R. takes K. Kt. P.

And White resigned.

Notes.

(a) There is no accounting for taste.

(b) Rather daring to play Evans's Gambit as second player; the move of "P. to K. R. third" is of advantage in this Gambit if properly made use of.

(c) Having played for the first move "P. to K. R. third," a move which is only made in order to prevent the Bishop from winning the Knight, White plays now the "Kt. to K. second." It would be useless to look further for reasons of the gallant Colonel's defeat.

Game between Mr. P. MORPHY and Mr. BARNES in consultation against Mr. HOWARD STAUNTON and ALTER.

White. (MORPHY and BARNES.)	*Black.* (STAUNTON and ALTER.)
1. P. to K. fourth	1. P. to Q. fourth (a)
2. P. takes P.	2. Q. takes P.
3. Q. Kt. to B. third	3. Q. to Q. square
4. P. to Q. fourth	4. K. Kt. to B. third
5. K. B. to Q. third	5. Q. Kt. to B. third
6. Q. B. to K. third	6. P. to K. third
7. K. Kt. to B. third	7. K. B. to Q. third
8. Castles	8. Castles
9. Q. to K. second (b)	9. P. to Q. Kt. third
10. Q. B. to Kt. fifth	10. Q. B. to Kt. second
11. Q. Kt. to K. fourth	11. K. B. to K. second
12. Q. Kt. takes K. Kt. (check)	12. K. B. takes Q. Kt.
13. Q. to K. fourth	13. P. to K. Kt. third
14. Q. to K. R. fourth	14. K. B. takes Q. B.
15. Kt. takes K. B	15. P. to K. R. fourth (c)
16. P. to Q. B. third	16. Q. to K. B. third
17. Q. R. to K. square	17. Kt. to K. second
18. P. to K. B. fourth	18. Kt. to K. B. fourth
19. Q. to K. R. third	19. K. R. to K. square
20. Q. R. to K. fifth	20. Q. R. to Q. square
21. K. R. to K. square (d)	21. Kt. to Kt. second
22. P. to K. Kt. fourth	22. P. to Q. B. fourth

23. B. to K. fourth	23. B. to R. third
24. Kt. P. takes R. P.	24. Kt. takes P.
25. B. to B. third	25. P. takes P.
26. B. takes Kt.	26. P. takes Kt.
27. Q. takes R. P.	27. Q. to Kt. second
28. K. to B. second (e)	28. Q. to B. sixth
29. Q. to R. fourth	29. B. to Q. sixth
30. Q. to Kt. third	30. B. to Kt. third
31. P. to K. B. fifth	31. B. takes P.
32. Kt. to K. fourth (disc. check)	32. Q. to Kt. third
33. Kt. to B. sixth (check)	33. K. to B. square
34. Q. takes Q.	34. B. takes Q.
35. Kt. takes K. R.	35. K. takes Kt.
36. P. to K. R. fourth	36. P. to Q. sixth
37. K. to K. third	37. K. to K. second
38. K. to Q. second	38. R. to Q. third
39. Q. R. to K. Kt. fifth	39. K. to B. third
40. K. R. to K. B. square (check)	40. B. to B. fourth
41. Q. R. to Kt. eighth	41. R. to Q. fourth
42. P. to K. R. fifth	42. R. to K. fourth
43. K. R. to B. second	43. R. to K. fifth
44. K. R. to R. second	44. B. to R. second
45. K. R. to K. R. eighth	45. K. to Kt. second
46. Q. R. to Q. R. eighth	46. K. to R. third
47. Q. R. takes R. P.	47. R. to K. B. fourth
48. Q. R. to Kt. seventh	48. P. to K. fourth
49. Q. R. takes P. (check)	49. P. to K. B. third
50. P. to Q. R. fourth	50. P. to K. fifth
51. Q. R. to K. sixth	51. R. to B. sixth
52. P. to Q. R. fifth	

And Black resigned.

Notes.

(a) Losing a move in a consultation game is never advisable; it seems, however, that the Black allies preferred to lose a move rather than expose themselves to the scientific opening of their antagonists.

(b) A very important move.

(c) Black had no other move.

(d) Threatening to win a Pawn.

(e) A very good combination, which finally wins the exchange.

Game between Mr. MORPHY and Mr. STANLEY of New York.

(*Evans's Gambit.*)

White. (Mr. MORPHY.)	*Black.* (Mr. STANLEY.)
1. P. to K. fourth	1. P. to K. fourth
2. Kt. to K. B. third	2. Kt. to Q. B. third
3. B. to Q. B. fourth	3. B. to Q. B. fourth
4. P. to Q. Kt. fourth	4. K. B. takes Q. Kt. P.
5. P. to Q. B. third	5. B. to Q. R. fourth
6. P. to Q. fourth	6. P. takes P.
7. Castles	7. P. to Q. third
8. P. takes P.	8. K. B. to Kt. third
9. Kt. to Q. B. third	9. Kt. to K. B. third (*a*)
10. P. to K. fifth	10. Q. P. takes P.
11. Q. B. to Q. R. third	11. K. B. takes Q. P.
12. Q. to Q. Kt. third	12. Q. B. to K. third
13. K. B. takes Q. B.	13. B. P. takes B.
14. Q. takes K. P. (check)	14. Q. Kt. to K. second
15. K. Kt. takes B.	15. K. P. takes Kt.
16. K. R. to K. square	16. Kt. to K. Kt. square
17. Kt. to Q. fifth	17. Q. to Q. second
18. B. takes Q. Kt.	18. Q. takes Q.
19. K. R. takes Q.	19. K. to Q. second
20. Q. R. to K. square	20. Q. R. to K. square
21. K. R. to K. fourth	21. P. to Q. B. third
22. K. R. takes Q. P.	22. B. P. takes Kt.
23. K. R. takes Q. P. (check)	23. K. to Q. B. third
24. K. R. to Q. sixth (check)	24. K. to Q. B. second
25. Q. R. to Q. B. square (check)	25. K. to Q. Kt. square
26. B. to K. B. fourth	26. Kt. to K. R. third
27. B. to K. Kt. third	27. K. to R. square
28. P. to K. R. third	28. Kt. to K. B. fourth
29. K. R. to Q. seventh	29. P. to K. Kt. third (*b*)
30. Q. R. to Q. B. seventh	30. Kt. takes B.
31. B. P. takes Kt.	31. Q. R. to Q. Kt. square
32. K. R. takes R. P.	32. K. R. takes K. R.
33. Q. R. takes K. R.	33. P. to Q. R. fourth
34. P. to K. R. fourth	34. R. to K. Kt. square
35. P. to K. Kt. fourth	35. P. to Q. Kt. fourth (*c*)

White	Black
36. P. to K. R. fifth	36. P. to Q. R. fifth
37. P. to K. R. sixth	37. P. to Q. Kt. fifth
38. R. to K. Kt. seventh	38. R. to K. R. square
39. P. to K. R. seventh	39. P. to Q. Kt. sixth
40. R. to Kt. eighth (check)	40. K. to Kt. second
41. R. takes R.	

And wins.

Notes.

(a) " B. to K. fifth" instead, would have been better.

(b) What an unlucky oversight, after having defended a bad game with great skill and perseverance, and brought it to an even game (nay, we should prefer Black in this position), to throw it away! " R. to K. second" would have at once freed Black from his embarrassing position. To allow White to bring the Rooks on a line was a grievous mistake.

(c) " K. to R. second" instead would have have given Black a chance of holding out; for

White.	Black.
36. P. to K. R. fifth	36. P. to Q. R. fifth
37. P. to K. R. sixth	37. P. to K. Kt. fourth
38. R. to K. Kt. seventh	38. R. to K. R. square
39. P. to K. R. seventh	39. R. to K. R. third

And Black has a chance of drawing the game.

Game between Mr. MORPHY and Mr. BODEN, played at the St. James's Chess Club: Mr. MORPHY playing, at the same time, four other games, against Mr. de RIVIERE, Mr. BARNES, Mr. BIRD, and Mr. LÖWENTHAL. (The game played by Mr. MORPHY against Mr. LÖWENTHAL was given in May number.)

(Scottish Opening.)

White. (Mr. MORPHY.)	Black. (Mr. BODEN.)
1. P. to K. fourth	1. P. to K. fourth
2. Kt. to K. B. third	2. Kt. to Q. B. third
3. P. to Q. fourth	3. P. takes P.
4. B. to Q. B. fourth	4. B. to Q. B. fourth
5. Castles	5. P. to Q. third
6. P. to Q. B. third	6. Kt. to K. B. third
7. P. takes P.	7. B. to Q. Kt. third
8. Kt. to Q. B. third	8. B. to K. Kt. fifth
9. B. to K. third	9. Castles
10. Q. to Q. third	10. Q. to Q. second (a)

11. K. Kt. to Q. second	11. Q. Kt. to K. second
12. B. to Q. Kt. third	12. P. to Q. fourth
13. P. to K. fifth	13. K. Kt. to K. square (b)
14. P. to K. R. third	14. Q. B. to R. fourth
15. P. to B. fourth	15. P. to K. B. fourth
16. K. to R. second	16. P. to Q. B. third
17. K. R. to K. Kt. square	17. K. to R. square
18. K. B. to B. second	18. B. to K. Kt. third (c)
19. K. Kt. to B. third	19. K. Kt. to Q. B. second
20. P. to Q. Kt. fourth	20. K. Kt. to K. third
21. K. Kt. to Q. second	21. Q. Kt. to K. Kt. square
22. K. Kt. to Q. Kt. third	22. Q. Kt. to K. R. third
23. Q. Kt. to Q. R. fourth	23. Q. to K. second
24. Q. Kt. to Q. B. fifth	24. Kt. takes Kt. (d)
25. Kt. P. takes Kt.	25. Kt. to Kt. fifth (check)
26. K. to R. square	26. Q. to K. R. fifth
27. K. R. to K. B. square	27. Kt. takes Q. B.
28. Q. takes Kt.	28. B. to Q. B. second
29. Kt. to Q. second	29. Q. to K. second
30. Kt. to K. B. third	30. Q. R. to K. square
31. Q. R. to Q. Kt. square	31. P. to Q. Kt. third
32. B. to R. fourth	32. P. to Q. Kt. fourth
33. B. to B. second	33. P. to Q. R. fourth
34. K. R. to K. Kt. square	34. Q. to K. third
35. P. to K. Kt. fourth	35. K. B. to Q. square
36. P. to K. Kt. fifth	36. K. to Kt. square
37. P. to K. R. fourth	37. P. to K. R. fourth
38. P. takes P. (en pass.)	38. K. R. to B. second
39. K. R. to Kt. second	39. Q. B. to K. R. fourth
40. Q. R. to K. Kt. square (e)	40. Q. takes R. P.
41. Kt. to Kt. fifth	41. K. B. takes Kt. (f)
42. R. P. takes P.	42. Q. to K. R. square
43. K. R. to K. R. second (g)	43. P. to K. Kt. third
44. Q. R. to K. Kt. third	44. K. R. to K. R. second
45. Q. R. to K. R. third	45. Q. R. to K. second
46. K. to Kt. square	46. B. to Kt. fifth
47. Q. R. to R. sixth	47. R. takes R.
48. R. takes R.	48. R. to K. R. second

49. R. takes P. (check)	49. K. to B. square
50. R. to R. sixth	50. R. takes R.
51. P. takes R.	51. Q. takes P.

And the game was given up as drawn.

Notes.

(*a*) " Kt. to Q. Kt. fifth," followed by " P. to Q. fourth," would have been Black's best play.

(*b*) " B. to K. B. fourth," followed by "Kt. to K. fourth," would have been better.

(*c*) This move makes the former move " K. to R." useless ; for if Black had no intention of pushing the K. Kt. P. forward, why lose a move with the King? It seems to us that " P. to K. Kt. fourth," and then " Kt. to K. Kt. third," would have given Black a formidable attack.

(*d*) If Black would have taken the Knight with the Bishop instead, he would have won at least a Pawn by the very skilful manœuvre which he conceived, and which, by having taken the Knight with the Knight instead of with the Bishop, turned out more ingenious than profitable.

(*e*) " P. takes P." would have won the game for White.

(*f*) Bad play ; Black ought to lose the game ; if Mr. Morphy had not had four other opponents at the time, he would have no doubt won it.

(*g*) " P. to K. Kt. fifth," would have easily won the game.

Games between Mr. ZYTOGORSKI and Mr. KENNY, played in 1854, Mr. ZYTOGORSKI giving the odds of Pawn and two moves.

GAME I.

White. (Mr. KENNY.)	*Black.* (Mr. ZYTOGORSKI.)
1. P. to K. fourth	
2. P. to Q. fourth	2. P. to K. third
3. B. to Q. third	3. B. to K. second
4. P. to K. fifth	4. P. to K. Kt. third
5. P. to K. R. fourth	5. P. to Q. fourth
6. P. to K. R. fifth	6. P. to K. Kt. fourth
7. P. to K. R. sixth	7. K. to Q. second
8. Q. to K. Kt. fourth	8. P. to Q. B. fourth
9. P. to Q. B. third	9. P. takes Q. P.
10. K. Kt. to B. third	10. P. takes Q. B. P.
11. Q. Kt. takes P.	11. Q. Kt. to B. third
12. K. B. to Q. Kt. fifth	12. K. to B. second
13. B. takes Q. Kt.	13. P. takes B.
14. B. to Q. second	14. B. to Q. second
15. Kt. takes Q. P.	15. K. P. takes Kt.

16. B. to R. fifth (check)   16. K. to B. square
17. B. takes Q.   17. B. takes Q.
18. B. takes B.   18. B. takes Kt.
19. B. takes K. Kt. P.   19. B. takes K. Kt. P.

And wins.

GAME II.

White. (Mr. KENNY.)	*Black.* (Mr. ZYTOGORSKI.)
1. P. to K. fourth	
2. P. to Q. fourth	2. P. to K. third
3. B. to Q. third	3. B. to K. second
4. P. to K. fifth	4. P. to K. Kt. third
5. P. to K. R. fourth	5. P. to Q. fourth
6. P. to K. R. fifth	6. P. to K. Kt. fourth
7. P. to K. R. sixth	7. K. to Q. second
8. Q. to K. Kt. fourth	8. P. to Q. B. fourth
9. P. to Q. B. third	9. P. takes P.
10. K. Kt. to B. third	10. Q. Kt. to B. third
11. Kt. takes K. Kt. P.	11. B. takes K. Kt.
12. B. takes B.	12. K. Kt. to K. second
13. Q. to K. R. fourth	13. P. takes P.
14. Q. Kt. takes P.	14. Q. Kt. takes K. P.
15. B. to Kt. fifth (check)	15. Q. Kt. to B. third
16. R. to Q. square	16. P. to Q. R. third
17. Kt. takes Q. P.	17. P. takes Kt.
18. R. takes Q. P.	18. Kt. takes R.
19. B. takes Kt. (check)	19. P. takes B.
20. B. takes Q.	20. R. takes B.
21. Castles	21. K. to Q. B. second
22. R. to Q. B. square	22. R. to Q. third
23. Q. to K. fourth	23. Kt. to K. B. third
24. Q. to K. fifth	24. P. to Q. R. fourth
25. R. to Q. square	25. Kt. to Q. fourth
26. R. takes Kt.	26. P. takes R.
27. Q. to K. seventh (check)	27. B. to Q. second
28. Q. takes K. R. P.	28. Q. R. to his third square
29. Q. to K. B. seventh	29. R. takes K. R. P.

30. Q. takes Q. P.	30. P. to R. fifth
31. P. to Q. Kt. fourth	31. Q. R. to Q. third
32. Q. to Q. B. fifth (check)	32. K. to Kt. second
33. P. to K. B. third	33. Q. R. to Q. eighth (check)
34. K. to B. second	34. Q. R. to Q. seventh (check)
35. K. to Kt. square	35. K. R. to Q. third
36. P. to Q. R. third	36. Q. R. to Q. eighth (check)
37. K. to B. second	37. K. R. to Q. seventh (check)
38. K. to Kt. third	38. Q. R. to Q. R. eighth
39. P. to Q. Kt. fifth	39. Q. R. to Q. R. seventh
40. K. to B. fourth	40. Q. R. to Q. Kt. seventh
41. Q. to K. seventh	41. Q. R. takes Q. Kt. P.
42. P. to K. Kt. fourth	42. Q. R. to Q. fourth
43. P. to K. Kt. fifth	43. K. R. to Q. fifth (check)
44. K. to Kt. third	44. R. to Q. eighth
45. P. to B. fourth	45. Q. R. to Q. sixth (check)
46. K. to B. second	46. K. R. to Q. seventh (check
47. K. to his square	47. Q. R. to Q. third
48. P. to K. B. fifth	48. K. to R. third
49. P. to K. B. sixth	49. B. to Q. Kt. fourth
50. Q. takes Q. R. (check)	50. R. takes Q.
51. P. to K. B. seventh	51. R. to Q. square
52. P. to K. Kt. sixth	52. B. to Q. B. fifth

And wins.

GAME III.

White. (Mr. KENNY.)	Black. (Mr. ZYTOGORSKI.)
1. P. to K. fourth	
2. P. to Q. fourth	2. P. to K. third
3. B. to Q. third	3. P. to Q. B. fourth
4. P. to K. fifth.	4. P. to K. Kt. third
5. P. to K. R. fourth	5. P. takes P.
6. P. to K. B. fourth	6. Q. to R. fifth (check)
7. B. to Q. second	7. Q. to Kt. third
8. B. to Q. B. square	8. Q. Kt. to B. third
9. P. to Q. R. third	9. K. to Q. square
10. P. to K. R. fifth	10. P. to K. Kt. fourth

11. Q. to K. Kt. fourth	11. P. takes P.
12. Q. takes K. B. P.	12. Q. to R. fourth (check)
13. Kt. to Q. second	13. Q. takes P. (check)
14. K. Kt. to K. second	14. Q. takes Q.
15. Kt. takes Q.	15. P. to Q. fourth
16. Q. Kt. to his third	16. K. Kt. to K. second
17. P. to K. Kt. fourth	17. P. to K. fourth
18. Kt. to K. R. third	18. B. takes K. Kt. P.
19. K. Kt. to his fifth	19. P. to K. fifth
20. B. to Q. Kt. fifth	20. K. to his square
21. Q. Kt. takes doubled P.	21. P. to Q. R. third
22. B. to Q. R. fourth	22. P. to K. R. third
23. K. Kt. to K. sixth	23. B. takes K. Kt.
24. Q. Kt. takes B.	24. R. to Q. B. square
25. R. to K. B. square	25. P. to Q. Kt. fourth
26. R. takes B. (check)	26. R. takes R.
27. Kt. takes R.	27. P. takes B.
28. Kt. to his sixth	28. Q. Kt. to Q. fifth
29. K. to Q. square	29. Kt. takes Q. B. P.
30. R. to Kt. square	30. K. Kt. to K. B. fourth
31. P. to Q. Kt. fourth	31. P. to Q. fifth
32. P. to Q. Kt. fifth	32. Q. Kt. to K. sixth (check)
33. B. takes Kt.	33. Kt. takes B. (check)
34. K. to his square	34. P. takes Q. Kt. P.
35. R. takes Q. Kt. P.	35. R. to Q. B. eighth (check)
36. K. to Q. second	36. R. to Q. B. seventh (check)
37. K. to his square	37. P. to Q. sixth
38. R. to Kt. eighth (check)	38. K. to Q. second
39. Kt. to K. fifth (check)	39. K. to Q. B. second
40. And White resigns.	

Game between two Amateurs.

White. (Mr. B.)	*Black.* (Mr. H.)
1. P. to K. fourth	1. P. to K. fourth
2. K. Kt. to B. third	2. Q. Kt. to B. third
3. P. to Q. fourth	3. P. takes P.
4. Kt. takes P.	4. Kt. takes Kt.
5. Q. takes Kt.	5. P. to Q. third

6. K. B. to Q. B. fourth
7. P. to K. B. fourth
8. Q. to Q. third
9. Castles
10. Q. takes B.
11. Kt. to B. third
12. Q. to Q. third
13. P. to B. fifth
14. B. to B. fourth
15. R. to Q. square
16. B. to Kt. third
17. P. takes P.
18. Kt. takes Kt.
19. Q. to K. second (check)
20. K. R. to K. square
21. Q. to B. third
22. R. to K. sixth
23. K. to R. square
24. Q. to R. fifth (check)
25. B. to Q. sixth
26. B. takes B.
27. R. takes P.
28. R. to Q. square
29. B. to Q. eighth
30. B. takes R. (check)

6. Q. B. to K. third
7. Q. to B. third
8. Q. to Kt. third
9. B. takes B.
10. Kt. to K. second
11. Q. to K. third
12. P. to Q. B. third
13. Q. to Q. second
14. R. to Q. square
15. P. to B. third
16. P. to Q. fourth
17. Kt. takes P.
18. P. takes Kt.
19. B. to K. second
20. K. to B. second
21. Q. to B. third
22. Q. to B. fourth (check)
23. K. R. to K. square.
24. K. to Kt. square
25. Q. takes P. at B. seventh
26. R. to Q. B. square
27. Q. to Kt. eighth (check)
28. Q. takes Kt. P.
29. P. to Kt. second
30. K. to B. second

And White mates in two moves.

Game between Herr FALKBEER and an AMATEUR.

(*Herr Falkbeer gives Mr. B. Pawn and two moves.*)

White. (Mr. B.)

1. Ps. to K. fourth and Q. fourth
2. P. to Q. B. fourth
3. P. to Q. fifth
4. P. to K. B. fourth
5. B. to Q. third
6. P. takes P.
7. P. to K. Kt. third

Black. (Herr FALKBEER.)

1. P. to K. third
2. P. to Q. B. fourth
3. P. to Q. third
4. K. Kt. to R. third
5. Q. Kt. to R. third
6. Q. to R. fifth (check)
7. Q. to B. third

8. P. to K. B. fifth	8. P. to K. Kt. third
9. Q. to R. fourth (check)	9. K. to Q. square
10. P. to K. R. fourth	10. Q. to Kt. second
11. P. to B. fifth	11. Q. to Q. B. second
12. B. takes Kt.	12. B. takes P.
13. B. to K. B. fourth	13. Q. to Kt. third
14. K. Kt. to B. third	14. Q. takes Kt. P.
15. Q. to Kt. third	15. Q. takes Q. R.
16. Q. takes Kt. P.	16. R. to Q. B. square
17. P. to K. fifth	17. Q. takes Q. R. P.
18. P. takes Q. P.	18. R. to Q. Kt. square
19. Q. to B. seventh (check)	19. K. moves

Mated with Pawn in four moves.

PROBLEMS FOR YOUNG PLAYERS.

No. 6. By DELTA, *North Shields.*

White.	*Black.*
K. at Q. Kt. fourth	K. at Q. fifth
R. at K. R. sixth	Kt. at K. fourth
B. at K. Kt. sixth	Ps. at Q. fourth, at
Ps. at K. R. fifth	Q. sixth, and K. B. fourth
K. B. third, and Q. second	

White to mate in three moves.

No. 7. By DELTA, *North Shields.*

White.	*Black.*
K. at Q. B. square	K. at Q. B. sixth
Q. at K. R. fourth	
Kt. at K. B. fifth	
B. at K. Kt. sixth	
P. at Q. R. second	

White to mate in three moves.

No. 8. By Mr. EDWIN GEAKE.

White.	*Black.*
K. at K. B. second	K. at K. B. fifth
R. at Q. sixth	Ps. at Q. B. second, Q. sixth,
B. at Q. R. square	K. B. fourth, and K. R. fifth
Kts. at K. B. seventh, and K. fifth	
Ps. at Q. B. second, & Q. B. sixth,	
Q. fourth, and K. R. third	

White to mate in three moves.

SOLUTIONS TO PROBLEMS.

No. 21.   *Page.* 191.

White.	*Black.*
Kt. to Q. R. fifth (check)	K. to Q. Kt. fourth
Kt. to Q. Kt. seventh (best)	R. to K. B.
Kt. to Q. sixth (check) (best)	K. to Q. B. seventh
Kt. to Q. B. fourth (check)	R. to Q. square
Kt. to Q. R. fifth (check)	K. to Q. Kt. fourth
Kt. to Q. Kt. seventh	R. to Q. second

And wins.

It must be here observed, that the Knight can never leave the neighbourhood of the King, or he will be cut off and captured by the adverse Rook and King.

No. 22.   *Page* 191.

White.	*Black.*
1. Kt. to K. B. second (disc. ch.)	1. Q. or R. takes R.
2. Q. to K. fourth (check)	2. Q. or R. takes Q.
3. B. mates	

No. 23.   *Page* 192.

White.	*Black.*
1. Q. to Q. R. eighth	1. Q. takes Q. or (A.)
2. Kt. to K. second	2. Anything
3. Kt. or B. mates	

A.

	1. Kt. takes Kt.
2. B. to Q. fifth (check)	2. Q. takes B.
3. Q. takes Q. mates	

No. 24.   *Page* 192.

White.	*Black.*
1. Q. to K. Kt. fourth (check)	1. K. to R. second
2. Kt. to K. B. sixth (check)	2. Q. takes Kt.
3. Q. to K. Kt. eighth (check)	3. R. takes Q.
4. P. to K. B. eighth (check) and mates.	

No. 25.   Problem by J. G. CAMPBELL, Esq.

BLACK

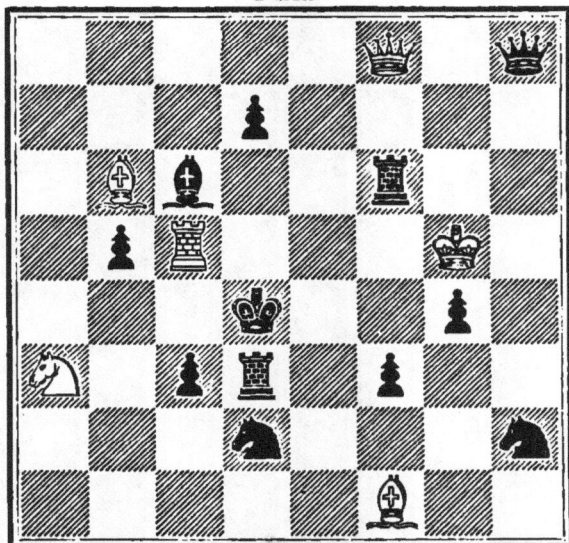

WHITE.

White to mate in three moves.

No. 26. Problem by DELTA, North Shields.

BLACK.

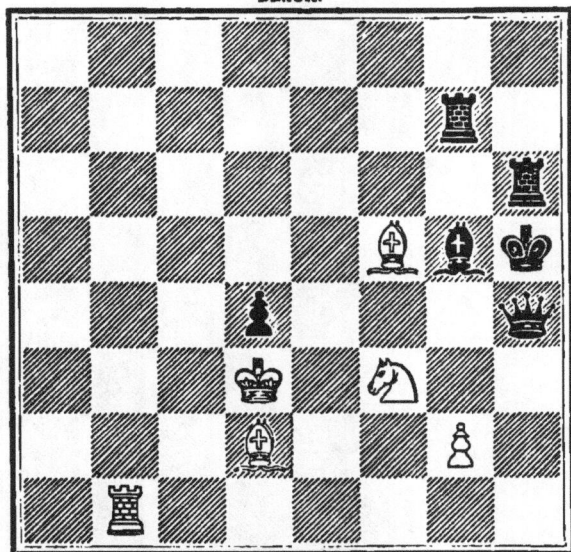

WHITE.

White to mate in three moves.

No. 27. Problem by J. A. CONROY, Esq., Dublin.

BLACK.

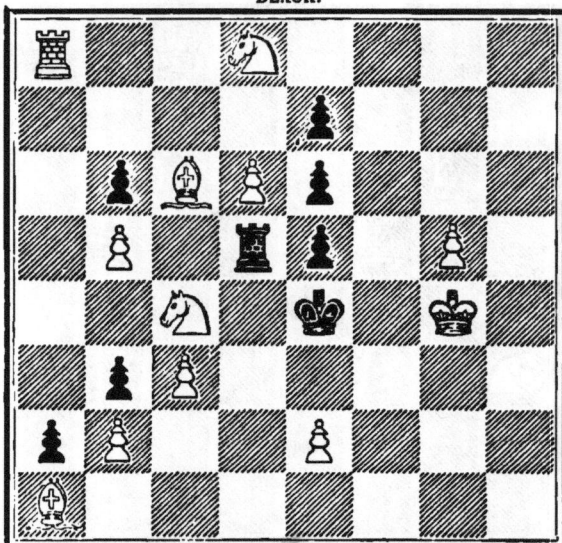

WHITE.

White to move and mate in four moves.

No. 28. Problem by — PERCIE, Esq.

BLACK.

WHITE.

White to move and mate in four moves.

CHESS TOURNAMENTS.

Amongst the causes that contribute to the extension of Chess, Tournaments stand in the foremost rank. The publicity which is generally given to them greatly enhances their interest, and produces among the disciples of Caissa that emulation which is so necessary to success in general, and to the progress of our noble game in particular. But in order to make them fully effective, they ought to be a fair trial of the skill of all those engaged in them. Now, this, as far as we are aware, has never been the case, especially as regards the second, third, and other prizes; for, according to the arrangements which have been made in former tournaments, what was more likely than, nay, it invariably so happened, that the two best, or next best, players met in the first or second tourney, and thus the persons who ought to have been the winners of the second and third prizes, were at once declared nonsuited. Few Chess players, we suppose, have paid serious attention to the arrangement of Chess Tournaments, else the incongruity of the thing would have struck them at once. Chance had so great a share in it, that in a tournament of thirty-two persons, the player to whom sixteen out of the number could have given odds, might have won the second prize, and this, even supposing that every one played up to the full standard of his skill. In all former tournaments, therefore, it is only the winner of the first prize who is entitled to full credit for his skill; the others owed more or less to chance, the prizes that fell to their share.

In order to leave as little as possible to chance, we propose the following simple arrangements, by which the prizes must necessarily come to the best players, if they play up to their standard.

Let us suppose sixteen players.

First Tourney.

A	B	C	D	E	F	G	H	(winners)
				versus				
A1	B1	C1	D1	E1	F1	G1	H1	(losers)

Second Tourney.

A	B	C	D	(winners)	A1	B1	C1	D1	(winners)
	versus					and	*versus*		
E	F	G	H	(losers)	E1	F1	G1	H1	(losers)

15

In this second tourney, the losers, E1, F1, G1, H1, having been twice beaten, retire from the field, and only twelve players remain.

Third Tourney.

A1	B1	C1	D1	(winners)	A	B	(winners)
	versus			and		*versus*	
E	F	G	H	(losers)	C	D	(losers)

In this tourney, the losers, E, F, G, H, having been twice beaten, retire from the field, and only eight players remain.

Fourth Tourney.

A1	B1	C1	(winners)	A
	versus		and	*versus*
D1	C	D	(losers)	B

In this tourney four players also retire from the field, A, as the winner of the first prize, and D1, C, and D, as losers, whilst only four remain, each of them having only lost one tourney.

Fifth Tourney.

A1	B1	(winners)
	versus	
C1	D	(losers)

In this tourney A and B retire, both having lost twice.

Sixth Tourney.

A1	(winner)	winning the second prize.
	versus	
B1	(loser)	winning the third prize.

What a different result this gives from the Tournament played in the old style; both A1 and B1, the winners of the second and third prizes, would have been excluded after the first tourney from any further participation in the Tournament, whilst here they have fairly earned their laurels. It is clear that the first and second prizes have been necessarily awarded to the best players; the only doubt can be about B, who has only been beaten by A and A1. It ought, therefore, be stipulated if such an event should happen, that if one of the players were only beaten by the winners of the first and second prizes, he be entitled to play an additional tourney for the third prize with the till then successful competitor, who in this case is B1, who was only beaten by A1 and B.

In a Tournament of eight players the following would be the arrangement :—

First Tourney.

| A | B | C | D | (winners) |

versus

| E | F | G | H | (losers) |

Second Tourney.

| E | F | | A | B | (winners) |

versus   and   *versus*

| G | H | | C | D | (losers) |

Third Tourney.

(G, H, having lost twice, are out.)

| E | F | A | (winners) |

versus

| B | C | D | (losers) |

Fourth Tourney.

(C, D, out, having been beaten twice.)

| A | B | (winners) |

versus

| E | F | (losers) |

Fifth Tourney.

A (winner)   winning the first prize.

versus

B (loser)   winning the second prize.

E and F, having been beaten twice, are out, or play for the third and fourth prizes if there be any.

This method seems to us more to the purpose, and will, we hope, be adopted in all future tournaments. It necessarily gives the first prizes to the best players, and effectually prevents inferior players from getting a prize. It must, however, not be forgotten, that if it be the object of the promoters of the Tournament to bring as many players together as possible, the old method is preferable, for it leaves the second, third, and fourth prizes to chance, and therefore more readily induces the weaker players to join in them, who, relying on the saying, *audaces fortuna juvat*, trust rather to their fortune than their skill.

TO THE EDITOR OF THE CHESS PLAYER'S CHRONICLE.

SIR,—It is generally supposed that CAXTON's *Game and Player of the Chess* was the first book ever printed in England, although some writers no doubt mention it as being the second. I give you below the names of two works printed in 1468 and 1471 respectively, which, if they are correctly described, would seem to prove that CAXTON's translation of JACOBUS DE CESOLIS, which bears the date of 1474, is entitled to rank as only third in the list of our printed books.

The first is mentioned by TWISS in his *Chess* (Part I. p. 46), in the following terms :—

"The next book on Chess was printed in 1474 by W. CAXTON, and according to AMES's *Typographical Antiquities*, was the first book printed in England, though the editors of the *Encyclopædia* printed at Edinburgh, say there is a small quarto volume of forty-one leaves in the public library at Cambridge, entitled *Exposicio Sancti Jeronimi in Simbolum Apostolorum ad Papam Laurentium Impressa Oxonia et finita Anno Domini* MCCCCLXVIII. XVII *die Decembris.* This is said to have been printed with wooden types, but CAXTON was the first who printed with metal types."

The title of the second is thus given by DIBDIN in his *Bibliomania* (vol. ii. p. 533), *Recule of the Historyes of Troy :* printed by CAXTON, 1471, folio.

DIBDIN informs us that both of the above works were disposed of by auction in 1786, at the sale of the library of " that judicious and tasteful bibliomaniac, MARK CEPHAS TUTET ": on which occasion the *Exposicio* brought £16. 5s., and the *Recule,* which was a very fine copy, realized 20 guineas.

While the pen is in my hand I cannot help expressing a hope that Professor FORBES will ere long give us a continuation of his remarks on Eastern Blindfold Play which appeared in your June number. There are, besides this, many deficient links in the History and Antiquities of Oriental Chess, which he, and he alone, of all our writers on the game, is competent to supply. I would specially instance that interesting part of the subject, of which at present little or nothing is generally known—I mean the progress of Chess from the time of its leaving Persia, until it reached Arabia and the Byzantine Empire. We were promised, some time since, by way of sequel to Professor FORBES's *Treatise on the Origin and Progress of Chess,* a disquisition on the introduction and advance of Chess in Europe, from the joint pens of Sir F. MADDEN and Mr. STAUNTON ; but this *desideratum* in the literature of the game has not yet been made good.

When these gaps shall have been filled up, there will then exist an almost unbroken succession of materials for some future Chess MA-

CAULAY to mould into a large and comprehensive history of the royal
game.   His narrative—commencing with the very childhood of the
human race, when, fifty centuries ago, the white-robed Brahmin first
meditated Chaturanga by the waters of his broad-flowing Gunga—
would unfold in its course down the stream of time many a strange
and wondrous incident of Chess prowess and Chess adventure, and,
extending itself to our day, record how in Europe PAUL MORPHY
emulated the deeds of his great namesake PAULO BOI, and by the
electric power of his genius kindled an enthusiasm for Chess in his
native land, which has spread like wildfire over every state in the
American Union.

I am, sir, yours faithfully,

BATH, *July* 20, 1859.   H. A. KENNEDY.

A GAME AT CHESS.

PLAYED AND WRITTEN BY ROBERT BENNETT, OF WISBECH.

OF mighty deeds in mimic fight,
'Twixt val'rous hosts of Black and White,
And war, and all its train of woes,
Where Nene [1] with rapid current flows,
The muse essays the picture to disclose.

Behold then, first, the scene of fight,
A field of chequers, eight times eight ;
Each corner by a massive Tower
Is flanked against the hostile power.
Backward, forward, from side to side,
These towers, across the champaign wide,
Rush, acting near or acting far,
The dread artillery of war.
Four mounted Knights of noble mien
Adjoining these are to be seen,
Who, o'er the plain curvetting light
From White to Black, from Black to White,
Forth on their deadly mission go
And deal destruction to the foe.
A martial Bishop guards each King,
Or sallies forth with oblique spring ;
A martial Bishop guards each Queen,
And well his high behest I ween
He doth perform.   The central space
The Monarchs and their consorts grace.

[1] The name of the Wisbech River.

Each King doth his bold front oppose
To him who leads his gallant foes,
And, trusting to his subjects' love,
With regal dignity doth move
One solemn step on every side,
Content the *grand design* to guide,
Relying on his Generals' skill
To save his *distant* force from ill.
The stately Queens their Lords attend
Till the harsh shouts of battle rend
The air, when, rushing madly forth,
They charge the foe with murd'rous wrath,
Careering swiftly o'er the plain
And strewing it with hostile slain;
Or, stealthily, with covert wiles,
Th' unwary foeman each beguiles,
And, step by step manœuvring slow,
Achieves at length their overthrow.
A soldier of *plebeian race*
Attends before each nobler piece.
Yet, Pawn of humble birth! thy name
And deeds full well are known to fame,
Nor wile nor gallantry can charm,
Or self-devotedness can warm
A patriot heart, shall strain of mine
Need eulogize a deed of thine?
One step, or two, he moves forthright,
Confiding in his arm of might.
Beginning thus his march, no more
He rushes two steps as before,
But cautiously, with steady tramp,
He threatens the opposing camp,
And when, relentless in his hate,
He seals an enemy's sad fate,
Obliquely must the vengeful steel
That enemy is doomed to feel,
Pierce to the heart the vanquished wight,
Or tow'rds the left, or tow'rds the right.

Thus organized, and thus encamped
(When erst the plains of Nene were swamped
By wintry floods), contending hosts
Each occupied their several posts.
But ah! what warrior there so bold
Whose blood would not run icy cold

To put the battle in array
And peril life to win the day?
Not one but felt the pow'rful spell,
Yet all resolved to bear them well.

With fiery haste, in rising wrath,
Two steps a White Pawn sallied forth
('Twas he who, by his monarch graced,
Had been in his pavilion placed),
This valiant spearman cried aloud,
And thus proclaimed his challenge proud;
" Ye coward slaves! let any dare
To meet me here in battle fair,
His fellows soon shall see him slain,
By me stretched lifeless on the plain."

Provoked, the swarthy Queen's Pawn cried,
" Such boundless insolence and pride
Must be chastised;" he said no more,
But, rushing on two steps before
The foremost rank, he took his stand,
And charged his foeman hand to hand.
Not bards more deadly strife have sung,
Nor long the strife uncertain hung,
For fortune smiled upon the White,
And Black soon " bade this world ' good night.' "
Then, hurling far his foe's remains,
The White that foe's position gains,
A post of danger, as of trust,
Who holds it, soon must bite the dust.
Enraged at what had late befell
The faithful guard she loved so well,
The sable Queen a mighty bound
(Regardless of her foes around)
Achieved, and with one sturdy blow
She laid the vaunting conqu'ror low.
Beware! beware! for thou art seen
By one devoted to his Queen,
Thy mortal enemy, a Knight
Of courage bold, " Sir Harry " hight.
He, leaping forth, hath aimed a stroke
Would cleave the soundest heart of oak.
The Queen his gage of combat spurns,
And wisely to her tent returns.
The White King's Bishop, with his shield
Uplifted high, then takes the field.

Ah! hapless Black! if none shall warn
Thy King to guard his Bishop's Pawn,
Too late for remedy thou 'lt find
Thy hopes all scattered to the wind.
The Knight who guards the sable throne
Forth issues next, with haughty tone,
Defying all the host of White
To meet him there in single fight,
Supported as he was by two
Brave Pawns as ever weapon drew.
Roused by the taunts, so fierce exprest,
The White King's Knight set lance in rest,
And, rushing to King's Bishop's third,
Took the rash warrior at his word.
But fate ordained these subjects leal
Should not each other's vengeance feel.

As yet, so little blood had flown,
That Black Queen's Knight, impatient grown,
Goaded his courser to a square*
Committed to his special care,
In hopes that deeds of high emprise
Would quickly on the field arise.
Nor vain that wish, though yet denied,
Ere long 'twas fully gratified.

The Pawn attendant on White Queen
Advancing one square next is seen,
The Bishop next, of Ethiop hue,
To his lov'd Queen and country true,
Fierce rushing into closest fight,
Makes prisoner the White King's Knight.
That monarch, fearful of his power,
Retreats behind th' embattled Tower.
The Black Queen's Knight in fury now
Gave utterance to a sacred vow,
That either that poor captive Knight
Should bite the dust, or he would bite;
And, springing to his King's fourth square,
He rushed th' adventurous deed to dare.
Oh God! what torture racked the breast
Of that pinned Knight, whose fallen crest
Proclaimed him recreant, or unskilled
In deeds his high-souled monarch willed.

* The Queen's Bishop's third.

"Oh! sad disgrace! unwept to fall,
Nay more, to die despised by all,
To be from fame, from favor, torn,
To leave my King, of glory shorn,
Nor know to avoid a doubled Pawn :
Yet stay! good Heavens! it cannot be ;
And yet it is, —what do I see?
Salvation to the fair-haired host!
But oh! at what a mighty cost!
Dear consort of my reverenced lord,
Our honor cannot be restored
Save at the hazard of thy life,
Yet, sure as thou'rt a faithful wife,
That hazard thou wilt gladly run,
Ere thou wilt see thy lord undone."
Thus spake that Knight, and burst his chains,
Nor from fierce combat long refrains.
The Black Queen's Knight did instant feel—
Felt but to die by—his keen steel.
The White King's consort, thus exposed,
Her sad career was swiftly closed,
The Bishop by one furious thrust
Transfixed her to her native dust.
" Still, ye survivors of the White,
Be not cast down, I yet can fight,"
The White-robed Bishop cries, and on
He dashes at the Bishop's Pawn.
" The battle is not with the strong,"
He shouts, as he careers along,
One stroke 's enough. That hapless Pawn
Had better never have been born.
He dies,—his lord finds all too late,
That that fell Bishop gives " checkmate."

The following are the moves of the game :—

White. (R. B.)	*Black.* (Mr. H.)
1. P. to K. fourth	1. P. to Q. fourth
2. P. takes P.	2. Q. takes P.
3. Q. Kt. to B. third	3. Q. to her square
4. K. B. to Q. B. fourth	4. K. Kt. to B. third
5. K. Kt. to B. third	5. Q. Kt. to B. third
6. P. to Q. third	6. Q. B. to K. Kt. fifth
7. Castles	7. Q. Kt. to K. fourth
8. Kt. takes Kt.	8. B. takes Q.
9. B. takes K. B. P.	Mate.

GAME IV.

Match between Mr. MORPHY and Herr LÖWENTHAL.

	Black. (Mr. MORPHY.)		White. (Herr LÖWENTHAL.)
1.	P. to K. fourth	1.	P. to K. fourth
2.	P. to K. B. fourth	2.	B. to Q. B. fourth
3.	K. Kt. to K. B. third	3.	P. to Q. third
4.	P. to Q. B. third	4.	B. to K. Kt. fifth
5.	K. B. to K. second	5.	B. takes Kt.
6.	B. takes B.	6.	Kt. to Q. B. third
7.	P. to Q. Kt. fourth	7.	B. to Q. Kt. third
8.	P. to Q. Kt. fifth	8.	Q. Kt. to K. second
9.	P. to Q. fourth	9.	P. takes B. P. (a)
10.	Q. B. takes P.	10.	Q. Kt. to K. Kt. third
11.	Q. B. to K. third	11.	K. Kt. to B. third
12.	Q. Kt. to Q. second	12.	Castles
13.	Castles	13.	P. to K. R. third
14.	P. to Q. R. fourth	14.	P. to Q. B. third
15.	Q. to K. second	15.	K. R. to K. square
16.	Q. to Q. third (b)	16.	P. to Q. fourth
17.	P. to K. fifth	17.	K. Kt. to Q. second
18.	K. B. to K. R. fifth (c)	18.	R. to K. third (d)
19.	P. to Q. R. fifth (e)	19.	B. to Q. B. second
20.	R. takes K. B. P.	20.	K. takes R. (f)
21.	Q. to K. B. fifth (check)	21.	K. to K. second
22.	B. takes Kt.	22.	Q. to K. Kt. square
23.	Q. B. to K. B. second	23.	Kt. takes K. P. (g)
24.	Q. P. takes Kt.	24.	Q. R. to K. B. square
25.	B. to Q. B. fifth (check)	25.	K. to Q. square
26.	B. takes Q. R.	26.	R. takes P.
27.	Q. to K. B. second	27.	Q. to K. third
28.	P. to Q. Kt. sixth	28.	P. takes P.
29.	P. takes P.	29.	Q. takes B.
30.	P. takes B. (check)	30.	K. takes P.
31.	R. to Q. Kt. square		

Resigns.

Notes.

(a) The books recommend here, "P. takes Q. P.," but the move in the text may be adopted without disadvantage.

(*b*) This was the proper play, providing for White's intended attack of "P. to Q. fourth," &c.

(*c*) The commencement of a combination of much merit.

(*d*) This was an error arising from Herr Löwenthal seeing only when too late the threatened attack.   "Q. to K. B. fifth" would have given White at least as good a game as Black.

(*e*) The sacrifice of the Rook at once would have been equally good.

(*f*) Badly played, "Kt. to R. square" would have been much better.

(*g*) A useless sacrifice, deciding White's fate at once. "Kt. to K. B. square" might have given Black a chance of drawing. Thus:—

	23. Kt. to K. B. square
24. B. to K. R. fourth (check)	24. K. to Q. second
25. B. to K. B. seventh	25. P. to K. Kt. third
26. B. takes Q. (best)	26. P. takes Q.
27. B. takes R.	27. K. takes B.

Leaving Black only a Pawn ahead.

The presence of Herr HARRWITZ in the metropolis enables us to present our readers with some of the games which he has played, we therefore give in this number only one of the games in the above match.

Games played at the PHILIDORIAN CHESS ROOMS, between Herr HARRWITZ and Mr. CAMPBELL, July 21, 1859.

GAME I.

Black. (Herr HARRWITZ.)	*White.* (Mr. CAMPBELL.)
1. P. to K. fourth	1. P. to R. fourth
2. Kt. to K. B. third	2. Kt. to Q. B. third
3. B. to Q. B. fourth	3. B. to Q. B. fourth
4. P. to Q. Kt. fourth	4. B. takes P.
5. P. to Q. B. third	5. B. to Q. R. fourth
6. P. to Q. fourth	6. P. takes P.
7. Castles	7. B. to Q. Kt. third
8. P. takes P.	8. P. to Q. third
9. P. to Q. fifth	9. Q. Kt. to K. second
10. P. to K. fifth	10. B. to K. Kt. fifth
11. B. to Q. Kt. second	11. P. takes P.
12. B. takes P.	12. Kt. to K. B. third
13. Q. to Q. R. fourth (check)	13. B. to Q. second
14. Q. to Q. Kt. third	14. Castles
15. B. takes Kt.	15. P. takes B.
16. Q. Kt. to Q. second	16. Kt. to K. Kt. third
17. K. R. to K. square	17. P. to K. B. fourth
18. Q. to Q. B. third	18. R. to K. square

19. Kt. to K. B. square	19. Kt. to K. R. fifth
20. Kt. to K. fifth	20. P. to K. B. fifth
21. Q. R. to Q. square	21. Q. to K. Kt. fourth
22. P. to K. Kt. third	22. R. takes Kt.
23. Kt. to Q. second	23. R. takes R. (check)
24. R. takes R.	24. P. takes P.
25. R. P. takes P.	25. Q. takes Kt.

And Black resigns.

GAME II.

White. (Mr. CAMPBELL.)	*Black.* (Herr HARRWITZ.)
1. P. to K. fourth	1. P. to K. fourth
2. Kt. to K. B. third	2. P. to Q. third
3. P. to Q. fourth	3. P. takes P.
4. Q. takes P.	4. Kt. to Q. B. third
5. B. to Q. Kt. fifth	5. B. to Q. second
6. B. takes Kt.	6. B. takes B.
7. B. to K. Kt. fifth	7. Kt. to K. B. third
8. B. takes Kt.	8. Q. takes B.
9. Q. takes Q.	9. P. takes Q.
10. Kt. to Q. B. third	10. Castles on Q. side
11. Castles on Q. side	11. R. to K. square
12. K. R. to R. square	12. P. to K. R. fourth
13. Kt. to Q. fourth	13. B. to K. R. third (check)
14. K. to Q. Kt. square	14. B. to K. B. fifth
15. Kt. takes B.	15. P. takes Kt.
16. P. to K. Kt. third	16. B. to K. R. third
17. P. to K. R. fourth	17. K. R. to K. Kt. square
18. R. to Q. fourth	18. P. to K. B. fourth
19. R. to Q. B. fourth	19. K. to Q. second
20. R. to Q. square	20. R. to K. Kt. fifth
21. R. to Q. B. fifth	21. P. takes P.
22. Kt. to K. second	22. P. to Q. fourth
23. P. to Q. B. fourth	23. K. to Q. third
24. P. to Q. Kt. fourth	24. R. to K. fourth
25. Kt. to Q. fourth	25. P. to K. sixth
26. P. to K. B. fourth	26. B. takes P.
27. P. takes B.	27. R. takes P.

28. Kt. to K. second	28. R. takes R. P.
29. K. to Q. B. second	29. P. to K. B. fourth
30. P. takes P.	30. P. takes P.
31. K. to Q. third	31. R. takes Q. Kt. P.
32. R. to Q. B. square	·32. R. to Q. Kt. seventh
33. R. to Q. B. sixth (check)	33. K. to K. second
34. R. takes P. (check)	34. K. to K. B. third
35. R. from Q. B. seventh to sixth (check)	35. K. to K. second
36. R. to Q. B. seventh (check)	36. K. to K. B. third
37. R. from Q. B. seventh (check)	37. R. to K. third
38. R. takes R.	38. K. takes R.
39. Kt. to K. B. fourth (check)	39. K. to K. fourth
40. K. takes P.	40. R. takes P.
41. R. to Q. B. fifth	41. R. to Q. R. sixth (check)
42. Kt. to Q. third (check)	42. K. to Q. third
43. R. to Q. B. eighth	43. P. to K. B. fifth (check)
44. K. to Q. second	44. R. to Q. R. seventh (check)
45. K. to Q. B. third	45. R. to Q. R. sixth (check)
46. K. to Q. second	46. R. to Q. R. fifth
47. R. to K. B. eighth	47. R. to Q. fifth
48. R. takes P.	48. R. takes R.
49. Kt. takes R.	49. K. to Q. B. fourth
50. R. takes B. P.	50. R. takes R.
51. Kt. takes R. P.	

And the game was drawn.

We give the three following games, not on account of their intrinsic merit (they having been played during the stay of Herr HARRWITZ at Mr. BRIEN's on a friendly visit), but, having been played by well-known players, they may be interesting to some of our readers, especially as few of the games of Herr HARRWITZ have been printed of late years in England.

White. (BRIEN.)	*Black.* (HARRWITZ.)
1. P. to K. fourth	1. P. to K. fourth ·
2. Kt. to K. B. third	2. P. to Q. third
3. P. to Q. fourth .	3. P. takes P.

4. Q. takes P.	4. Kt. to Q. B. third
5. B. to Q. Kt. fifth	5. B. to Q. second
6. Q. to Q. square	6. Kt. to K. B. third
7. Kt. to Q. B. third	7. B. to K. second
8. Castles	8. Castles
9. B. to K. B. fourth	9. P. to Q. R. third
10. B. to Q. third	10. P. to Q. Kt. fourth
11. Q. to Q. second	11. B. to K. third
12. K. R. to K. square	12. Kt. to Q. second
13. Kt. to Q. fifth	13. P. to K. B. third
14. P. to Q. B. fourth	14. R. to Q. Kt. square
15. Q. R. to Q. B. square	15. P. to Q. Kt. fifth
16. P. to Q. B. fifth	16. B. takes Kt.
17. P. takes B.	17. Q. Kt. to K. fourth
18. P. takes P.	18. B. takes P.
19. Kt. takes Kt.	19. P. takes Kt.
20. B. to K. Kt. fifth	20. Q. to Q. B. square
21. Q. to K. second	21. Kt. to Q. B. fourth
22. B. to Q. Kt. square	22. Q. to K. square
23. B. to K. third	23. R. to Q. Kt. fourth
24. Q. to K. Kt. fourth	24. Q. to K. B. second
25. Q. to K. R. fourth	25. P. to K. Kt. third
26. B. to K. R. sixth	26. Q. to K. B. third
27. B. to K. Kt. fifth	27. Q. to K. B. second
28. R. to K. third	28. Q. takes Q. P.
29. R. to K. R. third	29. Q. to K. B. second
30. R. to K. B. third	30. Q. to Q. second
31. B. to K. B. sixth	31. P. to K. fifth
32. B. takes P.	32. Kt. takes B.
33. Q. takes Kt.	33. R. to K. square
34. Q. to K. R. fourth (a)	34. R. to K. R. square
35. Q. to Q. B. fourth (check)	35. Q. to K. third
36. R. to K. third (b)	36. B. takes P. (check)
37. K. to K. B. square	37. Q. takes Q. (check)

And wins.

Notes.

(a) Evidently an oversight.　　　　(b) Another oversight.

GAME II.

White. (HARRWITZ.)	Black. (BRIEN.)
1. P. to K. fourth	1. P. to Q. fourth
2. P. takes P.	2. Q. takes P.
3. Kt. to Q. B. third	3. Q. to Q. R. fourth
4. P. to Q. fourth	4. B. to K. B. fourth
5. B. to Q. B. fourth	5. P. to K. third
6. K. Kt. to K. second	6. Kt. to Q. B. third
7. Castles	7. Castles
8. B. to K. third	8. Kt. to K. B. third
9. P. to Q. R. third	9. B. to K. Kt. third
10. B. to Q. Kt. fifth	10. Q. to Q. Kt. third
11. P. to Q. Kt. fourth	11. Kt. to Q. fourth
12. Q. to Q. B. square	12. Kt. takes Kt.
13. Kt. takes Kt.	13. Kt. takes Q. P.
14. R. to Q. square	14. P. to K. fourth
15. B. to K. B. square	15. Q. to Q. B. third (a)
16. B. takes Kt.	16. P. takes B.
17. Kt. to Q. Kt. fifth (b)	17. Q. takes Q. B. P.
18. Q. to K. B. fourth	18. B. to Q. third
19. Kt. takes B.	19. R. takes B.
20. Q. R. to Q. B. square	

And resigns.

Notes.

(a) A very inconsiderate move, which loses the game.
(b) The winning move.

Game between Herr HARRWITZ and Mr. ZYTOGORSKI.

White. Herr HARRWITZ.)	Black. (Mr. ZYTOGORSKI.)
1. P. to K. fourth	1. P. to K. fourth
2. P. to K. B. fourth	2. P. takes P.
3. K. B. to Q. B. fourth	3. Q. to K. R. fifth (check)
4. K. to B. square	4. P. to Q. fourth
5. P. takes P.	5. P. to Q. B. third
6. Q. to K. second (check)	6. Q. to K. second
7. P. to Q. fourth	7. Kt. K. to B. third
8. Q. Kt. to B. third	8. P. to Q. Kt. fourth

9. K. B. to Q. Kt. third	9. P. to Q. Kt. fifth
10. Q. takes Q. (check)	10. B. takes Q.
11. Q. Kt. to K. second	11. Kt. takes P.
12. B. takes Kt.	12. P. takes B.
13. Kt. takes P.	13. B. to Kt. second
14. K. Kt. to B. third	14. Kt. to Q. second
15. Q. B. to Q. second	15. Castles on K. side
16. P. to K. Kt. fourth	16. P. to Q. R. fourth
17. K. to Kt. second	17. Kt. to B. third
18. P. to K. R. third	18. K. B. to Q. third
19. Q. Kt. to Q. third	19. Kt. to K. fifth
20. B. to B. fourth	20. Q. R. to B. square
21. Q. B. to B. square	21. K. R. to K. square
22. K. R. to K. square	22. P. to K. B. third
23. B. takes B.	23. Kt. takes B.
24. Kt. to B. fifth	24. B. to B. third
25. K. Kt. to Q. second	25. K. to B. second
26. K. to B. third	26. P. to K. Kt. third
27. K. to B. second	27. Kt. to K. fifth (check)
28. Q. Kt. takes Kt.	28. P. takes Kt.
29. Kt. to B. fourth	29. K. R. to Q. square
30. P. to Q. B. third	30. P. to Q. R. fifth
31. K. to K. third	31. P. takes P.
32. P. takes P.	32. R. to B. second
33. Kt. to Q. second	33. P. to K. B. fourth
34. R. to K. B. square	34. B. to Q. second
35. P. to Q. B. fourth	35. K. to Kt. second
36. P. takes P.	36. B. takes P.
37. K. R. to Q. square	37. R. to Q. Kt. square
38. P. to Q. B. fifth	38. R. to Kt. seventh
39. P. to Q. fifth	

And Black resigned.

Game between Mr. HARRWITZ and Mr. BIRD.

Black. (Mr. BIRD.)	White. (Mr. HARRWITZ.)
1. P. to K. fourth	1. P. to K. fourth
2. Kt. to K. B. third	2. P. to Q. third
3. P. to Q. fourth	3. P. takes P.

4. Q. takes P.	4. Q. Kt. to B. third
5. K. B. to Q. Kt. fifth	5. B. to Q. second
6. B. takes Kt.	6. B. takes B.
7. Castles	7. Kt. to K. B. third
8. B. to K. Kt. fifth	8. B. to K. second
9. Kt. to Q. B. third	9. P. to K. R. third •
10. B. to K. R. fourth	10. Castles
11. Q. R. to Q. square	11. Kt. takes K. P.
12. B. takes B.	12. Q. takes B.
13. K. R. to K. square	13. P. to K. B. fourth
14. K to Q. second	14. Q. to K. B. third
15. Q. to Q. B. fourth (check)	15. K. to R. square
16. K. Kt. takes Kt.	16. P. takes Kt.
17. Q. to Q. fourth	17. Q. R. to K. square
18. K. R. to K. second	18. Q. R. to K. fourth
19. Q. takes Q. R. P.	19. P. to Q. fourth
20. Q. to Q. fourth	20. K. R. to K. square
21. Q. R. to K. square	21. Q. to K. R. fifth
22. R. to K. third	22. R. to K. B. square (a)
23. R. to K. R. third	23. Q. to K. second
24. R. to K. Kt. third	24. Q. to K. B. second
25. R. to K. second	25. R. to K. B. fourth
26. Kt. to Q. square	26. P. to Q. Kt. third
27. P. to K. R. third	27. B. to K. Kt. fourth
28. R. to Q. second	28. P. to Q. B. fourth
29. Q. to K. third	29. Q. to K. third
30. Q. to Q. Kt. third	30. B. to Q. B. fifth
31. Q. to Q. R. third	31. P. to Q. fifth
32. P. to Q. Kt. fourth	32. Q. to K. fourth
33. K. to R. second	33. P. to K. R. fourth
34. K. to K. Kt. square (b)	34. P. to K. R. fifth
35. R. to K. Kt. fourth	35. P. to K. Kt. fourth
36. P. takes P.	36. P. takes P.
37. Q. to Q. Kt. second	37. P. to K. sixth
38. Kt. takes P.	38. R. takes K. B. P.
39. R. takes R.	39. Q. takes Kt.
40. P. to Q. B. third	40. Q. to K. eighth (check) (c)
41. K. to R. second	41. Q. takes R.

16

42. Q. takes Q.	42. R. takes Q.
43. P. takes P.	43. P. takes P.
44. R. takes Q. P.	44. B. takes P. (d)
45. R. to K. Kt. fourth	45. R. to K. B. fourth
46. P. to K. Kt. third	

And the game was drawn.

Notes.

(a) A very well conceived move, which can only be parried by the move in the text; for if Black had played the obvious move, "R. to K. Kt. third," White would have replied by "P. to K. sixth"; if "Q. takes Q.," White mates in two moves; if "P. takes P.," then "Q. takes Q." and wins; if, thirdly, "Q. takes R.," then "P. takes P. (check)," "K. to B. square," "P. takes R. (dis. check)," "K' takes P.," "R. to K. square," wins.

(b) "P. to K. R. fourth" would have been bad, for White would have replied by "Q. to K. B. fifth."

(c) "P. takes P.," followed by "Q to K. eighth (check)," and then R. takes R. would have led to a speedy and favorable termination for White; for

Black.	White.
	41. P. takes P.
42. Q. to Q. B. second (best)	42. Q. to K. eighth (check)
43. K. to R. second	43. R. takes R.
44. Q. to K. fourth (best)	44. Q. takes Q.
45. R. takes Q.	45. R. takes P. (check)
46. K. takes R.	46. B. to Q. fourth
47. K. to B. third	47. P. to Q. B. seventh

And wins.

(d) "B. to K. third" would have still won the game.

Game between Herr HARRWITZ and Mr. MEDLEY, Hon. Secretary of the London Chess Club. Played at the London Chess Club, June 28, 1859.

White. (Mr. MEDLEY.)	Black. (Herr HARRWITZ.)
1. P. to K. fourth	1. P. to K. fourth
2. K. Kt. to B. third	2. P. to Q. third
3. P. to Q. fourth	3. P. takes P.
4. Q. takes P.	4. Q. Kt. to B. third
5. K. B. to Q. Kt. fifth	5. B. to Q. second
6. B. takes Kt.	6. B. takes B.
7. Castles (a)	7. K. Kt. to B. third
8. Q. Kt. to B. third	8. K. B. to K. second
9. Q. B. to K. B. fourth	9. Castles
10. Q. B. to K. Kt. third (b)	10. Kt. to R. fourth

11. Q. Kt. to Q. fifth	11. P. to K. B. fourth
12. Q. Kt. takes B. (check)	12 Q. takes Kt.
13. P. takes P.	13. B. takes Kt.
14. P. takes B.	14. R. takes P.
15. Q. to K. fourth	15. Q. to Q. second
16. Q. R. to K. square	16. Q. R. to K. B. square
17. Q. R. to K. third	17. K. R. to K. Kt. fourth
18. Q. to K. seventh	18. Q. takes Q.
19. R. takes Q.	19. K. R. to Q. B. fourth
20. P. to Q. B. third	20. Q. R. takes P.
21. K. R. to Q. square	21. P. to K. R. third
22. K. to Kt. second	22. R. to B. second
23. R. to K. eighth (check)	23. K. to R. second
24. R. to Q. fourth	24. P. to Q. R. fourth
25. P. to Q. R. fourth	25. P. to Q. Kt. third
26. R. to K. sixth	26. Kt. to B. third
27. B. to R. fourth	27. Kt. to R. fourth
28. B. to Kt. third	28. K. R. to B. fourth
29. R. to K. second	29. P. to K. Kt. fourth
30. K. R. to K. fourth	30. Kt. to Kt. second
31. R. to K. seventh	31. K. to Kt. third
32. R. takes R.	32. K. takes R.
33. R. to K. fourth	33. Kt. to K. third
34. K. to B. square	34. R. to Q. fourth
35. K. to K. second	35. Kt. to B. fourth
36. R. to Q. B. fourth	36. P. to K. R. fourth
37. P. to K. B. third	37. P. to K. R. fifth
38. B. to B. second	38. R. to K. fourth (check)
39. K. to Q. second	39. P. to Q. fourth
40. R. to K. Kt. fourth	40. Kt. to K. third
41. B. to K. third	41. P. to Q. B. fourth
42. P. to K. R. third	42. K. to Kt. third
43. K. to Q. third	43. K. to B. fourth
44. P. to Q. Kt. third	44. P. to Q. fifth
45. P. takes P.	45. P. takes P.
46. B. to Q. second (c)	46. R. to B. fourth
47. R. to K. fourth	47. R. to Q. B. square
48. R. to Kt. fourth	48. R. to Q. B. third

49. R. to K. Kt. square	49. Kt. to B. fourth (check)
50. K. takes P.	50. Kt. takes P. (check)
51. K. to Q. third	51. R. to Q. third (check)
52. K. to B. third	52. Kt. takes B. (d)
53. R. to Q. square	53. K. to B. fifth

And wins.

Notes.

(a) "B. to K. Kt. fifth" is the move generally played.

(b) "P. to K. R. third," to enable him to retreat the B., would have been better.

(c) If the B. had taken the P., Black would have been enabled to exchange pieces and win easily.

(d) Black might have saved the piece by playing "Kt. to Q. B. fifth," but the game was won as easily by the move in the text.

Game between Messrs. HARRWITZ and BIRD.

White. (Herr HARRWITZ.)	*Black.* (Mr. BIRD.)
1. P. to K. fourth	1. P. to K. fourth
2. Kt. to K. B. third	2. Kt. to K. B. third
3. B. to Q. B. fourth	3. Kt. takes P.
4. Kt. to Q. B. third	4. Kt. to K. B. third
5. Kt. takes P.	5. P. to Q. fourth
6. B. to Q. Kt. third	6. B. to Q. Kt. fifth
7. Castles	7. Castles
8. P. to Q. fourth	8. B. takes Kt.
9. P. takes B.	9. P. to Q. B. third
10. P. to Q. B. fourth	10. P. to K. R. third
11. P. to K. B. fourth	11. P. takes P.
12. Kt. takes P.	12. B. to K. third
13. P. to K. B. fifth	13. B. takes Kt.
14. B. takes B.	14. Q. Kt. to Q. second
15. B. to Q. Kt. third	15. Kt. to Q. Kt. third
16. P. to Q B. fourth	16. R. to K. square
17. Q. to Q. third	17. R. to K. fifth
18. B. to K. third	18. Q. to Q. B. second
19. R. to K. B. third	19. Kt. to K. Kt. fifth
20. Q. takes R.	20. Q. takes K. R. P. (check)
21. K. to B. square	21. Q. to K. R. eighth (check)

22. B. to K. Kt. square	22. Kt. to R. seventh (check)
23. K. to B. second	23. Kt. takes R.
24. Q. takes Kt.	24. Q. to R. fifth (check)
25. K. to K. B. square	25. R. to K. square
26. R. to Q. square	26. R. to K. fifth
27. B. to K. third	27. Kt. to Q. second
28. K. to K. Kt. square	28. Kt. to K. B. third
29. B. to Q. B. second	29. R. to K. Kt. fifth
30. B. to K. B. second	30. Q. to K. Kt. fourth
31. R. to K. square	31. Q. to Q. seventh
32. B. to Q. Kt. third	32. R. takes Q. P.
33. R. to Q. square	

And wins.

Herr HARRWITZ gives Q. R. to an AMATEUR.

White. (Herr HARRWITZ.)	*Black.* (AMATEUR.)
1. P. to K. fourth	1. P. to K. fourth
2. Kt. to K. B. third	2. Kt. to Q. B. third
3. B. to Q. B. fourth	3. B. to Q. B. fourth
4. P. to Q. Kt. fourth	4. B. takes Kt. P.
5. P. to Q. B. third	5. B. to Q. R. fourth
6. P. to Q. fourth	6. P. takes P.
7. Castles	7. Kt. to K. B. third
8. P. to K. fifth	8. P. to Q. fourth
9. B. to Q. Kt. fifth	9. Kt. to K. fifth
10. B. to Q. R. third	10. B. to Q. Kt. third
11. P. takes P.	11. B. to K. third
12. K. Kt. to Q. second	12. Kt. takes Kt.
13. Kt. takes Kt.	13. P. to Q. R. third
14. B. to Q. R. fourth	14. B. takes P.
15. B. takes Kt. (check)	15. P. takes B.
16. Q. to Q. R. fourth	16. B. takes K. P.
17. Q. takes Q. B. P. (check)	17. B. to Q. second
18. Q. takes Q. P.	18. B. to Q. third
19. B. takes B.	19. P. takes B.
20. R. to K. square (check)	20. B. to K. third
21. Q. to Q. B. sixth (check)	21. K. to K. B. square

22. Kt. to K. fourth	22. P. to K. Kt. third
23. Q. to Q. B. third	23. P. to K. B. third
24. Kt. takes K. B. P.	24. K. to K. B. second
25. Kt. to K. fourth	25. R. to K. square
26. P. to K. R. fourth	26. P. to K. R. third
27. Q. to Q. second	27. K. to K. Kt. second
28. Q. to Q. fourth (check)	28. K. to K. B. second
29. Kt. takes P. (check)	29. K. to K. second
30. R. to Q. square	30. R. to K. Kt. square
31. Q. to Q. B. fifth	31. Q. to K. B. square
32. Q. to Q. B. seventh (check)	32. K. to K. B. third
33. Kt. to K. fourth (check)	33. K. to K. B. fourth
34. P. to K. B. third	34. Q. to Q. Kt. square
35. Kt. P. mates	

Game between Mr. V. GREEN, in India, and the celebrated BRAHMIN, the latter giving the odds of Pawn and move.

(*Remove Black's K. B. P.*)

White. (Mr. GREEN.)	*Black.* (BRAHMIN.)
1. P. to K. fourth	1. P. to K. third
2. P. to Q. fourth	2. P. to Q. fourth
3. P. takes P.	3. P. takes P.
4. Q. (checks)	4. P. covers
5. Q. to K. fifth (check)	5. Q. covers
6. B. to K. B. fourth	6. B. to K. Kt. second
7. Q. takes Q. (check)	7. Kt. takes Q.
8. Kt. to K. B. third	8. P. to Q. B. fourth
9. P. to Q. B. third	9. P. takes P.
10. P. takes P.	10. Q. Kt. to B. third
11. B. to K. fifth	11. B. takes B.
12. P. takes B.	12. B. to K. Kt. fifth
13. Q. Kt. to Q. second	13. Castles Q. R.
14. B. to Q. Kt. fifth	14. P. to Q. R. third
15. B. to Q. R. fourth	15. Kt. to Q. Kt. fifth
16. Castles K. R.	16. Kt. to Q. sixth
17. Q. R. to Q. Kt. square	17. B. to K. B. fourth
18. B. to Q. B. second	18. Kt. to Q. B. third

19. P. to Q. R. third	19. Q. Kt. takes P.
20. B. takes B. (check)	20. P. takes B.
21. Kt. takes Kt.	21. Kt. takes Kt.
22. P. to K. B. fourth	22. Kt. to K. Kt. fifth
23. K. R. to K. square	23. K. R. to K. square
24. Kt. to K. B. third	24. R. to K. fifth
25. Q. R. to Q. B. square (check)	25. K. to Q. second
26. P. to K. R. third	26. Kt. to K. B. third
27. Kt. to K. fifth (check)	27. K. to his third
28. Kt. to K. B. third	28. K. to Q. third
29. Kt. to K. Kt. fifth	29. Q. R. to K. square
30. Kt. takes R.	30. K. B. P. takes Kt.
31. K. to B. second	31. P. to Q. fifth
32. P. to K. Kt. fourth	32. Kt. to Q. fourth
33. Q. R. to Q. square	33. K. to B. fourth
34. P. to K. B. fifth	34. R. to K. second
35. P. to K. Kt. fifth	35. P. to Q. sixth
36. P. to K. B. sixth	36. R. to K. fourth
37. P. to K. R. fourth	37. R. checks
38. K. to Kt. third	38. R. to K. B. sixth (check)
39. K. to Kt. fourth	39. K. to Q. fifth
40. K. to R. fifth	40. Kt. takes K. B. P.
41. P. takes Kt.	41. R. takes P.
42. R. to K. Kt. square	42. R. to K. B. fourth (check)
43. K. to R. sixth	43. R. to Q. Kt. fourth
44. P. to K. R. fifth	44. R. takes Q. Kt. P.
45. K. takes P.	45. R. to K. R. seventh
46. P. to K. R. sixth	46. P. to K. sixth
47. R. to K. R. square	47. P. to K. seventh
48. R. takes P. (check)	48. K. takes R.
49. R. takes R.	49. P. queens
50. R. to K. Kt. second	50. Q. to K. fifth (check)
51. R. covers	51. P. to Q. R. fourth
52. K. to Kt. seventh	52. Q. to K. second (check)
53. K. to Kt. eighth	53. K. to his fifth
54. P. to K. R. seventh	54. K. to B. fourth
55. R. to K. Kt. square	55. Q. to K. square (check)
56. K. moves	56. Q. to K. fourth (check)

57. K. to B. seventh	57. Q. to Q. B. second (check)
58. K. to Kt. eighth	58. Q. to Q. B. fifth (check)
59. K. to B. eighth	59. Q. to Q. B. fourth
60. K. to K. eighth	60. Q. to K. sixth (check)
61. K. to B. eighth	61. Q. takes R.
62. P. queens	62. Q. to B. fourth (check)

And wins.

The following game, perhaps the only one extant between Herr LÖWENTHAL and the late Dr. BLEDOW, has never appeared in the CHESS PLAYER'S CHRONICLE. It was printed in our Prussian contemporary in 1847.

White. (BLEDOW.)	Black. (LÖWENTHAL.)
1. P. to K. fourth	1. P. to Q. fourth
2. P. takes P.	2. Q. takes P.
3. Kt. to Q. B. third	3. Q. to Q. square
4. P. to Q. fourth	4. P. to Q. B. fourth
5. P. to Q. fifth	5. P. to K. fourth
6. P. to K. B. fourth	6. B. to Q. third
7. B. to Q. Kt. fifth (check)	7. B. to Q. second
8. Q. to K. second	8. Q. to K. second
9. Kt. to K. B. third	9. P. to Q. R. third
10. B. takes-B. (check)	10. Kt. takes B.
11. Kt. to K. fourth	11. P. to K. B. third
12. Kt. to K. R. fourth	12. P. to K. Kt. third
13. P. to K. B. fifth	13. Kt. to K. B. square
14. P. to Q. B. fourth	14. Castles
15. P. takes P.	15. Kt. takes P.
16. Kt. to K. B. fifth	16. Q. to K. B. square
17. Q. Kt. takes B. (check)	17. R. takes Kt.
18. Kt. takes R. (check)	18. Q. takes Kt.
19. Castles	19. K. Kt. to K. second
20. B. to K. R. sixth	20. P. to K. B. fourth
21. Q. to K. R. fifth	21. R. to K. Kt. square
22. R. takes K. B. P.	22. Kt. takes R.
23. Q. takes Kt. (check)	23. Q. to Q. second
24. R. to K. B. square	24. K. R. to K. square
25. B. to K. third	25. Q. takes Q.

26. R. takes Q.	26. P. to K. fifth
27. R. to K. B. seventh	27. Kt. to K. fourth
28. R. takes K. R. P.	28. Kt. takes P.
29. B. to K. B. fourth	29. P. to K. sixth
30. P. to Q. sixth	30. Kt. takes Q. P.
31. B. takes Kt.	31. P. to K. seventh .
32. B. to K. Kt. third	32. P. to K. eighth (queens, checking)
33. B. takes Q.	33. R. takes B. (check)
34. K. to K. B. second	34. R. to Q. Kt. eighth
35. P. to K. Kt. fourth	35. R. takes P. (check)
36. K. to K. third	36. K. to Q. square
37. P. to K. Kt. fifth	37. K. to K. square
38. P. to K. R. fourth	38. R. to Q. Kt. third
39. P. to K. R. fifth	39. R. to K. third (check)
40. K. to K. B. fourth	40. P. to Q. Kt. fourth
41. K. to K. B. fifth	41. R. to K. eighth
42. R. to Q. R. seventh	42. R. to K. second
43. R. takes R. (check)	43. K. takes R.
44. K. to K. Kt. sixth (a)	44. P. to Q. B. fifth
45. P. to K. R. sixth	45. P. to Q. B. sixth
46. P. to K. R. seventh	46. P. to Q. B. seventh
47. P. to K. R. eighth (queens)	47. P. to Q. B. eighth (queens)
48. Q. to K. B. sixth (check)	48. Q. to K. square

The game, we believe, terminated here, being given up as drawn.

Note.

(a) Although White cannot now lose the game, this is an evident mistake; "P. to K. R. sixth" would have won easily.

Two games played at Manchester, June 24th, in the Match between Mr. E. THOROLD and Mr. KIPPING.

(Evans' Gambit declined.)

White. (Mr. KIPPING.)	*Black.* (Mr. E. THOROLD.)
1. P. to K. fourth	1. P. to K. fourth
2. K. Kt. to B. third	2. Q. Kt. to B. third
3. K. B. to Q. B. fourth	3. K. B. to Q. B. fourth
4. P. to Q. Kt. fourth	4. B. to Q. Kt. third
5. Castles .	5. P. to Q. third

6. P. to Q. Kt. fifth	6. Kt. to Q. R. fourth
7. B. to K. second (a)	7. K. Kt. to K. second
8. P. to Q. B. third	8. P. to K. B. fourth
9. P. takes P.	9. Q. B. takes P.
10. P. to Q. fourth	10. P. to K. fifth
11. Kt. to K. R. fourth	11. Castles
12. Q. B. to K. Kt. fifth	12. P. to Q. fourth
13. P. to K. B. third	13. P. to K. R. third
14. B. to K. third	14. Q. to Q. third
15. P. takes P.	15. B. takes P.
16. Kt. to K. B. third	16. Kt. to K. B. fourth
17. B. to K. B. second	17. P. to Q. B. fourth
18. Q. Kt. to Q. second	18. P. to Q. B. fifth
19. K. Kt. to K. fifth	19. Q. R. to K. square
20. Kt. takes B.	20. P. takes Kt.
21. Kt. takes Q. B. P.	21. Kt. takes Kt.
22. B. takes Kt. (check)	22. K. to R. square
23. Q. to K. second	23. B. to Q. B. second
24. P. to K. Kt. third	24. Kt. to K. R. fifth
25. B. to K. third	25. Kt. to K. B. sixth (check)
26. K. to R. square	26. Q. to K. Kt. third
27. Q. to K. Kt. second	27. Q. to K. Kt. fifth
28. B. to K. second	28. K. R. to K. B. fourth
29. R. to K. B. second	29. Q. R. to K. B. square
30. Q. R. to Q. square	30. K. R. to K. R. fourth
31. P. to Q. fifth	31. Q. R. to K. B. fourth
32. P. to Q. sixth	32. B. to Q. square
33. B. takes Kt.	33. P. takes B.
34. Q. to K. Kt. square	34. R. takes Q. Kt. P.
35. Q. R. to Q. fourth	35. Q. to K. Kt. third
36. B. to K. B. fourth (b)	36. R. to Q. Kt. eighth
37. K. R. to K. B. square	37. R. takes R. P. (check)

And White resigns.

Notes.

(a) " B. to Q. Kt. third " would have been much better; this move paralyses both the movements of the B. and of the Q.

(b) Evidently an oversight; White ought to have played " R. takes K. B. P." with his Rook.

GAME II.

(*Ruy Lopez.*)

Black. (Mr. E. THOROLD.)	*White.* (Mr. KIPPING.)
1. P. to K. fourth	1. P. to K. fourth
2. K. Kt. to B. third	2. Q. Kt. to B. third
3. K. B. to Q. Kt. fifth	3. K. Kt. to K. second
4. P. to Q. third	4. K. Kt. to Kt. third
5. Castles	5. P. to Q. R. third
6. B. to Q. R. fourth	6. P. to Q. Kt. fourth
7. B. to Q. Kt. third	7. B. to Q. B. fourth
8. P. to Q. B. third	8. P. to Q. third
9. Kt. to K. Kt. fifth (*a*)	9. R. to K. B. square
10. Kt. takes R. P.	10. R. to R. square
11. Kt. to K. Kt. fifth	11. R. to K. B. square
12. Q. B. to K. third (*b*)	12. B. takes B.
13. B. takes B. P. (check)	13. R. takes B.
14. Kt. takes R.	14. K. takes Kt.
15. P. takes B. (dis. check)	15. K. to Kt. square
16. Q. to K. R. fifth	16. Q. Kt. to K. second
17. Q. Kt. to Q. second (*c*)	17. B. to K. third
18. Kt. to K. B. third	18. Kt. to K. B. square
19. Kt. to Kt. fifth	19. Q. Kt. to K. Kt. third
20. Kt. takes B.	20. Q. to K. second
21. Kt. to Kt. fifth	21. P. to Q. fourth
22. R. to K. B. third	22. P. takes P.
23. P. takes P.	23. Q. to Q. B. fourth
24. Q. R. to K. B. square	24. Kt. to K. B. fifth
25. Q. to K. B. seventh (check)	25. K. to R. square
26. K. to R. square	26. K. Kt. to Kt. third
27. P. takes Kt.	

And White resigns.

Notes.

(*a*) This seems to have been overlooked by White.

(*b*) This move, which was a mistake at the time, is not so disastrous as might at first appear.

(*c*) It is difficult for White to prevent the formidable advance of this Kt. to the K. Kt. fifth.

Game played in 1855 between Messrs. BRIEN and BODEN.

Black. (Mr. BODEN.)	*White.* (Mr. BRIEN.)
1. P. to K. fourth	1. P. to K. fourth
2. B. to Q. B. fourth	2. Kt. to K. B. third
3. P. to Q. third	3. B. to Q. B. fourth
4. P. to Q. B. third	4. P. to Q. third
5. Kt. to K. B. third	5. P. to Q. B. third
6. B. to Q. Kt. third	6. Castles
7. B. to K. Kt. fifth	7. B. to K. third
8. Q. Kt. to Q. second	8. Q. Kt. to Q. second
9. P. to K. R. third (a)	9. P. to Q. R. fourth
10. Castles	10. P. to K. R. third
11. B. to K. R. fourth	11. P. to K. Kt. fourth
12. B. to K. Kt. third	12. Kt. to K. R. fourth
13. P. to Q. fourth	13. Kt. takes B.
14. P. takes Kt.	14. B. to Q. Kt. third
15. K. to R. second	15. B. takes B.
16. Q. takes B.	16. K. to Kt. second (b)
17. P. to K. Kt. fourth	17. Q. to K. second (c)
18. Kt. to Q. B. fourth	18. R. to Q. R. third
19. Kt. to K. third	19. K. to R. second
20. Kt. to K. B. fifth	20. Q. to K. B. third
21. Q. R. to Q. square	21. K. R. to Q. square
22. K. to R. square	22. P. to Q. R. fifth
23. Q. to Q. B. fourth	23. B. to Q. B. second
24. P. takes P.	24. P. takes P.
25. Kt. takes P. (check) (d)	25. P. takes Kt.
26. Kt. to Q. sixth	26. Kt. to Q. Kt. third
27. Q. takes Q. R.	27. P. takes Q.
28. R. takes Q.	28. B. to Q. Kt. square
29. R. takes P. (check)	29. K. to Kt. square
30. R. to K. Kt. seventh (check)	30. K. to B. square
31. R. to Q. Kt. seventh	

And White resigns.

――――

Notes.

(a) Black could have won a Pawn by taking B. with B., and then playing "Q. to Q. Kt. third."

(b) "P. to Q. R. fifth" would have been White's best move under the circumstances.

(c) "Q. to Q. B. second" would have been a far better move.

(a) The subsequent moves were finely played by Black.

———

Game lately played in Paris between Herr HARRWITZ and Monsieur LAROCHE.

White. (LAROCHE.)	*Black.* (HARRWITZ.)
1. P. to K. B. fourth	1. P. to Q. fourth
2. P. to Q. B. fourth	2. P. to Q. fifth
3. P. to Q. third	3. P. to Q. B. fourth
4. P. to K. fourth	4. P. to K. third
5. B. to K. second	5. Kt. to Q. B. third
6. Kt. to K. B. third	6. P. to K. B. third
7. P. to Q. R. third	7. B. to Q. third
8. Castles	8. Kt. to K. R. third
9. B. to Q. second	9. Castles
10. P. to K. R. third	10. Kt. to K. B. second
11. Q. to K. square	11. Q. to Q. Kt. third
12. Q. to Q. B. square	12. B. to Q. second
13. B. to Q. square	13. K. Kt. to K. R. square
14. B. to Q. R. fourth	14. Q. B. to K. square
15. B. takes Kt.	15. B. takes B.
16. P. to Q. R. fourth	16. P. to Q. R. fourth
17. Q. to Q. B. second	17. K. R. to K. B. second
18. P. to Q. Kt. third	18. Kt. to K. Kt. third
19. Kt. to K. square	19. Q. to Q. B. second
20. P. to K. Kt. third	20. P. to K. R. fourth
21. Kt. to K. B. third	21. Q. to Q. second
22. B. to K. square	22. Q. R. to K. B. square
23. B. takes P.	23. P. to K. R. fifth
24. Kt. takes K R. P.	24. Kt. takes Kt.
25. P. takes Kt.	25. P. to K. fourth
26. P. to K. B. fifth	26. P. Kt. to K. third
27. B. to K. square	27. P. takes P.
28. R. takes P.	28. R. to K. Kt. second (check)
29. K. to K. R. second	29. Q. takes R.

And wins.

SOLUTIONS TO PROBLEMS.

No. 25. Page 223.

White.	Black.
Q. to Q. sixth (check)	R. takes Q.
K. to K. B. fourth	Any move
Kt. or B. mates	

No. 26. Page 223.

White.	Black.
R. to K. R. square	B. moves
B. to K. Kt. fifth	Anything
R. or P. mates	

No. 27. Page 224.

The White Pawn on Q. sixth was put there by mistake, and the mate is to be given in three moves.

White.	Black.
R. to Q. R. fifth	P. takes R.
Kt. to Q. Kt. seventh	P. moves
Kt. mates	

No. 28. Page 224.

White.	Black.
B. to Q. B. seventh	K. to Q. B. fifth
B. to Q. Kt. sixth	K. takes P.
P. to Q. third	K. to R. sixth
B. mates	

PAUL MORPHY, THE CHESS CHAMPION.—An account of his career in America and Europe; with a History of Chess and Chess Clubs, by an Englishman.—WILLIAM LAY, *King William Street, Strand.*
We have only been able to make a hasty perusal of the above volume, which appears to be written in a lively style, free from exaggeration, and therefore very likely to find favour with the general as well as the chess-loving public.

There has also been published by VEIT & Co., *Leipzig*, in two parts, the LIFE OF MORPHY, with a collection of all the games played by MORPHY that have appeared as yet in print. The notes, we believe, are by the editor of the Berlin *Schach-zeitung.*

Several Chess publications are announced to make their appearance before the end of the year.

The promised analysis of the positions, of which we gave the Diagrams in the Match between MORPHY and LÖWENTHAL in our last number, will be given in our next.

ERRATUM.

On page 196, *for* the Rev. W. Thorold, *read* Mr. E. Thorold.

No. 29.   Chess Study by F. HEALEY, Esq.

BLACK

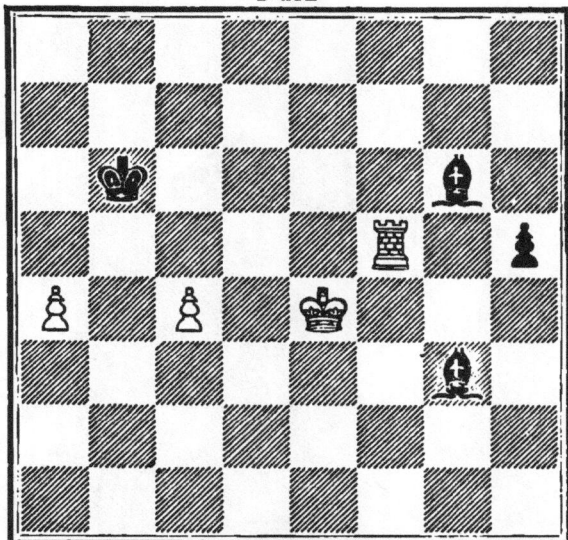

WHITE.
White, with the move, draws.

No. 30. Problem by F. HEALEY, Esq.

BLACK.

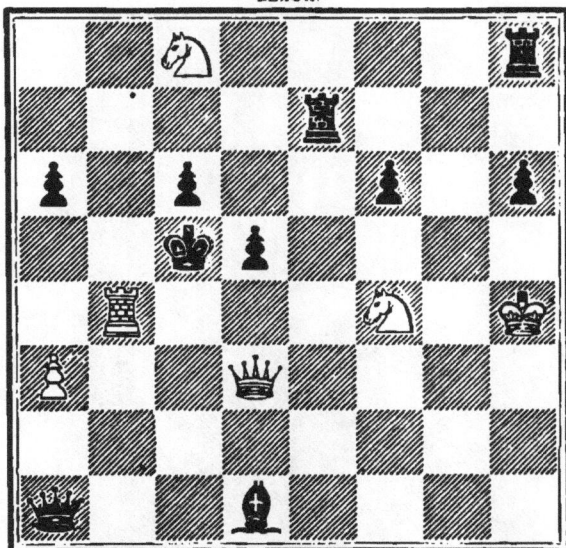

WHITE.
White to play, and mate in two moves.

No. 31. Problem by J. Law, Esq., M.D., Sheffield.

BLACK.

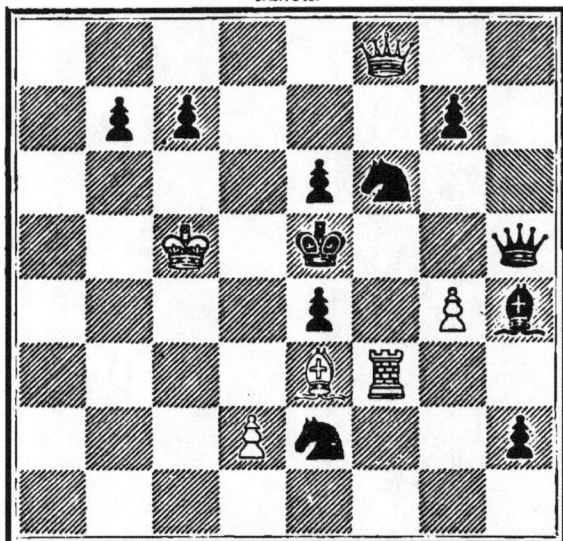

WHITE.

White to move, and checkmate in four moves.

No. 32. Problem by J. Law, Esq., M.D., Sheffield.

BLACK

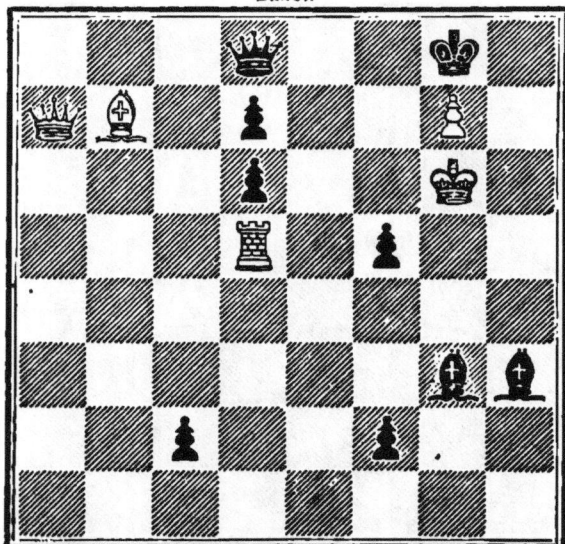

WHITE.

White to move, and checkmate in five moves.

THE GAME OF CHESS AND THE GAME OF LIFE.

It has been often and rightly asserted, that many of the phases of social life are faithfully, though perhaps allegorically, represented upon the chequered board in our noble game. The humble Pawn, in an obscure position in the lower ranks, where he is often sacrificed without having made his existence known, otherwise than by having been a protecting shield against the inimical shafts directed towards his betters, and falling a willing victim to his loyal zeal, has the material and stuff in him to reach the highest honours and dignities. When daringly leaping over the intermediate space at the risk of being taken *en passant*, and extinguished for ever, he boldly advances from post to post, attacking and displacing at every step, till he reaches the proposed goal. Next in dignity to the King, with a power surpassing that of his sovereign, does he not bring forcibly to mind the Cardinal Minister of a Henry VIII. or a Louis le Grand? Less daring perhaps, but not less subtle, another whom chance has placed in his menial condition next to his King, is aware of the advantage blind fortune has conferred on him, and never abandons the neighbourhood of his master for a moment, but stealthily pushing forward step by step, in turn leading and following his sovereign, always safe under his protection, till he reaches the top of the ladder, and yields a power far superior to that of the other grandees of the state—Knights, Bishops, or Viziers. He recalls the picture of Olivier le Dain accompanying Louis XI. with the leaden saints stuck in his worn-out hat. The daring and noble Knight, despising such obstacles as his own, his neighbour's, or enemy's vassals, leaps proudly over them, enters the opponents' camp, and, at the risk of having his retreat cut off, often takes single-handed, by surprise, an inimical Castle. His influence does not extend at a distance, but is strongly felt all around him, and he is the only power which, by a bold move, is enabled to threaten all the dignitaries in the state, and is equally and at the same time formidable to the King and the vassal. Supported by his bondmen, he becomes the most dangerous foe, and, unless attacked in front by the enemy's archers, cannot be dislodged, except in single combat, by an equally or more noble adversary. Bishop, Vizier, or even Prime Minister, must be often sacrificed to get rid of an inopportune Knight, who, through want of foresight, was allowed to get possession of a stronghold in the enemy's territory; and some-

17

times even no sacrifice will avail against a Knight supported by a brother Knight: a Tancred in Sicily, the country lies prostrate before him.

The mitred Bishop never uses his influence in a direct manner: his strokes come with a side-wind, and he is the most dangerous when seemingly least offensive : when his action is intercepted by a friendly piece, waiting for the opportune moment, he, by a sudden discovery, and by a double check, spiritual and temporal, completely prostrates and mates his adversary.   He represents diplomacy in all its tortuous windings, and has for his motto that of the Bishop of Autun—"Language is given to man to hide his thoughts." If Metternich had been a Chess player, he would have been unrivalled in the skilful use of his Bishops; as it was, he used them pretty well in the state.

The Castles are the grandees and the pillars of the state ; they are stiff and conservative to the backbone ; they always take the straight line ; their motto is *Frangor sed non flutor ;* their influence reaches to the most distant point of the territory, but, owing to their unwieldy nature, is often intercepted by their own underlings ; they fall an easy prey to Bishops, and are often surprised by Knights ; when, however, marching together upon the same line, or attacking the same point, their power is irresistible.   In the East they ride upon elephants; in our country, however, they are represented by castles, counties, or duchies.   SHERIDAN would have said, that according to this, the members of the Carlton Club ought to be the best Rook players.

The Queen, more properly called the Vizier in the East, is the Prime Minister and naturally belongs to the aristocracy ; but sometimes, as we have shown above, springs from the lowest ranks.   She has all the attributes of a Prime Minister, and stands in authority next to his majesty—   .   .   .   .

The King, whose person is sacred on the Chess board as well as in society at large.   His circle of action and his powers are limited, as they ought to be, in every country. Due respect is paid to him even by his enemies, when declaring war, by the polite announcement of it by the word *check ;* his person is unapproachable and inviolable ; and unless, after a decisive victory of the adverse party, he resigns the throne, even should he be defeated without war having been declared by the check, the battle is pronounced drawn by the international law of the stale mate.

To the Editor of the Chess Player's Chronicle.

Sir,—In reply to my excellent old friend, Captain H. A. KENNEDY, who writes *at* me in your number of this month, allow me to state that I *have* added several chapters to my *History of Chess* within the last four years. I expect that the whole will appear in a goodly octavo volume very soon, " much enlarged and improved," &c. &c., *of course,* as all new editions pretend to be. In the meanwhile I here send you a chapter on Chess among the Arabs, which is heartily at your service if you think it worth inserting.   Yours, &c.,

D. F.

58, *Burton Crescent, Aug.* 12, 1859.

SOME OBSERVATIONS ON THE ORIGIN AND PROGRESS OF CHESS.

By DR. DUNCAN FORBES.

(Continued from the Chess Player's Chronicle, July, 1855.)

CHAPTER XI.

Introduction of Chess from Persia to Arabia, and its probable Advancement to the Westward, through Northern Africa into Spain on the one hand, and through Naples and Sicily on the other.

HAVING now established, as we believe, beyond the possibility of cavil or doubt, that Chess was invented in India, and thence introduced into Persia in the reign of Naushīrawān, about the middle of the sixth century, we proceed to trace its further progress to the westward. We cannot determine the precise year or even decennium when the Indian embassy arrived at the Persian Court; for the reign of Naushīrawān extended over the lengthened period of forty-eight years—that is, from A.D. 531 to A.D. 579. We shall, therefore, assume the middle of that century as our starting-point, which cannot be very far from the mark; and, this being granted, we have excellent authority for saying that in the course of a little more than half a century afterwards the game became known to the Arabs. Early in the seventh century we find that it had reached the sacred cities of Mecca and Medina. The Prophet Muhammad clearly alludes to it in the fifth chapter of the Kurān; but, being himself ignorant of its precise nature, he gives it a place among sundry abominations to be carefully eschewed by the faithful in general. His words are, " O true believers, surely wine, and lots, and *images*, and divining arrows, are an abomination of the works of Satan, therefore avoid ye them, that ye may prosper."[1]   Now, all the

---

[1] *Kuran*, chapter v. page 135. We are told that this chapter was *revealed* at Medina, which in our plain English signifies that it was composed about, or

eminent Musalmān commentators on this psssage say that by " wine
and lots " are meant " all intoxicating drinks, and all games of chance."
By the term *images* they say that the Prophet alluded to " the game of
Chess," and that the interdict applied not to the game itself, in which
chance had no part, but to the little carved figures or images of men,
horses, elephants, &c., then used on the board as imported from India
and Persia, all of which savoured strongly of idolatry.

The Muhammadan casuists and expounders of the sacred text, with a
degree of sense and enlightenment much redounding to their credit, have
managed to rescue the game of Chess from the very degrading position
assigned to it by the Prophet, as one of the " abominations of Satan."
At the same time, the more rigid and orthodox among the " true
believers," such as the sect of the Sunnīs, including the Turks, the
Arabs, the people of Bukhāra, and the Afghāns of the present day, in
order to avoid all appearance of scandal, play with plain blocks of ivory
or wood variously cut, but bearing no resemblance to any living creature,
so that the term *images* may not apply.   The Shī'as, on the other hand,
including the Persians and Musalmāns of India, commonly called
Moguls, who are much more liberal in their ideas, and to the full as
free from idolatry as their more scrupulous coreligionists, still make
use of the old-fashioned and tastefully carved figures, such as they
existed at the courts of Kanoj and Susa in the sixth century. The following passage from the preliminary discourse of Sale's Kurān contains all
that need be said on this subject.   Sale, we may remark, was a most
sound and accurate oriental scholar, and everything he wrote was founded
on first-rate authorities.   The edition of his *Translation,* which I here
use, is that of Tegg, 2 vols. 8vo, 1825 : a very beautiful and accurately
printed work.   In the Preliminary Discourse, sect. 5, page 171, the
author says :—

" Under the name of *lots* the commentators agree that all other
games whatever, which are subject to hazard or chance, are compre-
hended and forbidden, as dice, cards, tables, &c.   And they are
reckoned so ill in themselves, that the testimony of him who plays at
them is, by the more rigid, judged to be of no validity in a court of

soon after, A.D. 622, when the Prophet executed his celebrated Hijra, or flight,
Friday, July 16 of that year.   In the second chapter, wine and gaming are in
like manner denounced, but nothing is there said of the images. The words are,
" They will ask thee concerning wine and *lots* (*i.e.,* games of chance) ; answer
them—In both there is great sin, and also something of use unto man ; but
their sinfulness is greater than their use."   Sale adds in a note, " From these
words some suppose that only drinking to excess, and too frequent gaming,
are prohibited ; and the moderate use of wine they also think is allowed from
the following words in the sixteenth chapter :—' *And from the fruits of palm-
trees and grapes ye obtain inebriating drinks, and also good nourishment.*' Verily
much may be said on both sides."

justice. Chess is almost the only game which the Mohammedan doctors allow to be lawful (though it has been a doubt with some)[1], because it depends wholly on skill and management, and not at all on chance ; but then it is allowed under certain restrictions, viz., that it be no hinderance to the regular performance of their devotions, and that no money or other thing be played for or betted ; which last the Turks and Sonnites religiously observe, but the Persians and Mogols do not.[2] But what Mohammed is supposed chiefly to have disliked in the game of Chess, was the carved pieces or men, with which the Pagan Arabs played, being little figures of men, elephants, horses, and dromedaries ;[3] and these are thought, by some commentators, to be truly meant by the *images* prohibited in one of the passages of the Koran [4] quoted above.

"That the Arabs in Mohammed's time actually used such images for chessmen appears from what is related in the Sonna of Ali, who, passing accidentally by some who were playing at Chess, asked them, *What images are these which you are so intent upon ?*[5] for they were perfectly new to him, that game having been but very lately introduced into Arabia, and not long before into Persia, whither it was first brought from India in the reign of Khosru Nushirwan.[6] Hence the Mohammedan doctors infer that the game was disapproved only for the sake of the images : wherefore the Sonnites always play with plain pieces of wood or ivory ; but the Persians and Indians, who are not so scrupulous, continue to make use of the carved ones.[7] The Mohammedans comply with the prohibition of gaming much better than they do with that of wine ; for though the common people, among the Turks more frequently, and the Persians more rarely, are addicted to play, yet the better sort are seldom guilty of it.[8]

"Gaming, at least to excess, has been forbidden in all well-ordered states. Gaming-houses were reckoned scandalous places among the Greeks, and a gamester is declared by Aristotle [9] to be no better than a *thief;* the Roman senate made very severe laws against playing at games of hazard,[10] except only during the *Saturnalia;* though the people played often at other times, notwithstanding the prohibition. The civil law forbade all pernicious games,[11] and though the laity were, in some cases, permitted to play for money, provided they kept within reasonable bounds, yet the clergy were forbidden to play at *tables*

---

[1] V. Hyde, de Ludis, Oriental in Proleg. ad Shahiludium.   [2] V. Eund. ibid.
[3] V. Eundem, ibid. and in Hist. Shahiludij, p. 135, &c.   [4] Chap. 5.
[5] Sokeiker al Dimishki, and Auctor libri al Mostatraf, apud Hyde, ubi sup. p. 8.
[6] Khondemir, apud cund. ib. p. 41.   [7] V. Hyde, ubi sup. p. 9.
[8] V. Eundem, in Proleg. and Chardin, Voy. de Perse, T. 2, p. 46.
[9] Lib. 4, ad Nicom.   [10] V. Horat. l. 3, Carm. Od. 24.
[11] De Aleatoribus. Novell. Just. 123, &c. V. Hyde, ubi sup. in Hist. Aleæ, p. 119.

(which is a game of hazard), or even to look on while others played.[1]
Accursius, indeed, is of opinion they may play at Chess, notwithstanding that law, because it is a game not subject to chance,[2] and being
but newly invented in the time of Justinian, was not then known in
the western parts. However, the monks for some time were not allowed
even Chess.[3]   As to the Jews, Mohammed's chief guides, they also
highly disapprove gaming : gamesters being severely censured in the
Talmud, and their testimony declared invalid."[4]

Within the two centuries immediately following the death of Muhammad, the Arabs, or, as they are more commonly styled, the Saracens, had extended their conquests to the eastward as far as the
Indus, and to the westward as far as the shores of the Atlantic.
Conquest and the acquisition of wealth introduced among them luxury
and a taste for all the refinements of life.   Under the munificent
patronage of the Abbáside Caliphs, many of the arts and sciences
advanced to a degree of perfection till then unknown in the world.
From the Hindús they obtained the decimal system of enumeration, so
vastly superior to the clumsy modes of reckoning previously in vogue :
modes through which any advancement in pure science was utterly impossible.   From the same quarter they obtained a knowledge of the elements of algebra and the elementary principles of trigonometry, which
acquisitions they cultivated with the keenest ardour.   Astronomy,
geometry, medicine, logic, and metaphysics, they had from the Greeks ;
but in all of these branches they made vast improvements of their own,
and to these same Arabs modern Europe was, soon after, indebted for
the first rays of its enlightenment from the dark cloud of barbarism,
ignorance, and superstition, under which it had lain prostrate for
several centuries.

During the eighth, ninth, and tenth centuries of our era, the game
of Chess had attained a high degree of perfection at the courts of the
eastern Caliphs, and elsewhere among the Saracenic people.   In this
period, lived, and played, and wrote on the subject, the far-famed
Al Súli, who may be justly styled the Arabian Philidor.   He was by
far the first player of his time, so that his name has become proverbial
to this day.   Like Philidor, he excelled in playing without seeing the
board, and against several adversaries at the same time.   He also
wrote a treatise on the theory and practice of the game.   His work is
now in all probability lost, but it is frequently cited as an authority by

---

[1] Authent. interdicimus, c. de episcopis.   [2] In com. ad Legem Præd.
[3] Du Fresne, in Gloss.   [4] Bava Mesia, 84. 1. Rosh hashana, and Sanhedr.
24, 2. V. etiam Maimon. in Tract. Gezila.   Among the modern civilians, Mas-
cardus thought common gamesters were not to be admitted as witnesses, being
infamous persons.   V. Hyde, ubi sup. in Proleg. et in Hist. Alew, § 3.

later writers.[1] Al Sūlī died in the city of Basra about A.D. 946. So great is his fame among the Arabs, that the unlearned among them will have it, that he must himself have been the inventor of Chess. They maintain, by a certain show of reason, that no man but the inventor of the game could have so excelled in its practice; and the highest compliment they can pay to any eminent player is, that he is a second Sūlī. Another celebrated master of the art, about, or a little before, this period, was 'Adalī al Rūmī. From the latter part of his name we may infer that he was a native of the Eastern Roman Empire, comprising what is now called European Turkey and Asia Minor, called Rūm by the Arabs to this day. To this country the game had (as we shall hereafter show) ere then passed either from Persia direct, which is the more probable supposition, or through the intercourse of the Arabs with the Byzantines, either in peace or in war. 'Adalī composed a work on the game, and is considered to have been nearly the equal of Al Sūlī in strength, both being of the class called 'Aliyat, or "first-rate." Next to these we read of Ibn Dandān and Al Kunāf, both of Bagdad, also of the highest class. With the Abbáside Caliphs themselves, Chess was a favourite amusement, and thence we may easily account for the remarkable progress made in the theory and practice of the game under that dynasty, and the high estimation in which distinguished players were held at that splendid court.

(*To be continued.*)

THE SEVEN AGES OF CHESS.—(*Continued from p.* 196.)

VI. CHESS IN AGE.

WE'RE in the evening of our lives, no doubt,
    I'm bald, and Julia's growing grey ;
But few by other signs would find it out,
    Or guess that we had reach'd mid-day.

A goodly show of "olive-branches" round
    Lend suppleness, and keep us young ;
Our life and joy in their young lives are found,
    Our gladdest utterance in their tongue.

Our hopes, our wishes, and our tastes, we see
    Renew'd in scions of our name ;
All fight on chequer'd field ; but all agree
    In reverence for the royal game.

[1] Numerous and copious extracts from the works both of Sūlī and 'Adalī are given in Dr. Lee's two MSS., lately in the possession of Mr. N. Bland, but of which, owing to most perverse circumstances, I have been unable to obtain a perusal, for reasons given in our eighth chapter.

Finding it pleasant still to take the lead,
   And patronize inferior skill,
The best Chess columns, on the sly, I read,
   In *Era*, *News*, and *Chronicle*.

New Morphy dodges, and bold Staunton strokes,
   Refined finesse from Harrwitz, Löwenthal,
1, smiling, play off on my foes, like jokes,
   And in our Club astonish all.

Our Club (I'm President) 'tis said, is slow ;
   Perhaps so, in these gambit days;
Our men (we date from thirty years ago)
   Impress you mildly—not amaze.

They love *piano* play, and the " close game ":
   When gambit visitors appear,
Who might declare the play a little tame,
   They 're made to face my conquering spear.

Thus, pleased and pleasing, do I still preside,
   Giving in turn the Pawn, Knight, Rook.
" Why not play Staunton ? " ask they in their pride,
   " Or bring Herr Löwenthal to book ? "

And we get up a correspondence game,
   Or send a deputy to town,
For hitherto we 've been quite lost to fame.
   " But bless me, Julia, what a frown ! "

" My dear," says Julia, " has it crossed your brains,
   That, since we 've had our governess,
Tom has been taking most unusual pains
   To teach the girl to play at Chess ?

" Look at them now : observe her downcast eyes !
   The girl is pretty, I confess ;
See how he worships that small hand—a prize
   I fear he values more than Chess.

" And see ! the game proceeds at a strange rate,
   Advantages he fails to seize,
Instead of giving, as he might, *checkmate*,
   He 's blindly left his Queen *en prise*."

" Too true," said I ; " and now, my dear, be calm ;
   Grieve not at Tom's first tender move,
But learn to say, with me, without a qualm,
   ' In Marriage, as in Chess, let all be done *for love*.' "

Games played at the PHILIDORIAN, between Messrs. CAMPBELL and
REEVES, Mr. CAMPBELL giving the Pawn and Move.

GAME I.

(Remove Black's K.B.P.)

White. (Mr. REEVES.)	Black. (Mr. CAMPBELL.)
1. P. to K. fourth	1. P. to K. third
2. P. to Q. fourth	2. B. to K. second (*a*)
3. B. to Q. third	3. Kt. to K. B. third (*b*)
4. P. to K. fifth	4. Kt. to Q. fourth
5. Q. (checks)	5. K. to B. square
6. K. B. takes P.	6. Q. to K. square
7. Q. takes Q.	7. K. takes Q.
8. B. to K. Kt. sixth (check)	8. K. to B. square
9. P. to Q. B. fourth	9. B. to Q. Kt. fifth (check)
10. B. covers	10. B. takes B.
11. Kt. takes B.	11. Kt. to K. B. fifth
12. B. to K. fourth	12. Kt. to Q. B. third
13. P. to K. Kt. third	13. Kt. to K. R. sixth (*c*)
14. Kt. to K. B. third	14. P. to Q. third
15. K. to B. square (*d*)	15. P. to K. Kt. fourth
16. B. takes Kt.	16. P. takes B.
17. P. takes P.	17. P. takes P.
18. Kt. to K. fourth	18. P. to K. Kt. fifth
19. Kt. to K. R. fourth	19. P. to Q. fourth
20. Kt. to Q. sixth	20. R. to R. third
21. Kt. takes B.	21. R. takes Kt.
22. P. to K. B. fourth (*e*)	22. R. to Q. Kt. square
23. P. takes P.	23. R. takes P.
24. P. takes Q. B. P.	24. R. to Q. B. seventh
25. R. to Q. Kt. square	25. R. takes P.
26. R. to Q. Kt. second	26. R. to Q. B. fifth
27. R. to Q. second	27. P. to K. fourth (*f*)
28. P. to Q. fifth (*g*)	28. R. takes Kt. (*h*)
29. P. takes R.	29. R. (checks)
30. K. to Kt. second	30. Kt. takes P. (check)
31. K. to Kt. third	31. R. takes R.
32. K. takes P.	32. K. to K. second
33. P. (checks)	33. K. to Q. second
34. P. to K. R. fifth	34. R. (checks)

35. K. to B. fifth	35. Kt. takes P.
36. K. takes P.	36. R. to K. Kt. fourth (check)
37. K. to K. fourth	37. Kt. to B. third (checks)
38. K. to B. fourth	38. R. to Q. R. fourth
39. P. to K. R. fourth	39. K. to K. third
40. K. to B. third	40. Kt. to Q. fourth
41. P. to R. fifth	41. K. takes P.
42. P. to R. sixth	42. K. to K. third
43. P. to R. seventh (*i*)	43. R. (checks)
44. K. to Kt. second	44. Kt. to B. fifth (check)
45. K. to B. second	45. R. to K. R. sixth
46. R. to Q. fourth	46. Kt. to Q. fourth
47. P. queens	47. R. takes Q.
48. R. to Q. R. fourth	48. R. to R. second
49. R. to R. sixth (check)	49. K. to K. fourth
50. K. to K. second	50. K. to Q. fifth
51. K. to Q. second	51. R. (checks)
52. K. to Q. B. square (*k*)	52. K. to Q. sixth
53. R. takes P. (*l*)	53. R. to Q. B. seventh (check)
54. K. to Q. Kt. square	54. Kt. to Q. B. sixth (check)
55. K. to R. square	55. R. to B. eighth (check)
56. K. to Kt. second	56. R. to Kt. eighth (check)
57. K. to Q. R. third	57. Kt. to Kt. fourth (check)

And White surrendered.

———

Notes.

(*a*) " P. to Q. fourth," though often played, is not better, as it loses at least a Pawn by checking with " Q. at K. R. fifth," &c. &c.

(*b*) This move causes the loss of a Pawn, and gives Black a bad game.

(*c*) Through this move the Knight for a long series of moves is completely out of play.

(*d*) In order to play K. to Kt. second, and bring the Rooks into co-operation.

(*e*) This bad move ultimately lost White the game.

(*f*) Probably, to free Knight, should White take with K. B. P.

(*g*) Another gross blunder, which loses a clear piece; had White taken Pawn with K. B. P. he could easily have won.

(*h*) Black properly avails himself of White's errors.

(*i*) By playing " R. to R. second " White might have drawn the game.

(*k*) If K. had moved to Q. square, " R. (check) takes P.," and on White's retaking, checks with Knight, and wins.

(*l*) White falls into this ingenious snare. " R. to Q. sixth " might still have drawn the game.

GAME II.
(*Remove Black's K.B.P.*)

White. (Mr. REEVES.)	*Black.* (Mr. CAMPBELL.)
1. P. to K. fourth	1. P. to K. third
2. P. to Q. fourth	2. P. to Q. fourth
3. P. to K. fifth (*a*)	3. P. to Q. B. fourth
4. P. to Q. B. third	4. Kt. to Q. B. third
5. B. to K. third	5. Q. to Q. Kt. third
6. Q. to Q. second	6. P. takes Q. P.
7. B. takes P.	7. Kt. takes B.
8. P. takes Kt.	8. B. to Q. Kt. fifth
9. Kt. to Q. B. third	9. Kt. to K. R. third
10. B. to Q. third	10. B. to Q. second
11. Kt. to K. B. third	11. Castles K. R.
12. Castles K. R.	12. Kt. to K. B. fourth
13. P. to Q. R. third	13. B. to K. second
14. Q. R. to Q. B. square	14. Q. R. to Q. B. square
15. B. to Q. Kt. square	15. K. to R. square (*b*)
16. Kt. to K. second	16. B. to Q. Kt. fourth
17. R. takes R.	17. R. takes R.
18. B. takes Kt. (*c*)	18. P. takes B.
19. R. to Q. B. square	19. R. takes R. (check)
20. Kt. takes R.	20. Q. to Q. B. third
21. P. to K. R. third	21. Q. to Q. B. fifth (*d*)
22. Kt. to K. R. second (*e*)	22. P. to K. R. third
23. P. to Q. Kt. third	23. Q. to Q. B. square
24. P. to Q. R. fourth	24. B. to Q. Kt. fifth
25. Q. to K. third	25. B. to K. square
26. P. to K. B. fourth	26. Q. to Q. B. seventh
27. Kt. to K. B. third	27. P. to Q. Kt. fourth
28. P. takes P.	28. B. takes P.
29. Kt. to K. square (*f*)	29. Q. to Q. eighth

And wins.

Notes.

(*a*) White ought to have checked with the Queen and won a Pawn at least.

(*b*) In order to begin an attack on Queen's Pawn with impunity.

(*c*) The object of these frequent exchanges was to break up Black's centre Pawns, and secure a passed Pawn.

(d) This move effectually confines White's Queen's Knight.

(e) " Kt. to K. square " would have brought his Knights into play.

(f) Had White now moved " K. to R. second," Black would reply with " B. to K. B. eighth," and win ; and any other move would be answered by " B. to Q. R. sixth," winning the Knight.

GAME III.
(*Remove Black's K.B.P.*)

White. (Mr. REEVES.)	*Black.* (Mr. CAMPBELL.)
1. P. to K. fourth	1. P. to K. third
2. P. to Q. fourth	2. P. to Q. fourth
3. P. to K. fifth (*a*)	3. P. to Q. B. fourth
4. B. to Q. third	4. P. to K. Kt. third
5. P. to Q. B. third	5. Kt. to Q. B. third
6. Kt. to K. B. third	6. P. to Q. B. fifth
7. B. to Q. B. second	7. B. to K. Kt. second
8. B. to K. Kt. fifth	8. K. Kt. to K. second
9. P. to K. R. fourth	9. Q. to Q. Kt. third
10. P. to Q. Kt. third	10. B. to Q. second
11. P. to K. R. fifth	11. Castles Q. R.
12. Q. Kt. P. takes P.	12. Q. to Q. Kt. seventh
13. P. takes Q. P.	13. Kt. takes P.
14. B. takes R.	14. R. takes B.
15. Kt. to Q. second	15. Q. takes Q. B. P. (*b*)
16. K. R. P. takes P.	16. Q. Kt. to Q. Kt. fifth
17. B. to K. fourth	17. Kt. to K. B. fifth
18. R. takes P. (*c*)	18. B. to Q. Kt. fourth
19. Q. to Q. Kt. square (*d*)	19. Kt. takes K. Kt. P. (check)
20. K. to Q. square	20. B. to Q. R. fifth (check)
21. Kt. to Q. Kt. third (*e*)	21. R. takes Q. P. (check)

And wins.

Notes.

(a) As we have said in the former games, White ought to have checked with the Q., and then played " Q. to K. fifth," and on Black's playing his best move, " Kt. to K. B. third," White pins the Kt. and wins Q. pawn.

(b) Far better than taking with Knight.

(c) White ought to have castled now.

(d) The only move. If " R. to R. second," Black wins Q. and the game ; if " K. to K. Kt. fifth," the result is the same.

(e) By moving K. to K. second, Black would be compelled to draw, his forces being so much reduced.

Match between Mr. MORPHY and Herr LÖWENTHAL.

GAME V.

(Petroff Defence).

White. (Herr LÖWENTHAL.)	*Black.* (Mr. MORPHY.)
1. P. to K. fourth	1. P. to K. fourth
2. Kt. to K. B. third	2. Kt. to K. B. third
3. Kt. takes P.	3. P. to Q. third
4. Kt. to K. B. third	4. Kt. takes P.
5. P. to Q. fourth	5. P. to Q. fourth
6. B. to Q. third	6. B. to K. second
7. Castles	7. Kt. to Q. B. third
8. P. to Q. B. fourth (*a*)	8. Q. B. to K. third
9. P. takes P. (*b*)	9. B. takes P.
10. Q. B. to K. third	10. Castles
11. Kt. to Q. B. third	11. P. to K. B. fourth
12. Kt. takes B.	12. Q. takes Kt.
13. B. to Q. B. second	13. K. to R. square
14. B. to Q. Kt. third ·	14. Q. to Q. third
15. P. to Q. fifth	15. Kt. to Q. R. fourth
16. Q. B. to Q. fourth	16. B. to K. B. third
17. K. R. to K. square (*c*)	17. Q. R. to Q. square
18. B. takes B.	18. Kt. takes B.
19. Kt. to K. Kt. fifth	19. K. Kt. to K. Kt. fifth
20. P. to K. Kt. third	20. Q. to Q. B. fourth
21. Q. to K. second	21. Q. Kt. takes B.
22. P. takes Kt.	22. Q. R. to K. square
23. Q. to K. B. third	23. Kt. to K. fourth
24. Q. to K. R. fifth	24. P. to K. R. third
25. Q. R. to Q. square (*d*)	25. Q. to Q. B. seventh
26. Kt. to K. sixth	26. Kt. to K. Kt. fifth
27. K. R. to K. B. square	27. Q. takes P. on Q. Kt. second
28. Kt. takes R.	28. R. takes Kt.
29. P. to K. R. third	29. Kt. to K. B. third
30. Q. takes K. B. P.	30. Q. takes Q. Kt. P.
31. P. to Q. sixth	31. P. takes P.
32. R. takes P.	32. Q. to K. B. second
33. Q. R. to Q. second	33. P. to Q. R. third

34. K. R. to K. square	34. P. to Q. Kt. fourth
35. Q. to Q. B. fifth	35. R. to K. square
36. Q. R. to K. second	36. R. takes R.
37. R. takes R.	37. Q. to Q. Kt. sixth
38. Q. to K. B. eighth (check)	38. Kt. to K. Kt. square
39. R. to K. seventh	39. Q. to Q. eighth (check)
40. K. to R. second	40. Q. to Q. fifth
41. R. to K. eighth	41. Q. to Q. B. fifth
42. R. to Q. R. eighth	42. P. to Q. Kt. fifth
43. R. to Q. R. seventh	43. Q. to Q. fifth
44. R. takes Q. R. P.	44. P. to Q. Kt. sixth
45. R. to Q. R. eighth	45. Q. to Q. fourth
46. R. to Q. R. seventh	46. Q. to Q. fifth
47. R. to Q. Kt. seventh	47. Q. to Q. B. sixth
48. Q. to K. B. seventh	48. K. to R. second (e)
49. R. takes Q. Kt. P.	49. Q. to K. fourth
50. R. to Q. Kt. seventh	50. P. to K. R. fourth
51. R. to Q. seventh	51. Kt. to K. R. third
52. Q. to Q. fifth	52. Q. to K. B. third
53. Q. to Q. third (check)	53. K. to R. square
54. R. to Q. eighth (check)	54. Kt. to Kt. square
55. Q. to Q. fourth	55. Q. to K. B. sixth
56. K. to Kt. square	56. K. to R. second
57. Q. to Q. fifth	57. Q. takes Q.
58. R. takes Q.	58. Kt. to K. B. third
59. R. to K. fifth	59. K. to Kt. third
60. P. to K. B. fourth	60. K. to B. second
61. K. to Kt. second	61. K. to Kt. third
62. K. to B. third	62. K. to B. second
63. R. to Q. R. fifth	63. K. to Kt. third
64. R. to Q. R. sixth	64. K. to B. second
65. P. to K. B. fifth	65. Kt. to Q. fourth
66. P. to K. Kt. fourth	66. P. takes P.
67. P. takes P.	67. Kt. to K. second
68. K. to B. fourth	68. Kt. to Q. fourth (check)
69. K. to K. fifth	69. Kt. to K. B. third
70. R. to Q. R. seventh (check)	

And Black resigned.

Notes.

(a) This time Herr Löwenthal made the correct move. In the third game of the match, however (see our July number, p. 204), he played "K. R. to K. square" at this point, a move which is far inferior.

(b) "Q. to Q. Kt. third" would have still more improved White's game.

(c) It is a fact well worth noticing, that the attack in this game was kept up by Herr Löwenthal with greater spirit and vigour than in any other of the preceding or following contests.

(d) A necessary precaution. Had he played "Kt. to K. sixth" instead (a move which at the first sight looks tempting), Black would have very properly replied to it with "Q. takes Q. P.," threatening to check with "Kt. on B. sixth."

(e) This is a forced move, as White threatened to play "R. to Q. Kt. eighth" on the next move.

GAME VI.
(Sicilian Opening.)

White. (Mr. MORPHY.)	*Black.* (Herr LÖWENTHAL.)
1. P. to K. fourth	1. P. to Q. B. fourth
2. P. to Q. fourth	2. P. takes P.
3. Kt. to K. B. third	3. Kt. to Q. B. third
4. Kt. takes P.	4. P. to K. fourth
5. Kt. takes Kt.	5. Kt. P. takes Kt.
6. B. to Q. B. fourth	6. Kt. to K. B. third
7. Castles (a)	7. P. to Q. fourth (b)
8. P. takes P.	8. P. takes P.
9. B. to Q. Kt. fifth (check)	9. B. to Q. second
10. B. takes B. (check)	10. Q. takes B.
11. R. to K. square	11. B. to Q. third
12. Kt. to Q. B. third	12. P. to K. fifth
13. B. to K. Kt. fifth	13. Kt. to K. Kt. fifth
14. Q. takes P.	14. B. takes R. P. (check)
15. K. to R. square	15. Q. takes Q.
16. Kt. takes Q.	16. Castles
17. P. to K. B. third	17. P. takes P.
18. P. takes P.	18. Kt. to K. fourth
19. R. to K. third	19. P. to K. B. third
20. K. takes B.	20. Q. R. to Q. square
21. R. takes Kt.	21. P. takes B.
22. K. to Kt. third	22. P. to K. R. third
23. P. to Q. B. fourth	23. R. to K. B. second

24. Q. R. to K. square	24. K. to B. square
25. P. to Q. B. fifth	25. P. to K. Kt. third
26. P. to Q. B. sixth	26. R. to Q. B. square
27. P. to Q. B. seventh	27. R. takes P.
28. R. to K. R. eighth (check)	28. K. to Kt. second
29. Kt. takes R.	

And wins. (c)

Notes.

(a) As White now has, evidently, the best position, it might have been, perhaps, quite as well for Black to have played on the third move, "P. to K. fourth," thus securing, at least momentarily, a Pawn, which to get back would have cost White some efforts.

(b) "Kt. takes P." instead, might have proved dangerous, for White could have replied to it with "R. to K. square," and if Black then plays "P. to Q. fourth," the first player, by taking Kt. with R., gains a decided advantage. The proper move in this position would have been "B. to K. second."

(c) Herr Löwenthal was probably out of spirits on that day, for this game is far below his average strength.

GAME VII.

(Philidorian Defence.)

White. (Herr LÖWENTHAL.)	*Black.* (Mr. MORPHY.)
1. P. to K fourth	1. P. to K. fourth
2. Kt. to K. B. third	2. P. to Q. third
3. P. to Q. fourth	3. P. takes P.
4. Q. takes P.	4. Q. B. to K. third
5. Kt. to Q. B. third	5. P. to Q. R. third
6. Q. B. to K. third	6. Kt. to Q. B. third
7. Q. to Q. second	7. Kt. to K. B. third
8. R. to Q. square	8. B. to K. second
9. B. to K. second	9. Castles
10. Castles	10. P. to Q. Kt. fourth
11. P. to Q. R. third	11. Q. Kt. to K. fourth
12. K. Kt. to Q. fourth	12. P. to Q. B. fourth
13. Kt. takes B.	13. P. takes Kt.
14. P. to K. B. fourth	14. Kt. to K. Kt. third
15. B. to K. B. third	15. R. to Q. Kt. square
16. Q. to K. second	16. Q. to Q. B. second
17. P. to K. R. fourth a)	17. Kt. takes K. R. P.

18. B. to K. Kt. fourth	18. Kt. takes B.
19. Q. takes Kt.	19. Q. to Q. B. square
20. P. to K. Kt. third	20. Kt. to K. Kt. third
21. R. to K. B. second	21. R. to K. B. third
22. Q. R. to K. B. square	22. P. to Q. Kt. fifth
23. P. takes P.	23. P. takes P.
24. Kt. to Q. R. fourth (*b*)	24. Q. to Q. B. third .
25. P. to Q. Kt. third	25. Q. takes K. P.
26. B. to Q. R. seventh	26. Q. R. to K. B. square
27. R. to K. second	27. Q. to Q. Kt. second
28. B. to K. B. second (*c*)	28. Kt. takes K. B. P.

And wins.

Notes.

(*a*) Evidently a premature attack. "P. to K. Kt. fourth," instead, might have been stronger; but still, if we may venture here to express our opinion, would not have decided the game in White's favour, there being still much resource left for the second player, as, for instance:—

17. Kt. to Q. second, or P. to K. Kt. fifth.

Amongst the lookers-on, however, the impression seems to have prevailed, that, up to this point, White had decidedly the better game, which, after close examination, will prove erroneous.

(*b*) After this move, the loss of a second Pawn was unavoidable.

(*c*) "B. to K. third" might have been answered with "Kt. to K. fourth." White's game is hopeless.

GAME VIII.
(*Philidorian defence.*)

White. (Mr. MORPHY.)	*Black.* (Herr LÖWENTHAL.)
1. P. to K. fourth	1. P. to K. fourth
2. Kt. to K. B. third	2. P. to Q. third
3. P. to Q. fourth	3. P. takes P.
4. Q. takes P.	4. Q. B. to Q. second
5. Q. B. to K. third	5. Kt. to K. B. third
6. Q. Kt. to B. third	6. B. to K. second
7. B. to Q. B. fourth	7. Q. Kt. to B. third
8. Q. to Q. second	8. Q. Kt. to K. fourth
9. Kt. takes Kt.	9. P. takes Kt.
10. Castles (K. R.) (*a*)	10. Castles
11. P. to K. B. fourth	11. K. B. to Q. third

18

12. P. to K. B. fifth	12. Q. B. to Q. B. third
13. Q. to K. second	13. P. to K. R. third (b)
14. Q. R. to Q. square	14. Q. to K. second
15. K. B. to Q. fifth	15. B. takes B.
16. Kt. takes B.	16. Kt. takes Kt.
17. R. takes Kt.	17. P. to K. B. third
18. Q. to K. Kt. fourth	18. P. to Q. B. third
19. R. to Q. third	19. B. to Q. B. fourth
20. Q. to K. Kt. third	20. Q. R. to Q. square
21. K. R. to Q. square	21. R. takes R.
22. R. takes R.	22. R. to Q. square
23. B. takes B. (c)	23. Q. takes B. (check)
24. Q. to K. B. second	24. Q. takes Q. (check)
25. K. takes Q.	25. R takes R.
26. P. takes R. (d)	26. P. to Q. B. fourth
27. P. to K. Kt. fourth	27. K. to B. square
28. P. to Q. R. fourth	28. P. to Q. Kt. third
29. K. to K. Kt. third	29. K. to B. second
30. K. to R. fourth	30. K. to B. square
31. K. to R. fifth	31. K. to B. second
32. P. to Q. Kt. third	32. K. to B. square
33. K. to Kt. sixth	33. K. to Kt. square
34. P. to K. R. third	34. K. to B. square
35. P. to K. R. fourth	35. K. to Kt. square
36. P. to K. Kt. first	36. R. P. takes P.
37. P. takes P.	37. P. takes P.
38. K. takes P.	38. K. to B. second
39. K. to R. fourth	39. K. to K. second
40. K. to Kt. fourth	40. K. to B. third
41. K. to R. fifth	41. P. to Q. R. third
42. K. to R. fourth	42. P. to K. Kt. third
43. P. to Q. R. fifth	43. P. takes Q. R. P.
44. P. takes K. Kt. P.	44. K. takes P.
45. K. to Kt. fourth	45. P. to Q. R. fifth
46. P. takes P.	46. P. to Q. R. fourth
47. K. to B. third	47. K. to B. third
48. K. to B. second	48. K. to B. second
49. K. to Kt. third	49. K. to Kt. second

50. K. to B. second	50. K. to B. third
51. K. to Kt. square	51. K. to Kt. fourth
52. K. to Kt. second	52. K. to B. fifth
53. K. to B. second	53. P. to Q. B. fifth
54. P. takes P.	54. K. takes P.
55. K. to K. second	55. K. to Q. fifth
56. K. to K. B. third	56. K. takes P.
57. K. to K. fourth	57. K. to Kt. fifth
58. K. takes P.	58. K. takes P.
59. K. to Q. fourth	59. K. to Kt. fifth
	And wins.

Notes.

(a) It seems to us, that Mr. Morphy here overlooked the advantage which he could have obtained by castling on Queen's side.

(b) It would certainly have been bad play on the part of Herr Löwenthal to take " K. P. with Kt.," for White would have replied by " Kt. takes Kt.," and then " P. to K. B. sixth " ; but whether he could not have taken the Pawn with the Bishop, seems to us not quite as clear ; for if Kt. takes B., Black Kt. takes Kt. ; and if, then, White plays " B. to Q. fifth," the second player, we should think, could safely retreat the Knight to K. B. third with the better position.

(c) " R. takes R." would have drawn the game. Thus :—

White.	Black.
23. R. takes R. (check)	23. Q. takes R.
24. B. takes B.	24. Q. to Q. eighth (check)
25. K. to B. second	25. Q. takes Q. B. P. (check)
26. K. to B. square	26. Q. takes B.
27. Q. to Q. Kt. B. (check)	27. K. to B. square
28. Q. takes Q. Kt. P.	

and the game is drawn by its nature.

(d) From this point the game is drawn, and can only be lost by a blunder on either side, which Mr. Morphy committed on the 51st move, by playing " K. to K. Kt. square."

GAME IX.
(Ruy Lopez.)

White. (Herr LÖWENTHAL.)	Black. (MR. MORPHY.)
1. P. to K. fourth	1. P. to K. fourth
2. Kt to K. B. third	2. Kt. to Q. B. third
3. B. to Q. Kt. fifth	3. B. to Q. B. fourth
4. P. to Q. B. third	4. Q. to K. second
5. Castles	5. P. to K. B. third (a)

6. P. to Q. fourth	6. B. to Q. Kt. third
7. Kt. to Q. R. third	7. Kt. to Q. square
8. Kt. to Q. B. fourth	8. Kt. to K. B. second
9. Kt. to K. third	9. P. to Q. B. third
10. Kt. to K. B. fifth	10. Q. to K. B. square (b)
11. B. to Q. third	11. P. to K. Kt. third
12. Kt. to K. Kt. third	12. P. to Q. third
13. P. to Q. R. fourth	13. Q. B. to K. Kt. fifth
14. P. to Q. R. fifth	14. B. to Q. B. second
15. P. to K. R. third	15. B. to Q. second
16. Q. to Q. Kt. third	16. Kt. to Q. square
17. K. R. to K. square (c)	17. B. to K. third
18. Q. to Q. B. second	18. Kt. to K. second
19. P. to Q. Kt. fourth	19. Q. to K. Kt. second
20. P. to Q. B. fourth	20. Castles
21. B. to K. third	21. Kt. to K. B. second
22. P. to Q. fifth	22. B. to Q. second
23. Q. R. to Q. square	23. K. to R. square
24. K. to R. square (d)	24. P. takes P.
25. K. P. takes P.	25. P. to K. B. fourth
26. Q. B. to Q. B. square (e)	26. Q. R. to K. square
27. B. to Q. Kt. second	27. Kt. to K. Kt. square
28. Q. to Q. B. third	28. Kt. to K. B. third
29. B. to Q. Kt. square	29. R. to K. Kt. square
30. R. to Q. second	30. Q. to K. R. third
31. Kt. to K. R. second	31. P. to K. B. fifth
32. Kt. to K. fourth	32. Kt. takes Kt.
33. B. takes Kt.	33. P. to K. Kt. fourth
34. P. to K. B. third	34. Q. to K. R. fifth
35. R. to K. B. square	35. Kt. to K. R. third
36. R. to K. second	36. Kt. to K. B. fourth
37. B. takes Kt.	37. B. takes B.
38. P. to Q. R. fifth (f)	38. Q. to K. R. third
39. K. R. to K. square (g)	39. K. R. to K. B. square
40. P. to Q. Kt. fifth	40. R. to Q. B. square
41. Q. to Q. R. third (h)	41. K. to Kt. square
42. P. to Q. Kt. sixth	42. P. takes Kt. P.
43. B. P. takes P.	43. B. to Q. square

44. R. to Q. B. square	44. R. takes R. (check)
45. B. takes R.	45. Q. to K. Kt. third
46. Q. to Q. Kt. fourth	46. B. to Q. sixth
47. R. to K. square	47. B. to K. second
48. Kt. to K. Kt. fourth	48. R. to K. square
49. B. to Q. Kt. second	49. P. to K. R. fourth
50. Kt. to K. B. second	50. P. to K. Kt. fifth
51. Q. to Q. B. third	51. B. to K. B. fourth
52. B. P. takes P.	52. P. takes P.
53. P. takes P.	53. B. takes P.
54. Kt. takes B.	54. Q. takes Kt.
55. R. to Q. B. square	55. K. to B. second
56. Q. to K. R. third (i)	56. Q. takes Q.
57. P. takes Q.	57. P. to K. B. sixth
58. R to K. B. square	58. P. to K. fifth
59. B. to Q. fourth	59. B. to K. B. third
60. B. to K. third	60. R. to Q. R. square
61. B. to Q. second	61. B. to Q. fifth
62. P. to K. R. fourth	62. K. to K. Kt. third
63. K. to K. R. second	63. R. to K. B. square
64. K. to K. Kt. third	64. P. to K. B. seventh
65. K. to K. Kt. second	65. P. to K. sixth
66. B. to K. square (j)	66. K. to K. R. fourth
67. K. to Kt. third	67. P. takes B. (queen's checking)

And White surrendered.

Notes.

(a) This move was first introduced into practice by Mr. Boden.

(b) Black's position gets very cramped now, and must remain so for many moves. Q. to her square, instead of the move in the text, might have rendered Black's game less intricate.

(c) We do not see the purport of this move, and believe there were more attacking ones at that moment. "B. to Q. B. fourth," followed by "P. takes P," eventually, might have been stronger play.

(d) On the preceding move Mr. Morphy was quite justified in moving his King; but this move, it seems, has no tangible object.

(e) The retreat of this Bishop is compulsory, but White ought to have played the Bishop to Q. Kt. second, at once on the twenty-first move.

(f) The correct move, which, however, unless we are mistaken, might have been made some moves before.

(g) Threatening to take the P. with P., and to sacrifice the Rook on the next move. The game abounds in interesting points.

(*h*) Instead of this move, "P. to Q. B. sixth" seems, to us, to win the game, and, unless a careful examination of this intricate position had deceived us, the following variations may have led to a successful result. Our opinion, we are given to understand, has been supported by that of several of the most distinguished Chess players, who analysed this position of the game at the termination of it; and although their researches did not lead to a decisive result, still their opinion appears to agree with ours. In the first place:—

White.	*Black.*
41. P. to Q. B. sixth	41. P. takes P. (best)
42. Q. P. takes P.	42. Q. to K. third

The only feasible moves in this position, which admit of a sound defence, seem to be either " Q. to K. third," or " Q. to K. B. third," or " R. to Q. Kt square."

43. P. to Q. Kt. sixth	43. P. takes P.
44. P. takes P.	44. B. takes P.
45. R. takes P.	45. P. takes R.
46. R. takes P.	46. Q. to K. B. third (the only move)
47. R. takes B.	47. Q. takes Q.
48. B. takes Q. (check)	48. K. to Kt. square
49. R. takes P. (check)	49. K. to B. second
50. Kt. to K. Kt. fourth, and must win.	

In the second place:—

41. P. to Q. B. sixth	41. P. takes P.
42. Q. P. takes P.	42. Q. to K. B. third
43. B. to Q. R. third	43. R. to Q. Kt. square (best)
44. R. to Q. Kt. second	44. K. R. to Q. square. (There seems no better move.)
45. Kt. to K. Kt. fourth	45. B. takes Kt. (or A)
46. B. P. takes B.	46. Q. to K. third
47. R. from K. sq. to Q. Kt. sq.	47. P. to K. fourth
48. P. to Q. Kt. sixth	48. P. takes P.
49. P. takes P.	49. P. to K. fifth
50. P. takes B., and wins.	

A.

	45. Q. to K. third
46. P. to Q. Kt. sixth	46. P. takes P.
47. P. takes P.	47. R. takes P. (or *a*)
48. R. takes R.	48. B. takes R.
49. P. to Q. B. seventh	49. R. to Q. B. square
50. Kt. takes P.	50. P. takes Kt. (best)
51. R. takes P.	51. R. takes P. (best)

(If Q. to K. B. third, instead, White plays B. to Q. Kt. second, and wins.)

52. Q. to Q. R. square	52. Q. to K. B. third
53. B. to Q. Kt. second, and wins.	

a

	47. B. takes P.
48. P. to Q. B. seventh, and wins easily.	

In the third place :—

41. P. to Q. B. sixth	41. P. takes P.
42. Q. P. takes P.	42. R. to Q. Kt. square
43. Q. to Q. Kt. fourth	43. Q. to K. third (best)
44. R. to Q. square (compulsory)	44. K. R. to Q. square

(If P. to K. R. fourth, then White plays " B. to Q. B. third," threatening to advance the Pawns on the left wing at the right moment ; if, however, " P. to Q. fourth," White takes the K. P. with the Rook (checking), and pinning the Bishop with the other Rook wins easily).

45. Kt. to K. Kt. fourth	45. B. takes Kt. (or A)
46. B. P. takes B.	46. K. to K. Kt. square
47. B. to Q. B. third	

The Pawns on the Queen's side, we think, ought to win. Whenever, in this variation, Black advances his Queen's Pawn, White, by replying with " B takes K. P.," followed, eventually, by " P. to Q. B. seventh," will soon gain the victory

A.

	45. P. to K. R. fourth
46. Kt. takes K. P.	46. P. takes Kt.
47. R. takes R. (check)	47. R. takes R.
48. P. to Q. Kt. sixth, and wins by force.	

(*i*) " Q. to K. B. third " may still have drawn the game.
(*j*) Desperate, but the game was past recovery.

GAME X.
(*French Opening.*)

White. (Mr. MORPHY.)	*Black.* (Herr LÖWENTHAL.)
1. P. to K. fourth	1. P. to K. third
2. P. to Q. fourth	2. P. to Q. fourth
3. P. takes P.	3. P. takes P.
4. K. Kt. to B. third	4. K. Kt. to B. third
5. K. B. to Q. third	5. K. B. to Q. third
6. Castles	6. Castles
7. Q. Kt. to B. third	7. P. to Q. B. third
8. Q. B. to K. Kt. fifth	8. P. to K. R. third
9. Q. B. to K. R. fourth	9. Q. B. to K. Kt. fifth
10. P. to K. R. third	10. B. takes Kt.
11. Q. takes B.	11. Q. Kt. to Q. second
12. K. B. to K. B. fifth	12. Q. to Q. B. second
13. Q. R. to K. square	13. Q. R. to K. square
14. Q. R. to K. third	14. K. B. to K. B. fifth
15. Q. R. to K. second	15. R. takes R.
16. Kt. takes R.	16. B. to Q. third

17. K. B. takes Q. Kt.	17. Kt. takes B.
18. Kt. to K. Kt. third	18. R. to K. square
19. Kt. to K. B. fifth	19. Kt. to K. B. square
20. B. to K. Kt. third	20. B. takes B.
21. P. takes B.	21. R. to K. fifth
22. P. to Q. B. third	22. Kt. to K. R. second (a)
23. P. to K. R. fourth	23. P. to K. R. fourth (b)
24. P. to Q. B. fourth (c)	24. Kt. to K. B. third (d)
25. Kt. takes K. Kt. P.	25. Kt. to Kt. fifth
26. Kt. takes R. P.	26. R. takes Q. P.
27. Kt. to B. sixth (check)	27. Kt. takes Kt.
28. Q. takes Kt.	28. R. takes B. P.
29. R. to K. B. fifth	29. R. to K. Kt. fifth
30. R. to K. fifth	30. Q. to Q. B. square
31. K. to K. seventh (e)	31. Q. to K. B. square
32. Q. to K. fifth	32. Q. to K. Kt. second (f)
33. R. to K. eighth (check)	33. K. to R. second
34. Q. to K. R. fifth (check)	

Black surrendered.

Notes.

(a) Black evidently here overlooked that he could never bring his Knight to B. third without the loss of a Pawn or two, for White's obvious answer " Kt. takes K. Kt. P." The proper move, therefore, would have been "Kt. to K. third."

(b) This is a trap move, which in our opinion gives Mr. Morphy the better game. Although the Pawn can obviously not be taken, eventually it must be lost.

(c) The proper answer to Black's last move, preventing the Rook from coming to K. Kt. fifth.

(d) An oversight, no doubt.

(e) It surprises us that Mr. M. here overlooked the obvious move, " R. to K. R. fifth," which would have won the game at once; for, after Black's only move R. to K. Kt. second, " Q. to K. R. sixth" settles the business.

(f) This is a suicidal move, whilst R. to K. fifth might yet have saved Black's game.

Game between Mr. CAMPBELL and Colonel SZABO, played at the Philidorian, July 23, 1859.

White. (Mr. CAMPBELL.)	Black. (Col. SZABO.)
1. P. to K. fourth	1. P. to K. fourth
2. Kt. to K. B. third	2. Kt. to Q. B. third
3. B. to Q. Kt. fifth	3. Kt. to K. second

4. Castles	4. Kt. to K. Kt. third
5. P. to Q. fourth	5. P. takes P.
6. Kt. takes P.	6. B. to Q. B. fourth
7. Kt. to K. B. fifth	7. Castles
8. Q. to K. R. fifth	8. P. to Q. third
9. Q. B. to K. Kt. fifth	9. P. to K. B. third
10. B. to B. fourth (check)	10. K. to R. square
11. Kt. to K. R. fourth	11. Kt. takes Kt.
12. B. takes Kt.	12. Kt. to K. fourth
13. B. to K. second	13. B. to K. third
14. Kt. to Q. B. third	14. B. to K. B. second
15. Q. to K. B. fifth	15. P. to Q. B. third
16. K. to R. square	16. P. to K. Kt. fourth
17. B. to Kt. third	17. B. to Kt. third
18. Q. to K. R. third	18. P. to K. R. fourth
19. P. to K. B. fourth	19. P. to K. Kt. fifth
20. Q. to K. R. fourth	20. B. to K. sixth
21. Q. R. to Q. square	21. Q. to Q. B. square
22. R. takes Q. P.	22. K. to Kt. second
23. P. takes Kt.	23. B. to Kt. fourth
24. P. takes P. (check)	24. R. takes P.
25. Q. takes B.	25. R. takes Q. R.
26. Q. to K. seventh (check)	

And Black resigns.

Consultation Game played between Messrs. FALKBEER and HORWITZ, against Messrs. ZYTOGORSKI and KLING, in 1855.

White. (F. and H.)	*Black.* (Z. and K.)
1. P. to K. fourth	1. P. to K. fourth
2. Kt. to K. B. third	2. P. to Q. third
3. B. to Q. B. fourth	3. B. to K. second
4. Castles	4. Kt. to K. B. third
5. Kt. to Q. B. third	5. P. to K. R. third
6. P. to Q. fourth	6. P. takes P.
7. Kt. takes P.	7. Castles
8. K. to K. R. square	8. B. to K. Kt. fifth
9. P. to K. B. third	9. B. to Q. second

White	Black
10. P. to K. B. fourth	10. Kt. to Q. B. third
11. Kt. takes Kt.	11. B. takes Kt.
12. B. to Q. third	12. Q. to Q. second (a)
13. P. to K. B. fifth (b)	13. Q. R. to K. square
14. R. to K. B. third	14. B. to Q. square
15. R. to K. Kt. third	15. K. to R. square
16. Q. to K. second	16. B. takes P.
17. Q. B. takes R. P. (c)	17. P. takes B.
18. Kt. takes B.	18. Kt. takes Kt.
19. B. takes Kt. (d)	19. Q. takes P.
20. Q. to Q. second (e)	20. Q. takes B. (f)
21. Q. takes P. (check)	21. Q. to K. R. second
22. Q. to Q. second	22. R. to K. fourth
23. Q. to Q. B. third	23. P. to K. B. third
24. R. to K. B. square	24. R. to K. R. fourth
25. Q. R. to K. B. third	25. R. takes P. (check)
26. K. to K. Kt. square	26. R. to R. eighth (check)
27. K. to B. second	27. Q. to R. fifth
28. K. to K. second	28. Q. to R. fourth
29. K. to Q. third	29. Q. to R. second (check)
30. K. to Q. second	30. Q. to K. fifth

And White resigns.

Notes.

(a) A good move, as it brings the Queen into play, and frees the Rooks.

(b) It would have been better not to push the Pawn for the present, and gaining time by playing Queen to K. B. third.

(c) From this point the game becomes very interesting.

(d) White ought to have taken Kt. with Kt., and the game would have probably been equal.

(e) This was very hazardous, to give up a piece in a consultation game.

(f) Black might have shortened matters by taking Bishop with Rook, thus gaining a tempo, and bringing the Rook into play at once.

Game played between Messrs. MONGREDIEN and GREENAWAY, in 1855.

White. (Mr. GREENAWAY.)	Black. (Mr. MONGREDIEN.)
1. P. to K. fourth	1. P. to K. fourth
2. P. to K. B. fourth	2. P. takes P.
3. Kt. to K. B. third	3. P. to K. Kt. fourth

4. P. to K. R. fourth	4. P. to K. Kt. fifth
5. Kt. to K. fifth	5. Kt. to K. B. third
6. B. to Q. B. fourth	6. P. to Q. fourth
7. B. takes P.	7. Kt. takes B.
8. P. takes Kt.	8. Q. takes K. P.
9. Q. to K. second	9. Q. to K. third (a)
10. P. to Q. fourth	10. P. to K. B. third
11. Kt. to Q. third	11. P. to K. B. sixth
12. P. takes P.	12. P. takes P.
13. Q. takes Q. (check)	13. B. takes Q.
14. K. to B. second	14. Kt. to Q. B. third
15. B. to K. third	15. Castles
16. R. to K. square	16. B. to K. B. fourth
17. Kt. to Q. B. third	17. B. takes Kt.
18. P. takes B.	18. Kt. takes P.
19. B. takes Kt.	19. R. takes B.
20. R. to K. eighth (check)	20. K. to Q. second
21. Q. R. to K. square	21. R. takes Q's P.
22. Kt. to Q. R. fourth	22. P. to Q. Kt. third (b)
23. R. to Q. R. eighth	23. R. to K. Kt. square
24. R. takes P.	24. B. to Q. B. fourth (check)
25. Kt. takes B. (check)	25. P. takes Kt.
26. R. to K. third	26. R. takes R.
27. K. takes R.	27. R. to K. Kt. seventh
28. R. to Q. Kt. seventh	28. P. to K. B. seventh
29. K. to K. second	29. R. to K. Kt. fifth
30. K. takes P.	30. R. to Q. Kt. fifth
31. R. takes R.	31. P. takes R.
32. K. to K. third	32. K. to Q. third (c)
33. P. to Q. R. fourth	33. P. to Q. Kt. sixth (d)
34. K. to K. fourth	34. K. to K. third
35. P. to Q. R. fifth	35. P. to K. P. fourth (check)
36. K. to B. fourth	36. K. to Q. third
37. K. takes P.	37. P. to Q. B. fourth (e)
38. K. to K. fourth	38. K. to B. third
39. K. to K. fifth	39. K. to Kt. fourth
40. K. to Q. fifth	40. P. to Q. B. fifth
41. K. to Q. fourth	41. K. takes P.

42. K. takes P.	42. K. to R. fifth
43. K. to B. third	43. P. to K. Kt. fourth ●
44. K. to B. fourth —	44. K. to R. fourth
45. K. takes P.	45. K. to Kt. fourth
46. K. to B. third	46. K. to B. fourth
47. K. to Q. third	

And Black resigns.

Notes.

(*a*) The best move in this position.

(*b*) It would have been better to have played Knight's Pawn two squares attacking the Knight, as it would, at least, have gained the exchange.

(*c*) Q. B. P. two squares, would have been the right move at that point.

(*d*) Here again Q. B. P. two squares should have been played, which would have ensured a victory.

(*e*) Here Black could draw the game by playing "K. to Q. B. fourth."

The blind Chess player, Mr. LUMLEY, has just arrived in London, and played, at the PHILIDORIAN CHESS ROOMS, three games at the same time. This blindfold performance is the more extraordinary, as this young man, being blind for several years, and having only learnt Chess since he became blind, has had, therefore, no opportunity of studying the game from books. We give one of the games as a specimen of his play, it was played against an Amateur, who is a Pawn and two moves player.

White. (Mr. LUMLEY.)	*Black*. (AMATEUR.)
1. P. to K. fourth	1. P. to Q. B. fourth
2. K. Kt. to B. third	2. Q. Kt. to B. third
3. P. to Q. B. third	3. P. to K. fourth
4. K. B. to Q. Kt. fifth	4. P. to Q. third
5. P. to Q. fourth	5. Q. B. P. takes Q. P.
6. P. takes P.	6. P. takes P.
7. Kt. takes P.	7. B. to Q. second
8. Q. Kt. to B. third	8. K. B. to K. second
9. B. takes Kt.	9. P. takes B.
10. Castles	10. Kt. to K. B. third
11. B. to K. Kt. fifth	11. P. to Q. R. third
12. Q. to K. B. third	12. Castles
13. Q. R. to Q. B. square	13. P. to K. R. third

14. B. takes Kt.
15. P. to K. fifth
16. Kt. takes Q. B. P.
17. Q. takes B.
18. Q. to K. fourth
19. R. to Q. B. second
20. Q. to Q. B. fourth (check)
21. Kt. to Q. fifth
22. Kt. to Q. B. seventh
23. R. takes Q.
24. Kt. to K. sixth
25. P. to K. Kt. third
26. K. R. to Q. B. square
27. R. to Q. B. eighth
28. R. to Q. B. seventh
29. K. R. to B. sixth
30. R. to K. B seventh
31. R. to Q. B. seventh
32. Kt. to K. B. fourth
33. P. takes P.
34. Kt. to K. R. fifth
35. K. to B. square
36. K. to K. second
37. K. to Q. third
38. P. to K. R. fourth
39. R. takes K. B. P.
40. K. to K. third
41. Kt. to K. B. sixth
42. K. to K. second
43. R. takes B.
44. R. from K. B. sixth to K. B. seventh
45. K. to B. second

14. B. takes B.
15. P. takes P.
16. B. takes Kt.
17. Q. to K. square
18. B. to K. Kt. fourth
19. P. to K. B. fourth
20. K. to R. square
21. Q. to Q. Kt. fourth
22. Q. takes Q.
23. Q. R. to R. second
24. K. R. to Q. Kt. square
25. B. to K. B. third
26. R. to K. Kt. square
27. Q. R. to Q. R. square
28. P. to K. fifth
29. B. takes P.
30. B. to K. B. third
31. Q. R. to K. square
32. P. to K. sixth
33. Q. R. takes P.
34. B. to Q. fifth
35. R. to K. B. sixth (check)
36. R. to K. B. seventh (check)
37. B. to Q. R. eighth
38. R. takes Q. R. P.
39. K. R. to Q. square (check)
40. P. to K. Kt. third
41. Q. R. to R. sixth (check)
42. B. takes Kt.
43. R. takes K. Kt. P.
44. Q. R. to K. square (check)
45. K. R. to K. third

And the game was ultimately drawn.

PROBLEMS FOR YOUNG PLAYERS.

No. 9. By Mr. EDWIN GEAKE.

White.	*Black.*
K. on K. third	K. on K. B. fourth
Q. on Q. Kt. fifth	B. on K. square
B. on K. Kt. fifth	Kt. on K. B. third
Kt. on Q. B. second	Kt. on K. R. eighth
P. on Q. fifth, K. Kt. second	P. on K. fifth, K. Kt. third
K. R. fourth and K. second	K. Kt. sixth, K. R. fourth

White to mate in three moves.

No. 10. By Mr. J. A. CONROY, *Dublin.*

White.	*Black.*
K. on Q. R.	K. on K. B. fifth
Q. on K. Kt. seventh	
B. on Q. fourth	
B. on K. R.	

White to mate in three moves.

SOLUTIONS TO PROBLEMS.

No. 29. *Page* 255.

White.	*Black.*
K. to K. B. third	B. takes R.
K. takes B.	K. attacks P.
K. attacks P.	B. defends P.
P. advances and draws.	

No. 30. *Page* 255.

White.	*Black.*
Q. to K. R. seventh	Anything.
K. or Q. mates	

No. 31. *Page* 256.

	Black.
B. to K. B. fourth (check)	Kt. takes B.
P. to Q. fourth (check)	P. takes P. *en passant*
R. mates	

No. 32. *Page* 256.

White.	*Black.*
Q. to Q. R. eighth	Q. takes Q.
B. takes Q.	P. to K. B. eighth
R. to K. R. fifth	B. (checks)
R. takes B.	Anything

mates next move.

No. 33.   Problem by Signor AsPA, of the Leamington Chess Club.

BLACK.

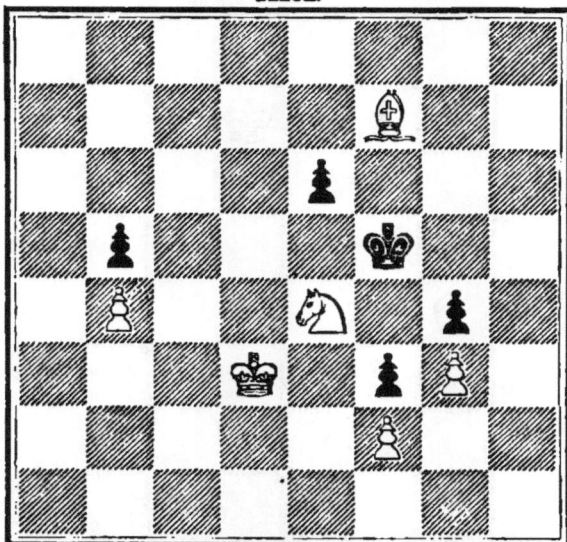

WHITE.
White to move, and checkmate in three moves.

No. 34.   Problem by Signor AsPA, of the Leamington Chess Club.

BLACK.

WHITE.
White to move, and checkmate in four moves.

No. 35.   Problem by Mr. EDWIN GEAKE.
BLACK.

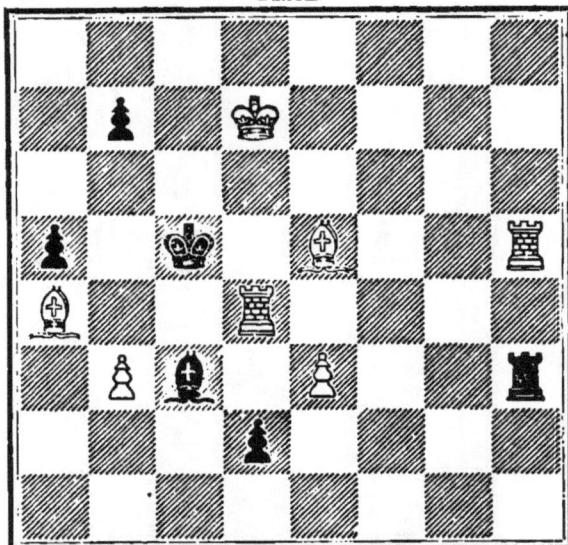

WHITE.
White to mate in two moves.

No. 36.   Problem by Mr. ROLL.
BLACK.

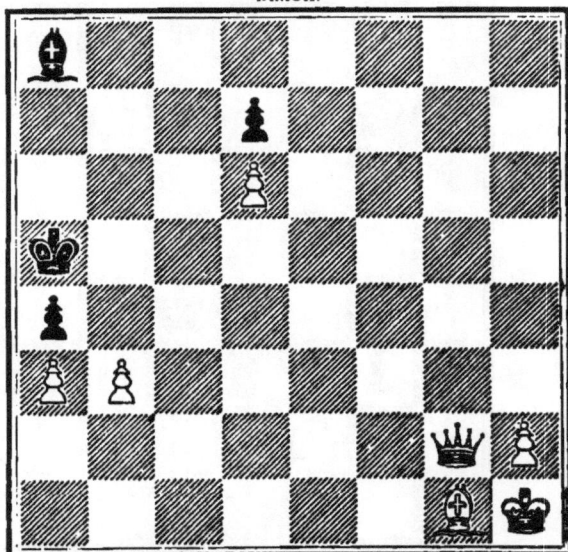

WHITE.
White compels Black to mate him in four moves.

PAUL MORPHY.

A SKETCH FROM THE CHESS WORLD.

SUCH is the title of the work before us. It was published some months ago at *Leipzig* by Messrs. VEIT & Co. in two volumes; the author is Herr MAX LANGE, the well-known editor of the Berlin *Schachzeitung*. We have received, at the same time, the proof-sheets of a translation of the above, by Herr ERNEST FALKBEER, which is to be presented to the public in a few days by the Chess publisher Mr. J. H. STARIE, of Rathbone Place, London.

The German edition is divided into fifteen chapters, of which the first volume contains ten, the second five; to each chapter are added notes, which the learned author, in contra-distinction to the notes of the games, calls glossaries. The style is entirely German, and perhaps too didactic for a Chess work, but on the whole, much valuable information may be gathered from it. The games, one hundred and twenty in number, are given in the German notation, and are very correctly printed. The notes to the games are generally to the purpose, and often elaborately disquisite. Particular care seems to have been bestowed on the analysis of the games in the match between ANDERSSEN and MORPHY, which fills half of the second volume. This section is analyzed in so masterly a manner, that we strongly suspect the German champion himself has furnished the necessary data to the notes.

In order to give our readers a more distinct idea of the work, we will here cite the contents of the different chapters, of which, however, the glossaries generally form the greater part.

Chapter I. treats of the chivalrous nature of the game. Chapter II. compares PAOLO BOI with PAUL MORPHY. Chapter III. gives five games played by MORPHY in his youth. Chapter IV. speaks of the Chess Congress in New York in 1857. Chapter V. relates MORPHY's triumphs in New York. Chapter VI. represents the American champion on his return to New Orleans. Chapter VII. narrates his voyage to, and his arrival in England. Chapter VIII. enumerates his victories over his English opponents. Chapter IX. is devoted to the match with Löwenthal, and the last Chapter of the first volume refers to the Chess Meeting at Birmingham.

In the second volume, the first chapter describes the youthful hero's reception and blindfold performance in the Café de la Regence in Paris.

19

The second contains the games with his French opponents. The third and fourth present a detailed account of the respective matches with HARRWITZ and ANDERSEN. The concluding chapter of the second volume expresses the author's own reflections on the American champion's extraordinary triumphs and future prospects.

These are the elements of which this work is composed, the merits of which we fully acknowledge; we cannot, however, conclude these remarks without animadverting to some points which must obtrude themselves to the English reader. First and foremost among them is the way in which the German author speaks of Morphy in the first volume; his praises sound like an *apotheosis*, no Roman poet ever addressed more flattering or high sounding epithets to his Cæsars. Even Caïssa's crown of glory seems to grow pale before this new-born light. No living Chess player, nay, even none of our dead celebrities could be compared to him, whose rising reputation is, as yet, in its first phase, and whom, when in his full glory, no Pantheon could hold, nor Westminster Abbey enshroud. Far less high sounding, however, are the praises meted out to the youthful hero in the cantos of the second volume, at the end of which there seems to be even an inkling of the possibility that some player may yet be found whose lance may not be shivered upon the unconquered breast-plate of this fearful paladin. Similar discrepancies on other points may be found in the two volumes. Although we fully agree with MAX LANGE in the estimate of ANDERSSEN's play, and think with him that in his match with MORPHY he has played considerably below his strength, we cannot but disagree with him in his estimate of HARRWITZ's play, who, as he seems to infer, has played up to his strength. Whoever peruses the games between MORPHY and HARRWITZ must easily see that in the latter part of the match, HARRWITZ laboured under some inimical influence, moral or physical, whatever that might have been, we leave it to him to explain.

In the glossaries we have found much interesting matter, and many details with which we were, as yet, unacquainted, especially as to the match between ANDERSSEN and MORPHY; as to these, however, we must refer our reader to the book itself, or the English translation by Herr ERNEST FALKBEER, which has united the two volumes into one, added a goodly number of games to the original edition, and enriched it with translator's notes, which, considering Herr FALKBEER's skill as a Chess player, must considerably augment the intrinsic value of the work. In comparing the English text with the German, we were struck with the correctness of the translation, especially in the notes, where redundant phrases and periphrastic style are the prevalent characteristics of the original, thus making an exact translation doubly difficult.

SOME OBSERVATIONS ON THE ORIGIN AND PROGRESS OF CHESS.

BY DR. DUNCAN FORBES.

CHAPTER XI.—(*Continued from our last Number*).

Who among our readers has not read that veracious and enchanting history called the *Arabian Nights' Entertainments?* Who has not heard of the "Commander of the Faithful," Harūn al Rashīd (pronounced by schoolboys, *Hairown al Raskid*)? Who has not read of the Wazīr Ja'far, and of Masrūr the Chief of the Eunuchs, and of the merry adventures of the trio through the city of Bagdad, at that time the most civilised place on the face of the earth? Well, then, Harūn was a fair Chess player, but his sister Abbāsiya was a still *fairer* player, and used to beat the Caliph at every game. So did the Wazīr Ja'far; only Harūn was a man of sense, and felt no mortification at being beaten at Chess either by his sister or his minister. In fact, he would have thoroughly despised any of his courtiers if he thought the latter lost to him a game out of mere courtesy, or under the idea that it would be anyways agreeable to the "successor of the Prophet" (on whom be peace). So Harūn bethought him that he would like to see a regular *match* between his sister and the Wazīr Ja'far. He accordingly had them married, with a proviso inserted for state reasons, that they should not cohabit without his consent, for as yet he had no heir of his own to succeed him.[1] Thenceforward Abbāsiya and Ja'far frequently played with alternate success in the presence of the Caliph; and we must confess the truth, still more frequently in his absence. The youthful lovers—I should like to know, who can blame them—entirely forgot or overlooked the clause about cohabitation, and the result was the disgrace and ultimately the death of Ja'far.

Al Amīn, the first of Harūn's sons, who succeeded him in A.D. 809, was devotedly fond of Chess. It is related of him, that when the city of Bagdad was besieged and on the point of being captured by the forces of his brother, Al Māmūn, he was intently occupied in a game of Chess with his friend Kūthar. In the meantime, a messenger entered in great haste, and said, "O Commander of the Faithful, this is not the time for play; pray arise, and attend to matters of more serious importance." To this, Al Amīn coolly replied, "Have patience, my friend, I am just going to give checkmate to Kūthar."[2]

---

[1] The simple English reader will here wonder why Abbāsiya and Ja'far could not play their game, at least, their Chess game—like any Christian lady and gentleman, without being married. The reason is, that a Musalmān female of any respectability is not allowed to converse with any of the male sex except her husband and her nearest blood relations, such as her father, brothers, and sons.

[2] *Historia Saracenica Arabice et Latine*, fol. 1625; *Lugduni Batavorum*, page 129.

It is further related of Amîn, that he issued orders through all the provinces of the Empire, inviting to his court all such persons as were expert Chess players.   To these he allowed pensions, and passed the happiest hours of his life, either in contending with them over the board, or in witnessing their contests with one another.

Al Mâmûn, the second son in succession from Harûn, was distinguished for the patronage he bestowed on Chess, as well as on all the elegant arts that embellish life.   "He is generally regarded as the most magnificent of all the Abbáside Caliphs.   At his nuptials, we are told that a thousand pearls of the largest size were showered on the head of his bride; and gifts of lands and houses, scattered in lottery tickets among the populace, announced to the astonished recipients the capricious profusion of the royal bounty.   Before drawing his feet from the stirrups he gave away 2,400,000 gold dînârs (£1,110,000 of our money), being four-fifths of the revenue of a whole province.   In the encouragement of literature he was the Mæcenas of the East.   Learned men from all parts of the world were invited to resort to the court of Bagdad, where their talents were duly appreciated, and they themselves received the most distinguished tokens of imperial favour; and in return these happy scholars laboured to the utmost of their power in extolling the glory of their generous patron, and in gratifying his taste by collecting and presenting to him the most rare and curious productions of Oriental genius."[1]

Al Mâmûn, though very fond of Chess, was not a first-rate player. He used to say, "It is wonderful that I, who rule the world from the Indus in the East, to Andalûs in the West, should be unable to manage the thirty-two chessmen included within a square space of two cubits by two."

Al Mu'tasim, the third of Harûn's sons in succession, was a distinguished Chess player.   Two of his problems have been handed down to us; one of which we have already presented to the reader in our eighth chapter, and the other which occurred to him in actual play, is given in the Asiatic Society's MS. fol. 14b, but unfortunately the side of the diagram next to the Caliph is effaced, so that we cannot say where his King was placed or what additional piece or pieces he may have had on the horizontal file nearest him.

Al Mu'tasim has been designated by historians the "Octonary Caliph," owing to the following remarkable coincidences of the number *eight* applicable to his life and reign.   He was the *eighth* in descent from 'Abbâs the founder of the dynasty.   His reign was distinguished by *eight* important victories. *Eight* sons of sovereign princes were enrolled in his service.   He possessed *eight* thousand male and *eight* thousand female slaves.   He was proprietor of *eighty* thousand horses.   He had *eight* sons and *eight* daughters.   He left in his coffers *eight* millions of

---

[1] *Edin. Cabinet Library*, Arabia, vol. ii. p. 18.

golden dīnārs, and *eighteen* millions of silver dirhems. He lived to the age of *eight* and forty years. He reigned *eight* lunar years, *eight* months, and *eight* days. Lastly his Chess-board, which constituted the delight of his leisure hours, contained *eight* times *eight* squares.

The Abbāside Caliphate had attained its utmost splendour under Harūn; his three sons Al Amīn, Al Māmūn, and Al Mu'tasim; and his grandson, Al Wāthik (vulgarly called Vathek). This last, the son and successor of Al Mu'tasim, was a liberal patron of learned men, and a cherisher of the arts and sciences. He is said to have so mildly and justly ruled his people, that not a single beggar was to be met with throughout his wide domains during his whole reign. The Abbāside dynasty continued to flourish at Bagdad for nearly four centuries after the death of Al Wāthik; and it would require from us a bulky volume to enumerate the names of eminent Chess players, and the copious allusions to the game found in the Arabian writers of that period. Many of these have been recorded by Hyde, to whose very learned but very ill digested work, *De Ludis Orientalibus*, we refer our readers.

In the Christian year 1171, the renowned Salāh ud-Dīn, better known to us as Saladin, founded the Ayūbite dynasty in Egypt and Syria, having thrown off his allegiance to the Caliphs of Bagdad, whose wazīr or viceroy he had previously been. At his court we find that the game of Chess was held in high repute. The fine old Arabic manuscript in the British Museum, as we have already stated, is dedicated either to Saladin himself, or to his successor, most probably the former, for he was the only distinguished man of the family which did not continue to flourish for more than the brief period of eighty years.

Spain was one of the Muslim conquests that first detached itself from the eastern Caliphate. In the seventh century of our æra, the Arabs, or as they are better known in the west, the Saracens, swept like a whirlwind along the north of Africa (taking note of Naples and Sicily in their way), as far as Fez—crossed the Straits of Gibraltar, and established themselves in the sunny plains and shady groves of Andalūs. In the course of time the court of Cordova equalled, if not surpassed, in splendour and magnificence its gorgeous rival in Bagdad. The Ommiade Caliphs of Spain were most generous patrons of the arts and sciences, and under their liberal and enlightened sway Arabian learning shone with a brighter lustre, and continued to flourish to a later period, than in the far-famed schools of the East. Cordova, Seville, and Granada rivalled each other in the magnificence of their academies, colleges, and libraries; and the same may be said of Toledo, Malaga, Murcia, and Valencia.

We must now draw our chapter to a conclusion, and in so doing, we beg to state as a mere suggestion, that in all probability Chess was introduced into South Italy and Spain in the seventh or eighth century of our æra. It is a mere inference (for we have no positive proof), but it is a very legitimate one. We have seen that the Arabs were intimate with the game early in the seventh century; and we are free to infer that they carried their knowledge of it along with that of other arts and sciences wherever their conquests extended. We are much less acquainted with the treasures of Arabian literature now mouldering in the gloomy dungeons of the Escurial Library, and elsewhere, than we are with the productions of the East. We have excellent authority for saying that in the twelfth century Spain possessed more than a million of manuscript volumes, the produce of Arabian genius, in all departments of human knowledge. These were mostly destroyed by the bigoted and ignorant monks, and the still considerable number that escaped from the ruthless hands of these "Holy Vandals," lie buried and unnoticed in a few obscure libraries and monasteries. It is to be hoped that Spain, the land of the Cid, of Cervantes, and of Ruy Lopez, will yet rouse herself from her lethargy and reveal to an admiring world the hidden treasures which she possesses. Let us hope that she will once more rekindle the extinguished lamp which six centuries ago shed its benign rays on benighted Europe.

CHAPTER XII.

On the Introduction of Chess into the Lower Empire.

In the present day we believe that no man in Europe acquainted with Chess, and imbued with the least tincture of scholarship, will maintain that the ancient Greeks possessed any knowledge of the game. That they had a game of their own called πεττεια, played on a board with ruled lines or squares, by two persons, we are perfectly aware; but this bore no stronger resemblance to Chess than a coal-barge does to the Great Eastern. This game is said to have been invented by Palamedes at the siege of Troy, though we are warranted in concluding that it had been known before that period; for we find the suitors of Penelope playing at it in Ithaca previous to the return of Ulysses from Troy. The earliest mention of it occurs in the first book of Homer's *Odyssey*, verse 106 :—

> ——————— οἱ μὲν ἔπειτα
> Πεσσοῖσι προπάροιθε φυράων θυμὸν ἔτερπον,
> Ἥμενοι ἐν ρινοῖσι βοῶν, οὓς ἔκτανον αὐτοί.[1]

Homer's meaning here is quite clear, however obfuscated by his commentators. The suitors of Penelope "were amusing themselves with the 'Pessoi' (or the game called 'Petteia,') being seated in

[1] *Homeri Opera Omnia*—cura Jo. Augusti Ernesti, five volumes, 8vo Leipsic, 1824.

front of the palace gates, upon skins of oxen which they themselves had slaughtered;" for in those good old times it was requisite in a gentleman that he should be qualified to kill his own bullock, and cook his own rumpsteak.

The game here alluded to is clearly the "petteia," a *sedentary* game, played by two people on a board of twenty-five squares, each player having five πεσσοι, or counters.[1] This may be said to have borne a very faint resemblance to Chess, but, in reality, it was only the rudiments of our modern Draughts or Backgammon. The commentators on Homer, with regard to the above passage, refer us to Athenæus for ample light on this subject, "ubi ludus hic procorum particulatim describitur;" well then, Athenæus treats us to a description of an *active* game which cannot by any possibility apply to that alluded to by Homer, far less does it resemble Chess.[2] In the Latin versions of the Odyssey the word πεσσοιοι, is translated "talis," *i.e.* "dice," evidently confounding two distinct games, the πεττεια and the κυβεια. Pope, availing himself of the proverbial license conceded to the "*genus irritabile*" improves marvellously on the Latin version, for of the original Greek he is said to have known little. His words are,

> "On hides of beeves, before the palace gate
> (Sad spoils of luxury!) the suitors sate.
> With rival arts and ardour in their mien
> At CHESS they vie to captivate the queen." [3]

[1] Vide, Three Letters on the Pseudo-Chess of the Ancient Greeks and Romans in the *Chess Player's Chronicle* of March, April, and May, 1855, alluded to in our first chapter.

[2] Vide Bohn *Trans. of Athen.* vol. i. p. 27. A more complete exposure of the apathy or stupidity of commentators does not exist. The game described by Athenæus is not played by men "seated on skins," as Homer clearly states. It is played by two equal parties of the suitors, fifty-four on each side, and strongly resembles what Strutt describes (p. 383-4) as "Hop-Scotch" or "Taw," known to some schoolboys.

[3] Pope has much to answer for as the originator of a vast deal of rhetorical rubbish inflicted upon us in Chess lectures and Chess articles in periodicals. Here, for example, is a fine stereotype specimen of this sort :—"When and where Chess was invented is a problem which we believe never will be solved. The origin of the game recedes every day further back into the regions of the past and unknown. Individuals deep in antiquarian lore, have very praiseworthily puzzled themselves and their readers in vain, in their endeavours to ascertain to their satisfaction, how this wonderful pastime sprang into existence. Whether it was the product of some peaceful age, when science and philosophy reigned supreme; or whether it was nurtured amid the tented field of the warrior, are questions which it is equally futile and unnecessary now to ask. *Sufficient for us that the game exists; that it has been sung of by Homer*," &c. &c.!!! We recommend the above eloquent *morceau*, taken from a Chess periodical now defunct, to the attention of Chessmen at Chess reunions, Chess lectures, and those who are ambitious to *do a spicy* article for a Chess periodical.

THE SEVEN AGES OF CHESS.—(Continued from p. 264.)

VII.—CHESS IN OLD AGE.

THE days are dark, and drear, and chill,
And here, without the power or will
    To go abroad;
I rest me in my snug arm-chair,
And care not for the bitter air,
    Or frozen road.

I cannot see too well, 'tis true,
And shouting friends have cause to rue
    My deafen'd ears:
My books have grown a weariness,
But still the thoughtful game of Chess
    The silence cheers.

The young folks crowd about my knees,
With " Grandpapa, dear, if you please,
    Give me a game."
And so I take them in their turn,
And all the art of Chess-play learn,
    And seek for fame.

They seek to mate poor Grandpapa,
Whose play is not without a flaw,
    Or needless moves.
But who in favourable hours,
When mustering his former powers,
    Victorious proves.

Yet, playing ordinary men,
'Tis not perhaps one time in ten
    I get a game:
I'm out of sorts—have taken cold—
My board and men are very old—
    Headless my Queen!

These tell me, every time I play,
That they and I are on our way
    To our last move.
Thankful for recreation past,
I give my pieces to the last
    A kind of love.

They've served as innocent relief,
When press'd with care, or worn with grief,
    In this brief state.
No entrance will there be for care,
If once I reach the purer air
    Beyond Heaven's gate.

Game played at the PHILIDORIAN, September, 1859, between Mr. LUMLEY, the blind Chess player, and Mr. ZYTOGORSKI, the latter giving Pawn and Two Moves.

(*Remove White's K.B.P.*)

White. (Mr. ZYTOGORSKI.)	Black. (Mr. LUMLEY.)
1.	1. P. to K. fourth
2.	2. P. to Q. fourth
3. P. to K. third	3. B. to Q. third
4. P. to Q. B. fourth	4. P. to K. fifth
5. P. to K. Kt. third	5. P. to Q. B. third
6. P. takes P.	6. P. takes P.
7. Kt. to Q. B. third	7. Kt. to K. B. third
8. P. to Q. fourth	8. B. to K. third
9. Q. to Q. B. fourth (check)	9. Kt. to Q. B. third
10. B. to Q. Kt. fifth	10. Q. to Q. B. second
11. K. Kt. to K. second	11. Q. B. to R. sixth
12. Q. B. to Q. second	12. Q. B. to K. Kt. seventh
13. R. to K. Kt. square	13. Q. B. to K. B. sixth
14. Castles on Q. side	14. P. to Q. R. third
15. B. takes Kt. (check)	15. P. takes B.
16. Q. R. to K. square	16. Kt. to K. Kt. fifth
17. Q. Kt. takes Q. P.	17. Q. to Q. Kt. second
18. P. to K. R. fourth	18. Castles on K. side
19. Q. Kt. to K. B. fourth	19. Kt. to K. B. seventh
20. K. to Q. Kt. square	20. Q. R. to Kt. square
21. P. to Q. Kt. third	21. Kt. to Q. sixth
22. Kt. takes Kt.	22. P. takes Kt.
23. Kt. to K. B. fourth	23. B. to K. fifth
24. R. to Q. B. square	24. K. R. to Q. B. square
25. K. to Q. Kt. second	25. P. to Q. B. fourth
26. P. to Q. fifth	26. P. to K. B. fourth
27. P. to K. Kt. fourth	27. B. takes Kt.
28. P. takes B.	28. Q. takes P.
29. Q. to Q. B. fourth	29. Q. takes Q.
30. R. takes Q.	30. K. to B. second
31. P. takes P.	31. B. takes P.
32. K. R. to Q. B. square	32. K. to Kt. third
33. R. takes P.	33. R. takes R.

White	Black
34. R. takes R.	34. R. to Q. B. square
35. R. takes R.	35. B. takes R.
36. K. to Q. B. third	36. B. to K. B. fourth
37. B. to K. square	37. K. to R. fourth
38. K. to Q. fourth	38. K. to Kt. fifth
39. K. to K. third	39. P. to K. R. third
40. P. to Q. Kt. fourth	40. B. to K. third
41. P. to Q. R. fourth	41. B. to Q. B. fifth
42. K. to Q. fourth	42. B. to Kt. sixth
43. P. to Q. Kt. fifth	43. B. takes P.
44. P. takes P.	44. B. to Kt. fourth
45. P. to R. seventh	45. B. to Q. B. third (check)
46. K. to K. fifth	46. P. to Q. seventh
47. B. takes P.	47. K. takes P.
48. P. to K. B. fifth	48. K. to R. fourth
49. K. to K. B. fourth	49. B. to Q. R. square
50. B. to Q. B. third	50. P. to K. Kt. fourth (check)
51. K. to K. fifth	51. P. to Kt. fifth
52. P. to B. sixth	52. P. to Kt. sixth
53. P. to B. seventh	53. P. to Kt. seventh
54. B. to Q. fourth	

And wins.

Game between Mr. LUMLEY, the Blind Chess Player and Mr. KENNY,
played at the PHILIDORIAN, *September*, 1859.

White. (Mr. LUMLEY.)	*Black.* (Mr. KENNY.)
1. P. to K. fourth	1. P. to K. fourth
2. Kt. to K. B. third	2. Kt. to Q. B. third
3. P. to Q. B. third	3. P. to K. B. fourth
4. B. to Q. Kt. fifth	4. P. takes K. P.
5. B. takes Kt.	5. P. takes Kt.
6. B. takes P.	6. K. Kt. to B. third
7. P. to Q. third	7. P. to Q. fourth
8. Q. B. to Kt. fifth	8. P. to Q. B. third
9. Castles	9. B. to K. second
10. R. to K. square	10. Q. to Q. B. second

11. Q. to K. second	11. K. B. to Q. third
12. P. to K. R. third	12. Castles
13. Kt. to Q. second	13. Q. B. to K. B. fourth
14. Q. to K. third	14. Q. R. to K. square
15. B. takes Kt.	15. R. takes B.
16. Kt. to Q. Kt. third	16. Q. to K. B. second
17. Q. R. to Q. square	17. Q. B. takes K. R. P.
18. B. takes Q. P.	18. Q. B. P. takes B.
19. Q. takes B.	19. R. takes K. B. P.
20. Kt. to Q. second	20. K. R. to K. B. third
21. Q. to K. third	21. Q. to K. R. fourth
22. Kt. to K. B. third	22. P. to K. fifth
23. P. takes P.	23. P. takes P.
24. R. takes B.	24. K. R. takes R.
25. Kt. to Kt. fifth	25. K. R. to Q. eighth
26. Kt. to K. B. third	26. P. takes Kt.
27. Q. takes R. (check)	27. Q. takes Q.

And White resigns.

Game played in 1851 between Messrs. ANDERSSEN and ZYTOGORSKI.

White. (Mr. ANDERSSEN.)	*Black.* (Mr. ZYTOGORSKI.)
1. P. to K. fourth	1. P. to K. fourth
2. P. to K. B. fourth	2. P. takes P.
3. K. B. to Q. B. fourth	3. Q. to K. R. fifth (check)
4. K. to K. B. square	4. P. to Q. third
5. K. Kt. to B. third (a)	5. Q. to K. R. fourth
6. P. to Q. fourth	6. P. to Q. Kt. fourth
7. B. to K. second	7. P. to Q. B. third
8. Q. B. takes P.	8. P. to K. B. third (b)
9. K. Kt. to Kt. fifth (c)	9. Q. to R. fifth
10. P. to K. Kt. third	10. Q. to R. third
11. B. to K. R. fifth (check) (d)	11. P. to K. Kt. third
12. B. to K. Kt. fourth	12. P. takes Kt.
13. B. takes B.	13. P. takes B.
14. B. to Q. Kt. seventh	14. P. takes P.

15. K. to Kt. second	15. P. takes P.
16. R. takes P.	16. Q. to K. B. fifth (e)
17. Kt. to Q. second	17. B. to K. Kt. second
18. Kt. to K. B. third	18. Kt. to K. B. third (f)
19. B. takes R.	19. Kt. to Kt. fifth
20. Q. to Q. third	20. Kt. takes R.
21. Kt. takes Kt.	21. Castles
22. K. to K. R. square	22. R. to K. square
23. R. to K. square	23. P. to K. Kt. fourth
24. P. to Q. R. fourth	24. P. to Q. R. third
25. P. to Q. fifth	25. P. to Q. B. fourth
26. P. takes P.	26. P. takes P.
27. Q. takes P.	27. R. to K. B. square
28. B. to Q. B. sixth	28. B. to K. fourth
29. Q. to K. second	29. Q. to R. fifth
30. R. to K. Kt. square	30. R. to B. seventh
31. R. takes P. (check)	31. K. to R. square
32. R. to R. fifth	32. Q. to B. fifth

And White resigned:

Notes.

(a) Writers of treatises on Chess here recommend Cozio's move, "Q. to K. B. third."

(b) The result of this mode of play is not very obvious, but notwithstanding, to it White owes much of his subsequent embarassment.

(c) Had the Knight been moved at this point to K. fifth, White would in all probability have lost at least his centre Pawn, had he preferred a totally different line of play, Black could have completed his defence, with an excellent counter attack in reserve, by the simple retreat of "Q. to K. B. second."

(d) Here many would prefer "B. to K. Kt. fourth." But a deep examination will prove that thereupon occur positions of so critical a character that the balance is *more obviously* against White than it it is in the actual game.

(e) This move has the advantage over "Q. to K. Kt. fourth (check)," because it not only preserves the original attack on the diagonal assaulted by the Queen, but also obtains command of a new diagonal with a menace addressed immediately to the royal Pawn.

(f) Besides other objections to "Q. takes K. P.," it will be noticed that White may reply with "Q. to K. square," forcing the exchange of Queens.

Games lately played between Herr HARRWITZ and Mr. GROCHEY, the President of the Ipswich Club.

GAME I.

Black. (Mr. GROCHEY.)	_White._ (Herr HARRWITZ.)
1. P. to K. fourth	1. P. to K. fourth
2. P. to K. B. fourth	2. P. takes P.
3. Kt. to K. B. third	3. P. to K. Kt. fourth
4. P. to K. R. fourth	4. P. to K. Kt. fifth
5. Kt. to K. fifth	5. Kt. to K. B. third
6. Kt. takes Kt. P.	6. Kt. takes K. P.
7. P. to Q. third	7. Kt. to Kt. sixth
8. B. takes P.	8. Q. to K. second (check)
9. K. to B. second	9. Kt. takes R. (check)
10. K. to Kt. square	10. B. to Kt. second
11. Kt. to Q. B. third	11. P. to K. R. fourth
12. Kt. to Q. fifth	12. P. takes Kt.
13. Kt. takes Q.	13. B. to Q. fifth (check)
14. K. takes Kt.	14. R. takes P. (check)
15. B. to R. second	15. P. to Kt. sixth

And wins.

GAME II.

White. (Herr HARRWITZ.)	_Black._ (Mr. GROCHEY.)
1. P. to K. fourth	1. P. to K. fourth
2. P. to K. B. fourth	2. P. takes P.
3. B. to B. fourth	3. P. to Q. fourth
4. B. takes P.	4. K. Kt. to B. third
5. Q. Kt. to B. third	5. P. to Q. B. third
6. B. to Q. Kt. third	6. B. to Q. B. fourth
7. Kt. to K. B. third	7. B. to K. Kt. fifth
8. K. B. takes P. (check)	8. K. to B. square
9. B. to Q. Kt. third	9. Q. Kt. to Q. second
10. P. to Q. fourth	10. B. takes Kt.
11. P. takes B.	11. B. to Q. Kt. fifth
12. Q. B. takes P.	12. Kt. to K. R. fourth
13. B. to K. third	13. Q. to K. R. fifth (check)

14. B. to K. B. second	14. Q. to K. R. sixth
15. Q. to Q. second	15. Q. takes K. B. P.
16. K. R. to K. B. square	16. B. takes Kt.
17. P. takes B.	17. Q. takes P. (check)
18. B. to K. third (check)	18. K. Kt. to B. third
19. Castles	19. P. to Q. R. fourth
20. P. to Q. R. third	20. P. to Q. Kt. fourth
21. Q. R. to K. square	21. Q. to K. second
22. K. to Kt. second	22. Kt. to Q. Kt. third
23. B. to K. Kt. fifth	23. Q. to Q. third
24. R. takes Kt. (check)	24. P. takes R.
25. B. mates	

Games in the Match between Messrs. CAMPBELL and WORMALD, played at the PHILIDORIAN Chess Rooms.

GAME XIX.

White. (Mr. CAMPBELL.)	*Black.* (Mr. WORMALD.)
1. P. to K. fourth	1. P. to K. fourth
2. K. Kt. to B. third	2. Q. Kt. to B. third
3. B. to Q. Kt. fifth	3. P. to Q. R. third (a)
4. B. to Q. R. fourth	4. K. Kt. to B. third
5. Castles	5. P. to Q. Kt. fourth
6. B. to Q. Kt. third	6. B. to K. second
7. P. to Q. fourth	7. Kt. takes K. P.
8. P. to Q. fifth	8. Kt. to Q. R. fourth
9. K. R. to K. square	9. Kt. takes K. B.
10. Q. R. P. takes Kt.	10. Kt. to K. B. third
11. Kt. takes K. P.	11. Castles
12. P. to Q. B. fourth	12. B. to Q. Kt. second
13. Q. Kt. to B. third	13. P. to Q. third
14. Kt. to K. B. third	14. P. to Q. Kt. fifth
15. Kt. to K. second	15. Kt. to K. fifth
16. B. to K. third	16. B. to Q. B. square
17. Q. Kt. to Q. fourth	17. B. to Q. second
18. B. to Q. second	18. Kt. takes B.
19. Q. takes Kt.	19. P. to Q. R. fourth

20. R. to K. second	20. B. to K. B. third
21. Q. R. to K. square	21. P. to K. R. third
22. P. to K. R. third	22. Q. to Q. Kt. square
23. Q. to Q. third	23. Q. to Q. B. square
24. R. to Q. B. square	24. R. to K. square
25. R. takes R. (check)	25. Q. takes R.
26. R. to K. square	26. Q. to K. B. square
27. R. to Q. R. square	27. Q. to Q. Kt. square
28. Q. to K. third	28. Q. to Q. Kt. third
29. K. to B. square	29. R. to K. square
30. Q. to Q. third (*b*)	

And the game was abandoned as drawn,

Notes.

(*a*) Bringing out the K. Kt. at once, we think preferable, Mr. Morphy in several of his games played this move successfully.

(*b*) The game might have been continued for many moves, but if correctly played must have resulted in a draw.

GAME XX.

White. (Mr. WORMALD.)	*Black.* (Mr. CAMPBELL.)
1. P. to K. fourth	1. P. to K. third
2. P. to Q. fourth	2. P. to Q. fourth
3. P. takes P.	3. P. takes P.
4. B. to Q. third	4. B. to Q. third
5. K. Kt. to B. third	5. K. Kt. to B. third
6. Castles	6. Castles
7. B. to K. third	7. B. to K. third
8. Q. Kt. to B. third	8. Q. Kt. to B. third
9. P. to Q. R. third	9. P. to K. R. third
10. Q. to Q. second	10. Kt. to K. Kt. fifth
11. B. to K. B. fourth	11. B. takes B.
12. Q. takes B.	12. P. to K. Kt. fourth
13. Q. to Q. second	13. P. to K. B. fourth
14. Q. R. to K. square	14. Q. to Q. second
15. B. to Q. Kt. fifth	15. Q. R. to K. square
16. Kt. to Q. R. fourth	16. Q. to Q. third

17. Kt. to Q. B. fifth	17. B. to Q. B. square
18. B. takes Kt.	18. Q. takes B.
19. P. to K. R. third	19. Kt. to K. B. third
20. Kt. to Q. fifth	20. Q. to Q. third
21. Q. to Q. square	21. P. to Q. Kt. third
22. Q. Kt. to Q. third	22. P. to Q. B. fourth
23. Kt. to K. Kt. sixth	23. R. takes R.
24. R. takes R.	24. R. to K. square
25. R. takes R. (check)	25. Kt. takes R.
26. Q. to K. R. fifth	26. K. to Kt. second
27. K. Kt. to K. fifth	27. Q. to K. third (a)
28. P. to K. R. fourth	28. B. to Q. R. third
29. P. takes P.	29. B. takes Kt.
30. Q. takes P. (check) (b)	30. Q. takes Q.
31. P. takes Q. (check)	31. K. takes P.
32. Kt. takes B.	32. P. takes Q. P.
33. Kt. to Q. Kt. fourth	33. Kt. to Q. third
34. Kt. takes Q. P.	34. Kt. to Q. B. fifth
35. Kt. to K. seventh	35. K. to Kt. fourth
36. Kt. to Q. B. sixth	36. Kt. takes Q. Kt. P.
37. Kt. takes Q. R. P.	37. K. to B. fifth
38. K. to B. square	38. K. to K. fifth
39. K. to K. second	39. K. to Q. fourth
40. Kt. to Q. B. eighth	40. K. to Q. B. fourth
41. Kt. to K. seventh	41. K. to Q. B. fifth
42. Kt. takes K. B. P.	42. P. to Q. sixth (check)
43. P. takes P.	43. Kt. takes P.
44. P. to K. Kt. fourth	44. Kt. to K. fourth
45. P. to K. B. fourth	45. Kt. to K. Kt. third
46. K. to K. third	46. K. to Q. Kt. sixth
47. Kt. to Q. sixth	

And wins.

Notes.

(a) The only move.
(b) Better perhaps to have taken with Pawn.—*e.g.*

30. P. takes P. (check)	30. K. to R. second (best)
31. P. takes B.	31. Say P. takes P.
32. Kt. to K. B. seventh, winning	

N.B.—White could not instead of 31. "P. takes B.," play 31. "Kt. to B.

seventh," as in that case Black could insure a draw by " Q. to K. eighth (ch.)," and afterwards " K. Kt. to B. third," compelling White to draw by perpetual check.

Game lately played at Sheffield between the Rev. Mr. PIERPOINT and Mr. E. THOROLD.

(*Evans's Gambit.*)

White. (Rev. Mr. PIERPOINT.)	Black. (Mr. E. THOROLD.)
1. P. to K. fourth	1. P. to K. fourth
2. K. Kt. to B. third	2. Q. Kt. to B. third
3. B. to Q. B. fourth	3. B. to Q. B. fourth
4. P. to Q. Kt. fourth	4. B. takes P.
5. P. to Q. B. third	5. B. to Q. R. fourth
6. Castles	6. P. to Q. third
7. B. to Q. Kt. second	7. K. Kt. to B. third
8. P. to Q. fourth	8. Q. B. to K. Kt. fifth (*a*)
9. Q. Kt. to Q. second	9. P. takes P.
10. Q. to Q. Kt. third	10. P. takes P.
11. Q. B. takes P.	11. B. takes B.
12. Q. takes B.	12. B. takes Kt.
13. Kt. takes B.	13. Castles
14. K. R. to K. square	14. P. to Q. R. third
15. Q. R. to Q. square	15. P. to Q. Kt. fourth
16. B. to Q. Kt. third	16. Q. Kt. to K. second
17. P. to K. fifth	17. Kt. to K. R. fourth
18. Kt. to K. Kt. fifth (*b*)	18. P. to Q. fourth
19. Q. to K. B. third	19. P. to K. Kt. third
20. P. to K. Kt. fourth	20. Kt. to K. Kt. second
21. Q. to K. R. third	21. P. to K. R. fourth
22. P. takes P.	22. Kt. takes P.
23. B. to Q. B. second	23. K. to Kt. second
24. P. to K. sixth	24. P. to K. B. third
25. Kt. to K. B. seventh	25. Q. to Q. B. square
26. Q. to K. third	26. R. to K. R. square
27. Q. R. to Q. fourth	27. P. to Q. B. fourth
28. R. to K. Kt. fourth	28. Q. to Q. B. second
29. P. to K. B. fourth	29. P. to K. B. fourth
30. R. to K. B. fourth	30. P. to Q. fifth

20

31. Q. to K. B. third	31. P. to Q. B. fifth
32. B. to Q. square	32. Q. R. to Q. B. square
33. Q. to K. Kt. second	33. Kt. takes P.
34. Q. to K. Kt. fifth	34. Kt. to K. R. sixth (check)
35. R. takes Kt.	35. R. takes R.
36. R. to K. second	36. P. to Q. sixth
37. R. to K. Kt. second	37. P. to Q. B. sixth
38. Kt. to K. fifth	38. P. to Q. B. seventh
39. B. takes P.	39. P. takes B.
40. R. takes P.	40. Q. takes Kt.
41. Q. takes Kt. (check)	41. K. to R. third
42. R. to K. B. second	42. R. to Q. B. eighth (check)
43. K. to Kt. second	43. Q. takes P.

And Mates.

Notes.

(a) This seems to us far from being a strong move, castling would have been the safest.

(b) White ought to have played " P. takes P." first, and then moved the Knight to the above square.

Game played between Messrs. HARRWITZ and BARNES, Sept. 22, 1859.

White. (Mr. BARNES.)	*Black.* (Herr HARRWITZ.)
1. P. to K. fourth	1. P. to Q. fourth
2. P. takes P.	2. K. Kt. to B. third
3. B. to K. Kt. fifth (check)	3. B. to Q. second
4. B. to Q. B. fourth	4. P. to Q. Kt. fourth
5. B. to Q. Kt. third	5. P. to Q. R. fourth
6. P. to Q. R. third	6. B. to K. Kt. fifth
7. P. to K. B. third	7. B. to Q. B. square
8. Q. to K. second	8. B. to Q. R. third
9. P. to Q. B. fourth	9. P. takes P.
10. B. takes P.	10. Kt. takes P.
11. B. takes B.	11. R. takes B.
12. Q. to Q. Kt. fifth (check)	12. P. to Q. B. third
13. Q. to Q. R. fourth	13. P. to K. fourth
14. Kt. to K. second	14. B. to Q. B. fourth
15. Q. Kt. to Q. B. third	15. Castles

16. Q. Kt. to K. fourth	16. B. to Q. R. second
17. P. to Q. fourth	17. P. takes P.
18. Kt. takes P.	18. Kt. to Q. Kt. fifth
19. P. takes Kt.	19. P. takes P.
20. Q. takes B.	20. Kt. takes Q.
21. Kt. takes P.	21. Q. to Q. Kt. third
22. Kt. takes B.	22. Q. takes Kt.
23. K. to K. second	23. Q. to Kt. third
24. B. to K. third	24. Q. to K. Kt. fourth (check)
25. K. to B. second	25. P. to K. B. fourth
26. Kt. to Q. sixth	26. Q. to B. third
27. K. R. to Q. square	27. P. to K. B. fifth
28. B. to Q. R. seventh	28. Kt. to B. fourth
29. B. takes Kt.	29. Q. takes B. (check)
30. K. to B. square	30. R. to Q. square
31. Q. R. to B. square	31. Q. to Kt. third
32. Kt. to B. fourth	32. R. takes R. (check)
33. R. takes R.	33. Q. to Q. R. third
34. R. to Q. eighth (check)	34. K. to B. second
35. R. to Q. seventh (check)	35. K. to K. square
36. R. to Q. fourth	36. Q. to Q. R. eighth (check)
37. K. to K. second	37. Q. to K. Kt. eighth
38. R. takes P.	38. Q. takes P. (check)
39. K. to Q. third	39. Q. takes R. P.

And after a few more moves White resigned.

Game between Herr HARRWITZ and Mr. BODEN, played recently at the Grand Cigar Divan.

(King's Bishop's Opening.)

White. (Mr. BODEN.)	Black. (Herr HARRWITZ.)
1. P. to K. fourth	1. P. to K. fourth
2. B. to Q. B. fourth	2. Kt. to K. B. third
3. K. Kt. to B. third	3. Kt. takes P.
4. Q. Kt. to B. third	4. K. Kt. to B. third
5. Kt. takes P.	5. P. to Q. fourth
6. B. to Q. Kt. third	6. K. B. to Q. third

7. P. to Q. fourth	7. P. to Q. B. third
8. Castles	8. Castles
9. Q. B. to K. Kt. fifth	9. P. to K. R. third
10. B. to K. R. fourth	10. Q. B. to K. B. fourth
11. P. to K. B. fourth	11. K. B. to K. second
12. B. takes Kt.	12. B. takes B.
13. Q. to K. B. third	13. Kt. to Q. second
14. P. to K. Kt. fourth	14. B. to R. second
15. Q. R. to Q. square	15. B. takes Kt.
16. Q. P. takes B.	16. Q. to K. R. fifth
17. Q. to K. Kt. second	17. Q. R. to K. square
18. K. R. to K. B. third	18. P. to K. B. fourth
19. P. takes P.	19. B. takes P.
20. R. to K. Kt. third	20. K. to R. square
21. Kt. to K. second	21. B. to K. fifth
22. Q. to K. R. third	22. Q. to K. second
23. P. to Q. B. third	23. Kt. to Q. B. fourth
24. K. R. to K. third	24. Kt. to K. third
25. Q. R. to K. B. square	25. Q. to Q. B. fourth
26. Q. R. to K. B. second	26. K. to R. second
27. R. takes B.	27. Kt. to K. Kt. fourth
28. Q. to K. Kt. second	28. Kt. takes R.
29. B. to Q. B. second	29. R. to K. B. fourth
30. B. takes Kt.	30. P. takes B.
31. Kt. to Q. fourth	31. P. to K. sixth
32. R. to K. B. third	32. R. to K. B. second
33. Q. to K. second	33. Q. to Q. Kt. third
34. P. to Q. Kt. fourth	34. P. to Q. R. fourth
35. P. to Q. R. third	35. P. to Q. B. fourth
36. P. takes Q. B. P.	36. Q. to K. Kt. third (check)
37. K. to B. square	37. Q. to K. fifth
38. Q. takes P.	38. Q. R. takes K. P.
39. Q. takes Q. (check)	39. R. takes Q.
40. P. to K. B. fifth	40. R. to K. fourth
41. K. to Kt. second	41. R. takes Q. B. P.
42. K. to Kt. third	42. P. to Q. Kt. fourth
43. K. to Kt. fourth	43. R. to Q. B. fifth
44. R. to K. B. fourth	44. K. R. to Q. Kt. second

45. P. to K. R. fourth	45. Q. R. takes P.
46. P. to K. B. sixth	46. P. takes P.
47. K. to K. B. fifth	47. K. R. to Q. Kt. third
48. Kt. to K. sixth	48. Q. R. to K. sixth
49. Kt. to B. eighth (check)	49. K. to Kt. second,
50. Kt. to Q. seventh	50. R. to Q. third

And White resigned.

From the match now going on at the PHILIDORIAN between Messrs. HARRWITZ and REEVES, the former giving the odds of Pawn and two Moves.—Score at present, Herr HARRWITZ, 1; Mr. REEVES, 2; drawn 1.

GAME I.

(Remove Black's K. B. P. from the Board.)

White. (Mr. REEVES.)	*Black.* (Herr HARRWITZ.)
1. { P. to K. fourth { P. to Q. fourth	1. P. to K. third
2. K. B. to Q. B. third	2. P. to Q. B. fourth
3. P. to Q. fifth (*a*)	3. P. to Q. third
4. Kt. to K. B. third (*b*)	4. P. takes P.
5. P. takes P.	5. Kt. to K. B. third
6. P. to Q. B. fourth	6. B. to K. second (*c*)
7. Castles	7. Castles
8. P. to K. R. third	8. Q. Kt. to Q. second
9. R. to K. square	9. R. to K. square
10. Q. B. to K. B. fourth	10. Q. Kt. to K. B. square
11. Q. to Q. B. second	11. P. to Q. R. third
12. P. to Q. R. fourth	12. B. to Q. second
13. Kt. to Q. B. third	13. Q. to Q. B. square
14. R. to K. third	14. Q. to Q. B. second
15. P. to K. Kt. fourth	15. K. B. to Q. square
16. R. takes R.	16. B. takes R.
17. Q. to K. second	17. Q. B. to K. B. second
18. R. to K. square	18. P. to K. R. third
19. Q. B. to K. Kt. third	19. P. to Q. Kt. third
20. Kt. to K. R. fourth	20. P. to K. Kt. third
21. P. to K. B. fourth	21. Q. R. to R. second
22. P. to K. B. fifth	22. P. to K. Kt. fourth
23. Kt. to K. B. third	23. Q. to Q. Kt. square

24. Q. to K. R. second (*d*)	24. R. to Q. second
25. K. Kt. to Q. second	25. Q. Kt. to K. R. second
26. K. Kt. to K. fourth	26. B. to K. second
27. Q. to Q. B. second	27. Kt. takes Kt.
28. Kt. takes Kt.	28. Kt. to B. third
29. Q. to Q. Kt. third	29. Kt. takes Kt.
30. R. takes Kt.	30. B. to K. B. third
31. Kt. to Kt. second	31. K. to Kt. second
32. B. to Q. Kt. square	32. Q. to Q. Kt. second
33. K. B. to Q. R. second	33. Q. to Q. Kt. square
34. Q. B. to K. square	34. R. to Q. Kt. second
35. B. to Q. B. third	35. Q. to Q. square
36. Q. to Q. B. second	36. P. to Q. Kt. fourth
37. R. P. takes P.	37. P. takes P.
38. P. to Q. Kt. third	38. B. takes B.
39. Q. takes B. (check)	39. Q. to K. B. third
40. Q. takes Q. (check)	40. K. takes Q.
41. R. to K. second	41. R. to K. second
42. R. takes R.	42. K. takes R.

The game was continued a few more moves, but finally given up as drawn.

Notes by Herr Falkbeer.

(*a*) " P. to K. fifth " is considered the stronger move.

(*b*) " P. to Q. B. fourth," prior to castling, is recommended by the books.

(*c*) We should think that " Q. B. to K. Kt. fifth " instead, would have been more to the purpose. It would have brought the Bishop into the field, and effectually have prevented Black's pieces being crowded through a long series of moves.

(*d*) From this point the game is carefully played on both sides, and becomes equally interesting and instructive.

GAME II.

(*Remove Black's K. B. P. from the Board.*)

White. (Mr. REEVES.)	*Black.* (Herr HARRWITZ.)
1. { P. to K. fourth { P. to Q. fourth	1. P. to K. third
2. Q. B. to K. third	2. P. to Q. B. fourth
3. P. to Q. fifth	3. P. to Q. third

4. P. to Q. B. fourth	4. Q. Kt. to R. third
5. P. to Q. R. third	5. P. to K. Kt. third
6. P. to K. R. fourth	6. Kt. to Q. B. second
7. Kt. to Q. B. third	7. B. to K. Kt. second
8. P. to K. R. fifth (a)	8. B. takes Kt. (check)
9. P. takes B.	9 Q. to K. B. third
10. Q. to Q. Kt. third	10. K. Kt. to K. second
11. K. Kt. to B. third	11. P. to K. fourth
12. Q. B. to K. Kt. fifth	12. Q. to B. second
13. P. to K. R. sixth	13. P. to Q. Kt. third
14. K. R. to R. fourth	14. Castles
15. Q. to Q. Kt. second	15. B. to Q. second
16. Kt. to K. R. second	16. Q. Kt. to K. square
17. Q. to K. second	17. Q. Kt. to K. B. third
18. Q. R. to R. second	18. Q. Kt. to K. R. fourth
19. P. to K. Kt. third	19. P. to Q. R. third
20. Q. to K. B. square	20. P. to Q. Kt. fourth
21. P. takes P.	21. B. takes P.
22. B. takes B.	22. P. takes B.
23. Q. takes P.	23. Q. R. to Q. Kt. square
24. Q. to Q. third	24. P. to Q. B. fifth
25. Q. to Q. B. second	25. R. to Q. Kt. sixth
26. Kt. to K. B. square	26. Kt. to Q. B. square
27. Kt. to K. third	27. Q. to K. B. sixth
28. K. R. to R. third (b)	28. Kt. to K. B. fifth
29. B. takes Kt. (c)	29. P. takes B.
30. Kt. to Q. square	30. Q. to K. Kt. seventh
31. R. to R. fourth	31. P. takes P. (d)
32. P. to K. B. fourth	32. Q. to Kt. eighth (check)
33. K. to Q. second	33. Q. to K. B. eighth
34. K. to Q. B. square	34. K. R. takes K. B. P.
35. R. takes R.	35. Q. takes R. (check)
36. Q. to Q. second	36. Q. takes K. P.
37. R. to Q. B. second	37. Kt. to K. second
38. Q. to K. Kt. fifth	38. Kt. to K. B. fourth
39. Q. to Q. eighth (check)	39. K. to B. second
40. Q. to K. R. eighth	40. Q. to K. B. fifth (check)
41. R. to Q. second	41. Q. takes P.

And after a few more moves White resigned.

Notes.

(*a*) " Q. B. to Q. second " would have been stronger.
(*b*) This move, weak though it seems, was compulsory on account of the threatened check of the Queen on K. R. eighth.
(*c*) Another forced move, as Black threatened to check with Kt. on Q. sixth.
(*d*) This is excellent play indeed. The game was masterly played throughout by Herr Harrwitz.

Match between Mr. MORPHY and Herr LÖWENTHAL.

GAME XI.

(*Sicilian Opening.*)

White. (Herr LÖWENTHAL.)	*Black*. (Mr. MORPHY.)
1. P. to K. fourth	1. P. to Q. B. fourth
2. P. to Q. fourth	2. P. takes P.
3. Kt. to K. B. third	3. P. to K. third
4. Kt. takes P.	4. Kt. to Q. B. third
5. Kt. to Q. Kt. fifth	5. P. to Q. R. third (*a*)
6. Kt. to Q. sixth (check)	6. B. takes Kt.
7. Q. takes B.	7. Q. to K. second
8. Q. to K. Kt. third (*b*)	8. Kt. to K. B. third
9. Kt. to Q. B. third	9. P. to Q. fourth
10. P. to K. fifth	10. Kt. to K. R. fourth
11. Q. to K. B. third	11. P. to K. Kt. third
12. P. to K. Kt. fourth	12. Q. Kt. takes K. P. (*c*)
13. Q. to K. second	13. Q. Kt. takes P.
14. Q. takes Kt.	14. P. to K. fourth
15. Q. to Q. R. fourth (check)	15. B. to Q. second
16. Q. to Q. Kt. third	16. P. to Q. fifth
17. Q. takes Q. Kt. P.	17. Castles
18. Kt. to Q. fifth	18. Q. to Q. third
19. B. to K. Kt. second	19. P. to K. fifth
20. P. to Q. B. fourth (*d*)	20. P. to K. B. fourth
21. Q. to Q. Kt. fourth	21. Q. to K. fourth
22. Q. to K. seventh	22. B. to K. third
23. Q. to Q. B. seventh	23. Q. to K. Kt. second
24. Q. takes Q.	24. Kt. takes Q.
25. Kt. to Q. Kt. sixth (*e*)	25. Q. R. to Q. Kt. square
26. P. to Q. B. fifth	26. Kt. to K. R. fourth

27. P. to Q. Kt. fourth	27. K. to B. second
28. Castles	28. P. to K. Kt. fourth
29. R. to Q. square	29. K. R. to Q. square (*f*)
30. B. takes K. Kt. P.	30. K. R. to K. Kt. square
31. P. to K. R. fourth	31. R. to K. Kt. third
32. R. takes P.	32. Q. R. to K. Kt. square
33. Kt. to Q. seventh	33. R. takes B.
34. P. takes R.	34. R. takes P.
35. K. to R. second	35. Kt. to K. B. fifth
36. B. to K. B. square	36. R. to R. fourth (check)
37. K. to Kt. third	37. Kt. to Q. fourth
38. P. to K. B. fourth	38. P. takes P. (*en passant*)
39. Kt. to K. fifth (check)	39. K. to B. third
40. Kt. takes P.	40. R. to R. third
41. Q. R. to K. square	41. R. to Kt. third (check)
42. K. to B. second	42. Kt. to Q. B. sixth
43. B. to Q. third	43. B. to Q. fourth
44. B. takes Q. R. P.	44. R. to Kt. second
45. K. R. to K. B. fourth	45. B. takes Kt.
46. R. takes B. (*g*)	

And wins.

Notes by Herr Falkbeer.

(*a*) If "P. to Q. fourth," White answers with "P. takes P.," and if then "K. P. takes P.," White retakes with Q., winning a Pawn.

(*b*) White could have also played "P. to K. fifth." Black's game is very confined already, in consequence of the defence he chose, and his following move does not serve to improve it.

(*c*) Black thus gives up a piece—a venturesome sacrifice, which can only be explained by his cramped position, there being no other means to free his pieces.

(*d*) This game is again played with great care and consummate skill by Herr Löwenthal. We deeply regret, therefore, the inconsistency of his play on the whole.

(*e*) This is stronger than "Kt. to Q. B. seventh."

(*f*) "Q. R. to Q. square" might be preferable.

(*g*) This game began on August 12, and was finished in two sittings.

GAME XII.
(*French Opening.*)

White. (Mr. MORPHY.)	Black. (Herr LÖWENTHAL.)
1. P. to K. fourth	1. P. to K. third
2. P. to Q. fourth	2. P. to Q. fourth
3. P. takes P.	3. P. takes P.
4. Kt. to K. B. third	4. Kt. to K. B. third
5. B. to Q. third	5. Q. B. to K. third
6. Castles	6. B. to Q. third
7. Kt. to Q. B. third	7. P. to Q. B. third
8. Kt. to K. fifth	8. Q. to Q. Kt. third
9. Q. B. to K. third	9. Q. Kt. to Q. second (*a*)
10. P. to K. B. fourth	10. B. takes Kt.
11. B. P. takes B.	11. Kt. to K. Kt. fifth
12. Q. to Q. second	12. Kt. takes B.
13. Q. takes Kt.	13. Q. takes Q. Kt. P. (*b*)
14. Kt. to K. second	14. Q. to Q. R. sixth
15. Kt. to K. B. fourth	15. Q. to K. second (*c*)
16. Q. R. to Q. Kt. square	16. Castles on Q's. side (*d*)
17. B. to K. second	17. Kt. to Q. Kt. third
18. Q. to Q. Kt. third	18. R. to Q. second
19. Kt. to Q. third	19. Kt. to Q. B. fifth
20. Kt. to Q. B. fifth	20. R. to Q. B. second
21. Q. to Q. R. fourth	21. P. to Q. Kt. third
22. B. takes Kt.	22. P. takes Kt.
23. B. to Q. R. sixth (check)	23. K. to Q. second
24. B. to Q. Kt. seventh	24. R. to Q. square
25. B. takes P. (check)	

And Black resigned.

Notes by Herr Falkbeer.

(*a*) It was not advisable to take the Q. Kt. P. at this moment. White's best answer, we think, would have been, 10. "Q. Kt. to K. second," and if Black then plays "Q. to Q. Kt. third," 11. "P. to Q. B. fourth."

(*b*) Again, either castling on King's side, or "P. to Q. R. fourth," would have been safer play.

(*c*) This move was forced, as White threatened to take B. with Kt. and if "P. takes B." to win the Queen on the next move, by checking with B. on K. Kt. sixth.

(*d*) Black's last move was probably made with the intention of securing the

Q. Kt. P., as we can imagine no other reason for this suicidal step. Castling on the Queen's side at this critical point, and thus giving a most welcome opportunity for the display of Morphy's characteristic brilliancy of style, and eminently attacking power, is something far beyond our comprehension. There were several other means to protect the Pawn, far safer than the one adopted, as for instance, "Kt. to Q. Kt. third," which, we believe, is the best; for if White then takes B. with Kt., Black retakes with P., having a safe defence with a Pawn ahead.

Game between Mr. MORPHY and Mr. BARNES.

(Irregular Opening.)

White. (Mr. MORPHY.)	Black. (Mr. BARNES.)
1. P. to K. fourth	1. P. to K. third
2. P. to Q. fourth	2. P. to K. third
3. B. to Q. third	3. K. Kt. to K. second
4. Q. B. to K. third	4. P. to Q. fourth
5. Kt. to Q. B. third	5. P. takes P.
6. Kt. takes P.	6. Kt. to Q. fourth
7. Kt. to K. R. third	7. K. B. to K. second
8. Q. to K. R. fifth (check)	8. P. to K. Kt. third
9. Q. to R. sixth	9. B. to B. square
10. Q. to R. fourth	10. B. to K. Kt. second
11. Castles	11. Castles
12. P. to Q. B. fourth	12. Kt. takes B.
13. P. takes Kt.	13. P. to K. B. fourth
14. Q. Kt. to K. Kt. fifth	14. P. to K. R. third
15. Q. Kt. to K. B. third	15. P. to K. R. fourth
16. Q. takes Q.	16. R. takes Q.
17. B. to Q. B. second	17. P. takes P.
18. P. takes P.	18. B. takes P. (check)
19. Kt. takes B.	19. R. takes Kt.
20. K. R. to K. square	20. K. to B. second
21. P. to Q. B. fifth	21. B. to K. third
22. Q. R. to Q. square	22. Kt. to Q. B. third
23. R. takes R.	23. Kt. takes R.
24. B. to Q. R. fourth	24. P. to K. Kt. fourth
25. R. to Q. square	25. R. to Q. square
26. P. to Q. R. third	26. P. to K. B. fifth
27. Kt. to B. second	27. Kt. to K. seventh (check)

28. K. to B. square	28. R. takes R. (check)
29. B. takes R.	29. Kt. to Q. fifth
30. K. to K. square	30. K. to B. third
31. K. to Q. second	31. Kt. to Q. Kt. sixth (check)
32. B. takes Kt.	32. B. takes B.
33. Kt. to Kt. fourth (check)	33. K. to Kt. third
34. P. to K. Kt. third	34. P. to K. R. fourth
35. Kt. to B. second	35. K. to B. fifth
36. K. to Q. B. third	36. B. to Q. fourth
37. K. to Q. fourth	37. P. to Q. B. third
38. P. to Q. Kt. fourth	38. B. to K. Kt. seventh
39. P. takes P.	39. K. takes P.
40. P. to Q. R. fourth	40. B. to K. B. eighth
41. Kt. to K. fourth	41. P. to K. R. fifth
42. Kt. to Q. second	42. B. to K. seventh
43. Kt. to K. fourth	43. P. to K. Kt. fifth
44. Kt. to K. B. second	44. K. to B. sixth
45. Kt. to K. fourth	45. B. to K. B. eighth
46. K. to K. fifth	46. B. to Q. sixth
47. Kt. to K. Kt. fifth (check)	47. K. to Kt. seventh
48. K. to Q. sixth	48. K. takes P.
49. K. to Q. B. seventh	49. K. to Kt. sixth
50. K. takes P.	50. P. to K. R. sixth

And wins.

Game between Mr. BODEN and Mr. MORPHY.
(*Philidorian Defence.*)

White. (Mr. BODEN.)	*Black.* (Mr. MORPHY.)
1. P. to K. fourth	1. P. to K. fourth
2. Kt. to K. B. third	2. P. to Q. third
3. P. to Q. fourth	3. P. takes P.
4. Q. takes P.	4. Q. B. to Q. second
5. Q. B. to K. third	5. Kt. to Q. B. third
6. Q. to Q. second	6. Kt. to K. B. third
7. K. B. to Q. third	7. K. B. to K. second
8. Kt. to Q. B. third	8. Castles
9. Castles (K. R.)	9. P. to K. R. third

10. P. to K. R. third	10. Kt. to K. R. second
11. P. to K. Kt. fourth	11. P. to K. R. fourth
12. Kt. to K. R. second	12. P. takes P.
13. P. takes P.	13. Q. Kt. to K. fourth
14. P. to K. B. third	14. P. to K. Kt. fourth
15. K. to Kt. second	15. P. to Q. B. fourth
16. K. B. to R. square	16. K. to Kt. second
17. Kt. to B. square	17. K. R. to R. square
18. Kt. to Kt. third	18. P. to K. B. third
19. Q. Kt. to Q. fifth	19. K. Kt. to B. square
20. K. Kt. to R. fifth (check)	20. K. to B. second
21. Q. R. to Q. square	21. K. Kt. to K. Kt. third
22. K. B. to K. second	22. K. Kt. to K. R. fifth (check)
23. K. to B. second	23. Q. B. to Q. B. third
24. Kt. takes B.	24. Q. takes Kt.
25. Q. takes P.	25. P. to Q. Kt. third
26. Q. takes Q. (check)	26. K. takes Q.
27. Kt. to K. Kt. third	27. K. to B. second
28. R. to Q. sixth	28. K. to K. second
29. R. to Q. second	29. K. to B. second
30. P. to K. B. fourth	30. P. takes P.
31. B. takes P.	31. K. Kt. to K. Kt. third
32. Q. B. to R. sixth	32. R. to R. second
33. K. to K. third	33. Q. R. to K. R. square
34. Kt. to B. fifth	34. Kt. to K. second
35. Kt. takes Kt.	35. K. takes Kt.
36. P. to K. Kt. fifth	36. K. to K. third
37. K. R. to Q. square	37. P. takes P.
38. R. to Q. sixth (check)	38. K. to B. second
39. K. B. to K. R. fifth (check)	39. K. to K. second
40. Q. B. takes P. (check)	40. K. to B. square
41. K. R. to K. B. square (check)	

And Black resigned.

PROBLEMS FOR YOUNG PLAYERS.

No. 11.   By Mr. ABBOTT, *of Southampton.*

White.	*Black.*
K. on Q. B. fifth	K. on K. B. fourth
Q. on Q. Kt. second	B. on Q. Kt. eighth
Kt. on K. second	P. on Q. R. seventh
B. on Q. square	
P. on K. third	

White to mate in three moves.

No. 12.   By Mr. GROSDEMANGE, ST. DIE (*Vosges.*)

White.	*Black.*
K. on Q. R. fifth	K. on Q. B. fifth
R. on K. Kt. sixth	Kt. on K. R. seventh
B.'s on Q. Kt. third and K. fifth	B. on Q. Kt. eighth
Kt.'s on K. third and K. B. second	P. on Q. R. sixth

White to mate in three moves.

SOLUTIONS TO PROBLEMS.

No. 33.   *Page* 287.

White.	*Black.*
K. to Q. fourth	P. to Q. fourth (check)
K. to Q. B. fifth	K. takes Kt.
B. mates	

No. 34.   *Page* 287.

On the diagram in our last number, there was a Bishop left out on King's square. Please, therefore, to place a Black Bishop on Black King's square, and the following is the solution:—

White.	*Black.*
Kt. to K. Kt. fifth (check)	K. takes R.
Q. to Q. B. fifth (check)	K. takes Q.
Kt. to K. fourth (double check)	K. to Q. B. fifth
R. mates	

No. 35.   *Page* 288.

White.	*Black.*
R. to K. Kt. fourth	Anything
R. or B. mates, or	
B. discovers mate	

No. 36.   *Page* 288.

White.	*Black.*
P. to Q. Kt. fourth (check)	K. to Q. Kt. fourth
Q. to Q. fifth (check)	K. to Q. B. third
Q. to Q. Kt. seventh (check)	K. takes Q.
P. to Q. Kt. fifth	K. discovers mate

No. 37. Problem by Herr KLING.
BLACK.

WHITE.
White to move, and mate in three moves.

No. 38. Problem by Mr. WORMALD.
BLACK.

WHITE.
White to move, and mate in three moves.

No. 39.   End Game by Mr. BROWN, of Leeds.
BLACK.

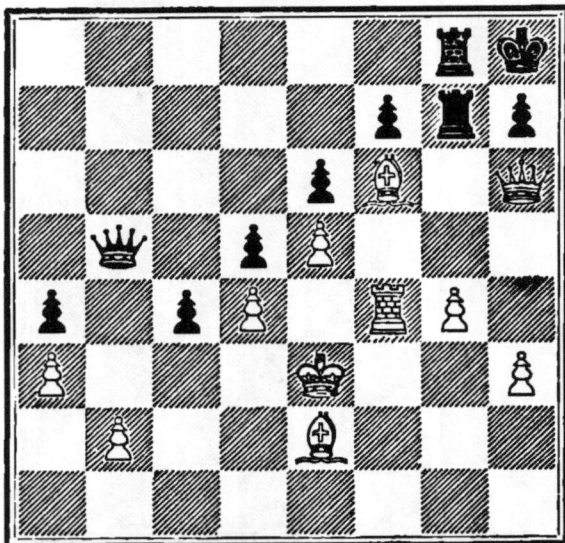

WHITE.
White to move, and mate in six moves.

No. 40.   End Game by Mr. ZYTOGORSKI, from actual play.
BLACK.

WHITE.
White to move and win.

PAUL MORPHY; A SKETCH FROM THE CHESS WORLD.

HERR FALKBEER'S TRANSLATION OF MAX LANGE'S WORK.

THE English public has been presented last week with the above-mentioned book, of which we have already given a short review in our last number, but a more minute perusal of its contents induces us to make a few more remarks upon this subject. The author of the German work is Herr MAX LANGE, the editor of the Berlin *Schachzeitung ;* the translator of it is Herr ERNEST FALKBEER, late editor of the Vienna *Schachzeitung,* and at present editor of the Chess columns in the *Sunday Times.* In perusing, therefore, the English edition of the work, we obtain the views of the two chief representatives of the German periodical press, and thus, most probably, the opinions of the majority of German Chess players. A not less interesting feature of the book, is, that we get a sort of peep behind the scenes in the grand Chess drama which Mr. MORPHY performed before his European audience. It is not part of our task (nor have we the slightest intention at present to do so) to initiate our readers in the secrets of gaining or keeping a Chess reputation, we simply want to show that we hold opinions common with the strongest Chess players, at home and abroad. Thus, the *Chess Monthly,* which is under the joint direction of Messrs. MORPHY and FISKE, was very bitter in its July number against the *Chronicle* for stating that most of the European opponents of Mr. MORPHY encountered him at great disadvantages, and that very few of them played up to the standard of their skill, and that some of the very strongest English and Foreign Chess players had not contended with the American champion at all. Now let us see how far we are borne out in our assertions. As to the English players, a comparatively small number of them have at all played with Mr. MORPHY, it is not, therefore, upon the victories over them he can found his extraordinary reputation, it is rather upon those victories which he might have had if he had played with them, he rests his claims. It is, therefore, upon his achievements against the three foreign players he prides himself. The three players are LÖWENTHAL, HARRWITZ, and ANDERSSEN. As to the first, Herr LÖWENTHAL, it cannot be denied, he is an excellent player ; but his play has one great defect, that is, uncertainty ; he works with great skill to obtain a winning position, which some way or other

21

he manages to turn afterwards into a losing one ; according to his own notes to his games, he ought to have won the majority of them. In his match he only won three games to MORPHY's nine. This is, apparently, a grand result for the American, but it dwindles down to nothing when we compare it with the match between LÖWENTHAL and HARRWITZ, where out of the last twenty games, LÖWENTHAL only scored a single game. As to the second, Herr HARRWITZ, out of the eight games he played with MORPHY, he won only three, and lost five, there remains a balance of two games in favor of MORPHY, but it must not be forgotten that Herr HARRWITZ was ill at the time, and asked for a respite of a few days, which was granted, and when after resuming, he found he was as yet too unwell to play, and asked for another respite, the request was refused, on the plea of Mr. MORPHY's inability to stay any longer in Paris. Thereupon Herr HARRWITZ gave up the match, and Mr. MORPHY remained six months longer in the French metropolis. We do not blame Mr. MORPHY for not granting to Herr HARRWITZ the required time, especially, as with his wonderful memory, he must have well recollected HARRWITZ's match with LÖWENTHAL, in which, as in that with MORPHY, HARRWITZ won the two first games, and then lost seven games running—mind seven—not five; being obliged to play according to stipulations every other day, and finding himself too unwell to continue the match, he daringly gave up two more games, thus being only two games to LÖWENTHAL's nine. After a week's sojourn in the country, he resumed the match, and won it by the odd game, having, as we said above, lost only one game out of twenty played. With this feat in his recollection, Mr. MORPHY was quite right not to grant Mr. HARRWITZ the required time. As to the third, Professor ANDERSSEN, there certainly the *American Monthly* ought to find no fault with us, as they wrote themselves a few months before, that ANDERSSEN was completely out of play, and, therefore, not fit to oppose MORPHY. In the same article, the *Monthly* also confesses that there are stronger German players than either LÖWENTHAL, HARRWITZ, or ANDERSSEN, and, therefore, Mr. MORPHY has not even encountered the strongest German players.

We here quote the following extract from the American Chess periodical, which cannot be mistaken :—

" Germany, unlike France, exhibits no decline in Chess. The generation which succeeded KOCH and ALLGAIER was indeed a generation of giants, and for the last twenty years the practice and theory, the literature and history of Chess, have been nowhere better illustrated than by Teutonic writers and players. The rise of the famous Berlin school, marked one of the most important epochs in the annals of the game, and led to larger views and grander developments in every department of Chess. Though some of the earlier members of that school, MENDHEIM, BLEDOW, BILGUER, and HANSTEIN have been called to a higher sphere, some of its brightest ornaments, HEYDEBRAND VON DER LASA, MAYET, and ANDERSSEN still remain. The Austrian dominions lost, either by death or absence, many of the players who formerly adorned the clubs of Southern Germany and Hungary. SZÈN is dead ; LÖWENTHAL and FALKBEER are in London, and HAMPE now plays but little. Of German players, not to say European, we should be inclined to place VON DER LASA foremost ; but he is now Prussian Minister at Rio Janeiro, and for many years has had little or no practice. ANDERSSEN, with the exception of his rather unfortunate visit to Manchester last August, has played but rarely of late. But a new man has arisen within a few years, who, to judge from his published games, and his power of analysis, as displayed in several theoretical essays, is worthy to be ranked among the very first of living players. We refer to Mr. MAX LANGE, the present chief editor of the *Berlin Schachzeitung*. We believe our young champion will find in Europe no more worthy and able antagonist than Mr. LANGE. Berlin and Leipzig both possess flourishing clubs. The latter will celebrate, in December, its tenth anniversary, at which LANGE and ANDERSSEN will be present, and to which Mr. MORPHY has been invited. Among the strong players of Germany, to whom we have not already alluded, may be mentioned FRANZ, DUFRESNE, WILLBERG, of Berlin ; FRIEDLÄNDER, of Breslau ; POLLMAECHER, VITZTHUM, and WIGAND, of Leipzig ; BEZZEL, of Ansbach, and RECSI, of Pesth. Besides the *Berlin Schachzeitung*, the periodical literature of Chess is represented by excellent columns in the *Illustrirte Familien-Journal* (edited by POLLMAECHER) and the *Illustrirte Zeitung* (edited by PORTIUS), both published in Leipzic. In the branch of problem-making, the labours of such living composers as BAYER, WILLMERS, PONGRACZ, DELLA TORRE, KUIPER, NOWOTNY, and others, have given to their country a position not equalled by any other nation. German analytical works, such as the *Handbuch*, VON DER LASA's *Leitfaden*, and LANGE's *Kritik*,

have acquired a lasting reputation, and exercised an universal influence.
We should like to speak of Russia and Italy next to Germany and
France, the two greatest Chess playing nations on the Continent; but
our space forbids, and our object to enable our readers to follow with
a better understanding the continental career of Mr. MORPHY, is now
,fulfilled; for, however much both the world and himself may desire
such a *denouement* to Mr. MORPHY's European tour, it is hardly
possible that he will at present be able to encounter the PETROFFS,
JAENISCHES, SCHUMOFFS, and URUSSOWS of the Czar's dominions, or
the DUBOIS and CENTURINIS of the Italian peninsula."

Herr MAX LANGE himself is of opinion, that HEYDEBRAND VON
DER LASA is decidedly the strongest German player; he calls him the
grandmaster of Germany.   The German author's decided opinion is,
that ANDERSSEN has played far below his strength, from various circumstances, and he thinks that, in another encounter, if duly prepared
for the contest, he has a good chance to come off the conqueror; this
is also the opinion of ANDERSSEN, who intends to play a return match
should the occasion offer.   An interesting insight into the manœuvres
employed to give Mr. MORPHY a European reputation, will be found
in the following passage :—

" To this must be added that certain parties abroad, not satisfied
with the influence exercised by the press, tried to bring the intrigue to
an issue by direct communications.   Letters were all at once addressed
by the companion of the American champion to several of the German
clubs, with the announcement that the transatlantic master was making
preparations for his return to his native country, a fact which in itself
would be of the utmost indifference to Germany; to this was joined the
very presumptuous request to ask him for a continuance of his stay
in Paris.

" Thus nothing less was required but that Germany should address
a petition to a foreign young Chess player, as yet not personally known,
and whose own ardent desire ought naturally to have been to meet the
German masters, just to enable the French players to enjoy for some
time longer the pleasure of his play in Paris.   This was certainly the
most preposterous request that foreigners could dare to make to
Germany.   Still there were to be found some German Chess amateurs
who entertained the above demand.   The Berlin Chess club, however,
unanimously repudiated the suggestion, and in a simple but dignified

answer expressed their regret not to be able to take part in the desired petition."

The following is the original letter :—

" Vous apprendrez, sans doute, avec regret que le beau joueur d'Echecs Américain M. PAUL MORPHY se dispose en ce moment de quitter l'Europe dans une quinzaine de jours et aussi qu'il est bien probable que nous ne le reverrons plus que dans plusieurs années. Rien n'est plus malheureux pour tous les vrais amateurs d'Echecs ; car déja plusieurs forts joueurs se disposaient à se rendre à Paris pour se mésurer avec lui et le trop prompt départ de M. MORPHY va nous priver de magnifiques parties qui auraient été jouées entre lui et ces illustres champions. M. MORPHY tout le premier regrette vivement l'obligation où il se trouve de retourner aux Etats Unis et il préfererait, j'en suis convaincu, de passsr l'hiver en Europe. Mais il craint de mécontenter sa famille en prolongeant trop son séjour parmi nous.— Dans cet état des choses tous les amateurs d'Echecs de Paris se sont décidés à lui écrire collectivement une lettre pour l'engager à rester, au nom de l'intérêt des Echecs. Déja plusieurs clubs de Londres et de Paris se mettent en train de suivre cet exemple et s'empressent de lui écrire dans le même sens. Et si votre cercle veut bien lui adresser pendant cette semaine (!) le même voeu, il n'y à aucun doute que Mr. MORPHY se rende à ce désir unanime, en se réservant de présenter à sa famille ces puissantes raisons qui lui ont fait différer son départ. J'ai eu le plaisir de voyager avec Mr. MORPHY depuis son arrivée en Europe et je suis convaincu qu'il cédera à un voeu aussi imposant et unanime. De cette façon, etc."

It is the opinion of most German Chess players, that if ANDERSSEN had played the match in Breslau, where the laurel seeking MORPHY had every reason to go and meet him, the result would have been a different one. There seems to have been a sort of fatality which induced ANDERSSEN to go to Paris, when nearly all the German players were opposed to his proceeding there, as shown by the following letter of MAX LANGE to ANDERSSEN :—

" My dear Sir and Friend,—Your much esteemed lines of yesterday bring me the confirmation of news, which till now I neither believed well founded, nor possible. You, the mature master of high renown, really intend to undertake a journey to Paris, and thus make the first

advances towards a meeting with the youthful champion, who came to
Europe to establish his reputation.

" If for a moment the flattering hope of adding fresh laurels to, or
to consolidate your well-earned renown has seized entirely upon your
mind, and banished for a time, perhaps, every other regard, your
natural good sense and tact has, no doubt, soon' shown you several
points worthy of grave reflection ; and I trust your determination is the
result of serious and mature thought.   After this most probable supposition, I should perhaps abstain from saying anything else, but
simply express my best hopes for your success, wishing you sincerely
a continuation of the well-being of your body and intellect, and a never
failing presence of the powers of your mind.

" The peculiar circumstances of the case, however, demand a decided
and unvarnished opinion, the more so as your determination is of great
consequence to the Chess circles in general, and as it is our duty firmly
to pronounce the sentiments of our country in the face of the presumptuous foreigner.

" If you were to be welcomed in Paris as the representative of
German championship, I should be obliged to protest against such a
misconception in the name of German mastership. Neither our grandmaster HEYDEBRAND VON DER LASA—who but lately repudiated the
suppositions of the daily press concerning him, with proud energy—
nor the German Clubs—especially that of Berlin, known to advantage
equally well at home and abroad—would, under present circumstances,
consider your journey to the foreign country necessary or advisable.

" The long established reputation of German mastership, stands in
the opinion of all good Chess players in the world, so high and im-
movable, that it does not require confirmation in a contest of our own
seeking ; and, considering the supercilious pretensions with which
foreigners are in the habit of regarding our country, it behoves the
proud consciousness of national power, not to imperil our dignity by
making the first step towards the stranger.   This first step should be
the farther from our mind, the more there is a necessity for the ambitious young master himself to issue the challenge; and when you were
the first to throw down the gauntlet, you had then passed already the
limits prescribed by national pride.   But now, as you are prepared to
go still farther, there remains nothing even for your personal position,
than the single chance of a complete and decisive victory, as the only

excuse for that deeply founded consciousness of superiority, which alone could have reasonably induced you to make the first step to meet the foreigner.

"That this chance may be realised, allow me now, and chiefly for your own sake, confidently to hope, and to give to that confidence the strongest expression, by my stating to you, that in this combat of *your own seeking*, you *must*, under any circumstances, carry a decisive victory.

"If the iron power of will, which counts for so much in Chess, could, steeled in the fire of that necessity, yet gain in hardness and resistance, then it will be my greatest triumph to have spoken that word, as it is my heartfelt wish, that your high genius may safely guide you.

"In sincere devotedness, your's truly,

"Professor Anderssen. MAX LANGE."

From the above, our readers will see that the book is interesting, not only on account of the one hundred and forty-eight games contained therein, but also by its biographical, historical, and other notes, which are copiously interspersed among the games.

SOME OBSERVATIONS ON THE ORIGIN AND PROGRESS OF CHESS.

BY DR. DUNCAN FORBES.

CHAPTER XII.—(*Continued from our last Number*).

Now looking at these couplets of Pope's, or rather of Pope's workmen, we have no hesitation in saying that they are the least worthy of his name that ever were written. It is well known that Pope himself did not *do* the *Odyssey*. He may have touched off the rhymes of his scribblers or so, leaving the sense to come as it might. The parenthesis in the second line is not only, *not* Homer's, but it is downright nonsense. We really see no very alarming "symptoms of luxury" in a man's making a seat, aye and a bed too, of a bullock's skin, particularly as the said man had previously killed and flayed the beast with his own hands. The third and fourth lines are not in Homer at all, so it would be simply ridiculous to waste time upon them. I have only to add that this passage, *not of Homer's*, but of Pope's Grub Street Hacks, has been quoted and appealed to "usque ad nauseam" as a *proof* of the antiquity of Chess in "early Greece."

The Byzantine, or Neo-Hellenic term for Chess, that is, "bona fide Chess," is ζατρίκοιν, a word unknown in the classic period of the Greek language, and incapable of satisfactory derivation from any Greek root. It is a pure exotic in the language (like the terms Chatrang and Shatranj in the languages of Persia and Arabia) where it serves as a mere puzzle to exercise the ingenuity of the Lexicographers. The fact is, as we have already shown in our fifth chapter, that the Sanskrit compound "Chatur-anga" is the real root of Chatrang, Shatranj, and as we shall immediately point out of ζατρικιον in like manner. The term ζατρικιον is simply a barbaric or foreign word with a Hellenic termination. The Greek alphabet had no letter or combination of letters capable of expressing the sound of the Persian "ch" (like our "ch" in "church") and as the nearest approximation, they employed for that purpose the letter (zeta) ζ; hence Chatrang became ζατρανκ, or ζατρινκ, or Hellenized, ζατρανκιον or ζατρινκιον. Again the middle ν of the last form is thrown out in conformity with a very prevalent usage of the language well known to every Greek scholar, hence the form ζατρικιον which is applied to Chess only, and never to the πιττιια, or any other species of game. As instances of the elision of the letter ν in foreign words introduced into the Hellenic, we may mention the Roman term "Castrense," which becomes καστρισιον; and "Armenta," which becomes ἑρμητα. So much for the derivation of ζατρικιον, the third in descent from Chaturanga through the Persian Chatrang.

In the more recent Byzantine writers we meet with another modification of the term ζατρικιον, viz., σαντραζ, which is evidently taken from the Arabic "Shatranj." In the first place σαντραζ is a mere transposition of σατρανζ, per metathesin, another usage very common in the Greek language, especially in the adopting of foreign words. For instance, the plain Arabic word "Tarjumān," or "Targumān," is in Greek metamorphosed into τρόγομᾶνος, δραγομᾶνος, or δρογομᾶνος, &c. Well, with regard to the Arabic Shatranj, the Greek alphabet had neither the initial nor the final sound of the word. For the former they made use of the (sigma) σ as the nearest approximation; and for the latter, the (zeta) ζ, as in the case of the Persian "ch;" for the ch and j being cognate sounds both were represented, when necessary in Greek by ζ; hence the term σατρανζ, or per metathesin, σαντραζ, which is the fourth in descent from Chatur-anga through the forms "Chatrang" and "Shatranj" respectively. I have dwelt thus particularly on the etymological or philological part of our argument, because, if sound, and I cannot see any flaw in it, we are warranted in drawing thence several important conclusions.

1. In the first place, we have shown that the term ζατρικιον the older form under which it appears in the Byzantine writers, is derived solely from the Persian "Chatrang," and not from the Arabic "Shatranj." The obvious inference then is, that the Greeks received the game of Chess, along with the older term ζατρικιον, directly from the Persians and not through the intervention of the Arabs. This event may pos-

sibly have occurred during the reign of Naushīrwān, who repeatedly carried his conquests into Syria and Asia Minor, but it is much more probable that it took place some thirty or forty years later, during the reign of Khusrū Parvīz, or Chosroes II., as we shall hereafter point out.

2. In the second place, the Byzantines must have received the term ζατρικιον, and consequently the game of Chess from the Persians at a period when the latter made use, in their language, of the older term "Chatrang," and not after they had adopted the Arabic modification "Shatranj." This must have happened some time before the middle of the seventh century, when the language of Persia was greatly changed or modified, and the ancient religion of Zoroaster gave place to that of Muhammad, in consequence of the conquests of the Saracens. Under the command of the Caliph 'Umar, these temperate and hardy sons of the desert, with the Kurān in one hand, and the sword in the other, had possessed themselves of the whole country extending from the Euphrates to the Oxus and Indus, about A.D. 640. The hitherto comparatively pure language of Persia became then largely intermixed with words and phrases from the Arabic; and the term "Shatranj," the only one in use by Persian writers of modern times, then superseded the older form "Chatrang." All this leads us nearly to the same conclusion as before, viz., that the Byzantines received the game of Chess from the Persians at least as early as the first quarter of the seventh century.

3. Lastly, if we could ascertain the earliest mention of the word ζατρικιον among the Byzantine writers, we should have a certain landmark by which to steer our course. We might rest assured that the game of Chess had, ere then, become known to the Greeks. We are told that the word occurs for the first time in the *Alexiad of Anna Comnena*,[1] which was written early in the twelfth century. The term is also used by a mediæval scholiast on *Theocritus*, but I am unable to ascertain the period at which the scholiast wrote. In *Theocritus*[2] *Idyll.* vi. 18, the following passage occurs, which clearly alludes only to the game of πεττεία, viz., καὶ τὸν ἀπὸ γραμμᾶς κινεῖ λίθον, "he moves away the pebble from the [sacred] line," meaning that "he has the worst of the contest." Now, for our further enlightenment, the scholiast tells us that "that this is a figurative expression borrowed from the phraseology of those who play at the game commonly called ζατρικιον, or Chess!" whereupon Hyde exclaims, in the genuine commentator style, "*quantum hallucinatus est Scholiastes!*" One thing, however, we may safely infer, which is this, that the scholiast wrote,

---

[1] We are by no means sure that this is the first time that it is mentioned in the Byzantine writers; and even if it should be so, it proves nothing against the fact of the game being known there for four or five centuries previously.

[2] *Theocritus Bion et Moschus* &c., edit. A Valpy, 2 tom. 8vo, Londini, 1829.

not earlier than the eighth century; but whether before or after the days of Anna Comnena is uncertain.

Having thus endeavoured to establish on etymological grounds that Chess had reached Byzantium within a century after its introduction into Persia, we shall proceed to investigate such historical evidence— at least presumptive evidence—as comes within our reach. It is true, we have not in this case such positive and incontestable proofs to rely on, as we had in our last chapter respecting the introduction of Chess among the Arabs. We must therefore content ourselves, in the first place, with such fair and legitimate inference as an unprejudiced mind can scarcely fail to accept. This course is frequently adopted, in the absence of positive testimony, by those who endeavour to clear up obscure or doubtful points of history.

We observed in a note (Chap. VI.) respecting Sergius, the Greek interpreter at the Court of Naushīrwān, that Chess *might* have reached Byzantium even in the days of Justinian. This bare *possibility* amounts to a strong *probability* some quarter of a century later under the reign of Khusrū Parviz, the grandson of Naushīrwān, and the contemporary of the Byzantine emperors Maurice, Phocas, and Heraclius. Khusrū, or as the Greeks styled him Chosroes II., ascended the Persian throne in A.D. 591, and reigned thirty-seven years. His father, Hormuz, was assassinated by Bahrām, an able, but unscrupulous general, who himself aimed at sovereign power. The young prince Khusrū became an exile at the court of the Emperor Maurice, and to the generous (or politic) friendship of the latter he was solely indebted for his restoration to his crown and sceptre. During the life of Maurice the strictest intimacy existed between the courts of Persia and Constantinople. Khusrū married a Grecian princess by name Sira, or as the Persians called her, Shīrīn, a lady celebrated for her wit and beauty, who is generally supposed to have been Maurice's daughter. Out of compliment to the Greek emperor and his daughter, Khusrū maintained for several years in his service as a select body-guard a thousand Byzantine youths; while his court was thronged by eminent men from the Lower Empire who had befriended him in his exile, and by whose aid he ultimately succeeded to the throne of his ancestors.

This state of things continued till the death, or rather the assassination of Maurice, early in the seventh century, after which event Khusrū declared war against the Roman empire, then ruled over by the weak and contemptible Phocas. It does not fall within our province to follow the Persian monarch in his career of conquest for the next twenty years. It is sufficient to say that he possessed himself of Asia Minor, all Syria, Egypt, and the north of Africa; and had he possessed a sufficient naval power he would have overrun eastern Europe. A Persian camp was maintained for more than ten years in sight of Constantinople; but the days of reverse and extinction were fast approaching. During the last six years of his reign Khusrū was stripped of all his recent conquests by the Emperor Heraclius.

It is now time we should resume our argument respecting the progress of Chess. We know from history that the game was a favourite pastime with Khusrū and his courtiers. Majdī, a Persian historian, states in describing the magnificence of Khusrū's court that, "he had a Chess board of which one half of the pieces were of solid ruby, and the other half of emerald." A later Arabian historian alluding to the same subject, gives us some idea of their value. He says "that the very least of the pieces was worth 3000 golden dinars or ducats." Now if such was the value of each pawn, we may safely estimate the superior pieces at 30,000 dinars each, amounting altogether to a quarter of a million sterling! At the present day they would be worth a million.

Let us now sum up the results of our argument founded on etymological grounds and historical inference respecting the early introduction of Chess into the Lower Empire. In the first place we have shown etymologically that the Byzantines received the game of Chess from the Persians, and that too, at a period when the older term Chatrang was still in use in the language of the latter. All this indicates the early part of the seventh century. In the second place we have shown historically, that Khusrū Parvīz was a Chess player, that he passed sometime at the court of the Emperor Maurice before he succeeded, by the aid of the latter, to the throne of his ancestors, and that there existed, at least during the lifetime of Maurice, the closest friendship and intimacy between the two courts. All this being taken into account, it is impossible for us not to arrive at the conclusion that the Byzantines received the game of Chess direct from Persia in the reign of Khusrū Parvīz, and this again harmonises in point of time with what we have already deduced from etymological grounds, viz., the early part of the seventh century.

We are told by Hyde, that the princess Anna Comnena in the *Alexiad*, a work written by her in the beginning of the twelfth century, states "that the Emperor (Alexius) her father, in order to dispel the cares arising from affairs of state, occasionally played Chess (ζατρικιον,) at night, with some of his relations or kinsfolk." She then says that "*this game had been* (originally) *brought into use among the Byzantines from the Assyrians.*" The fair historian says nothing as to the time *when* the game came from Assyria, which may have been five centuries before she wrote; her statement, however, proves that it came from Persia, and not from Arabia, for Assyria formed an important portion of the Persian Empire under the Sassanian Dynasty; and in fact it was alternately occupied by the Persians and Romans, as victory swayed to one side or the other. The term Assyria is used here in a well known figurative sense, "*per synecdochen,*" a part taken for the whole, just as the term Fārs is employed at this day to denote the whole of Persia, whereas it is only the name of a single insignificant province of that kingdom. Finally, the once splendid empires of Assyria, of Media, and of Persia, had all passed away long before Anna Comnena wrote, so that one name is just as good as another.

Passing on to the end of the eighth century, we meet with a valuable historical proof not only that the game of Chess was then well-known to the Greeks, but that it must have been familiar to them for a considerable period of time previously. In the *Annals of the Muslims*, by Abu-l-Fidā,[1] we have on record a letter addressed to the Caliph Harūn Rashīd by the Greek Emperor Nicephorus, immediately after the latter had succeeded the 'Empress Irene, the contents of which run thus:— " From Nicephorus Emperor of the Romans to Harūn, Sovereign of the Arabs." After the usual compliments, the epistle proceeds :—" The Empress (Irene) into whose place I have succeeded, looked upon you as a *Rukh*,[2] and herself as a mere *Pawn;* therefore she continued to pay you a tribute more than the double of which she ought to have exacted from you. All this has been owing to female weakness and timidity. Now, however, I insist that you, immediately on reading this letter, repay to me all the sums of money you ever received from her. If you hesitate, the sword shall decide the claim."

In reply to this pithy epistle, Harūn in great wrath wrote on the back of the leaf :—" In the name of God the merciful and generous. From Harūn the Commander of the Faithful to Nicephorus, the Dog of the Romans. I have read thine epistle, thou son of an infidel mother. My mode of answering it thou shalt *see*, not *hear*." We may add that Harūn kept his word. He instantly marched as far as Heracleia, wasting the Roman territories with fire and sword, and soon made Nicephorus sue for peace and consent to pay the tribute as before.

This laconic correspondence took place A.D. 802, and we may safely infer from it that both Greeks and Arabs had long previously become acquainted with the game; for it requires some TIME before its allusions and phraseology become thus " familiar as household words " in the language of a people. The Arabs, as we have shown in our last chapter, had most probably received it nearly two centuries before this period ; and the familiar allusions made to it by the scribe of Nicephorus confirms all that we have said respecting its early introduction into Byzantium. We may then conclude by stating as our unbiased conviction, that both the Arabs and the Greeks received the game of Chess from the Persians very nearly at the same time, that is about, or soon after, the commencement of the seventh century of the Christian æra.

[1] *Abulfedae Annales,* tom. ii. p. 85, 4to, Hafn. 1790—also Leipsic Edition, tom. i. p. 166, 4to, 1778.

[2] It is needless for us to say that the Rukh was the strongest piece on the Chess board down to the beginning of the sixteenth century.

Two last Games in the Match between Mr. MORPHY and Herr
LÖWENTHAL.

GAME XIII.

(*Petroff's Defence.*)

White. (Herr LÖWENTHAL.)	*Black.* (MORPHY.)
1. P. to K. fourth	1. P. to K. fourth
2. Kt. to K. B. third	2. Kt. to K. B. third
3. Kt. takes P.	3. P. to Q. third
4. Kt. to K. B. third	4. Kt. takes P.
5. P. to Q. fourth	5. P. to Q. fourth
6. K. B. to Q. third	6. K. B. to K. second
7. Castles	7. Kt. to Q. B. third
8. P. to Q. B. fourth	8. Q. B. to K. third
9. P. takes P.	9. Q. B. takes P.
10. Kt. to Q. B. third	10. Kt. takes Kt.
11. P. takes Kt.	11. Castles
12. Q. B. to K. B. fourth	12. K. B. to Q. third
13. B. takes B.	13. Q. takes B.
14. Kt. to Kt. fifth	14. P. to K. B. fourth
15. P. to Q. B. fourth (a)	15. B. takes K. Kt. P.
16. K. takes B.	16. Q. to K. Kt. third
17. P. to K. B. fourth	17. P. to K. R. third
18. P. to Q. fifth	18. Kt. to Q. square
19. P. to K. R. fourth	19. P. takes Kt.
20. R. P. takes P.	20. Kt. to K. B. second
21. Q. to K. B. third	21. Kt. to R. third (b)
22. Q. to Kt. third	22. Kt. to B. second
23. P. to Q. B. fifth	23. Q. R. to Q. square
24. B. to Q. B. fourth	24. P. to Q. Kt. fourth
25. B. to Kt. third	25. P. to Q. R. fourth
26. Q. R. to K. square	26. K. R. to K. square
27. Q. R. to K. sixth	27. R. takes R. (c)
28. P. takes R.	28. K. to B. square
29. P. takes Kt.	29. P. to Q. R. fifth
30. R. to Q. square	30. R. takes R.
31. B. takes R.	31. Q. to Q. B. third (check)
32. B. to B. third	32. Q. takes P.
33. P. to K. Kt. sixth	33. Q. to Q. third

34. Q. to K. Kt. fifth	34. Q. to Q. seventh (check)
35. K. to R. third	35. Q. to Q. sixth
36. Q. to R. fifth	36. K to K. second
37. Q. to R. fourth (check)	37. K. to Q. second
38. K. to Kt. third	38. Q. to Q. third
39. Q. to K. R. eighth (d)	39. Q. takes K. Kt. P. (check)
40. K. to B. second	40. Q. takes B. P.

Drawn game.

Notes.

(a) From this point Herr Löwenthal plays extremely well up to move 38.

(b) This loses Mr. Morphy two moves, and in consequence he gets a lost game.

(c) There is nothing better for him to do.

(d) Once more does Herr Löwenthal make one of those unaccountable mistakes which characterise his match play. "Q. to Kt. fifth" must have won the game in a few moves.

GAME XIV.
(*Ruy Lopez.*)

White. (Mr. MORPHY.)	*Black.* (Herr LÖWENTHAL.)
1. P. to K. fourth	1. P. to K. fourth
2. K. Kt. to B. third	2. Q. Kt. to B. third
3. B. to Q. Kt. fifth	3. P. to Q. R. third
4. B. to Q. R. fourth	4. Kt. to K. B. third
5. P. to Q. fourth	5. P. takes P.
6. P. to K. fifth	6. Kt. to K. fifth
7. Castles	7. K. Kt. to Q. B. fourth
8. B. takes Q. Kt.	8. Q. P. takes B.
9. Kt. takes P.	9. Kt. to K. third
10. Kt. takes Kt.	10. B. takes Kt.
11. Q. to K. second	11. B. to Q. B. fourth
12. Q. Kt. to B. third	12. Q. to K. second (a)
13. Kt. to K. fourth	13. P. to K. R. third
14. B. to K. third	14. B. takes B.
15. Q. takes B.	15. B. to K. B. fourth
16. Kt. to K. Kt. third	16. B. takes P. (b)
17. P. to K. B. fourth	17. P. to K. Kt. third (c)
18. P. to K. sixth (d)	18. B. to K. B. fourth

19. Kt. takes B.	19. P. takes Kt.
20. P. takes P. (check)	20. K. takes P.
21. Q. to K. R. third	21. Q. to K. B. third
22. Q. R. to K. square	22. K. R. to K. square (e)
23. R. to K. fifth	23. K. to K. Kt. third
24. K. R. to K. square	24. R. takes R.
25. R. takes R.	25. R. to Q. square
26. Q. to K. Kt. third (check)	26. K. to R. second
27. P. to K. R. third	27. R. to Q. second
28. Q. to K. third	28. P. to Q. Kt. third
29. K. to K. R. second	29. P. to Q. B. fourth
30. Q. to K. second	30. Q. to K. Kt. third
31. R. to K. sixth	31. Q. to K. Kt. second
32. Q. to K. R. fifth	32. R. to Q. fourth
33. P. to Q. Kt. third	33. P. to Q. Kt. fourth
34. R. takes Q. R. P.	34. R. to Q. third
35. Q. takes P. (check)	35. Q. to K. Kt. third
36. Q. takes Q. (check)	36. K. takes Q.
37. R. to Q. R. fifth	37. R. to Q. Kt. third
38. P. to K. Kt. fourth	38. P. to Q. B. third
39. K. to Kt. third	39. P. to K. R. fourth
40. R. to Q. R. seventh	40. P. takes P.
41. P. takes P.	41. K. to B. third
42. P. to K. B. fifth	42. K. to K. fourth
43. R. to K. seventh (check)	43. K. to Q. third
44. P. to B. sixth	44. R. to Kt. square
45. P. to K. Kt. fifth	45. R. to K. B. square
46. K. to B. fourth	46. P. to Q. B. fifth
47. P. takes P.	47. P. takes P.
48. K. to B. fifth	48. P. to B. sixth
49. R. to K. third	

And Black resigned. (f)

Notes.

(a) Black's forces are now completely developed, a fact which, in our opinion, is highly creditable to the second player, considering the strong attack he has to contend against in the *Ruy Lopez*. Surely the game deserved a better fate, if it were only for the great skill with which, up to this point, it was conducted by Herr Löwenthal, whose perfect knowledge of the openings surpasses that of nearly every other player of his own strength and experience.

(b) This is a very weak move, the Bishop, after White's following move, which could have easily been foreseen, being placed in imminent jeopardy. The safer course would have been to play " B. to Q. second," and if then follows " P. to K. B. fourth," to play " P. to K. B. fourth " in answer.

(c) This purely defensive move, of which White does not fail to take the utmost advantage by his energetic reply, is now unavoidable on account of White's obvious threat to advance the K. B. P., followed by "K. R. to Q. B. square." In order, therefore, to rescue the Bishop, the above move, precarious though it may be, appears the only plausible one under the circumstances ; for castling on Queen's side could have been replied to with "Q. to Q. R. seventh," whilst in answer to "P. to K. R. fourth," or "Q. to Q. third," White could have equally played " P. to K. B. fifth," with great advantage.

(d) Threatening to move "Q. to Q. B. third," if Black captures the Pawn.

(e) Apparently the best move.

(f) This game was played at the London Chess Club on August 21, shortly before the commencement of the Meeting of the British Chess Association in Birmingham, to which place Morphy repaired a few days afterwards. His Birmingham exploits and the great feat which he there performed for the first time during his stay in Europe, of playing eight games simultaneously without sight of board and men, have been recorded in Chapter X. With regard to the above game, which concluded the match, we quote the following graphic remark from a London contemporary :—" Mr. Morphy's play is so superior to anything latterly seen of Chess in England, that his adversary throughout, appeared under a cloud ; bewildered and stumbling beneath the blows of his opponent."

Game between Herr HARRWITZ and Mr. STOREY, *of Liverpool.*

(Remove Queen's Rook from the Board.)

White. (Herr HARRWITZ.)	*Black.* (Mr. STOREY.)
1. P. to K. fourth	1. P. to K. fourth
2. P. to K. B. fourth	2. P. to Q. fourth
3. P. takes Q. P.	3. K. B. to Q. B. fourth
4. K. Kt. to B. third	4. Q. B. to K. Kt. fifth
5. Q. Kt. to B. third	5. K. Kt. to B. third
6. P. takes P.	6. Kt. takes P.
7. K. B. to Q. B. fourth	7. B. takes Kt.
8. Q. takes B.	8. Q. to K. R. fifth (check)
9. P. to K. Kt. third	9. Q. takes B.
10. Kt. takes Kt.	10. Kt. to B. third
11. P. to Q. B. third	11. Castles (K. R.)
12. P. to Q. fourth	12. B. takes P.
13. B. to K. R. sixth	13. Q. R. to K. square
14. P. takes B.	14. Kt. takes Q. P.

And White announced mate in seven moves.   (See Diagram.)

BLACK.

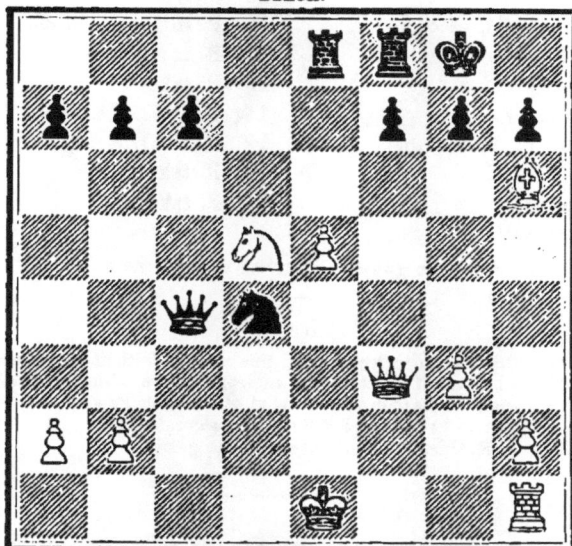

WHITE
To mate in seven moves.

Game lately played at the PHILIDORIAN between Messrs. MUCKLOW and JANSSENS.

(Evans's Gambit.)

White. (Mr. MUCKLOW.)	*Black.* (Mr. JANSSENS.)
1. P. to K. fourth	1. P. to K. fourth
2. Kt. to K. B. third	2. Kt. to Q. B. third
3. B. to Q. B. fourth	3. B. to Q. B. fourth
4. P. to Q. Kt. fourth	4. B. takes P.
5. P. to Q. B. third	5. B. to Q. B. fourth
6. P. to Q. fourth	6. P. takes P.
7. P. takes P. (*a*)	7. B. to Q. Kt. third
8. P. to Q. R. fourth	8. P. to Q. third
9. Castles	9. Kt. to K. B. third
10. P. to Q. fifth	10. Kt. to Q. R. fourth (*b*)
11. B. to Q. third	11. P. to K. R. third

22

12. P. to K. R. third	12. Castles
13. B. to Q. Kt. second	13. P. to Q. B. third
14. B. to Q. B. second	14. B. to Q. second
15. Q. to Q. third	15. P. takes P.
16. P. takes P.	16. P. to K. Kt. third
17. Kt. to K. R. fourth	17. R. to Q. B. square
18. Kt. takes K. Kt. P.	18. R. takes B.
19. Q. takes R.	19. P. takes Kt.
20. Q. takes P.	

And the game was given up as drawn.(*c*)

———

Notes.

(*a*) We should not like to recommend this move, White having given a Pawn has no equivalent attack if Black plays the proper move, which is checking with the B., White ought to have castled instead of retaking Pawn.

(*b*) Black ought to have played " Kt. to K. second."

(*c*) " R. to Q. R. third " would have won the game.

———

Consultation game played at the PHILIDORIAN, October 21st, 1859.

Black. (Herr HARRWITZ.)	*White.* (Messrs. REEVES and SMITH.)
1. P. to Q. fourth	1. P. to K. B. fourth
2. P. to Q. B. fourth	2. P. to K. third
3. Q. Kt. to B. third	3. K. Kt. to B. third
4. P. to Q. R. third	4. B. to K. second
5. K. Kt. to B. third	5. P. to Q. third
6. P. to K. third	6. P. to Q. Kt. third
7. K. B. to Q. third	7. P. to Q. B. fourth
8. P. to Q. Kt. fourth	8. P. takes Q. P.
9. K. Kt. takes P.	9. P. to K. Kt. third
10. Q. to K. B. third	10. P. to Q. fourth
11. P. takes P.	11. P. takes P.
12. B. to Q. Kt. fifth (check)	12. K. to B. second
13. Q. B. to Q. Kt. second	13. Q. B. to Q. Kt. second
14. Q. R. to Q. square	14. Q. Kt. to Q. second
15. Q. to K. Kt. third	15. R. to Q. B. square
16. Castles	16. P. to K. R. fourth

17. P. to K. B. fourth	17. P. to K. R. fifth
18. Q. to K. R. third	18. K. Kt. to K. Kt. fifth
19. P. to K. fourth	19. B. to K. B. third
20. P. to K. fifth	20. Q. Kt. takes P.
21. P. takes Kt.	21. B. takes P. .
22. Q. takes Kt.	22. Q. to K. B. third
23. K. Kt. takes P.	23. P. takes Kt.
24. K. R. takes P.	24. B. takes Kt.
25. B. takes B.	25. R. takes B.
26. R. takes Q. (check)	26. K. takes R.

And Black announced mate in four moves.

Game played between Herr HARRWITZ and Messrs. GUIBERT and LEQUESNE, the only gentlemen who drew their games in Mr. MORPHY's blindfold performance at Paris.

Black. (Herr HARRWITZ.)	*White.* (The Allies.)
1. P. to K. fourth	1. P. to K. third
2. P. to Q. fourth	2. P. to Q. fourth
3. P. takes P.	3. P. takes P.
4. P. to Q. B. fourth	4. P. to Q. B. third
5. Q. Kt. to B. third	5. K. Kt. to B. third
6. K. Kt. to B. third	6. K. B. to K. second
7. K. B. to Q. third	7. Q. B. to K. Kt. fifth
8. Q. B. to K. third	8. Castles
9. P. to K. R. third	9. B. to K. R. fourth
10. Castles	10. P. to Q. R. fourth
11. R. to Q. B. square	11. Q. Kt. to R. third
12. P. takes P.	12. Kt. takes P.
13. P. to K. Kt. fourth	13. B. to K. Kt. third
14. B. takes B.	14. B. P. takes B.
15. K. Kt. to K. fifth	15. Q. Kt. to B. second
16. Q. to Kt. third	16. R. to Q. Kt. square
17. P. to K. B. fourth	17. K. to R. square
18. Q. Kt. to K. second	18. K. B. to Q. third
19. K. to Kt. second	19. Kt. takes B. (check)
20. Q. takes Kt.	20. Kt. to Q. fourth

21. Q. to K. fourth	21. Q. to K. second
22. Kt. to Q. B. third	22. Kt. to K. B. third
23. Q. to K. second	23. Q. R. to Q. square
24. Q. R. to Q. square	24. Q. to Q. B. second
25. Q. to Q. B. fourth	25. Q. R. to B. square
26. P. to Q. R. fourth	26. Q. R. to Q. square
27. Q. R. to K. square	27. Q. R. to B. square
28. K. R. to B. third	28. Q. R. to Q. square
29. Q. R. to K. second	29. Q. R. to B. square
30. Q. to K. sixth	30. Q. R. to K. square
31. Q. to Q. Kt. third	31. R. to K. second
32. Kt. to K. fourth	32. Kt. to Q. fourth
33. Q. R. to K. B. second	33. K. R. to K. square
34. Q. to Q. third	34. K. to Kt. square
35. Kt. to Q. B. third	35. Kt. to K. B. third
36. Q. to Q. B. fourth (check)	36. K. to R. square
37. P. to K. Kt. fifth	37. Kt. to R. fourth
38. Kt. to K. fourth	38. R. to K. B. square
39. P. to K. R. fourth	39. Q. to Q. Kt. square
40. Q. to Q. B. third	40. B. to Q. Kt. fifth
41. Q. to K. third	41. Q. to Q. square
42. Kt. to Q. B. third	42. R. to K. B. fourth
43. Q. to K. fourth	43. K. to Kt. square
44. Kt. to Q. square	44. B. to Q. third
45. Kt. to K. third	45. R. to B. square
46. P. to K. B. fifth	46. B. takes Kt.
47. P. takes B.	47. P. takes P.
48. Kt. takes P.	48. Q. R. to K. square
49. P. to K. sixth	49. Q. to Q. B. second
50. P. to K. seventh	50. R. takes Kt.
51. R. takes R.	51. Q. to Kt. sixth (check)
52. K. to B. square	

Resigns.

Game played between Messrs. HARRWITZ and MAUDE, the former giving the odds of Pawn and two moves.

(Remove Black's K. B. P. from the Board.)

White. (Mr. MAUDE.)	*Black.* (Herr HARRWITZ.)
1 { P. to K. fourth	1. P. to K. third
{ P. to Q. fourth	
2. K. B. to Q. third	2. P. to Q. B. fourth
3. P. to K. fifth	3. P. to K. Kt. third
4. P. to K. R. fourth	4. Q. B. P. takes P.
5. P. to K. B. fourth	5. Kt. to K. second
6. Kt. to Q. second	6. P. to Q. fourth
7. P. takes P. (*en passant*)	7. Kt. to Q. fourth
8. Kt. to K. fourth	8. B. takes P.
9. P. to K. R. fifth	9. B. to Q. Kt. fifth (check)
10. K. to B. square	10. R. to K. B. square
11. Q. to K. Kt. fourth	11. Kt. to K. second
12. P. takes P.	12. P. takes P.
13. Q. to K. Kt. fifth	13. Q. to Q. R. fourth
14. Kt. to B. sixth (check)	14. K. to Q. square
15. Q. to K. R. sixth	15. Kt. to K. B. fourth
16. Q. takes P.	16. Kt. to Q. second
17. Kt. to K. R. seventh	17. Kt. to K. fourth
18. Q. to Kt. fifth (check)	18. B. to K. second
19. B. takes Kt.	19. B. takes Q.
20. Kt. takes R.	20. B. to K. second
21. Kt. takes P. (check)	21. B. takes Kt.
22. R. to R. eighth (check)	22. K. to Q. B. second
23. R. takes R.	23. B. to K. R. fifth
24. P. to K. Kt. third	24. B. takes P.
25. K. to Kt. second	25. Q. to K. eighth
26. Kt. to K. R. third	26. B. to Q. fourth (check)
27. B. interposes	27. B. takes B. mate

Games in the match between Herr HARRWITZ and Mr. REEVES.

GAME III.

(Remove Black's K. B. P. from the Board.)

White. (Mr. REEVES.)	*Black.* (Herr HARRWITZ.)
1 { P. to K. fourth { P. to Q. fourth	1. P. to Q. third
2. P. to K. B. fourth	2. P. to Q. B. fourth
3. P. to Q. fifth	3. P. to K. fourth
4. K. Kt. to K. B. third	4. Q. B. to K. Kt. fifth
5. P. to K. R. third	5. B. takes Kt.
6. Q. takes B.	6. Q. Kt. to Q. second
7. P. to K. B. fifth	7. K. Kt. to K. B. third
8. B. to Q. third	8. B. to K. second
9. P. to K. Kt. fourth	9. P. to K. R. third
10. P. to Q. B. fourth	10. K. Kt. to K. R. second
11. Q. B. to K. third	11. B. to K. R. fifth (check)
12. K. to K. second	12. Q. to Q. Kt. third
13. P. to Q. Kt. third	13. K. Kt. to K. Kt. fourth
14. Q. to K. Kt. second	14. Castles (Q. R.)
15. Q. Kt. to B. third	15. P. to Q. B. third
16. K. R. to Q. Kt. square	16. Q. to Q. R. fourth (*a*)
17. Q. B. to Q. second	17. Q. to Q. B. second
18. P. to Q. Kt. fourth (*b*)	18. P. to K. R. fourth
19. P. to Q. Kt. fifth	19. P. to Q. R. fourth
20. P. to Q. Kt. sixth	20. Kt. takes P.
21. Kt. to Q. Kt. fifth (*c*)	21. Q. to Q. Kt. square
22. B. takes Q. R. P.	22. Kt. to Q. R. square
23. B. takes R.	23. K. takes B.
24. P. to Q. B. fourth	24. K. to K. second
25. P. to Q. R. fifth	25. K. Kt. to K. B. second
26. P. to Q. R. sixth	26. P. to Q. Kt. third
27. P. to Q. R. seventh	27. Q. to Q. B. square
28. R. to Q. Kt. second	28. B. to K. Kt. fourth
29. P. takes P.	29. R. takes P.
30. Q. to K. Kt. fourth	30. R. to R. square
31. P. to K. B. sixth (check)	31. B. takes P.
32. Q. takes Q.	32. R. takes Q.

33. Kt. to Q. B. third	33. K. to Q. second
34. R. to Q. R. sixth	34. Kt. to K. Kt. fourth
35. Kt. to Q. R. fourth	35. B. to Q. square
36. K. to K. third	36. Kt. takes R. P.
37. B. to K. second	37. B. to K. Kt. fourth (check)
38. K. to B. third	38. Kt. to Kt. eighth (check)
39. K. to Kt. fourth	39. B. to Q. square
40. B. to B. square,	40. B. to Q. B. second
41. Kt. takes Q. Kt. P. (check)	41. B. takes Kt.
42. K. R. takes B.	42. K. to Q. B. second
43. R. to Q. B. sixth (check)	43. K. to Kt. second
44. R. takes R.	44. K. takes K. R.
45. R. takes Q. P.	

And wins.

Notes.

(*a*) This seems loss of time, the Queen being compelled to retreat on the next move. It appears from the present game that Mr. Harrwitz, at the commencement of the match, underrated his youthful opponent's strength. He fully acknowledged it, however, in the following games, three of which were played with the greatest care, and consecutively scored by the eminent Prussian player.

(*b*) White very cleverly takes advantage of his opponent's confined position.

(*c*) Winning the exchange by force.

GAME IV.

(Remove Black's K. B. P. from the Board.)

White. (Mr. REEVES.)	*Black.* (Herr HARRWITZ.)
1 { P. to K. fourth { P. to Q. fourth	1. P. to Q. third
2. B. to Q. third	2. Q. Kt. to B. third
3. P. to Q. B. third (*a*)	3. P. to K. fourth
4. P. to Q. fifth	4. Q. Kt. to K. second
5. B. to K. Kt. fifth	5. P. to Q. R. third
6. P. to Q. B. fourth	6. P. to Q. B. third
7. Q. Kt. to B. third	7. Q. to Q. Kt. third
8. Q. to K. second	8. Q. Kt. to K. Kt. third
9. P. to K. Kt. third	9. B. to K. second
10. B. to K. third	10. P. to Q. B. fourth

White	Black
11. P. to K. R. fourth	11. P. to K. R. fourth
12. P. to K. B. third	12. Kt. to K. B. third
13. Q. to K. Kt. second	13. B. to Q. second
14. P. to Q. Kt. third	14. Q. to Q. B. second
15. K. Kt. to K. second	15. Castles (Q. R.)
16. Castles (K. R.)	16. K. to Q. Kt. square
17. K. R. to Q. Kt. square	17. K. to R. square
18. P. to Q. Kt. fourth	18. P. to Q. Kt. third
19. P. to Q. R. fourth	19. R. to Q. Kt. square
20. P. to Q. R. fifth	20. P. takes Q. R. P.
21. R. takes P.	21. R. takes P.
22. R. takes R. P. (check)	22. K. to Kt. second
23. K. R. to Q. R. square (b)	23. K. to Q. B. square
24. Kt. to Q. Kt. fifth	24. B. takes Kt.
25. P. takes B.	25. B. to Q. square
26. R. to R. eighth (check)	26. K. to Q. second
27. Q. R. to R. seventh	27. K. to K. square
28. R. takes Q.	28. B. takes R.
29. Q. to K. R. third	29. Kt. to K. second
30. R. to R. eighth (check)	30. B. to Q. square
31. Q. to K. sixth	31. Kt. to Q. second
32. B. to K. Kt. fifth	

And wins.

Notes.

(a) "P. to Q. fifth" is stronger. If Black then moves the "Kt. to K. fourth," or to "Q. Kt. fifth," the first player will keep up a vigorous attack by playing "P. to K. B. fourth."

(b) White has now a splendid attack, and follows up his advantage with great skill and perseverance.

GAME V.

(*Remove Black's K. B. P. from the Board.*)

White. (Mr. REEVES.)	*Black.* (Herr HARRWITZ.)
1 { P. to K. fourth / P. to Q. fourth	1. P. to K. third
2. K. B. to Q. third	2. P. to Q. B. fourth
3. P. to K. fifth	3. P. to K. Kt. third

4. P. to K. R. fourth	4. P. takes P.
5. P. to K. B. fourth˙	5. K. Kt. to K. second
6. P. to K. R. fifth	6. R. to K. Kt. square
7. P. takes P.	7. P. takes P.
8. Q. to K. Kt. fourth	8. P. to Q. third
9. Kt. to K. B. third	9. Q. Kt. to B. third
10. P. to Q. R. third	10. Q. to Q. B. second
11. Q. Kt. to Q. second	11. P. to Q. fourth
12. K. R. to R. seventh	12. Q. B. to Q. second
13. Kt. to K. Kt. fifth (a)	13. Kt. to Q. square
14. Q. Kt. to K. fourth (b)	14. P. takes Kt.
15. Kt. takes P. on K. fifth	15. K. Kt. to Q. fourth
16. Kt. to Q. sixth (check)	16. B. takes Kt.
17. P. takes B.	17. Q. takes Q. P.
18. B. takes P. (check)	18. K. to B. square
19. Q. to K. Kt. fifth	19. Q. to K. second (c)
20. Q. to R. sixth (check)	20. Q. to Kt. second
21. R. takes Q.	21. R. takes R.
22. P. to K. B. fifth	22. Kt. to K. B. second
23. Q. to R. fifth	23. Kt. to K. B. third
24. Q. to R. fourth	24. K. to K. second
25. Q takes P.	25. P. takes P.
26. B. takes Kt.	26. K. takes B.
27. B. to Q. second (d)	27. Q. R. to K. square (check)
28. K. to B. square	28. B. to Q. B. third
29. P. to K. Kt. third	29. R. takes P.
30. R. to K. square	30. R. to B. sixth (check)
31. K. to Kt. square	31. R. to K. Kt. square (check)
32. K. to R. second	32. Kt. to Kt. fifth (check)
33. Q. takes Kt. (e)	33. R. takes Q.

And wins.

Notes.

(a) The prelude to a very ingenious manœuvre.

(b) An admirable move, which ought to have won the game.

(c) The only resource. "R. takes B.," instead, would have been answered with "Q. takes R.," and nothing could then have saved Black's game.

(d) After having made so many splendid efforts, White seems to have become exhausted at this point. The correct move was "B. to K. third," in order to castle on the next move.

(e) Had he moved the King, Black would have mated in a few moves. .

Game between Herr HARRWITZ and Mr. CAMPBELL, played at the PHILIDORIAN.

(*Allgaier Gambit.*)

Black. (Herr HARRWITZ.)	*White.* (Mr. CAMPBELL.)
1. P. to K. fourth	1. P. to K. fourth
2. P. to K. B. fourth	2. P. takes P.
3. K. Kt. to K. B. third	3. P. to K. Kt. fourth
4. P. to K. R. fourth	4. P. to K. Kt. fifth
5. Kt. to K. fifth	5. K. Kt. to K. B. third
6. K. B. to Q. B. fourth	6. P. to Q. fourth
7. P. takes P.	7. K. B. to Q. third
8. P. to Q. fourth	8. K. B. takes Kt.
9. Q. P. takes B.	9. K. Kt. to K. R. fourth
10. Q. to Q. fourth	10. Q. Kt. to Q. B. third
11. K. B. to Q. Kt. fifth	11. Castles
12. K. B. takes Kt.	12. P. takes B.
13. P. to Q. B. fourth	13. P. to K. B. third
14. K. P. takes K. B. P.	14. R. takes P.
15. Q. Kt. to Q. B. third	15. Q. to K. second (check)
16. K. to Q. square	16. P. to Q. B. fourth
17. Q. to K. fourth	17. Q. to K. B. second
18. K. R. to K. square	18. K. to K. B. square
19. Q. to K. fifth	19. Q. B. to K. B. fourth
20. P. to Q. Kt. third	20. Q. R. to Q. square
21. Q. B. to Q. R. third	21. K. to K. Kt. square
22. K. to Q. B. square	22. Q. to Q. second
23. Q. B. takes P. (*a*)	23. K. R. to K. third
24. Q. takes R.	24. B. takes Q.
25. R. takes B.	25. R. to K. square
26. R. takes R. (check)	26. Q. takes R.
27. K. to Q. second	27. Kt. to K. Kt. sixth
28. R. to K. square	28. Q. to K. R. fourth
29. R. to K. seventh	29. Q. takes R. P.
30. R. takes Q. B. P.	30. Kt. to K. B. eighth (check)
31. K. to K. second	31. Q. to K. R. eighth
32. P. to Q. sixth	32. Q. takes P. (check)
33. K. to Q. third	33. Q. to Q. seventh (check)
34. K. to K. fourth	34. Kt. to K. Kt. sixth (check)

35. K. to K. fifth	35. Q. takes Kt. (check)
36. B. to Q. fourth	36. Q. to Q. sixth
37. B. takes Q. R. P.	

And White mates in two moves.

Note.

(a) Evidently an oversight.

Game played lately at the PHILIDORIAN, between Messrs. CAMPBELL and F. HEALEY.

White. (Mr. CAMPBELL.)	*Black.* (Mr. HEALEY.)
1. P. to K. fourth	1. P. to K. fourth
2. Kt. to K. B. third	2. P. to Q. third
3. P. to Q. fourth	3. P. to K. B. fourth
4. P. takes K. P.	4. B. P. takes K. P.
5. Kt. to K. Kt. fifth	5. P. to Q. fourth
6. P. to Q. B. fourth	6. B. to K. second
7. P. to K. R. fourth	7. P. to Q. B. third
8. Kt. to Q. B. third	8. B. to Q. Kt. fifth
9. Q. to Q. Kt. third	9. B. takes Kt. (check)
10. P. takes B.	10. Kt. to K. second
11. B. to Q. R. third	11. P. to K. R. third
12. Kt. to K. R. third	12. Q. to Q. Kt. third
13. B. takes Kt.	13. Q. takes Q.
14. P. takes Q.	14. K. takes B.
15. P. takes P.	15. P. takes P.
16. Kt. to K. B. fourth	16. R. to Q. square
17. Castles	17. B. to K. third
18. B. to Q. B. fourth	18. Kt. to R. third
19. Kt. takes P. (check)	19. B. takes Kt.
20. B. takes B.	20. Kt. to Q. B. fourth
21. B. to Q. B. fourth	21. R. takes R.
22. R. takes R.	22. R. to Q. B. square
23. K. to B. second	23. R. to K. B. square
24. R. to Q. second	24. R. to K. B. fourth
25. P. to Q. Kt. fourth	25. Kt. to Q. second
26. P. to K. sixth	26. Kt. to Q. Kt. third
27. B. to Q. Kt. third	27. P. to Q. R. fourth

28. P. takes P.	28. R. takes P.
29. R. to K. second	29. Kt. to R. fifth
30. B. takes Kt.	30. R. takes B.
31. K. to Kt. third	31. R. to B. third
32. R. takes P.	32. R. to Q. third
33. P. to K. Kt. fourth	33. R. takes P.
34. R. takes R.	34. K. takes R.
35. K. to K. Kt. fourth	35. K. to K. fourth
36. K. to Q. Kt. fifth	36. K. to K. B. fifth

And the game was ultimately drawn.

Game between Herr HARRWITZ and Mr. GOCHER.

Black. (Mr. GOCHER.)	*White.* (Herr HARRWITZ.)
1. P. to K. fourth	1. P. to K. fourth
2. K. Kt. to B. third	2. P. to Q. third
3. P. to Q. fourth	3. P. takes P.
4. Q. takes P.	4. Q. Kt. to B. third
5. K. B. to Q. Kt. fifth	5. B. to Q. second
6. B. takes Kt.	6. B. takes B.
7. Q. B. to K. Kt. fifth	7. K. Kt. to B. third
8. Q. Kt. to B. third	8. B. to K. second
9. Castles (Q. R.)	9. P. to K. R. third
10. B. to K. R. fourth	10. Castles
11. Q. R. to K. square	11. Kt. to K. Kt. fifth (a)
12. B. takes B.	12. Q. takes B.
13. Kt. to Q. fifth	13. B. takes Kt.
14. P. takes B.	14. Q. to Q. second
15. Kt. to Q. second	15. Q. R. to K. square
16. P. to K. R. third	16. Kt. to K. fourth
17. P. to K. B. fourth	17. P. to Q. B. fourth
18. Q. to K. B. second	18. Kt. to Kt. third
19. P. to K. B. fifth	19. Kt. to K. fourth
20. P. to K. B. sixth (b)	20. P. to K. Kt. third
21. Q. to K. R. fourth	21. K. to R. second
22. Kt. to K. fourth	22. K. R. to K. R. square
23. Kt. to Kt. fifth (check)	23. K. to Kt. square

24. Kt. to K. B. third (c)	24. Kt. takes Kt.
25. P. takes Kt.	25. K. to R. second
26. R. to K. seventh	26. R. takes R.
27. P. takes R. (d)	27. K. to Kt. second (e)
28. R. to K. square	28. R. to K. square
29. Q. to K. fourth	29. Q. takes K. R. P.
30. P. to K. B. fourth	30. P. to Q. Kt. fourth
31. P. to Q. R. fourth	31. P. to Q. R. third
32. P. takes P.	32. P. takes P.
33. Q. to K. second	33. Q. to K. R. fifth
34. Q. to K. third	34. P. to Q. Kt. fifth
35. P. to Q. B. third	35. P. takes P.
36. Q. takes P. (check)	36. Q. to K. B. third
37. Q. to K. third	37. Q. to K. B. fourth
38. Q. to Q. B. third (check)	38. P. to K. B. third
39. Q. to Q. second	39. K. to B. second
40. R. to K. sixth	40. R. takes P.
41. R. takes P.	41. R. to K. fifth
42. P. to Q. Kt. third	42. R. takes K. B. P.
43. R. to Q. seventh (check)	43. K. to K. square
44. Q. to K. second (check) (f)	44. K. takes R.
45. Q. to Kt. fifth (check)	45. K. to Q. third
46. Q. to Q. B. sixth (check)	46. K. to K. fourth
47. Q. to K. eighth (check)	47. K. to Q. fifth
48. Q. to Q. R. fourth (check)	48. K. to K. sixth
49. Q. to K. eighth (check)	49. Q. interposes

And wins.

Notes.

(a) In the Morphy and Harrwitz match, the latter now played "Kt. to K. square."

(b) Well played; Black has now the attack.

(c) Allowing the Knights to be exchanged is injudicious, as it weakens Black's attack.

(d) This Pawn thus far advanced must be eventually lost.

(e) To prevent B. Q. going to K. B. sixth.

(f) A vain attempt to draw the game by perpetual check.

A Match has just commenced between Mr. F. RAINGER of Norwich, and Mr. ATKINS of Weymouth; the winner of the first eleven games to be the victor.

SOLUTIONS TO PROBLEMS.

No. 37.　Page 319.

White.	Black.
B. to K. eighth	P. to Q. B. seventh (best)
B. to Q. R. fourth	K. to Q. eighth
R. to Q. Kt. eighth (check)	

and mates.

No. 38.　Page 319.

White.	Black.
R. to K. Kt. seventh (check)	B. takes R. (best)
R. to K. B. sixth	Anything.
Kt. mates.	

No. 39.　Page 320.

In our last number it was, by mistake, printed two moves instead of six.

White.	Black.
P. to Q. Kt. fourth	R. P. takes P. (*en pass.*) (best)
P. to K. Kt. fifth	Anything.
Q. takes K. R. P. (check)	K. takes P.
R. to K. R. fourth (check)	K. to Kt. third
R. to K. R. sixth (check)	K. to B. fourth
B. to K. Kt. fourth (check)	

and mates.

No. 40.　Page 320.

White.	Black.
P. to Q. Kt. seventh	R. to Q. Kt. second (best)
R. to Q. R. fifth	R. to Q. Kt. square
P. to Q. Kt. seventh	

and wins.

SOLUTIONS OF PROBLEMS FOR YOUNG PLAYERS.

No. 9.　Page 286.

White.	Black.
K. to Q. fourth	Kt. to K. Kt. fifth
Q. takes B.	Anything
Q. or Kt. mates	

No. 10.　Page 286.

White.	Black.
Q. to K. fifth (check)	K. to Kt. fifth
B. to K. B. second	K. to R. fifth
Q. to K. R. fifth, mates	

No. 41.　Problem by F. HEALEY, Esq.

BLACK.

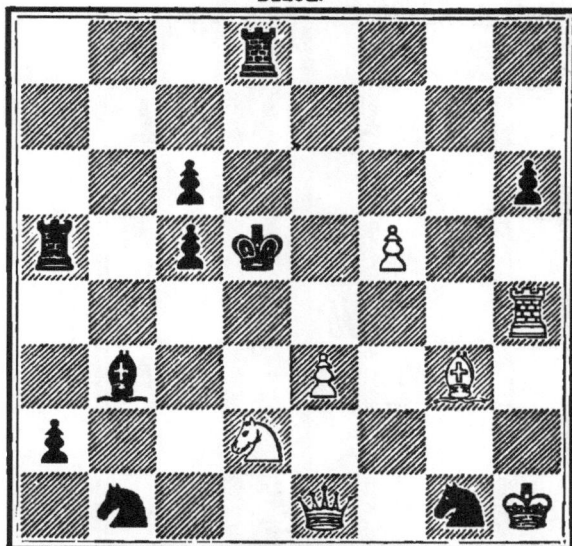

WHITE.

White to move, and mate in four moves.

No. 42.　Problem by F. HEALEY, Esq.

BLACK.

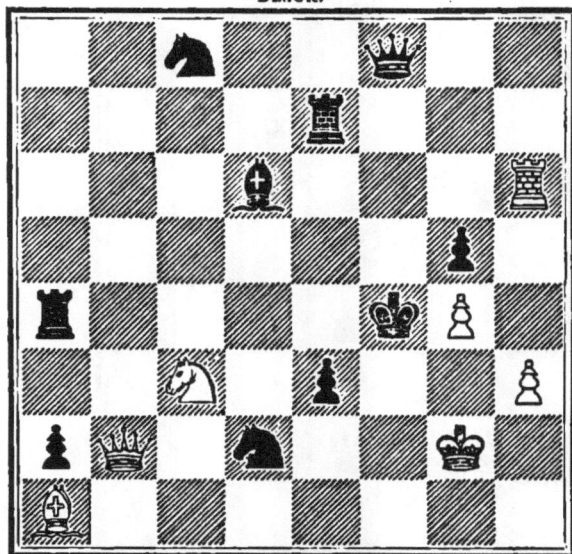

WHITE.

White to move, and mate in four moves.

No. 43.   Problem by Herr HARRWITZ, from actual play.

BLACK.

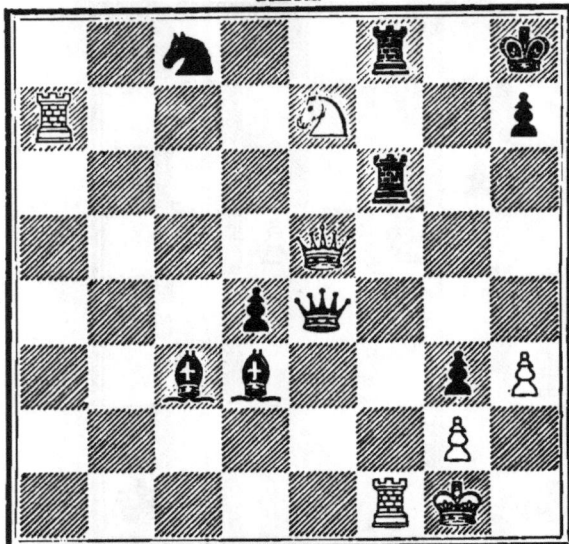

WHITE.

White to mate in four moves.

No. 44. Interesting Problem by M. GROSDEMANGE, St. Die (Vosges).

BLACK.

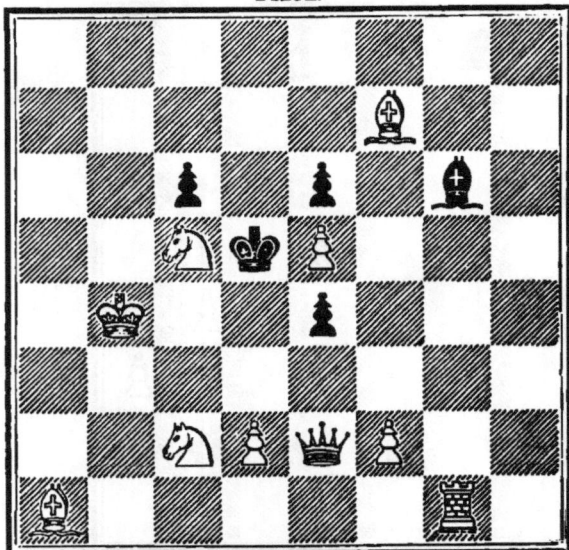

WHITE.

White engages to checkmate Black in seven moves with any of the
Pawns he may choose.

THE STATE OF CHESS IN ENGLAND IN 1859.

It is but natural that, in presenting our readers with the last number of the first volume of the third series of the CHESS PLAYER'S CHRONICLE, we should throw a retrospective glance upon the Chess events of the year. In thus taking a cursory review, we cannot help observing that, wherever we may turn, we invariably meet with the name of MORPHY. The American champion, although some months separated from us by the broad Atlantic, still keeps a fast hold on the imagination of the English Chess player. Chess editors, of all sizes and colours, players of every degree and station, publish or read his games. His name has become a household word with every follower of Caissa. In the annals of Chess there is no parallel to be found to his popularity. No PHILIDOR, DESCHAPPELLES, LABOURDONNAIS, or MACDONNELL, could boast of the hundredth part of his renown. This fact, and an uncontested and incontestable fact it is, leads us to inquire, if the young American's extraordinary reputation be owing solely to his superior powers as a player—superior even to all players before him—or to other and accidental reasons. This interesting question we shall try to answer in a future number; at present we must content ourselves with noticing the fact, as far as it influenced the state of Chess. In the latter part of last year, and in the first part of this, PAUL MORPHY's presence in Europe gave a sort of impulse to English play; the Chess localities were better frequented, and several of the weekly papers opened their columns to Chess, in consequence, we believe, of the rekindled interest in the game.

With the transatlantic hero's departure, however, a kind of reaction took place; and, as far as we remember, Chess has never been so languishing in the metropolis, as in the latter part of the present year. Not even the presence of Herr HARRWITZ was able to enliven the evident apathy of the Chess players. Match play has been at a discount during the year, and excepting the match between Messrs. CAMPBELL and WORMALD, which began in December, 1858, and has not yet terminated, we can only mention the little match between Messrs. HARRWITZ and REEVES, at the odds of pawn and two moves, which was concluded a few days ago. Why this should be so, we are unable to explain; in vain have we searched for the reasons. There are more Chess players now in England than in former times; the

23

number of strong players has also decidedly increased. We say decidedly, for, in looking over the first volume of the first series of the CHESS PLAYER'S CHRONICLE, which was published seventeen years ago, we were glad to find that in the phalanx of former heros, but few gaps were made, that in the last twenty years, but four names were erased from the list of players whose games were generally recorded.[1] That even the veterans who were already known to fame in the first quarter of the century are still in the enjoyment of health. That the gap which death has made, was not only filled up, but that the ranks were strengthened by such names as BARNES, BIRD, BODEN, BRIEN, CAMPBELL, GREENAWAY, HEALEY, MEDLEY, OWEN, WORMALD, &c.&c. That among the foreign Chess players resident in London, since the CHESS PLAYER'S CHRONICLE started, we had to regret the death of POPERT, but had to rejoice in the arrival of the Herren HORWITZ, HARRWITZ, LÖWENTHAL, and FALKBEER, who now reside in England. This clearly proves that the number of strong Chess players has considerably increased, and that it is not the want of players or even of strong players, which has occasioned the present lull in the English Chess world. Other causes have concurred, and other influences have contributed to produce this effect. To find out the causes and to remove, if possible, the noxious influences, shall be our task in the next year.

[1] Messrs. Daniels, Perigal, Tuckett, and Williams.

SOME OBSERVATIONS ON THE ORIGIN AND PROGRESS OF CHESS.

BY DR. DUNCAN FORBES.

CHAPTER XIII.

On the Introduction of Chess into Central Europe.

IN the 9th, 11th, and 24th volumes of the *Archæologia* will be found some very interesting disquisitions on the origin of Chess, the names of the pieces, and the introduction of the game into Europe. All these essays have been reproduced in the first volume of the *Chess Player's Chronicle*, 1841, to which we refer the reader, as the Archæological transactions are perhaps less accessible. The paper on this subject in Vol. IX. is by the Hon. Daines Barrington, who is strongly inclined to confer the honour of the invention on the Chinese, to which we have only to say at present, *not proven.* The honourable gentleman's discussion on the games of the ancient Greeks and Romans is sound and satisfactory, proving that none of their sedentary games bore the least resemblance to Chess. On the subject of the introduction of Chess into Europe, we think Mr. Barrington has been less successful. He appears to have adopted a very common but erroneous notion, that we received our earliest knowledge of the game from Constantinople, through the Crusaders, and that Italy was the first country in Western Europe where it became known. He seems to have altogether ignored the authority of our early chronicles and romances; so that in fact he is three or four centuries behind in his reckoning. He also falls into errors from inacquaintance with the manner in which the game was played both in Asia and in Europe till the beginning of the sixteenth century. For instance, he says, "the piece of the greatest power was by the Persians styled Pherz, or General." This is a decided mistake; for the piece called by the Persians "Farz," or "Farzīn," and by Europeans "Ferzia, "Dame," or "Queen," continued to be one of the weakest pieces on the board—not worth half a Rook—till a little more than three hundred and fifty years ago.

Vol. XI. contains a very interesting paper on the names of the European Chessmen, by Francis Douce, Esq., who was a very sound and sensible antiquarian, deeply read in early mediæval lore. His concluding paragraph is well worth quoting, viz., "I shall conclude with a wish that the foregoing observations may be in any degree serviceable or acceptable to those who may interest themselves in the most excellent game that the wit of man has yet devised. The subject is certainly difficult, and I am not without apprehension that future researches may convict me of many errors. To have drawn forth such a conviction, may, nevertheless, have its use; and it should be remembered, that in speculative inquiries like the present, the truth is seldom attained till many visionary systems have been destoyed." In all this we heartily agree with Mr. Douce, more especially with what he states in his concluding sentence. We have only to add further that Mr. Douce attributes the invention of Chess to the Hindūs, a conclusion at which every unprejudiced mind must arrive after perusing the writings of Dr. Hyde and Sir William Jones.

In Vol. XXIV. we have from the pen of Sir Frederic Madden, by far the best essay on this subject that has yet appeared, either in our own country or abroad. It occupies from pp. 203 to 291 of the volume, and is entitled, *Historical Remarks on the Introduction of the Game of Chess into Europe, and on the ancient Chess-men discovered in the Isle of Lewis; by* FREDERIC MADDEN, Esq., F.R.S.[1] It would be

---

[1] A few copies were struck off separately for the author's own use, but these are now very rare.

superfluous and indeed presumptuous in us to add a word more, respecting the merits of this dissertation.   We shall have occasion frequently to refer to it as we proceed, chiefly with a view to confirm, or place in a new light, what the author has already stated.

I believe I shall be able, in this chapter, to show that the game of Chess was known in France at least *eleven hundred years* ago.   I shall in proof of this, insert here the earliest Chess anecdote which I have yet seen in reference to central Europe, and if the circumstance there related can be established not only as highly probable, but historically authentic, the correctness of all subsequent anecdotes, &c., respecting the game, found in our old chronicles and romances before the time of the Crusaders, will need no further confirmation.   The story to which I allude is given by Augustus, Duke of Luneburg, in his great work on Chess,[1] p. 14.   It is extracted from an old Bavarian chronicle then in the Library of Marcus Welser, and states, that Okarius [Okar, or Otkar] prince of Bavaria, had a son of great promise residing at the court of King Pepin.   One day Pepin's son, when playing at Chess with the young prince of Bavaria, became so enraged at the latter for having repeatedly beaten him, that he hit him on the temple [with one of the Rooks] so as to kill him on the spot.

As the authenticity of this anecdote is of the utmost importance to our argument in determining the earliest appearance of Chess in central Europe, let us examine it more fully.   I here insert the original Latin as given by the Duke of Luneburg, together with his additional references to other works in confirmation of the same.

" Okarius filium habuit, in curiâ Pipini, bonis moribus plus quam filius Pipini, adornatum : quod Invidiæ fomitem administrabat ; quoniam ex Fortunâ sæpe crescit Invidia.   Et dum Filii dictorum Principum in Scaco luderent, Filius Okarii semper Pipini Filium vicit.

---

[1] *Das Schach oder Koenig-Spiel, von Gustavo Seleno,* &c., fol. Leipsic, 1616. Augustus (then styled Augustus Junior) Duke of Brunswick-Luneburg is better known to the collectors of rare Chess books as " Gustavus Selenus."   Gustavus is merely an anagram of " Augustus," and " Selenus," is apparently a far-fetched *Hellenization* of " Luneburg," or " Lunaburgensis," similar to the transformation of " Schwartserdt " into " Melancthon."   This great work on Chess was published at Leipsic, 1616, folio, pp. 495, and some copies appear to have received a new title page, dated 1617, but the text is precisely the same in both. The greater part of it consists of a translation of the work of Rui Lopez into German.   I happen to possess a rare copy of the work in the original binding, with the Brunswick arms stamped in gold on the outside, together with the following superscription in large capitals.   " Augustus Junior D. G. Dux B. et Luneb. Dono dedit. Johani Finx O. B. Z. Z. L.   Anno 1624."   The decipherment of the letters in capitals following the name, I must leave to antiquaries more learned than myself in such weighty matters.   For aught we know, the worthy " Johan " may have been in his own day a distinguished Chess player.—*Vixere fortes ante Agamemnona.*

Pipini tamen Filius de potentiâ Patris præsumens, Filium Ducis per tempora Percutiens, interfecit."

"Okarius had a son at the court of Pepin, who was more highly endowed with good qualities than the son of Pepin. This proved an incitement to envy; for envy often arises from good fortune. Now, when the sons of the said princes were playing at Chess, the son of Okarius always conquered the son of Pepin; this latter, however, presuming on the power of his father, struck the Bavarian prince on the temples and killed him."

In further confirmation of this story, Augustus of Luneburg, cites the following passage from a work in verse by Metellus of Tegernsee, entitled *Quirinalia*, or the *Acts of Saint Quirin*, composed about A.D. 1060 :—

> ——————— " Duci nempe tener filius extitit,
> Urbanos sales, intra genus tum puer inbibit,
> Huic Ludo Tabulæ,[1] Regis erat filius obvius,
> Donec doctior hic, obtinuit promptiùs Aleam.
> Rixam victus agit corde Patris forté potentius
> Et Rocho jaculans mortiferè ——— ——— adegerat,
> Sublatum puerum consequitur mors properantior,
> Clam funus tegitur."

The Latinity and metre of these lines may not be of the most faultless sort; but fortunately the meaning is clear enough. The duke then cites two other old chronicles alluding to the same subject, viz., *Chronicon Bavariæ, Andreæ Presbyteri, Ratispon. a Marq. Frehero editum*, p. 17, &c. Also another old Bavarian chronicle mentioned by H. Albrecht and H. Glarus, in which it is said that the Bavarian

---

[1] The four middle lines in the above extract are quoted by Sir Frederic Madden in his *Dissertation*, p. 206. The blank (which occurs in *Gustavus Selenus*), in the last of the four, is filled up by the word "vulnus," which I have no doubt is quite correct. Sir F. by an oversight, gives the date of the composition of the *Quirinalia*, 1160, instead of 1060. The latter date is of some consequence, as it proves that we had Chess at least long before the time of the Crusaders. Another oversight made by Sir Frederic is of a more serious nature. It is the idea he attaches to the word "Roch," in the line "Et Rocho jaculans," &c. where he conceives *Roch* to be the Bavarian prince's name; but I am inclined to think that it means the piece which we call the Rook. The construction is "Et Rocho jaculans [illum, puerum vel principem, understood], and smiting or aiming at [him] with a Rook, he mortally wounded him." A similar construction occurs in Ovid, viz., "Jupiter igne suo lucos jaculatur et arces." The importance arising from the express mention of the Rook here, is, that it proves beyond a doubt that the game played at by the two young princes was really CHESS; otherwise, the vague expression "Huic Ludo Tabulæ," &c. in a previous line might be construed so as to denote the game pf "Tables," or Backgammon, which is frequently alluded to in the old romances, along with Chess, thus, "Puis apriet il as *tables* et *eschacs* joier," as quoted by Strutt from the Romance of *Parise la Duchesse*.

prince was an only son, and that he was killed with the Chess *board*, not the Chess *Rook*, which in reality amounts to the same thing, so far as our argument is concerned.   As the passage is very short we give it in the original as quoted by the noble duke.   " Die Zween Firsten, hetten nit mer dan einen Sun der ward erschlagen, in seinen Jungen Tagen, mit einem Schach-Zabelpret, an König Pipinus Hofe von Frankrich, von einem andern Jungen Firsten."

" These two princes (*i.e.*, the prince and princess of Bavaria), had no more than one son who was killed in his early days with a Chess board, at the court of King Pepin of France, by another young prince."

Now here we have an anecdote as well authenticated as any recorded in history ; therefore we are bound to receive it as a fact. The old chroniclers, to be sure, *did* tell many improbable and some impossible tales ; but this is not one of them.   For example, we heretics have some hesitation in believing the statement of Harduinus, and a whole host of other good and holy men respecting the edifying exit of St. Denis from this wicked world.   They tell us that "the Saint aforesaid was beheaded at Montmartre near Paris, and that he afterwards walked some three or four miles to the spot where the famous church bearing his name now stands."   As if this was not marvellous enough, we are further told, " that he, very accommodatingly, carried his own head in his hand the whole way, singing Halleluiahs as he went along."   Well then, these and such like *strong facts*, being of rather rare occurrence among us, we may reasonably be allowed to entertain some doubts on the score of their authenticity ; but no such objections can be raised against the story of King Pepin's passionate son and the prince of Bavaria.

Accepting the story then as a historical fact, and I see no reason why we should not, unless we disown at once the truth of all history, we have still remaining two points for consideration.   The first, which is not very weighty is, to determine the precise period, or nearly so, when the event took place.   This point fortunately falls within a narrow compass, that is, the reign of Pepin, from 752 to 768, a period of only sixteen years.   Sir Frederic Madden in a note, p. 206, states, that " this story is repeated in a fragment of a chronicle published by Canisius, in which it is referred to the year 746."   This is evidently an error, either on the part of the chronicler or of Canisius.   We know well from history that Charles was the *eldest* son of Pepin, and that he was born in 742.   Now although this " Baby Charles " became afterwards a very great man, it is not easy for us to believe that he was so exceedingly precocious as to have played Chess and committed murder when only four years old.   We must therefore consider the date 746, to be an oversight, probably for 756, or 766 ; and I would humbly suggest, that even then, we have no reason to suppose that either

Charles or his next brother Carloman was the culprit. It must have been a still younger son of Pepin's whose name appears not in history.

The second point for our consideration is much more difficult to determine in a satisfactory manner, viz., " through what channel did the game of Chess reach King Pepin's court ? " To this question we have two plausible though not positive answers, and it so happens that both of them may be quite correct in point of fact, and differing only as to time. We may say in the first place, that Chess was introduced among the Franks by the Saracens, immediately from Spain ; or secondly, we may say that it was brought among them through the intercourse of the early sovereigns of the Carlovingian dynasty with the court of Byzantium. Let us then carefully weigh each of these probabilities, for we have no decisive proof in favour of either assumption.

We have shown in our eleventh chapter, that the Arabs were acquainted with Chess at the time of Muhammad in the first quarter of the seventh century. Under their leader Tārik, they crossed the Strait of Gibraltar (i.e., " Jibal Tārik," or "Tārik's mountain,") about 711. Then in A.D 718, after having subdued the whole of Spain, they crossed the Pyrences and extended their conquests thence to the eastward as far as the Rhone, and northwards as far as the Loire ; and thus they kept possession of one half of France for the next twelve years. At their first irruption they were bravely resisted by Eudes, Duke of Acquitaine, who, being defeated, entered into an alliance with them, and even bestowed his daughter in marriage on the Amîr Munuza, one of the Saracen leaders. Now in consequence of this doubly *unholy* alliance (politic and matrimonial), one half of the people of France were accustomed to intermingle freely with the Saracens for a period of twelve years ; and this is the precise time at which I conceive it most probable that the Acquitanians acquired their knowledge of Chess. It accounts at once for the game being familiarly known some thirty or forty years later at Pepin's court ; and conversely, it confirms us in our belief of the authenticity of the anecdote cited from so many sources by the Duke of Luneburg.

The *Norfolk News* has commenced a Chess column under the editorship of Mr. F. G. RAINGER. the Secretary of the Norwich Chess Club.

A series of Tournaments have been commenced at the PHILIDORIAN which has excited considerable interest in the Chess community ; in a Tournament of eight, lately played, Mr. SISSON came off victor ; and, at the present time a Tournament of sixteen has just been arranged.

Game played between Mr. E. THOROLD and the Rev. Mr. PIERPOINT.

(Irregular Opening.)

Black. (Mr. THOROLD.)	White. (Mr. PIERPOINT.)
1. P. to K. B. fourth	1. P. to K. third
2. Kt. to K. B. third	2. P. to Q. fourth
3. P. to K. third	3. K. B. to Q. third (a)
4. P. to Q. fourth	4. K. Kt. to B. third
5. P. to Q. B. fourth	5. Kt. to K. fifth
6. P. to Q. B. fifth	6. B. to K. second
7. K. B. to Q. third	7. Castles
8. Castles	8. P. to K. B. fourth
9. Q. Kt. to B. third	9. Q. Kt. to B. third
10. P. to Q. R. third	10. R. to K. B. third
11. B. takes Kt.	11. K. B. P. takes B.
12. Kt. to K. Kt. fifth	12. R. to K. Kt. third (b)
13. K. Kt. takes P. at K. fifth	13. Q. P. takes Kt.
14. Kt. takes P.	14. B. to K. R. fifth
15. P. to Q. Kt. fourth	15. Q. to Q. fourth
16. Q. to K. B. third	16. B. to Q. second
17. K. to R. square	17. Q. R. to K. B. square
18. P. to K. Kt. fourth	18. Kt. takes Q. P.
19. P. takes Kt.	19. B. to Q. B. third
20. P. to Q. Kt. fifth	20. Q. takes Q. P.
21. P. takes B.	21. Q. takes R.
22. P. takes P.	22. Q. to Q. R. seventh
23. P. to K. B. fifth	23. P. takes P.
24. Q. takes P. (c)	24. K. R. to K. B. third
25. Kt. takes R. (check)	25. B. takes Kt.
26. P. to K. Kt. fifth	26. Q. to Q. Kt. sixth
27. P. to Q. B. sixth	27. B. to K. second
28. R. to K. B. third	28. Q. to Q. eighth (check)
29. R. to K. B. square	29. Q. takes R. (check)
30. Q. takes Q.	30. R. takes Q. (check)
31. K. to Kt. second	31. R. to K. B. square
32. B. to K. B. fourth	32. B. to Q. third
33. B. takes B.	33. P. takes B.
34. P. to Q. B. seventh	

And White resigns.

Notes.

(*a*) " P. to Q. B. fourth " would have been the correct move.

(*b*) He should have played " P. to K. R. third," which would have put the Knight out of play for some time.

(*c*) Capitally played ; from this point to the end, Black plays in a very superior style.

Game played in the American Chess Congress between Messrs. PAULSEN and PAUL MORPHY.

(*Irregular Opening.*)

White. (Mr. PAULSEN.)	*Black.* (Mr. P. MORPHY.)
1. P. to K. fourth	1. P. to K. fourth
2. Kt. to K. B. third	2. Kt. to Q. B. third
3. Kt. to Q. B. third	3. B. to Q. B. fourth
4. B. to Q. Kt. fifth (*a*)	4. P. to Q. third
5. P. to Q. fourth	5. K. P. takes P.
6. K. Kt. takes P.	6. Q. B. to Q. second
7. K. Kt. takes Q. Kt.	7. Kt. P. takes K. Kt.
8. K. B. to R. fourth	8. Q. to K. R. fifth (*b*)
9. Castles	9. Kt. to B. third
10. Q. to B. third	10. Kt. to Kt. fifth
11. Q. B. to K. B. fourth	11. Kt. to K. fourth
12. Q. to Kt. third	12. Q. to K. B. third
13. Q. R. to Q. square	13. P. to K. R. third (*c*)
14. K. to R. square	14. P. to K. Kt. fourth
15. Q. B. takes Kt.	15. Q. P. takes Q. B.
16. P. to Q. Kt. fourth (*d*)	16. K. B. to Q. third
17. Q. R. to Q. third	17. P. to K. R. fourth
18. K. R. to Q. square	18. P. to Q. R. third
19. Kt. to K. second	19. Q. R. to Q. square
20. P. to Q. R. third	20. P. to K. Kt. fifth
21. P. to Q. B. fourth	21. Q. to R. third
22. P. to Q. B. fifth	22. P. to K. R. fifth
23. Q. to K. third	23. K. B. to K. second
24. P. to K. B. fourth	24. K. P. takes P.
25. Q. takes P.	25. Q. takes Q.
26. Kt. takes Q.	26. K. R. to R. third
27. Kt. to K. second	27. P. to K. B. fourth (*e*)

28. P. to K. fifth	28. K. R. to K. third
29. K. Kt. to B. fourth	29. R. takes K. P.
30. Q. R. takes Q. B. (*f*)	30. Q. R. takes Q. R.
31. B. takes B. P.	31. B. to Q. third
32. P. takes B.	32. B. P. takes P.
33. K. to Kt. square	33. K. to Q. square
34. B. takes Q. R.	34. K. takes B.

And White wins.

Notes.

(*a*) This is a novel way of playing the Lopez gambit, and has the effect of neutralizing book knowledge to a certain extent.

(*b*) We should hardly have expected such a paltry attempt against so strong a player as Mr. Paulsen.

(*c*) Black could evidently not castle at this juncture, for if he castles on the Q's side, he would have lost the exchange by "B. to K. Kt. fifth"; and for the K's side, White would, by first taking the Knight, win the Q. B.

(*d*) Well conceived; if this P. be taken, White takes Q. B. with R., and then "Kt. to Q. fifth."

(*e*) This ill judged move loses the game at once. "B. to Q. B. square" would have been the proper move, and in that case, Black's game does not appear so hopeless.

(*f*) White plays this game throughout in a masterly style, maintaining the attack with rare skill and perseverance.

Game played at the Manchester Chess Meeting between Messrs. ANDERSSEN and HARRWITZ.

(*Gambit refused.*)

White. (Herr ANDERSSEN.)	*Black.* (Herr HARRWITZ.)
1. P. to K. fourth	1. P. to K. fourth
2. P. to K. B. fourth	2. B. to Q. B. fourth
3. Kt. to K. B. third	3. P. to Q. third
4. P. to Q. B. third	4. B. to K. Kt. fifth
5. B. to Q. B. fourth	5. Kt. to Q. B. third
6. P. to Q. third	6. K. Kt. to K. second
7. P. to K. R. third	7. B. takes Kt.
8. Q. takes B.	8. Q. to Q. second
9. P. to Q. Kt. fourth (*a*)	9. B. to Q. Kt. third
10. P. to Q. R. fourth	10. P. to Q. R. fourth
11. P. to Q. Kt. fifth	11. Kt. to Q. square

12. P. to K. B. fifth	12. P. to K. B. third
13. P. to K. Kt. fourth	13. Kt. to K. Kt. square
14. Kt. to Q. second (*b*)	14. Kt. to K. R. third (*c*)
15. B. to Q. R. third (*d*)	15. Q. Kt. to K. B. second
16. B. to K. sixth	16. Q. to K. second
17. P. to K. R. fourth	17. Castles
18. K. to K. second	18. K. to R. square
19. Kt. to Q. B. fourth	19. Kt. to Q. square
20. Q. B. takes P. (*e*)	20. P. takes B.
21. Kt. takes B.	21. Kt. takes B.
22. Kt. takes R.	22. Kt. to K. B. fifth (check)
23. K. to Q. second	23. R. takes Kt.
24. Q. R. to K. Kt. square	24. P. to Q. fourth (*f*)
25. P. to K. Kt. fifth	25. Kt. to K. B. second
26. R. to K. Kt. third	26. Q. P. takes P.
27. Q. takes P.	27. Kt. to Q. third
28. Q. to K. square	28. Kt. takes K. B. P.
29. P. takes P.	29. P. takes P.
30. R. to K. B. third	30. Q. to Q. R. sixth
31. Q. to Q. R. square	31. Q. takes Q.
32. R. takes Q.	32. K. Kt. takes R. P.
33. R. to K. B. second	33. R. to Q. square
34. P. to Q. fourth	34. Kt. from R. fifth to K. Kt. third
35. K. to K. third	35. Kt. to Q. fourth (check)
36. K. to Q. second	36. K. to Kt. second
37. K. to B. second	37. R. to Q. B. square
38. P. takes P.	38. R. takes P. (check)
39. K. to Kt. second	39. Kt. takes P.
40. R. to Q. B. second	40. Kt. to Q. sixth (check)
41. K. to Kt. square	41. R. to Kt. sixth (check)
42. K. to R. second	42. R. to Kt. fifth
43. K. to R. third	43. Kt. to Q. Kt. third
44. R. to K. Kt. square (check)	44. K. to B. second

And White resigned.

Notes.

(*a*) This attack seems to us rather premature, as it weakens White's Pawns on the Queen's side, without gaining a direct attack on the adverse King.

(b) We should have preferred this on the ninth move.

(c) Well played, as it brings the two Knights into communication.

(d) An ill judged *coup* to win the Q. P., this B. should rather have been preserved to have retarded the *certée* of the adverse Kt. to R. third.

(e) White evidently overlooked that Black's last move effectually prevented the sacrifice of the B., and although the combination dates from the fifteenth move, it was unsound.

(f) Very well played; has conducted this game throughout with great skill and foresight.

Game between EDMUND THOROLD, Esq., *of Sheffield*, and Mr. JOHN WATKINSON, *of Huddersfield*, played at the Annual Meeting of the Sheffield Chess Club, November 16, 1859.

(Ruy Lopez Opening.)

White. (E. THOROLD, Esq.)	*Black.* (Mr. WATKINSON.)
1. P. to K. fourth	1. P. to K. fourth
2. Kt. to K. B. third	2. Kt. to Q. B. third
3. B. to Q. Kt. fifth	3. Kt. to K. B. third
4. Castles	4. P. to Q. R. third
5. B. to Q. R. fourth	5. P. to Q. Kt. fourth
6. B. to Q. Kt. third	6. B. to Q. B. fourth
7. P. to Q. B. third	7. P. to Q. third
8. P. to Q. fourth	8. P. takes P.
9. P. takes P.	9. B. to Q. Kt. third
10. B. to K. Kt. fifth	10. B. to K. Kt. fifth
11. B. takes Kt.	11. Q. takes B.
12. P. to K. fifth	12. P. takes P.
13. P. takes P.	13. Q. to K. Kt. third
14. P. to K. sixth	14. P. takes P.
15. R. to K. square	15. Castles (a)
16. K. to R. square	16. Kt. to Q. fifth
17. Kt. to K. fifth (b)	17. B. takes Q.
18. Kt. takes Q.	18. B. takes B.
19. Kt. takes R.	19. R. takes Kt.
20. P. takes B.	20. Kt. to Q. B. seventh
21. Kt. to Q. B. third	21. Kt. takes Q. R.
22. R. takes Kt.	22. R. takes K. B. P. (c)
23. R. to Q. Kt. square	23. B. to Q. fifth
24. P. to K. R. third (d)	24. B. takes Kt.

25. P. takes B.	25. R. to Q. B. seventh
26. R. to Q. R. square	26. R. takes Q. B. P.
27. R. takes Q. R. P.	27. K. to K. B. second
28. P. to Q. Kt. fourth	28. R. to Q. B. eighth (check)
29. K. to K. R. second	29. R. to Q. B. fifth
30. R. to Q. R. seventh	30. K. to K. B. third
31. K. to K. Kt. third	31. K. to K. fourth
32. R. to Q. Kt. seventh	32. R. takes Q. Kt. P.
33. R. takes Q. B. P.	33. K. to K. B. third
34. P. to K. R. fourth	34. R. to Q. Kt. eighth
35. R. to Q. B. third	35. P. to Q. Kt. fifth
36. R. to K. B. third (check)	36. K. to K. second
37. K. to K. B. second	37. P. to Q. Kt. sixth
38. K. to K. second	38. P. to Q. Kt. seventh
39. R. to Q. Kt. third	39. R. to K. Kt. eighth

And Mr. THOROLD resigns.(e)

Notes.

(a) Black has now a fine game.

(b) A good move under the circumstances. The position is extremely complicated.

(c) The series of exchanges, followed up by this move, wins Black the game.

(d) White must have a loop-hole at any cost.

(e) For if White now takes P. with Rook, he obviously loses by Black playing 40. " R. takes K. Kt. P. (check) " &c.

Consultation game played between Messrs. ZYTOGORSKI and MUCKLOW against Messrs. CAMPBELL and F. HEALEY.

(Ruy Lopez.)

White. (Messrs. ZYTOGORSKI and MUCKLOW.)	*Black.* (Messrs. CAMPBELL and HEALEY.)
1. P. to K. fourth	1. P. to K. fourth
2. Kt. to K. B. third	2. Kt. to Q. B. third
3. B. to Q. Kt. fifth	3. P. to Q. R. third
4. B. to Q. R. fourth	4. Kt. to K. B. third
5. P. to Q. fourth	5. P. takes P.
6. P. to K. fifth	6. Kt. to K. fifth
7. Castles	7. B. to K. second
8. B. takes Kt.	8. Q. P. takes B.

9. Q. takes P.	9. B. to K. B. fourth
10. B. to Q. third	10. Castles
11. Kt. to Q. B. third	11. P. to Q. B. fourth
12. Q. takes Q.	12. Q. R. takes Q.
13. Kt. takes Kt.	13. B. takes Kt.
14. Q. R. to Q. B. square	14. B. takes Kt.
15. P. takes B.	15. R. to Q. fourth
16. P. to K. B. fourth	16. P. to Q. B. fifth
17. Q. R. to Q. square	17. K. R. to Q. square
18. R. takes R.	18. R. takes R.
19. R. to K. square	19. K. to B. square
20. K. to K. Kt. second	20. K. to R. square
21. K. to K. B. third	21. P. to Kt. third
22. K. to K. fourth	22. P. to Q. B. third
23. P. to K. B. fifth	23. P. to K. B. third
24. P. to K. B. fourth	24. K. to B. second
25. R. to K. Kt. square	25. P. takes K. P.
26. P. takes K. P.	26. B. to Q. B. fourth
27. P. takes P. (check)	27. P. takes P.
28. R. to K. B. square (check)	28. K. to K. square
29. B. takes B.	29. R. takes B.
30. R. to K. B. sixth	30. R. to Q. Kt. fourth
31. P. takes K. Kt. third	31. P. takes P.
32. R. P. takes P.	32. R. to Q. Kt. fifth (check)
33. P. to Q. B. fourth	33. R. takes Kt. P.
34. R. takes K. Kt. P.	34. R. to K. R. sixth
35. K. to K. Kt. fifth	35. R. takes P.
36. K. to K. sixth	36. K. to K. B. square
37. K. to Q. seventh	37. R. to K. B. seventh
38. P. to K. sixth	38. R. to Q. seventh (check)
39. K. to Q. B. second	39. P. to Q. Kt. fourth
40. P. to Q. B. fifth	40. P. to Q. Kt. fifth
41. K. takes Q. B. P.	41. P. to Q. Kt. sixth
42. R. to K. Kt. third	42. P. to Q. Kt. seventh
43. R. to Q. Kt. third	43. R. to Q. B. seventh

Drawn game.

GAMES PLAYED AT THE GRAND CHESS TOURNAMENT IN NEW YORK.

(From the book of the American Chess Congress, by D. Fiske.)

GAME I.

Between Mr. MONTGOMERY and Mr. ALLISON.

(Evans's Gambit.)

White. (Mr. MONTGOMERY.)	*Black.* (Mr. ALLISON.)
1. P. to K. fourth	1. P. to K. fourth
2. K. Kt. to B. third	2. Q. Kt. to B. third
3. K. B. to Q. B. fourth	3. K. B. to Q. B. fourth
4. P. to Q. Kt. fourth	4. K. B. takes Kt. P.
5. P. to Q. B. third	5. K. B. to Q. R. fourth
6. Castles	6. P. to Q. third
7. P. to Q. fourth	7. K. P. takes P.
8. B. P. takes P.	8. K. B. to Kt. third
9. P. to Q. fifth	9. Q. Kt. to R. fourth (a)
10. P. to K. fifth	10. Q. Kt. takes K. B.
11. Q. to Q. R. fourth (check)	11. Q. B. to Q. second
12. Q. takes Q. Kt.	12. Kt. to K. second
13. P. to K. sixth	13. B. P. takes P.
14. Q. P. takes P.	14. Q. B. to B. third
15. B. to K. Kt. fifth (b)	15. Castles (c)
16. Q. to K. R. fourth (d)	16. K. R. to K. square
17. Q. Kt. to Q. second	17. P. to K. R. third (e)
18. K. R. to K. square	18. R. P. takes B.
19. K. Kt. takes P.	19. Q. to Q. B. square
20. Q. to K. R. seventh (check)	20. K. to B. square
21. Q. to K. R. eighth (check)	21. Kt. to Kt. square
22. P. to K. seventh (check)	22. K. R. takes P.
23. K. R. takes K. R.	23. K. takes K. R.
24. Q. takes Kt. P. (check)	24. K. to Q. square
25. Q. takes Kt. (check)	25. Q. B. to K. square
26. R. to K. square	26. K. to Q. second
27. Q. Kt. to K. fourth	27. K. to Q. B. third
28. Q. to Q. B. fourth (check)	28. K. B. to B. fourth
29. Q. Kt. takes K. B.	29. P. takes Q. Kt.
30. R. to K. sixth (check)	

And Mr. MONTGOMERY wins in the First Section.

Notes.

(a) Not a good move, although frequently adopted at this point by M'Donnell in his games with La Bourdonnais. Black's play was to retreat his Queen's Knight to King's second.

(b) 15. "K. Kt. to Kt. fifth," strikes us as preferable. The move in the text afforded Black an opportunity (which he very injudiciously neglected) of exchanging his Queen's Bishop for White's King's Knight.

(c) He should have taken off the King's Knight thus :—

	15. Q. B. takes K. Kt.
16. Kt. P. takes B.	16. P. to K. R. third
17. Q. to K. R. fourth (best)	17. K. R. to Kt. square
18. B. takes Kt. (A.)	18. Q. takes B.
19. Q. to K. R. fifth (check)	19. P. to K. Kt. third
20. Q. takes K. R. P.	20. Castles
and Black has a fine game.	

A.

18. B. to Q. second	18. Kt. to K. B. fourth
and Black's game is good.	

(d) From this point to the end the first player conducts the attack with great vigor and determination.

(e) Black seems to have no better move on the board ; 17. "Q. B. to Q. Kt. fourth " would simply advance his adversary's game, while the capture of the King's Knight would now be utterly useless.

GAME II.

Between Mr. STANLEY and Mr. LICHTENHEIN.

(Giuoco Piano.)

White. (MR. STANLEY.)	Black. (MR. LICHTENHEIN.)
1. P. to K. fourth	1. P. to K. fourth
2. K. Kt. to B. third	2. Q. Kt. to B. third
3. K. B. to Q. B. fourth	3. K. B. to Q. B. fourth
4. P. to Q. fourth	4. P. to Q. third
5. P. to K. R. third	5. P. to K. R. third
6. K. Kt. to B. third	6. K. Kt. to B. third
7. K. B. to K. third	7. K. B. to Kt. third
8. Castles	8. Q. B. to K. third
9. K. B. to Kt. third	9. Castles
10. Q. to K. second	10. K. Kt. to R. second
11. K. Kt. to R. second (a)	11. Q. Kt. to Q. fifth
12. Q. to Q. second	12. Q. B. takes K. B.
13. R. P. takes B.	13. P. to K. B. fourth
14. K. P. takes P.	14. K. R. takes P.
15. K. Kt. to Kt. fourth	15. Q. to K. R. fifth

16. Q. Kt. to Q. fifth	16. Q. R. to K. B. square
17. Q. Kt. takes B.	17. R. P. takes Q. Kt.
18. B. takes Q. Kt.	18. K. P. takes B.
19. Q. R. to K. square	19. Kt. to Kt. fourth (b)
20. P. to K. B. fourth	20. P. to K. R. fourth
21. B. P. takes Kt.	21. R. P. takes Kt.
22. R. P. takes P.	22. Q. takes P. at Kt. fifth
23. K. R. takes K. R.	23. Q. takes K. R.
24. Q. to K. second	24. Q. takes Kt. P.
25. Q. to K. sixth (check)	25. R. to K. B. second
26. Q. to K. eighth (check)	26. R. to K. B. square
27. Q. to K. sixth (check)	27. K. to R. second
28. Q. to R. third (check)	28. K. to Kt. third
29. R. to K. fourth	29. Q. to B. eighth (check)
30. K. to R. second	30. R. to K. B. fourth
31. R. takes Q. P. (c)	31. Q. takes B. P.
32. Q. to K. Kt. fourth (check)	32. K. to B. third
33. R. to Q. B. fourth	33. Q. takes Q. P.
34. R. takes Q. B. P.	34. P. to K. Kt. third
35. Q. to K. R. fourth (check)	35. K. to K. fourth
36. Q. to K. R. eighth (check)	36. R. to K. B. third
37. R. to K. B. seventh	37. Q. to K. B. eighth
38. Q. to K. eighth (check)	38. K. to Q. fourth
39. R. takes R.	39. Q. takes R.
40. Q. to Q. Kt. fifth (check)	40. K. to K. third
41. Q. takes P.	41. Q. to K. fourth (check)
42. K. to Kt. square (d)	42. Q. to Q. B. fourth (check) (e)
43. Q. takes Q.	43. Q. P. takes Q.
44. K. to B. second	44. K. to B. fourth
45. K. to B. third	45. K. to Kt. fourth
46. K. to Kt. third	46. P. to Kt. third
47. K. to B. third	47. K. to R. fifth
48. K. to K. second (f)	48. K. to Kt. sixth

And Black wins. (g)

Notes.

(a) White appears to weaken his position, and lose time by this move, since it allows his adversary to play at once 11. "Q. Kt. to Q. fifth."

24

(*b*) Black now threatens to win a Pawn by

21. Kt. P. takes Q.	20. Q. takes R. P.
22. K. to Kt. second	21. Kt. to K. B. sixth (check)
	22. Kt. takes Q.

and can afterwards extricate his Knight by playing it to King's Bishop's sixth.

(*c*) We think that in this position White would have done better to check with the Rook at King's sixth, by which he probably could at least have drawn the game.

(*d*) "K. to Kt. third" was certainly preferable, as it prevented the exchange of Queens, and would have made it extremely difficult for Black to win.

(*e*) Black, by the hasty play of his adversary, not only thus effects an exchange of Queens, but also unites his two isolated Pawns on the Queen's side. With such an advantage, victory was sure to follow, sooner or later.

(*f*) This is bad, but any other move would not have affected the ultimate result. If 48. "K. to B. second," Black finally wins by being able, at the proper time, to gain a move with his Queen's Knight's Pawn.

(*g*) Time, two hours and a half.

GAME III.

Between the same opponents.

(*Scotch Gambit.*)

White. (Mr. LICHTENHEIN.)	*Black.* (Mr. STANLEY.)
1. P. to K. fourth	1. P. to K. fourth
2. K. Kt. to B. third	2. Q. Kt. to B. third
3. P. to Q. fourth	3. K. P. takes P.
4. K. B. to Q. B. fourth	4. K. B. to Q. B. fourth
5. P. to Q. B. third	5. P. to Q. sixth (*a*)
6. K. Kt. to Kt. fifth (*b*)	6. K. Kt. to R. third
7. Q. to K. R. fifth (*c*)	7. Q. Kt. to K. fourth
8. K. B. takes B. P. (check)	8. K. Kt. takes B.
9. K. Kt. takes K. Kt.	9. K. B. takes B. P. (check)
10. K. takes K. B.	10. Kt. takes K. Kt.
11. K. R. to K. B. square	11. Castles
12. K. to Kt. square	12. P. to Q. B. third
13. B. to K. third	13. P. to Q. third
14. Kt. to Q. second	14. B. to K. third
15. Q. R. to K. square	15. Q. to Q. second
16. P. to K. R. third	16. P. to Q. R. fourth
17. P. to Q. R. fourth	17. P. to Q. B. fourth
18. P. to Q. Kt. third	18 P. to Q. B. fifth
19. Kt. takes B. P.	19. B. takes Kt.

20. Kt. P. takes B.	20. Kt. to K. fourth
21. B. to Q. fourth	21. Q. takes Q. R. P.
22. P. to Q. B. fifth	22. P. to Q. seventh
23. K. R. takes K. R. (check) (*d*)	23. Q. R. takes K. R.
24. R. to Q. square	24. Kt. to K. B. sixth (check)

And Black wins.(*e*)

Notes.

(*a*) Not positively bad, but inferior to the move first suggested by Jænisch, of 5. "K. Kt. to B. third," reducing the game to a well-known position of the Giuoco Piano. The object of Black's fifth move is to prevent White from uniting his two Pawns in the centre of the board, and by leaving White's Queen's Bishop's Pawn where it now stands, to hinder the movements of the adverse Queen's Knight. He also appears to gain time by this move, for White must capture the Queen's Pawn within a few moves. But, notwithstanding this, we consider the line of play recommended by the distinguished Russian analyst as eminently safer for Black. It has, in fact, rendered the Scotch Gambit a much less popular game for the attack than formerly.

(*b*) 6. "P. to Q. Kt. fourth," followed by 7. "P. to Q. Kt. fifth," was the proper play.

(*c*) If 7. Kt. takes K. B. P. | 7. B. takes K. B. P. (check)
    8. K. takes B. | 8. Kt. takes Kt.
    9. B. takes Kt. (check) | 9. K. takes B.
White may now move 10. "R. to K. B. square," or 10. "Q. takes P.," with an even game. If he play 10. "Q. to Q. Kt. third (check)," Black replies 10. "K. to Kt. third," with a superior game.

(*d*) 23. "Q. R. to Q. square," was the proper play.

(*e*) Time, one hour and forty-five minutes.

GAME IV.

(*Queen's Gambit refused.*)

Between the same opponents.

White. (Mr. LICHTENHEIN.)	*Black.* (Mr. STANLEY.)
1. P. to Q. fourth	1. P. to Q. fourth
2. P. to Q. B. fourth	2. P. to K. third
3. Q. Kt. to B. third	3. Q. P. takes P.
4. P. to K. third	4. K. B. to K. second
5. K. B. takes P.	5. K. Kt. to B. third
6. K. Kt. to B. third	6. Castles
7. Castles	7. K. Kt. to Q. fourth
8. Q. to Q. Kt. third	8. K. Kt. takes Q. Kt.
9. Kt. P. takes Kt.	9. Q. Kt. to B. third

10. K. B. to Q. third	10. P. to Q. R. fourth
11. P. to Q. R. fourth	11. P. to Q. Kt. third
12. K. B. to K. fourth	12. Q. B. to Kt. second
13. Q. to B. second	13. P. to K. B. fourth
14. K. B. takes Kt.	14. Q. B. takes K. B.
15. Kt. to K. fifth	15. Q. to Q. fourth
16. P. to K. B. fourth	16. Q. to K. fifth
17. Q. takes Q.	17. Q. B. takes Q.
18. B. to R. third	18. K. B. takes B.
19. Q. R. takes K. B.	19. K. R. to Q. square
20. K. R. to K. B. second	20. P. to Q. B. fourth
21. Q. R. to Kt. third	21. B. P. takes P.
22. B. P. takes P.	22. K. R. to Q. B. square (a)
23. K. R. to Q. Kt. second	23. K. R. to B. eighth (check)
24. K. to B. second	24. K. R. to B. seventh (check)
25. K. to Kt. third	25. Q. R. to Q. B. square
26. Q. R. takes Kt. P.	26. K. R. takes K. R.
27. Q. R. takes K. R.	27. B. to Q. B. seventh
28. R. to Q. Kt. fifth	28. B. takes R. P.
29. R. takes R. P.	29. B. to Q. Kt. sixth
30. R. to Q. B. fifth	30. R. to Q. R. square
31. Kt. to Q. B. fourth	31. P. to K. R. third
32. Kt. to Q. Kt. sixth	32. R. to R. third
33. R. to Kt. fifth	33. R. to R. sixth
34. K. to R. fourth	34. B. to R. seventh
35. R. to K. fifth	35. R. to R. third
36. R. to Kt. fifth	36. R. to R. sixth
37. R. to Kt. second	37. B. to Kt. sixth
38. P. to K. R. third	38. K. to B. second
39. P. to K. Kt. fourth	39. B. P. takes P.
40. R. P. takes P.	40. K. to K. second
41. P. to K. fourth	41. K. to Q. third
42. P. to K. B. fifth	42. P. to K fourth
43. Q. P. takes P. (check)	43. K. takes P.
44. Kt. to Q. seventh (check)	44. K. to B. fifth
45. P. to K. fifth	45. R. to Q. R. seventh (b)
46. R. takes B.	

And Black resigned. (c)

Notes.

(a) The Queen's Knight's Pawn cannot be saved.

(b) Black evidently committed this error under the supposition, that if White captured the Bishop, he would mate with Rook at King's Rook's seventh. We think, however, that, in any case, the passed Pawn of White would have won in the end.

(c) Time, four hours.

GAME V.

Between Mr. PAULSEN and Mr. CALTHROP.

(Scotch Gambit.)

White. (Mr. PAULSEN.)	*Black.* (Mr. CALTHROP.)
1. P. to K. fourth	1. P. to K. fourth
2. K. Kt. to B. third	2. Q. Kt. to B. third
3. P. to Q. fourth	3. K. P. takes P.
4. K. B. to Q. B. fourth	4. K. B. to Q. B. fourth
5. P. to Q. B. third	5. K. Kt. to B. third (a)
6. Castles (b)	6. Q. Kt. to R. fourth (c)
7. B. P. takes P.	7. Q. Kt. takes K. B.
8. Q. P. takes K. B.	8. P. to Q. fourth
9. B. P. takes P. (en passant.)	9. Q. takes P.
10. P. to K. fifth	10. Q. takes Q.
11. K. R. takes Q.	11. K. Kt. to Q. second
12. P. to Q. Kt. third	12. Q. Kt. to Kt. third
13. B. to Q. R. third	13. K. Kt. to K. B. square
14. B. takes K. Kt.	14. K. R. takes B.
15. Q. Kt. to B. third	15. P. to Q. B. third
16. Q. Kt. to K. fourth	16. Kt. to Q. fourth
17. Q. Kt. to Q. sixth (check)	17. K. to K. second
18. K. Kt. to Q. fourth	18. P. to K. Kt. third
19. K. R. to K. square	19. Q. R. to Kt. square
20. Q. R. to Kt. square	20. Q. B. to Q. second
21. P. to Q. Kt. fourth	21. P. to K. B. third
22. Q. Kt. to Q. B. fourth	22. P. to Q. Kt. fourth
23. Q. Kt. to R. fifth	23. Q. R. to Kt. third
24. P. to K. sixth	24. B. to K. square
25. P. to Q. R. third	25. K. to Q. third
26. Q. R. to B. square	26. Kt. to K. second

27. K. R. to Q. square	27. K. to Q. B. second
28. K. Kt. to Q. Kt. third	28. P. to K. B. fourth
29. K. Kt. to Q. B. fifth	29. K. R. to B. third
30. K. Kt. to Q. seventh	30. K. R. takes K. P.
31. K. Kt. takes Q. R.	31. R. P. takes K. Kt.
32. Kt to Kt. third	32. R. to K. fourth
33. K. R. to K. square	33. R. takes K. R.
34. R. takes R.	34. K. to Q. third
35. Kt. to Q. fourth	35. P. to Q. B. fourth
36. Kt. to Q. B. second	36. B. to K. B. second
37. R. to Q. square (check)	37. Kt. to Q. fourth
38. Kt. to K. third	38. P. to Q. B. fifth
39. Kt. takes Kt.	39. B. takes Kt.
40. P. to K. B. fourth	40. P. to Q. B. sixth (*d*)
41. R. to Q. B. square	41. B. to Q. B. fifth
42. R. takes B. P.	

And White wins.(*e*)

Notes.

(*a*) The proper play; the same position arises in the Giuoco Piano, thus :—

1. P. to K. fourth	1. P. to K. fourth
2. K. Kt. to B. third	2. Q. Kt. to B. third
3. K. B. to Q. B. fourth	3. K. B. to Q. B. fourth
4. P. to Q. B. third	4. K. Kt. to B. third
5. P. to Q. fourth	5. K. P. takes P.

(*b*) Not so strong as 6. "P. to K. fifth."

(*c*) We are inclined to think that 6. "P. to Q. third," though more quiet, would have been better in the end. White could not then play "P. to K. fifth."

(*d*) Bad; he should have played 40. "K. to B. third," and then "B. to K. fifth," and his chances of a draw would have been very fair.

(*e*) Time, four hours.

GAME VI.

Between Mr. PAULSEN and Mr. MONTGOMERY.

(*Sicilian Opening.*)

White. (Mr. MONTGOMERY.)	*Black.* (Mr. PAULSEN.)
1. P. to K. fourth	1. P. to Q. B. fourth
2. P. to Q. fourth	2. B. P. takes P.
3. K. Kt. to B. third	3. Q. Kt. to B. third
4. K. B. to Q. B. fourth	4. P. to K. third

5. Castles	5. K. B. to Q. B. fourth
6. P. to Q. B. third	6. Q. P. takes P.
7. Q. Kt. takes P.	7. K. Kt. to K. second (a)
8. P. to K. fifth	8. K. Kt. to Kt. third (b)
9. Q. Kt. to K. fourth	9. Q. Kt. takes K. P. (c)
10 K. Kt. takes Q. Kt.	10. K. Kt. takes K. Kt.
11. Kt. takes K. B.	11. Q. to Q. B. second (d)
12. Q. to Q. fourth	12. Kt. takes K. B.
13. Q. takes Kt.	13. P. to Q. Kt. third
14. Kt. to K. fourth (e)	14. Q. takes Q.
15. Kt. to Q. sixth (check)	15. K. to K. second
16. Kt. takes Q.	16. B. to Q. B. third
17. P. to Q. Kt. third	17. P. to Q. fourth
18. B. to Q. R. third (check)	18. K. to B. third
19. Kt. to Q. sixth (f)	19. B. takes K. R.
20. R. takes B.	20. K. R. to Q. square
21. R. to Q. B. square	21. K. R. to Q. second
22. R. to Q. B. third	22. P. to K. Kt. fourth
23. R. to K. B. third (check)	23. K. to K. Kt. third
24. P. to K. Kt. fourth	24. Q. R. to Q. square
25. Kt. to Q. Kt. fifth	25. P. to Q. fifth
26. B. to Q. Kt. second	26. P. to K. fourth
27. Kt. to Q. R. third	27. K. R. to Q. fourth
28. R. to Q. third	28. P. to K. fifth
29. R. to Q. square	29. P. to K. sixth
30. K. to B. square	30. P. to K. B. fourth
31. Kt. to Q. B. second	31. P. to K. seventh (check)
32. K. takes P.	32. P. to Q. sixth (check)
33. K. to B. third	33. B. P. takes P. (check) (g)
34. K. to K. fourth	34. K. R. to K. B. fourth
35. Kt. to K. third	35. K. R. takes B. P.
36. B. to K. fifth	36. K. R. takes Q. R. P.
37. R. to K. B. square	37. K. R. to K. seventh
38. R. to K. B sixth (check)	38. K. to K. R. fourth
39. R. to K. sixth	39. P. to Q. seventh
40. B. to K. Kt. seventh	40. Q. R. to K. square (h)
41. R. takes Q. R. (i)	41. P. to Q. eighth (Q.)
42. B. to Q. fourth (k)	42. Q. to K. R. eighth (check)

43. K. to K. fifth	43. Q. to K. B. sixth
44. K. to Q. sixth	44. Q. to K. B. fifth (check)
45. K. to Q. fifth	45. Q. to K. B. second (check)
46. R. to K. sixth	46. R. to Q. seventh
47. K. to K. fifth	47. R. takes B.

And White resigns.(*l*)

Notes.

(*a*) We should certainly have preferred 7. "P. to Q. third."

(*b*) 8. "P. to Q. fourth" would have been better Chess, freeing his game at once.

(*c*) Black ought to have played, at this stage, 9. "K. B. to K. second."

(*d*) If Black now play

	11. Kt. takes K. B.
12. Q. to Q. fourth	12. P. to Q. fourth
13. Q. takes K. Kt. P.	13. K. R. to B. square
14. B. to K. R. sixth	

and White must win.

(*e*) By simply playing 14. "Q. to K. fourth," White would have preserved his advantage in position. If Black then moved 14. "P. to Q. fourth," White would have answered with 15. "Q. to Q. R. fourth (check)."

(*f*) The position is an instructive one. White should now have availed himself of the opportunity presented for drawing the game, thus:—

19. B. to Kt. second (check)	19. K. to K. second (best)
20. B. to R. third (check)	20. K. to B. third (best)

and the game is drawn by perpetual check. If the Black King moves to any other squares than those indicated, White frees his Knight and Rook.

(*g*) He ought rather to have captured the Knight at once.

(*h*) Elegantly played; from this point to the end, the second player conducts the attack with great vigor and accuracy.

(*i*) White has no better move.

(*k*) If 42. "R. to K. sixth," Black would play 42. "Q. to Q. B. seventh (check)," and either win both Rook and Knight, or mate in a few moves.

(*l*) Time, six hours.

GAME VII.
Between Mr. MORPHY and Mr. LICHTENHEIN.
(*Queen's Gambit refused.*).

White. (Mr. LICHTENHEIN.)	*Black.* (Mr. MORPHY.)
1. P. to Q. fourth	1. P. to Q. fourth
2. P. to Q. B. fourth	2. P. to K. third
3. Q. Kt. to B. third	3. K. Kt. to B. third
4. K. Kt. to B. third	4. P. to Q. B. fourth
5. P. to K. third	5. Q. Kt. to B. third

6. P. to Q. R. third	6. K. B. to Q. third
7. Q. P. takes P.	7. K. B. takes P.
8. P. to Q. Kt. fourth	8. K. B. to Q. third
9. Q. B. to Kt. second	9. Castles
10. Q. Kt. to Kt. fifth	10. K. B. to K. second
11. Q. Kt. to Q. fourth	11. K. Kt. to K. fifth
12. Q. Kt. takes Q. Kt.	12. Kt. P. takes Q. Kt.
13. K. B. to Q. third	13. P. to Q. B. fourth
14. Kt. to Q. second	14. Kt. takes Kt.
15. Q. takes Kt.	15. Q. P. takes P.
16. K. B. to K. fourth	16. Q. takes Q.
17. K. takes Q.	17. Q. R. to Kt. square.
18. Q. B. to K. fifth (a)	18. Q. R. to Kt. fourth
19. K. B. to Q. B. sixth	19. Q. R. to Kt. third
20. P. to Q. Kt. fifth	20. Q. B. to Kt. second
21. Q. B. to B. seventh	21. P. to B. sixth (check)
22. K. takes P.	22. Q. B. takes K. B.
23. Q. B. takes R.	23. K. B. to B. third (check)
24. K. to Q. second	24. R. P. takes B.
25. Kt. P. takes Q. B.	25. B. takes Q. R.
26. R. takes B.	26. R. to Q. B. square
27. P. to Q. R. fourth	27. R. takes B. P.
28. P. to Q. R. fifth	28. Kt. P. takes P.
29. R. takes P.	29. P. to K. Kt. third
30. P. to K. B. third	30. R. to Q. Kt. third (b)
31. R. takes B. P.	

And the game was eventually drawn. (c)

Notes.

(a) He would have done better in the end if he had now taken measures to bring his Rooks into play.

(b) Failing by an oversight to score a game which his extra Pawn ought to have insured him.

(c) Time, four hours and a half.

Game between Col. MICHAELS, President of the Cercle des Echecs, Brussels, and Mr. F. DEACON of Bruges.

(King's Bishop's Gambit.)

White. (Mr. DEACON.)	*Black.* (Col. MICHAELS.)
1. P. to K. fourth	1. P. to K. fourth
2. P. to K. B. fourth	2. P. takes P.
3. B. to Q. B. fourth	3. Q. to K. R. fifth (check)
4. K. to B. square	4. P. to K. Kt. fourth
5. Kt. to Q. B. third	5. B. to K. Kt. second
6. P. to Q. fourth	6. P. to Q. third
7. Kt. to K. B. third	7. Q. to K. R. fourth
8. P. to K. fifth	8. P. takes P.
9. Kt. to Q. fifth	9. K. to Q. square
10. P. to K. R. fourth	10. P. to K. R. third
11. K. to Kt. square	11. Q. to K. Kt. third
12. Kt. takes K. P.	12. Q. to K. B. fourth
13. Q. to K. R. fifth	13. B. to K. third
14. K. R. P. takes P.	14. P. to Q. B. third
15. B. to Q. third	15. Q. takes K. Kt. P.
16. Kt. takes K. B. P. (check)	16. B. takes Kt.
17. Q. takes B.	17. P. takes Kt.
18. R. to K. R. fifth	18. Q. to K. second
19. Q. takes Q. P. (check)	19. Kt. to Q. second
20. B. to Q. second	20. R. to Q. B. square
21. R. to K. square	21. Q. to K. B. third
22. Q. takes Q. Kt. P.	22. Kt. to K. second
23. B. to Q. R. fifth (check)	23. Kt. to Kt. third
24. R. takes Kt.	24. Q. takes R.
25. R. to Q. fifth (check)	25. K. to K. square
26. B. to K. Kt. sixth (check)	26. K. to B. square
27. B. to Q. Kt. fourth	

And wins.

Game between Mr. F. DEACON, and Signor DISCART, of Sienna.

White. (Mr. DEACON.)	*Black.* (Signor DISCART.)
1. P. to K. fourth	1. P. to K. fourth
2. Kt. to K. B. third	2. Kt. to Q. B. third

3. B. to Q. B. fourth	3. B. to Q. B. fourth
4. P. to Q. Kt. fourth	4. B. takes Kt. P.
5. P. to Q. B. third	5. B. to Q. R. fourth
6. Castles	6. Kt. to K. B. third
7. Kt. to K. Kt. fifth	7. Castles
8. Q. to Q. Kt. third	8. Q. to K. second
9. P. to K. B. fourth	9. B. to Q. Kt. third (check)
10. K. to R. square	10. Kt. to K. Kt. fifth
11. Kt. takes K. B. P.	11. R. takes Kt.
12. B. takes R. (check)	12. Q. takes B.
13. Q. takes Q. (check)	13. K. takes Q.
14. P. takes P. (dis. check)	14. K. to K. third
15. P. to Q. fourth	15. Kt. to Q. R. fourth (a)
16. P. to K. R. third	16. Kt. to R. third
17. B. takes Kt.	17. P. takes B.
18. K. R. to B. sixth (check)	18. K. to K. second .
19. Kt. to Q. second	19. P. to Q. third
20. Q. R. to Q. B. square	20. B. to K. third
21. P. to Q. fifth	21. B. to K. Kt. square
22. P. to K. sixth	22. P. to B. third
23. R. to K. B. seventh (check)	23. B. takes R.
24. R. takes B. (check)	24. K. to K. square
25. R. takes K. R. P.	25. R. to Q. square
26. Kt. to K. B. third	26. B. to K. R. seventh
27. P. to K. Kt. fourth	27. Kt. to Q. B. fifth
28. K. to Kt. second	28. B. to K. sixth
29. Kt. to K. R. fourth	29. B. to K. Kt. fourth
30. Kt. to K. Kt. sixth	30. B. to K. B. third
31. R. to K. B. seventh	

And wins.

Note.

(a) "Kt. takes Q. P." would have been the correct move.

Game between Mr. CAMPBELL and Mr. JANSSENS, played recently at the PHILIDORIAN.

White. (Mr. JANSSENS.)	*Black.* (Mr. CAMPBELL.)
1. P. to K. fourth	1. P. to K. fourth
2. K. Kt. to B. third	2. Q. Kt. to B. third

3. B. to Q. B. fourth	3. B. to K. B. fourth
4. P. to Q. B. third	4. K. Kt. to B. third
5. P. to Q. third	5. P. to Q. third
6. Castles	6. Q. to K. second
7. P. to K. R. third	7. Castles
8. P. to Q. Kt. fourth	8. B. to Kt. third
9. P. to Q. R. fourth	9. P. to Q. R. fourth
10. P. to Q. Kt. fifth	10. Kt. to Q. square
11. B. to K. Kt. fifth	11. B. to K. third
12. Q. Kt. to Q. second	12. B. takes B.
13. Kt. takes B.	13. Kt. to K. third
14. Kt. to K. third (a)	14. Kt. takes B.
15. Kt. takes Kt.	15. B. takes Kt.
16. P. takes B.	16. P. to Q. fourth
17. P. takes P.	17. Kt. takes P.
18. Q. to R. fifth	18. P. to K. R. third
19. Kt. to B. third	19. Q. R. to K. square
20. P. to Q. fourth	20. Kt. takes K. P.
21. K. R. to K. square	21. P. takes P.
22. P. takes P.	22. Q. to Q. third
23. Q. R. to Q. B. square	23. Q. to Kt. sixth
24. R. to K. second	24. R. to K. fifth
25. R. to Q. B. fifth	25. K. R. to K. square
26. R. to K. fifth	26. K. R. takes R.
27. P. takes R.	27. R. takes Q. R. P.

And wins.

Note.

(a) A weak move, of which Black takes due advantage.

CHESS SOIRÉE.—This Soirée took place on Wednesday last, in the New Hall, and proved one of the most successful gatherings that have been held. Visitors assembled in the morning, and the mimic warfare was kept up between various combatants until nearly midnight. Among the company, which included gentlemen from Abingdon, Henley, Southampton, Uxbridge, and other towns, were G. WHITE, Esq., the celebrated composer of problems, known as "C. W.," and Mr. LUMLEY, the blind player, &c. The play of the last-named gentleman attracted much attention.—*Reading Mercury, Nov.* 26.

SOLUTIONS TO PROBLEMS.

No. 41. *Page* 351.

White.	Black.
1. Kt. to Q. B. fourth	1. R. to Q. Kt. fourth (best)
2. Q. to Q. R. fifth	2. K. R. to Q. second (*a*)
2. Kt. to Kt. sixth (check)	3. R. takes Kt.
4. R. mates	

(*a*)

	2. K. R. to Q. Kt. square
3. Q. to Q. B. seventh	

and mates next move.

No. 42. *Page* 351.

White.	Black.
1. R. to K. sixth	1. R. takes R. (*a*)
2. Q. to Kt. seventh	2. P. to K. seventh (*b*)
3. Q. to K. fourth (check)	3. R. or Kt. takes Q.
4. Kt. mates	

(*a*)

	1. B. to K. fourth
2. Kt. to Q. fifth (check)	2. K. moves
3. Q. to B. second (check)	3. K. takes Kt.
4. Q. to B. sixth, and mates	

(*b*)

	2. K. to K. fourth, or R. to Q. fifth
3. Kt. to K. second (check)	3. Anything
4. B. takes R., and mates	

No. 43. *Page* 352.

White.	Black.
1. R. takes R.	1. Q. to K. sixth or eighth (ch.)
2. R. covers check	2. Q. takes Q.
3. Kt. to Kt. sixth (check)	3. B. or P. takes Kt.
4. R. takes R. (check), and mates	

No. 44. *Page* 352.

White to checkmate with King's Pawn.

White.	Black.
1. R. takes B.	1. P. to K. sixth
2. R. takes P.	2. P. takes P.
3. R. takes P. (check)	3. K. takes R.
4. Q. to Q. R. sixth (check)	4. K. to B. second
5. Q. to K. Kt. seventh (check)	5. K. to Q. square
6. P. to K. sixth	6. P. Queens
7. P. to K. seventh	

and mates.

White to checkmate with Bishop's Pawn.

White.	Black.
1. B. takes B.	1. P. to K. sixth
2. P. to B. third	2. P. takes P.
3. R. to Q. Kt. square	3. P. to Q. eighth

Becoming either a Queen, Rook, Knight, or Bishop. If Queen or Rook, Queen checks on Queen's third, and Pawn mates in two or three moves. If Pawn becomes a Bishop, thus,

4. R. to Q. Kt. third	4. B. takes Q.
5. R. to Q. third (check)	5. B. takes R.
6. B. checks	6. B. takes B.
7. P. mates	

If Pawn becomes a Knight, then,—

4. B. to K. B. fifth	4. Kt. to Q. Kt. second (best)
5. B. takes Kt.	5. P. takes B.
6. Q. to Q. fourth (check)	6. P. takes Q.
7. P. mates	

White to checkmate with Queen's Pawn.

White.	*Black.*
1. B. takes B.	1. P. to K. sixth
2. P. to Q. third	2. P. takes P.
3. R. to K. Kt. third	3. P. Queens

becoming either Q., R., Kt., or B.

If Queen, P. checkmates in three moves; if Rook, Pawn mates in three moves; if Bishop, also in three moves; if Knight, thus,—

4. Kt. to K. third (check)	4. Kt. takes Kt.
5. Q. to Q. R. second (check)	5. Kt. interposes
6. P. mates	

SOLUTIONS OF PROBLEMS FOR YOUNG PLAYERS.

No. 11.   *Page* 318.

White.	*Black.*
Q. to K. Kt. seventh	K. to K. fifth, (or A. B. C.)
Kt. to Q. B. third (check)	Anything.
Q. or B. mates.	

A.

	P. Queens.
Kt. to K. Kt. fifth (check)	K. to K. third
B. mates	

B.

	B. to Q. B. seventh
B. takes B. (check)	K. to K. third
Kt. mates.	

C.

	B. to Q. sixth
Kt. to Q. fourth (check)	K. to K. fifth
Q. to K. seventh, mates.	

No. 12.   *Page* 318.

Black King ought to be placed on Q. B. fourth, not on Q. B. fifth, as printed by mistake in our last number.

White.	*Black.*
B. to Q. fifth	B. to K. Kt. third
Kt. to Q. third (check)	B. takes Kt.
R. mates.	

No. 45.   Problem by F. HEALEY, Esq.

BLACK.

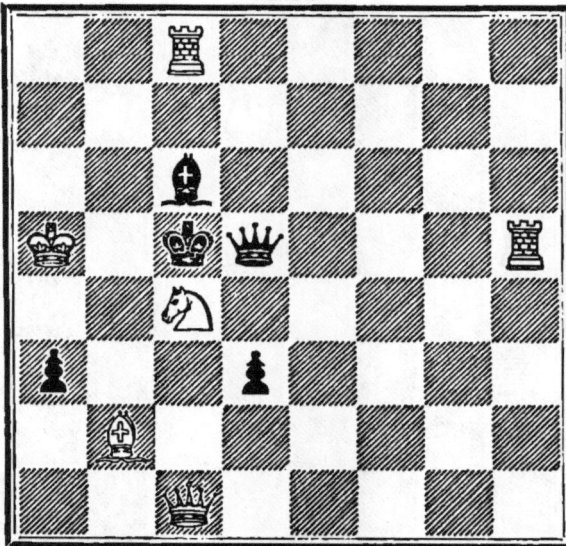

WHITE.

White to move, and mate in two moves.

No. 46.   Problem by I. O. HOWARD TAYLOR, Esq., Norwich.

BLACK.

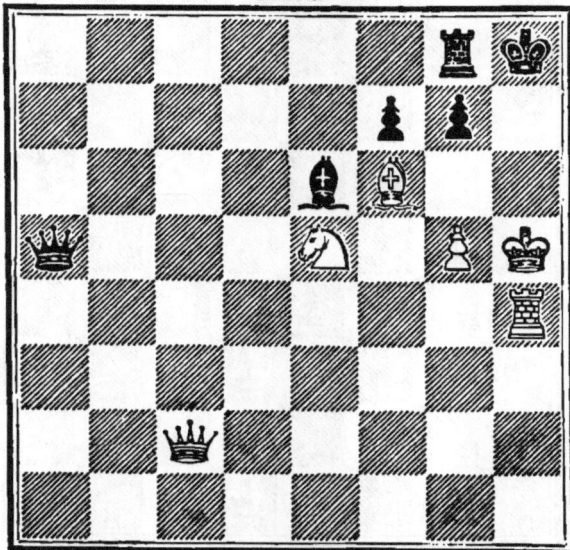

WHITE.

White to move, and mate in two moves.

No. 47.　Problem by M. GROSDEMANGE, St. Die (Vosges).

BLACK.

WHITE.

White to mate in three moves.

No. 48.　Problem by F. HEALEY, Esq.

BLACK.

WHITE.

White to play, and mate in four moves.